Black Blood Brothers

The History of African American Religions

UNIVERSITY PRESS OF FLORIDA

Florida A&M University, Tallahassee
Florida Atlantic University, Boca Raton
Florida Gulf Coast University, Ft. Myers
Florida International University, Miami
Florida State University, Tallahassee
New College of Florida, Sarasota
University of Central Florida, Orlando
University of Florida, Gainesville
University of North Florida, Jacksonville
University of South Florida, Tampa
University of West Florida, Pensacola

Black Blood Brothers

Confraternities and Social Mobility for Afro-Mexicans

NICOLE VON GERMETEN

Foreword by Stephen W. Angell and Anthony B. Pinn, Series Editors

University Press of Florida
Gainesville/Tallahassee/Tampa/Boca Raton
Pensacola/Orlando/Miami/Jacksonville/Ft. Myers/Sarasota

Published in the United States of America

First cloth printing, 2006
First paperback printing, 2026

31 30 29 28 27 26 6 5 4 3 2 1

A record of cataloging-in-publication data is available from the Library of Congress.

ISBN 978-0-8130-2942-9 (cloth) | ISBN 978-0-8130-8179-3 (pbk.)

The University Press of Florida is the scholarly publishing agency for the State University System of Florida, comprising Florida A&M University, Florida Atlantic University, Florida Gulf Coast University, Florida International University, Florida State University, New College of Florida, University of Central Florida, University of Florida, University of North Florida, University of South Florida, and University of West Florida.

University Press of Florida
PO Box 140239
Gainesville, FL 32614
floridapress.org

GPSR EU Authorized Representative: Mare Nostrum Group B.V, Doelen 72, 4831 GR Breda, The Netherlands, gpsr@mare-nostrum.co.uk

Contents

Tables and Graphs

Parral
Zacatecas
San Luis Potosí
León
Celaya
Querétaro
Valladolid
Mexico City
Toluca
Puebla
Veracruz
Orizaba
Taxco
Antequera
Acapulco

Series Foreword

The shelves of libraries are lined with volumes that address the mechanics of slavery in the Americas, including the nature of labor, living arrangements, family structures, religious developments, and forms of rebellion. However, missing from many such treatments of slavery is attention to more-nuanced dimensions of life, the tone of slave society that cannot be captured so easily through flat attention to statistics, archaeological findings, written texts, and the like. Yet scholars have recently realized with a sense of urgency the importance of capturing the tone of slave society in order to unpack the nature of African identity in the New World as well as the implications of assimilation for this identity.

They have also come to understand that recovering the complexities of life and identity within slavery in the Americas requires that we examine these materials with questions geared toward the subtle dimensions of life. The manner in which levels of nuance can best be understood and portrayed awaits discovery.

It is because this volume makes advances in addressing such dimensions of nuance and subtlety that we are pleased to present it as an important addition to this series and to scholarship on the African presence in the New World in general. Giving primary attention to African involvement in confraternal organizations, Nicole von Germeten provides significant insights into the complexities of African identity in colonial Mexico. Through a comparative examination of case studies in Mexico City, Valladolid, and Parral, she presents a rich depiction of piety and religiosity particularly within the environment of the confraternities and among what she calls the "Afromexicans" of colonial Mexico.

Particularly illuminating is her depiction of the early involvement of Afromexican women, the social significance of African and mulatto confraternities in Mexico City, the connection of confraternal organizations to rebellions, and the push for respectability attendant on efforts to assimilate. Overall, the author creatively and carefully depicts the shifting religious and larger cultural life patterns of Afromexicans. By highlighting the similarities and differences in the ways various confraternities in various locations in colonial Mexico understood, responded to, and shaped issues of identity, race, gender, and religion, she points to the significant role played by those of African descent in shaping socioeconomic and religious life in a very vital area of the New World.

This series aims to enrich and expand scholarship that mines the thick and complex nature of religious life in the Americas. We are pleased to count Nicole von Germeten's book among its distinguished volumes.

Stephen W. Angell and Anthony B. Pinn, Series Editors

Preface and Acknowledgments

This book explores changes in social, family, economic, and religious life experienced by Africans and their descendants living in New Spain from the sixteenth to the late eighteenth centuries. At first most Africans and their children suffered under the harsh conditions of slavery, which prevented them from achieving social and economic success in the Hispanic world. Often baptized as "without known fathers" or as orphans in the seventeenth century, Afromexicans (labeled *negros*, *morenos*, *pardos,* or *mulatos* in colonial documentation) created fictive families for themselves by joining confraternities, or lay religious brotherhoods. The confraternities provided social connections, charity, and status for their members within towns throughout New Spain. Confraternities led by men and women of African descent flourished in the 1600s in Veracruz, Mexico City, Zacatecas, San Luis Potosí, Taxco, San Miguel Allende, and Querétaro. Often penitent (practicing public processional flagellation in honor of the Passion of Christ) and dedicated to popular Spanish and African advocations, Afromexican confraternities enjoyed success and prestige in the baroque religious milieu of seventeenth-century New Spain.

Male confraternity leaders, even if they were enslaved or were given colonial racial labels, achieved limited prosperity from the mid-seventeenth century onward in towns such as Morelia and Mexico City. Gradually, individuals with African ancestry were less likely to be enslaved and were generally labeled *mulato*, indicating strong social, cultural, and familial connections to the Hispanic world. Children described as mulatto in eighteenth-century baptismal records were twice as likely to have both parents present at their baptism as their seventeenth-century ancestors, and their parents' unions were officially recognized as "legitimate" by the colonial authorities. Eighteenth-century mulattos were likely to be born free (without an enslaved mother), and some individuals inherited their fathers' trades, which helped them attain social and economic status in their professional and personal lives. Confraternities played a strong role in this long-term upward mobility by providing an acceptable way for members to take part in public rituals and celebrations of local life in New Spain. However, racial hierarchies varied by town and region. This book will examine Mexico City, Parral, and Morelia to show the varying success individuals living in a racially divided colonial society experienced. Despite legal distinctions and divisions, by the end of the colonial era, individuals descended from African slaves in New Spain had achieved a limited degree of status in Hispanic society. Confraternities were a crucial institution that facilitated this process.

I would like to acknowledge the generosity of my dissertation advisor William B. Taylor, who helped me complete this project in many tangible and intangible ways. The inspiration of his scholarship and integrity offers a high standard for all historians. He was always generous with advice on ways of thinking about colonial Mexico. Practically, Professor Taylor gave me his notes on documentation, which were crucial in tracking down confraternities, especially his notes about seventeenth-century pastoral visits. This was one among many other ways he helped me focus and expedite my research. His wise insights add a new dimension of complexity to my work.

Professors Sarah Cline and Margaret Chowning were also instrumental to this project. Professor Cline, at the University of California, Santa Barbara, mentored my early projects on Parral and Alonso de Sandoval, SJ, and has offered dependable help since 1996. She also read early chapter drafts. Professor Chowning introduced me to the Casa de Morelos, the archive of the diocese of Michoacán. Without her knowledge and guidance at the Casa de Morelos and the notarial archive in Morelia, this book would not have been possible.

I am grateful to Professors Randolph Starn and Thomas A. Brady, who expanded my confraternal horizons a great deal through their courses on early modern European history. Walter Brem trained me in scholarly bibliography, an important tool for my research. Christopher Lutz kindly sent me his work on *casta* populations in colonial Guatemala. Douglas Cope, Ben Vinson, and Patrick Carroll not only offer historians superior studies on Africans and their descendants in New Spain but were willing to provide expedient long-distance assistance to a researcher they had not, at that time, met. Without the inspiration of their work, especially their footnotes and archival references, my research would not have been possible. Dr. Carroll also read several versions of this book. His suggestions greatly improved the finished product. Dr. Vinson has fostered a circle of Afromexicanists, and I am proud to have the honor to associate with it due to his unstinted encouragement and support. I can only hope that this work lives up to the high standard these scholars have set for the study of Africans in Mexico.

Mabel Lee, Barbara Hayashida, and Sandy Richmond were considerate, helpful, and extremely professional members of the Department of History at the University of California, Berkeley. The Muriel McKevitt Sonne and Peder Sather History Department Endowed Chairs funded my time at Berkeley, and the Graduate Division of the University of California, Berkeley, provided travel grants. A Fulbright-Garcia Robles Grant funded my research in Mexico. The Ford Foundation funded the Program on Women and Religion in the African Diaspora at Princeton University, where I had the chance to do much revision.

Karen Melvin and Rachel Chico helped me keep my sense of humor through ups and downs in coursework, teaching, writing, and research and were dependable friends from my first day at Berkeley. It would be hard not to have high standards when working with colleagues like them. Karen gave me many archival and printed references and read early drafts of several chapters. Rachel sacrificed her own work to aid me with her professional editing at short notice. In Mexico, Matt O'Hara, Martin Nesvig, and Edward Wright-Rios provided much-needed help in accessing archives.

My colleagues at the History Department of Oregon State University and the Center for the Study of Religion at Princeton University have also helped me with their comments on my work and by offering the time and space to complete this book. I would especially like to thank Paul Farber, Marie Griffiths, Amy Koehlinger, Maureen Healy, Paul Kopperman, Anita Kline, and Ron Doel. I am also grateful for the research assistance provided by Adam Neff, one of the first-rate undergraduate history majors at Oregon State University.

Very little would be known about Afromexican confraternities if it were not for the trust and patience of the dozens of staff members who allowed me access to archives, churches, dioceses, convents, and archdioceses from Parral to Oaxaca. I apologize for not remembering the name of every person I encountered. Berenice Bravo Rubio and Marco Antonio Pérez Iturbe made the Archivo Histórico del Arzobispado de México a refuge in Mexico City and a gateway to many other archives. Dr. Yolia Tortolero Cervantes at the Registro Nacional de Archivos in the Archivo General de la Nación also helped me gain access to parish archives. The entire staff of the Archivo General de Notarías in Mexico City and Morelia was helpful and professional. The staff of the Casa de Morelos provided documents for several visits. Fray Alfredo Vega was a generous archivist in the Franciscan archive in Celaya. Working in more than twenty parishes and ecclesiastical archives was an experience I will never forget, one that would not have been possible without the gracious help of parish office secretaries, priests, and the numerous bishops' assistants who contacted parishes for me. Although every person generously took time from their regular work to help a stranger, I especially remember Ricardo Sánchez at the parish of San Miguel in Orizaba, the staff of the Archdiocese of San Luis Potosí, and Judith Marin, the archivist in the Church of Santo Domingo in Zacatecas. When access to a church's records was not possible, I could always depend on the excellent records of the Church of Jesus Christ of the Latter Day Saints, a resource many historians of Mexico have appreciated. Dr. Linda Arnold, Eugenio Cortés Hernández (of the Baden-Powell Language Institute in Morelia), and Dr. Alicia Mayer also provided personal and professional help in Mexico.

My parents Joan and Jim von Germeten and my sister Ann von Germeten have in many ways helped me complete this work, especially by making my time in Mexico more enjoyable by thoughtfully visiting me in Veracruz, Morelia, and Oaxaca. Through the continuous efforts of my husband, Brent Ayrey, I had a peaceful and well-equipped space for writing and was able to include tables and graphs that would have been impossible without his knowledge of statistics and graphs. He is always willing to drop everything to help in my graph and table emergencies. His patience, care, knowledge, optimism, and generosity greatly improved my experience of researching and writing this book.

Introduction

Care in sickness, a decent burial, and a "good death," wrote Alonso de Sandoval (1576–1651), were desperately needed to offset the deep humiliations African slaves suffered in seventeenth-century Latin America. In his 1627 book *De instauranda aethiopum salute*, Sandoval described the piles of slaves' bodies left unburied "as if they were beasts, mouths dropped open, looking up and full of insects [como si fuesen bestias, las bocas hacia arriba, abiertas y llenas de moscas]."[1] Sandoval observed with horror that even the lifelong masters of slaves would not spend a small amount of money on their burial, instead leaving their bodies exposed.[2] Sandoval's focus on burial was in line with the Jesuit concern for "a good death," but it opens our eyes to the lives of seventeenth-century slaves and their descendants in Latin America. Sandoval praised the lay brotherhoods, or confraternities [*cofradías*], that slaves and free Africans maintained as the only way for slaves to achieve care in their times of greatest need, salvation, a good death, and burial. Throughout Latin America, Africans and Afro-Latinos founded confraternities under the auspices of religious orders and parish churches and, less officially, on haciendas in order to meet the needs identified in Sandoval's observations.

Spaniards arriving in the New World brought with them the long-established tradition of the confraternity. Laypeople, priests, and friars all organized confraternities that were recognized by the ecclesiastical hierarchy through its approval of a confraternity's constitution. The primary function of a confraternity was to celebrate a saint's day or honor a less-tangible religious doctrine, such as the holy sacrament or the rosary or a moment in the passion of Christ. Confraternity members cared for an image of their advocation that was usually located in a parish or convent church or chapel. The members cleaned, dressed, and decorated their image. Every year on the holiday connected to the advocation, the image could be taken out for a procession or celebrated with masses, sermons, and fiestas. Majordomos were elected during the yearly fiesta to take charge of accounts and confraternity activities. Penitent confraternities focused their activities on processions during Holy Week. People joined confraternities by paying a small fee, having their name entered in a confraternity record book [*libro*], or receiving a patent that stated the benefits they would receive through membership. Confraternity members [*cofrades*] depended on their brotherhood to pay for their funeral mass and burial, and they especially trusted other members to pray for their soul.

Historians have taken an interest in Afro-Latino confraternities in Brazil, Cuba, and Peru, but they mention them only in passing in New Spain.[3] This study, based on documentation from more than sixty confraternities led by Africans and their descendants, wills, sacramental records, and judicial records, will establish the place of Afro-Latino confraternities in New Spain, the most important Spanish colony. This exploration of the involvement of African slaves and their descendants in this basic social and religious institution will also place them in Hispanic society and show how people of African descent first struggled for survival and later attained acceptance and social improvement within the dominant system of Hispanic values.

Historians of Europe and the New World have interpreted confraternities as having a wide variety of social and political functions. These differing interpretations depend on each historian's methodology, era, and analytical framework. Confraternities have been viewed as proselytizing tools of empire or the Catholic church, methods of social control or organization, demonstrations of local pride, extensions of labor organizations, precursors to political formation, providers of social welfare and a kind of life insurance, sites of polycentric baroque ritual and piety, and, finally, outlets for emotional and spiritual needs.[4]

Confraternities—Hispanic institutions that had been enmeshed in local societies in Spain for centuries by the seventeenth century—were brought to the New World by the laity, the mendicant religious orders, and the secular clergy to help convert and educate non-European populations and continue traditions that were familiar to Spanish immigrants from their lives in their hometowns and villages. As Hispanic ideas about local government, religion, and social organization came to New Spain, confraternities also came and re-created in a new land the local institutions of Spain. As in Spanish cities, confraternities both brought together local residents and separated them by profession, parish, or place of origin.

Although Spanish confraternities were based on local identities and social divisions, the confraternal system adapted to incorporate non-Spanish populations in the medieval period. Confraternities based on African origins existed in Spain as early as the 1400s. Medieval confraternities were established in towns such as Toledo that had been newly colonized as Spain slowly came back into Christian hands after centuries of Islamic control. When a creole society began to grow after a generation or two of settlement in New Spain, confraternities based on place of origin were affected by new divisions of birth or lineage, whether indigenous, Spanish, African, mestizo, or *mulato*.[5] Confraternities in Spain and New Spain were always connected to some kind of social

division, and in the New World they became part of the process and formation of a racially divided society. The fact that confraternities had labels such as "*de los mulatos*" [mulattos], "*morenos*" and "*pardos*" [browns], "mestizos," and "*negros*" [blacks] indicates that this institution contributed to racial divisions and to an idea of what each of these race-based labels meant. Many towns in New Spain had several different racially designated confraternities, and the racial labels they used might have attracted a range of members in each locale. Confraternities were part of social divisions and social mobility. While this study explores other aspects of confraternal culture, such as local pride, baroque piety, and charity, the emphasis here is on the social aspects of confraternities and the role they played in the changes Africans and their descendants experienced from the sixteenth to the nineteenth centuries, especially as they moved up the social ladder from slaves to more-prosperous colonial subjects.

Recently, scholarship on Africans and their descendants has grown. Laura Lewis's work *A Hall of Mirrors: Power, Witchcraft, and Caste in Colonial Mexico* analyzes hundreds of Inquisition cases from central Mexico and offers interpretations that complicate the idea of race in the seventeenth century.[6] Herman L. Bennett's *Africans in Colonial Mexico* argues for the existence of a conscious racial identity during the process of creolization.[7] Several Mexican historians have also broadened regional knowledge of Afromexican history.[8]

This book depends most on the issues and methodologies put forward in two excellent studies: Ben Vinson's *Bearing Arms for His Majesty*[9] and R. Douglas Cope's *The Limits of Racial Domination*.[10] Vinson's work brings to life the social dignity and identity free people of color attained through the institution of the militia. I hope to emulate Vinson's broad chronological and geographic coverage, a breadth that is essential if we are to reach an understanding of the diverse experiences of Africans and their descendants in New Spain. While Vinson proves that a sense of racial identity existed among what he calls "free-colored" militiamen, he qualifies this assertion by arguing that race was generally used as a tool for attaining privilege and that race-based associations were readily denied when they were no longer convenient.[11] Vinson emphasizes that racial identity always worked hand in hand with "corporate privilege" and does not forget that gains made by militiamen were always at the expense of retaining their colonial status as inferior due to racial labels they were assigned within the militia.[12] Many of these issues also apply to the corporate institution of the confraternity.

R. Douglas Cope argues that racial divisions in lower-class society had decreased by the end of the seventeenth century in Mexico City and sees the rise of a class-based society during this period. This "class versus caste" argument has long been a central concern in Latin American historical studies and has evolved into the concept of *calidad* [quality], which takes into account a variety of aspects of an individual's reputation and heritage.[13] However, the degree to which race declined as a factor in a person's identity varied enormously depending on the specific region of New Spain, an urban or rural setting, and the kind of economy in which a man or woman labored (plantation, mining, craft, or free).

Scholars have interpreted Afro-Latino confraternities from two extremes, as an imposition of colonial ecclesiastical authority and as an expression of African identity. These extremes may be more or less accurate depending on the era and location of the confraternity. For New Spain, in the earlier era of the second half of the sixteenth century and for most of the seventeenth century, confraternities helped Afromexicans survive the debilitating conditions of enslavement. African slaves, who had little or no hope of improving their circumstances, modified the Spanish institution and marked it with their concepts of gender, religiosity, and sociability. Hispanic authorities recognized that slaves had little status or wealth to lose, and thus they allowed this degree of autonomy to exist and even encouraged it. However, gradually the children and grandchildren of African slaves gained their freedom, through purchasing it from their masters, receiving it in a testamentary bequest, or being born to a free mother, and eventually they began to fill jobs that carried a limited degree of social prestige, as tailors, painters, builders, or shoemakers.[14] Through this occupational and social improvement, men of African descent were able to emulate Hispanic norms of familial behavior and change their confraternities in imitation of the Hispanic male-dominated brotherhoods. Rather than arguing for a permanent African identity or an instant voluntary or forced assimilation, this study examines the gradual transition from religious and social expressions influenced by Africa to greater concern for Hispanic society and religious practice. These will be explored through the lenses of work, family life, and confraternal life.

This book uses racial labels throughout; such usage must be consistent and have a theoretical and historical justification. Some authors easily slip into the black-and-white dichotomies common in the United States.[15] However, these terms do not necessarily apply well to New Spain: in New Spain, someone normally labeled *pardo* or *morisco* would have been insulted and confused if they were called *negro* or black. Vinson uses the term "free-colored" to refer to people given the labels "*pardo*," "*moreno*," and "*mulato*" to "most faithfully capture the spirit of colonial referencing," which often used the word "*libre*" to describe people of color.[16] While Vinson's approach makes sense for his work, I chose to use the more general term "Afromexican," which does not appear in colonial documents, to refer to the group of people, both slave *and* free, of African or mixed racial heritage, who lived in New Spain from the sixteenth to the nineteenth centuries. My purpose in using this term is to suggest that a diverse range of individuals of African descent contributed individually and collectively to many aspects of life in New Spain through their own version of religious piety, especially in the seventeenth century. African descent had different meanings at different times and in different places in the colonial period and may have changed dramatically at independence. The term "Afromexican" connotes a fluid group and is meant to highlight the long-term presence of people of African ancestry and suggest that they influenced the development of Mexican religion and society. The term also implies the existence of a sense of racial connection that might have not always existed in all settings in colonial life. In the context of confraternities that were given labels that indicated that their members had African descent, I argue for the tentative existence and awareness among such members of a variety of changing conceptions of what it meant to be of African descent in New Spain; "Afromexican" captures these subtleties of meaning.[17]

When I use "Afromexican" to describe confraternities, I mean organizations that officially carried the labels of *cofradía de los mulatos, cofradía de los pardos, cofradía de los morenos*, or *cofradía de los negros*. I use the term to describe individuals who were labeled *negro, mulato*, or *pardo* consistently in their lifetime. This label does not mean that these people were unquestionably of genetically African descent, but it does mean that they presented themselves or were designated by colonial authorities as having this heritage because of their appearance, associations, and family or confraternity connections.

The words used to designate race in New Spain reveal much about the status of those who carried these labels. Laura Lewis observes that Africans, unlike Indians, "were labeled with a color term, *negro* (black) . . . [considered to be] an 'unlucky and sad' color."[18] Lewis argues that while the term "mestizo" implies that Spaniards and Indians could successfully *mezclar* [mix], the result when an African procreated with a member of another race was a *mulato* [mule], the impotent offspring of a horse and a donkey. For this reason, the term "*mulato*" always carried a derogatory connotation in New Spain. When authorities referred to criminal behavior, they used the term "*mulato*," but even in the seventeenth century, they used the term "*pardo*" to refer with a degree of respect to some literate, high-status mulattos, especially those born in Spain.[19] "*Pardo*" became more common in the eighteenth century, although "*mulato*" remained a common racial designation. The use of "*moreno*," "*pardo*," "*negro*," and "*mulato*" also varied according to region.

Another term used in the colonial period to designate people of African and/or indigenous heritage was "*casta*," a term that includes people with indigenous ancestry. The term "*casta*" implies both a lower economic and social level and a mixed racial heritage. It could be used to refer to people who did not fit into the legal divisions of the *repúblicas de indios* and *españoles*, and it identified a group that increased in size throughout the colonial era. Confraternities whose membership included plebeians with African and indigenous heritage could be considered *casta cofradías*. However, I do not use this term to describe confraternities or other groups in the population unless I am discussing a racially mixed group that was made up of a variety of individuals of African *and* indigenous heritage. The Confraternity of the Immaculate Conception in Parral was a group of this kind; it had working-class mestizo, Indian, and mulatto members.

All racial labels used in colonial Mexico imply a certain social, economic, legal, and political status that went far beyond biological conceptions of race. Racial labels used in the text follow usage in the colonial records of each particular case being discussed. Specific terms such as "*pardo*," "*moreno*," "*negro*," and "*mulato*" signified specific social and personal identities to both the colonial authorities and the people who were assigned these labels according to time and place and must be used and interpreted in their proper contexts.

Before coming to America, people called *negros* in the New World had a variety of self-definitions based on where they lived and how they fit into their local world. These identities were difficult or impossible to maintain when they were forced to travel and live far from their original homes. The overarching label of "African" or "*negro*" was a colonial identity, similar to the colonial label "*indio*" applied to those who were descended from people indigenous to Mexico.[20] Because I use many colonial labels for individuals of African descent, I also follow colonial documentation and use the term *indio*. Similar to mulatto, this term may offend us today, but is accurate in the colonial context. Some Indians in Mexico were able to hold onto pre-conquest identities that were connected to where they lived, but only one group of Africans, Zapes, tried to maintain its cultural identity in seventeenth-century Mexico City by forming a confraternity.[21]

Connections formed in Afromexican confraternities were not the only influence on black and mulatto identities within colonial society. People of African descent also had social, personal, and economic ties with Indians, mestizos, and poor and rich Spaniards through their work and families. Individuals who were given every possible racial label, especially mulattos, intermarried and had children with other racial groups. In urban work settings, mulattos, mestizos, and Indians may have worked together and formed guilds, although confraternities seem to have been a more popular way of organizing. Rural labor forces were also composed of a variety of groups. Confraternities of the Holy Sacrament brought together every racial group in a given town.

A sense of connection to a specific African cultural identity was no longer possible by the eighteenth century, after the slave trade into New Spain ended. "Mulatto" was a more widely used racial label in the eighteenth century, replacing "black" or "*negro*" and references to African origins such as "Congo" and "Angola." People described as *mulatos* may have had Indian, mestizo, or even poor Spanish parents and grandparents. Individuals designated as mulattos in the eighteenth century were often urban tradesmen who practiced a variety of trades with varying success. The choice to lead a mulatto confraternity helped solidify an individual's connection to this racial category. However, a person who made this choice would almost never be addressed as "Don" or "Doña," no matter how much wealth or influence they achieved.

This study focuses on case studies in Mexico City, Valladolid, and Parral, communities that offer a range of settings from the viceregal capital to a smaller provincial city to an isolated mining town. The three locales produced very different stories of Afromexican society and confraternities. Mexico City's seventeenth-century confraternities were implicated in rebellions but also, especially from the late seventeenth to the early eighteenth centuries, sought to present themselves as respectable Hispanic institutions. Some individuals of African descent achieved fame and wealth in the seventeenth century through close ties to the Spanish elite. Mulattos sought and had sometimes achieved social respectability by the eighteenth century in Valladolid, as confraternities created by African slaves in the seventeenth century evolved into brotherhoods of dignified tradesmen. While Parral's *pardo* Confraternity of the Immaculate Conception, which was formed by hacienda workers in the seventeenth century, also evolved into a tradesmen's group in the eighteenth century, it did not achieve the success or local recognition of the mulatto Confraternity of the Rosary in Valladolid (modern-day Morelia).

The towns this book studies owed their existence to a silver-based economy and the structures of colonial government, and they were all founded and flourishing by the 1600s, coinciding with the era of widespread practice of baroque forms of religiosity. Carlos M. N. Eire's analysis of Spanish testaments demonstrates that confraternities, shrines, processions, and flagellation flourished in sixteenth-century Spain and that lavish baroque death rituals had peaked in Madrid by 1600.[22] This approach to religion reached Mexico early in the 1600s and extended to provincial capitals and the distant outposts of the empire.

This book begins with two thematic chapters that present the characteristics of confraternal piety as experienced by seventeenth-century Africans living in towns and villages all over New Spain, from the far northern mining towns to southern sugar haciendas. In these places, confraternity members worked as slaves, miners, or free laborers. The first chapter will introduce a particularly Afromexican baroque religiosity that flourished in the seventeenth century that celebrated the humble, publicly penitent, even slave-like confraternity member, a model that a range of people honored, including the Spanish elite. The chapter explores advocations, rituals, and ties to religious orders and other religious aspects of confraternities, emphasizing the penitential nature of these early brotherhoods and their strong sense of African community and connections to African heritage. Because confraternities emerged from Spanish religious traditions brought to New Spain and were modified to suit the new situation in America, the overview of Afro-Hispanic confraternities will begin in medieval Spain.

Chapter 2 looks at the role Afromexican women played in confraternities and introduces the theme of social and religious change from the seventeenth to the eighteenth centuries. In the seventeenth century, African women led and were founding members of confraternities, and their participation was one of the fundamental and unique aspects of baroque public piety as practiced by people of African heritage in New Spain. By the eighteenth century, they were more likely to be on the receiving end of confraternal charity as better-off, well-established free men took the leadership roles. As Afromexican men became more successful and gained their freedom, they modeled their lives and confraternities after Hispanic patriarchal models, a change that meant a loss of public authority for women.

African and mulatto confraternities flourished in the diverse and pious public life of seventeenth-century Mexico City. Chapter 3 shows how Afromexican confraternities were part of social movements and pious practices in the capital city. A 1608 rebellion of African slaves, which was organized around confraternal connections, demonstrates that religious organizations were not always successful instruments of Hispanization. This chapter also looks at a few very successful Afromexicans and their enthusiasm for baroque religious practices.

Although Africans in Mexico City rapidly integrated into the Spanish world, this was also the location for a confraternity that maintained ties between Africans of a specific language and cultural group, the Zapes.

Chapters 4 and 5 highlight the change from the rebellious group consciousness and baroque exuberance of the seventeenth century to eighteenth-century respectability in a case study of Valladolid in Michoacán. These chapters use sacramental and notarial records to analyze general and individual life patterns for Valladolid's *castas*, whose social position changed greatly from 1600 to 1800. The history of the two main confraternities people of African descent led in Valladolid mirrors the changes in the lives of specific individuals. The early slave confraternities in Valladolid embraced humiliating, self-mortifying baroque piety, mirroring the slave status of their members. By the eighteenth century, when these confraternities became more established, many mulattos in Valladolid had shed their status as slaves, instead working as free tradesmen. They began to show a sense of connections across the boundaries created by racial labels and confraternity affiliations.

Chapter 6 presents a case study from the mining town of San Joseph del Parral, modern-day Hidalgo del Parral, Chihuahua. The formation, struggle, and survival of the Confraternity of the Immaculate Conception there reveals much about the role of patronage and lineage in towns settled by Spaniards and their servants and slaves. This chapter presents Parral, whose bonanza began in 1631, as a late and modest outpost for the 1600s baroque culture seen in greater opulence in the larger and wealthier mining centers of Zacatecas, San Luis Potosí, and Taxco. The brown lower class in Parral experienced a social improvement over time similar to that found in Valladolid but did not create strong or lasting confraternities. Although their confraternity was very weak, eighteenth-century *castas* in Parral found limited social acceptance through their professions and confraternity membership.

The final chapter of the book returns to the inherent racial conflicts built into colonial society and brings together what is known about black and mulatto confraternities throughout New Spain, exploring areas other than mining towns, the capital, and Valladolid: Veracruz, Toluca, Oaxaca, San Miguel el Grande (now Allende), Celaya, Puebla de los Angeles, Querétaro, Orizaba, and several hacienda-based settlements in the state of Michoacán that supported African and mulatto confraternities. Each of these towns and villages provided unique religious, economic, and social settings that led to the creation of different kinds of confraternities. This chapter will especially emphasize the race-based conflicts and struggles and racial divisions implicit in confraternity constitutions in many areas of New Spain. It will show how confraternities, although they were formed in Europe, where race was less relevant to day-to-day society, and were meant to foster universal lay participation in Christianity, increased racial distinctions and even furthered a sense of racial identity in New Spain, especially at a local level. Although confraternities began as communal and charitable groups that helped African slaves survive the early difficult years of their life in America, Afromexicans engaged with Catholic society and perpetuated racial divisions through their participation in confraternities, ultimately increasing their own status in and integration into the Hispanic world.

Mexico City, Parral, Valladolid, and most of the other settlements considered here were some of the most Hispanized areas of New Spain. Any town from Parral to Veracruz lay along the main transportation artery of the silver economy and drew a population that sought to re-create patterns of Spanish society; some functioned as centers of colonial government.[23] Valladolid and other areas of the Bajío region were also connected to the mining economy through agriculture. Only two Afromexican confraternities have been documented for towns that were not involved in or profited from the silver economy: the Confraternity of Our Lady of the Snow founded by Africans in early seventeenth-century Antequera and the Confraternity of San Nicolás in San Cristobal de Chiapas, although it is probable that confraternities existed in Mérida, Yucatán, that were led by members of the large population of African and mulatto craftsmen.[24]

Confraternities that were founded and led by people of African descent in New Spain bring to light complex issues of identity, community, race, religion, and gender that went far beyond the basic spiritual necessities Alonso de Sandoval described. While the study of confraternities illuminates one kind of social connection and one facet of the process of Hispanization that non-European colonial subjects experienced, it suggests that the presence of an African population in New Spain led to complex social, economic, and religious results, not unlike the complicated results of contact between indigenous peoples and Spaniards. It also suggests the variety of Afromexican experiences in colonial Mexico and the changes in these experiences from the sixteenth to the nineteenth centuries.

1

Blood Brothers

Afromexican Confraternities in the Seventeenth Century

In seventeenth-century New Spain, Spanish institutions and African traditions and needs coincided to create a unique religious expression best identified as Afromexican baroque piety. During this century, most Afromexicans had left Africa only one or two generations before and many were still enslaved. They struggled to survive in the harsh conditions of forced labor and violence, but at the same time, in many areas of New Spain, including Taxco, Zacatecas, San Luis Potosí, Veracruz, Mexico City, and the diocese of Michoacán, African participation in confraternities reached its apex, leading to a distinctly Afromexican ritual expression best seen in public displays such as alms-collecting, flagellant processions, lavish processions, and fiestas.

By taking part in confraternities, Africans and their descendants embraced Christianity in their own ways that were informed by African sensibilities but also in ways that received full approval by the Spanish church. They held positions of leadership in confraternities, such as the office of majordomo, while maintaining associations with African culture. The power structure in African confraternities thwarted Spanish patriarchy, granting women authority as founding members and as major donors. This kind of confraternity reached its apex before the end of the seventeenth century. In this chapter, elements of Afromexican baroque piety will be explored in detail.

The term "baroque" in this work refers to a way of practicing religion as a physical, emotional, and public experience. The writings of early Jesuits, such as Ignatius of Loyola's *Spiritual Exercises*, elucidate this triadic or baroque experience:

> the share of sentiment and imagination in the psychology of belief, laying great stress on the "composition of place" and the use of the senses as aids to the imagination with the object of arousing an emotion.[1]

Brian Larkin not only stresses the sensory experience of baroque religious practice and rituals but also alludes to their social implications, writing that they

> privileged the direct experience of God's presence through contact with his many physical manifestations in the world, liturgical gesture, and a lavish and dramatic ornamentation of sacred space . . . [also encompassing] communal religiosity, collective participation in religious rituals, fraternity among the faithful, and collective responsibility for salvation.[2]

Latin American baroque religiosity can also be thought of as open to diverse local influences, especially those that came from indigenous cultures and even, as argued in this chapter, from African slaves coming to Latin America.

Seventeenth-century baroque piety as experienced and practiced by Africans and their descendants and the Spanish population celebrated humility and thus opened up a new ritual space for its practitioners. This group, which included slaves and other poor Africans and mulattos, achieved a kind of special sacred status. In New Spain, wealthier people of Spanish heritage showed their acceptance of and even devotion to the religious practices of blacks and mulattos in the seventeenth century by leaving pious bequests to their confraternities. Sometimes Spaniards requested posthumous membership in these confraternities. The ritual of public flagellation created a public forum for Afromexican religious expression and changed colonial Catholicism.

While Afromexican confraternities evolved to meet the needs of their members, Spanish models and influence can be seen in the existence of this institution itself, the popularity of flagellation, and the dedication to particular saints. Priests and friars who came to the New World encouraged the worship of certain saints, especially the African saints who appealed to their enslaved parishioners such as Saint Benedict of Palermo and Saint Ephigenia. The existence of African and mulatto brotherhoods in early modern Spain also contributed to the popular and official approbation similar confraternities enjoyed in New Spain. In the late seventeenth century, Archbishop Francisco Aguiar y Seixas was particularly supportive of confraternities, and he gave written approval to many confraternity constitutions throughout the Archdiocese of Mexico and the diocese of Michoacán. The mix of Spanish religious practice and Afromexican public ritual expression is far too complex to argue that confraternities were institutions entirely imposed upon slaves or, on the other hand, that confraternities were nothing more than an expression of African communal identity. Here instead is an intricate mix and intertwining of people and religion from Spain, Africa, and Mexico that led to a new interpretation of public piety.

Change over time also complicates these simple dichotomies. Confraternities were not a static institution nor did their members' lives remain unchanged, trapped in permanent enslavement. By the eighteenth century, people of African descent were most often labeled mulatto regardless of their heritage. Very few were still enslaved, and the slave trade from Africa to New Spain had almost entirely ceased. Eighteenth-century mulattos usually worked as free craftsmen, sometimes even as professionals practicing high-status trades such as architecture. Baptismal records show that eighteenth-century *mulatas* tended to have fewer illegitimate children than their seventeenth-century ancestors. As people of African descent became more respectable, their confraternities became more conservative. They depended less on alms and more on income from properties, and they deemphasized flagellation. Confraternities became organizations of tradesmen, modeled more closely on Hispanic confraternities, and men rather than black and *mulata* women began to lead religious brotherhoods. Members rejected the particularly sacred status Afromexican confraternities had earlier enjoyed, becoming more secular and distant from the extreme humility of the seventeenth century. In other words, by the eighteenth century, Afromexican society showed signs that its members were making choices that brought their lives as close to the standards of Hispanic society as they could. But for one century, even as Afromexicans enthusiastically embraced a Spanish institution, practicing confraternal piety did not mean assimilation to Hispanic norms or rejection of African values.

The institution of the Christian confraternity originally developed when larger cities began to reappear in Europe in the late middle ages. Cities on the Italian peninsula, especially Bologna, were at the forefront of founding confraternities, which celebrated local piety, community, and popular saints. Early confraternities often functioned as prayer groups inspired by a particular preacher, who would leave behind the guidelines for continuing religious enthusiasm in the institutional form of a brotherhood. While first meant to unite local people, confraternities, like all other organizations, soon began to represent specific groups in society.

Long before the settlement of Latin America, urban Afro-Hispanic confraternities existed in Spain, especially in Seville. Brotherhoods made up of people of African descent flourished in several Spanish cities in Andalusia: Granada, Cádiz, Triana, and Jaen.[3] The existence of Afro-Hispanic confraternities in these cities can be attributed to their large African population. Although fewer Africans lived in Madrid and Toledo than in the port cities or southern regions of Spain, these cities in central Spain also had resident Africans. In 1590, Phillip II is said to have attended a dance and fiesta organized by blacks in Madrid.[4]

Seville, which had a large slave and African population, enjoyed an active and diverse confraternal infrastructure. From 1503, Seville was a major port of departure for Spaniards, other Europeans, and slaves destined for New Spain.[5] No Spanish city had a larger percentage of slaves in residence; in the mid-1500s, close to 10 percent of the Sevillian population was described as "Moors," blacks, or mulattos. The small African presence may have seemed larger than it was; observers said that the city appeared to be "a giant chessboard containing an equal number of black and white chessmen."[6] Confraternities were so common in Seville that Miguel de Cervantes's 1614 "exemplary novel" *Rinconete and Cortadillo* describes a confraternity formed by a group of thieves.[7] Some of Seville's most famous brotherhoods designated their members as blacks or mulattos.

It is likely that Spaniards, especially those from Seville, saw Africans and their confraternities as normal elements of urban life and that they brought these preconceptions to New Spain. Sevillians had a strong presence in Mexico City: approximately 10 percent of the seventeenth-century wills preserved at the General Notarial Archive in Mexico City were made by people who claimed Sevillian birth or parents. Although none of these testators was labeled mulatto, *pardo*, or black, some Sevillian testators might have had African ancestors, and they were certainly aware of Seville's famous black and mulatto confraternities.

The two best-known Afro-Sevillian brotherhoods were the confraternities Presentation of Our Lady and Our Lady of Angels. The foundations of these black and mulatto confraternities in Seville slightly anticipated but formed part of the same chronological trend seen in the development of confraternities with African leadership in New Spain. Although the black Confraternity of Our Lady of Angels claimed to have been founded before 1400, its first official documentation and constitution date from 1554.[8] The mulatto Confraternity of Presentation of Our Lady was founded in 1572.[9] The *moreno* Confraternity of the Rosary in Cádiz was also founded in the late sixteenth century. All three Afro-Hispanic confraternities were officially founded one to two generations before many Afromexican confraternities. Seville's Afro-Hispanic and Afromexican confraternities declined in the eighteenth century. In the 1700s, Sevillian brotherhoods were no longer given the labels *de los negros* or *de los mulatos*, and their membership was no longer of African descent.

Confraternities flourished in Spain in the sixteenth and seventeenth centuries, influencing the development of confraternal piety in New Spain as a fundamental part of Latin American baroque culture. The confraternal traditions that thrived in sixteenth- and seventeenth-century Spain helped create urban piety as practiced in New Spain. While Spaniards may have brought confraternal piety to New Spain, confraternities continued to experience changes and modifications throughout the viceregal era. Spanish confraternal culture as a whole changed when it arrived in New Spain and as it came under the direct influence of Archbishop Francisco Aguiar y Seixas.

Spanish influence on confraternities in New Spain, which emanated from the general population of Iberian immigrants, peaked in the late sixteenth and early seventeenth centuries.[10] However, individual leaders, especially Francisco Aguiar y Seixas, who was bishop of Michoacán for five years before he was promoted to archbishop of Mexico in 1682, continued to encourage confraternities into the late seventeenth century. The archbishop, most famous for his extreme misogyny and role in the life of Sor Juana Inez de la Cruz, was an active religious leader who recognized, categorized, and catalogued confraternal piety.[11] Aguiar y Seixas's pastoral visits to smaller towns outside Valladolid and Mexico City provide the greatest evidence of his promotion of confraternities throughout his jurisdiction. He frequently traveled around his diocese and later his archdiocese to officially recognize and approve informal organizations and confirm confraternity constitutions. Aguiar y Seixas demonstrated his support for confraternities in smaller towns with pastoral visits from the late 1670s and early 1680s, which are documented in the Archivo Histórico del Arzobispado de Mexico and the Casa de Morelos, the archive of the colonial Diocese of Michoacán. Though these archives have no older visits to compare to those of Aguiar y Seixas, he was probably one of the first bishops to heavily emphasize new confraternities and provide official approval for their constitutions. Among the archbishops of Mexico who made documented pastoral visits, Aguiar y Seixas was the most careful to apply racial labels to confraternities; bishops and archbishops in the eighteenth century gradually discarded these labels. He approved many of the confraternities referred to here, including the Confraternity of Saint Efigenia in Toluca, the Confraternity of the Precious Blood of Christ in Apaseo, the Confraternity of the Tránsito in Querétaro, and the Confraternity of Saint Nicolás Tolentino in Acapulco.[12] Aguiar y Seixas also visited the Confraternity of Saint Nicolás Tolentino in Taxco in 1684.[13] His penchant for confraternities led him to occasionally join new and humble brotherhoods as their first *asiento* [member].[14]

While pastoral inspections reveal Aguiar y Seixas's concern with officially recognizing confraternities with specific racial designations, few sources provide insights into his motivation and his personal thoughts on racial identity in New Spain. Although the archbishop hated and avoided any contact with women (a point his confessor/biographer Joseph Lezamis emphasized to demonstrate his chastity), he was not, as were other viceregal authorities earlier in the century, fearful of *castas*. Lezamis wrote that Aguiar y Seixas's courtesy and humility extended to "mestizos, mulattos and even Indians," whom he allowed to sit in his presence.[15] This attitude extended to his belief that all races should enjoy the benefits of confraternities.

Aguiar y Seixas's instructions to confraternities illustrate his more general attitude toward these organizations. Many of these guidelines were copied into confraternities' books. He frequently condemned wasteful spending. Perhaps his desire to promote confraternities with strict regulations was connected to his notorious hatred of gambling, cockfights, and bullfights. Lezamis writes that the archbishop stringently forbade majordomos to spend any confraternity money on these kinds of fiestas, and he also banned such celebrations and other entertainments for the general population, which led to intense hatred of him and his policies.[16]

Aguiar y Seixas described confraternal indulgences "as such a great treasure, and confraternities so necessary for the instruction of the Christian doctrine to all kinds of people."[17] Confraternities gained indulgences through papal approval, and members believed that they would help shorten their time in purgatory. The archbishop stressed how confraternities could provide routes to salvation and viewed education as one of their main responsibilities, "extremely necessary for all kinds of people, in particular the very small [*pequeñuelos*], coarse people, and those of less understanding, of which there are many in the towns of the Archbishopric." He added that special care had to be taken in *obrajes* [primitive factories] and mines, "because experience has shown that owners care more for worldly gain then the spiritual life of the people in their care, resulting in the total ruin and perdition of their souls." He preached against church approval of marriages for Spaniards, Indians, or slaves who did not know Christian doctrine because they would not be able to pass it on to their children. He also stressed that confraternity membership was open to all. He wrote, "All can join as members, any person of both sexes, of any age, state, quality or condition" adding that "any type of person, if they are Spanish or otherwise, and know how to read" should receive published indulgences from priests. The archbishop attempted to breathe new life into the teaching of Christian doctrine to a broad spectrum of the population, especially people living in small towns and villages outside the capital and diocesan seats. As viceregal society matured, it became clear to Aguiar y Seixas that work in mines, *obrajes*, and other common economic enterprises did not foster spiritual growth for the poor and *castas*. Not unlike Alonso de Sandoval, Aguiar y Seixas viewed confraternities as a beneficial and successful institution that was useful in achieving the original goals of spiritual conquest.

Although confraternities led by blacks and mulattos continued to thrive after the end of the seventeenth century, Aguiar y Seixas was perhaps the last archbishop of Mexico to officially advocate the founding of new confraternities. Authorities in the early eighteenth century left confraternities alone, and eventually many became defunct and were officially extinguished during the era of Bourbon reforms due to low membership or lack of funding. This downturn culminated in the severe depletion of confraternity resources in the 1804 consolidation of *vales reales* [royal loans].

Spaniards who came to New Spain in the sixteenth and early seventeenth centuries, active religious leaders such as Aguiar y Seixas, and mendicant friars all promoted Afromexican confraternities by providing them with official ecclesiastical approval, altars, and chapels for confraternity images. Despite these strong Spanish influences and the models of Afro-Hispanic confraternities in Seville and other Spanish towns, Afromexican confraternities developed along a unique trajectory that was possible only because of the conditions of religious, social, and economic life in New Spain.

The issue of African confraternity advocations illustrates how difficult it is to determine the degree to which friars and priests controlled Afromexican religiosity and the degree to which it evolved according to the parishioners' sense of African identity. Confraternities were organized in both convent and non-convent churches. Friars played an instrumental role in supporting confraternities among colonial subjects in New Spain and actively promoted certain confraternity advocations. What these advocations meant to confraternity members is open to speculation. While of course they remained Christian, some of these saints had African associations and friars might have viewed them as appealing to Africans in New Spain. Some advocations were popular among the population in general, and Afromexican confraternities followed wider trends in piety by adopting these advocations, especially the very popular advocation of the rosary. It seems most likely that friars suggested or promoted advocations but that some of these grew to have special significance for Africans and evolved into a publicly displayed representation of their heritage.

As can be seen in appendix 1, no particular devotion dominated Afromexican confraternities. Most confraternities drew their advocations from their location, a connection to a particular religious order, or a penitent function. Afromexican confraternities were founded in parish churches and convent churches and at the College of the Holy Spirit of the Jesuits in Puebla.[18] Popular among the twenty-seven known Afromexican confraternity advocations were saints with African origins, including Saint Benedict and Saint Efigenia. Other saints, such as the Augustinian saint Nicolás Tolentino, were popular in particular mendicant orders, and confraternities dedicated to such saints clustered in regions where these orders were prominent. All racial groups in New Spain, including Africans and their descendants, showed confraternal devotion to advocations connected to the Virgin, including the Virgin of the Sorrows, the Virgin of the Immaculate Conception, and Virgin of the Rosary. Finally, African confraternities often had advocations associated with the Passion of Christ because of the popularity of flagellant activities.

Popular confraternity advocations often emerged from the combined influences of location, the particular devotion of a religious order, and/or accepted characteristics of a saint. For example, thirteen confraternities had the advocation of Saint Nicolás Tolentino, the patron of the Augustinian province of Michoacán. While four of these confraternities were located in Augustinian convent churches, nine more were located in parish or Franciscan churches in this province. Augustinians may have chosen this advocation deliberately for more-humble confraternities, or perhaps groups of blacks and mulattos developed a devotion to this popular saint and founded confraternities dedicated to him without prompting from the friars. Saint Nicolás Tolentino, an Augustinian friar who died in 1305 and was canonized in 1446, preached to the humble on the streets of Tolentino in Italy.[19] Friars may have repeated this story to make Saint Nicolás appealing to the faithful, or they may have seen themselves in the place of Saint Nicolás, dedicated to the spread of Christianity to the poor.

While appendix 1 shows that friars from the orders of Saint Augustine, Saint Francis, Our Lady of Mercy, and Saint John of God supported several confraternities each in various areas of New Spain, this activity can be attributed more to the particular demographics of regions where certain orders were dominant than to any order's special sense of mission regarding catechizing slaves and free people of color. For example, while Jesuits in South America, especially in Lima and Cartagena, had missions to catechize slaves, they did not play a large role in educating slaves in New Spain. Instead, other orders in areas with a large black and mulatto population sponsored Afromexican confraternities. Some orders, such as the Dominicans, did not leave substantial evidence of interaction with New Spain's African population. Dominican convent churches were not a common location for confraternities led by blacks or mulattos, with the exception of one group of Africans that tried to found a flagellant confraternity in the viceregal capital in the early 1600s. However, Dominicans may have fostered Afromexican confraternities in the rural areas of the Dioceses of Oaxaca or Yucatán. The Dominican influence remained strong through its advocation of the rosary, one of the most popular in New Spain, and the advocation of the mulatto Confraternity of the Rosary in Valladolid. Convent churches of other orders and parish churches throughout Mexico often served as headquarters for confraternities dedicated to the rosary, which were founded in imitation of the original confraternity in the Dominican convent in Mexico City.

Bringing Africans into the institutional church took unique forms in several centers of Spanish rule. In contrast to Mexico City, Lima, the capital of the viceroyalty of Peru, had a larger number than New Spain did of enduring confraternities led by people of African descent with different advocations and a distinct pattern of support from religious orders. Frederick Bowser lists fifteen African and mulatto confraternities based in Lima in 1619.[20] Lima had a large population of African descent (Bowser cites sources that claim that up to 25,000 Africans lived there), and authorities tolerated an active religious and social life among these residents. Jesuits in Lima and in other areas of South America played a much more active role in the religious education of Afro-Peruvians. They supported a confraternity dedicated to the Savior in Lima, but they did not support any black or mulatto confraternities in Mexico City. Limeño Dominicans also reached out to this segment of the population, sponsoring a mulatto and black rosary confraternity. As they did in Mexico City, Franciscans worked with African people and maintained two confraternities with the advocations of Our Lady of Kings (for mulattos) and Saint Juan of Buenaventura (for blacks). Our Lady of Kings was also the advocation of the medieval black confraternity in Seville, so perhaps Limeño Franciscans were looking more directly to Spain as a model. The fact that Franciscans in Lima felt the need to make a division between black and mulatto confraternities within one church, which was also a custom in Brazil, indicates the high numbers of Afro-Peruvians in Lima's population. As in Mexico City, Limeño Mercedarians also sponsored two African confraternities, one dedicated to Our Lady of Loreto and the other to Our Lady of the Holy Water. The Franciscans and the Mercedarians in Mexico City supported confraternities dedicated to African saints, including Saint Efigenia and Saint Benedict, a trend not seen in Lima. Important confraternities in Seville and other towns in Spain probably influenced the organization of similar devotion in the viceregal capitals, but local conditions and the concerns of local religious leaders clearly also played a role.

Those confraternities not located in convent churches tended to favor advocations that emphasized humble and self-deprecating piety. Common advocations for parochial confraternities included Our Lady of the Solitude, Saint John of the Penitence, and the Tears of Christ; the names of the last two refer to the penitent activities of these brotherhoods. It is possible that confraternities in parish churches, as opposed to those in convent churches, enjoyed more latitude in choosing their advocations and elected to emphasize the sorrowful side of their piety.

Several confraternities chose or were assigned advocations directly associated with the African background of their members. Even if the friars decided what saint a confraternity honored, popular African saints could then become a focus for displaying African corporate identity. These popular African saints included Saint Efigenia (Iphigenia), the patron of three confraternities, including two in Mercedarian churches. Saint Efigenia is an African saint connected with John the Baptist who has now fallen into relative obscurity. However, around 1700 in Valladolid and other areas of New Spain, women and men were frequently given the name Efigenia or Efigenio.[21] While only a few confraternities in Mexico City, Toluca, and Aguascalientes officially centered their devotion on Saint Efigenia, the Confraternities of Saint Benedict in Querétaro and San Miguel and the Confraternity of Saint John of the Penitence in Zacatecas all carried an image of Saint Efigenia in their processions. In the two confraternities of Saint Benedict, carrying Saint Efigenia in processions called further attention to the African identity designated by their advocations. The combination of Saint Efigenia and the penitential function of the confraternity in Zacatecas married participants' African heritage with their emphasis on humble and self-punishing piety.

Within the regulations of the church, Africans forged a space to display pride in their heritage and gender roles. African and *mulata* women carried images of Saint Efigenia, a saintly African woman who offered them an example and inspiration. The act of these women carrying their own female African saint and their public and unashamed recognition of African heritage must have made an impression on spectators. If the purpose of processions was to be seen and to even conquer urban public spaces, processions carrying Saint Efigenia made a strong statement regarding the important and large presence of women of African heritage in towns throughout New Spain.[22] Contrast this to 1827 New York, where African voluntary society brothers "decided against parading to protect people of color from the white toughs who roamed the city streets."[23]

The popular Franciscan Saint Benedict of Palermo (1526–1589) exemplifies a particular religious order's emphasis on a specific saint to fit the needs of congregants. Saint Benedict was the patron of three confraternities in Franciscan churches in Querétaro, Veracruz, and San Miguel el Grande (now Allende). Catholics of African descent in North America also honor this Franciscan saint, who is called Saint Benedict the Black in English-speaking countries.[24] Saint Benedict grew up in Sicily in the sixteenth century, a child of slaves. As a child he was called "*il moro santo*," the holy Moor, although he was not a "*moro* [Islamic]."[25] Other legends indicated that Saint Benedict was only half-African but prayed to appear more humble and to have a darker appearance. His images almost always show him with a dark complexion.[26] Although he was very self-abnegating, Saint Benedict held positions of authority in the Franciscan Order. This was possible because Saint Benedict lived in Italy: in Spain, he would have been officially forbidden from entering the order because he was not of "pure" Christian descent. Despite his lack of pure heritage, according to Spanish ideals of *limpieza de sangre* [purity of blood], Saint Benedict enjoyed great popularity in Spain. In 1606 or 1607, Lope de Vega wrote a comedy dedicated to and about Saint Benedict called *El Santo Negro: Rosambuco de la ciudad de Palermo* as a celebration of the arrival in Spain of the Afro-Italian saint's relics.[27] Saint Benedict was an African holy man who fit all the Spanish requirements for colonial subjects.

Lope's play and its excellent analysis by Baltasar Fra-Molinero help clarify how Africans such as Saint Benedict could be viewed as saintly by Spaniards in the seventeenth century and why Spaniards were so eager to embrace a new saint who was the son of African slaves. To avoid his Spanish audience's concern over Saint Benedict's "tainted" heritage, Lope had Saint Francis himself intervene when conflicts arose regarding Saint Benedict's progress through the Franciscan Order. In the play, "to be black, to be humble and to be a saint were closely connected." The play explained the seeming paradox of blackness and sainthood by emphasizing the virtue of humility.[28] The main character of El Santo Negro, a noble Moor, renounces his power and struggle against Christianity to become a Franciscan. Fra-Molinero interprets the decision as a plan to become a slave voluntarily by taking the vows of poverty and obedience. He writes that the Moor became

> the best possible captive. . . . The slave could only reach dignity by voluntarily accepting captivity, serving as an example for masters and other slaves. . . . Benito is a slave because, as a slave, he understands the mystery of his condition: slavery is a necessity for salvation, and masters are a divine instrument.[29]

This message may have been exactly what friars wanted to pass along to their parishioners and may have been how they promoted Saint Benedict as an appealing image for confraternities to honor. The seventeenth century began and ended with harshly punished rebellions in Mexico City, and Saint Benedict's surrender to religious authorities was a useful message for friars to impart to slaves, at least from the perspective of the authorities. Fra-Molinero suggests that El Santo Negro's black skin came to signify Franciscan virtue, humility, and poverty rather than the prevalent seventeenth-century associations of dark skin with sin and rebellion.[30] Despite the fact that this saint seems to typify humble submission, he could also represent an effective statement of African corporate identity. Through his very humility, he achieved a place in the religious hierarchy and the devotion of those who considered their lineage to be superior to his.

Far more popular than the devotion to these African saints, devotion to the advocation of the rosary went beyond the three confraternities dedicated to Our Lady of the Rosary based in Valladolid, Sultepec, and Tlaxcala that are listed in appendix 1. In contrast to the African heritage that some advocations signified, the advocation of the rosary declared faith in the most mainstream and important Spanish devotion. Pastoral inspections of the Archdiocese of Mexico and the Diocese of Michoacán left documents that show that almost every town in these regions had a confraternity dedicated to the rosary.[31] In Europe, the Dominican Order promoted devotion and recitation of the rosary from the fifteenth century, and it continued to found new such confraternities for more than five centuries.[32] Rosary confraternities today still encourage devotional exercises and prayer in order to earn indulgences for members.

From its founding in the Dominican convent in Mexico City in 1537, the Archconfraternity of the Rosary was created and led by the elite of the capital. However, membership was open to all.[33] The archconfraternity organized and pushed for widespread devotion to the rosary; it extended beyond towns with a Dominican presence by encouraging the numerous other rosary confraternities that had been founded throughout New Spain and by selling pamphlets that described the official rules and papal indulgences granted to rosary members. The Confraternity of the Rosary in Valladolid was one of many whose constitution followed the model of the Mexico City archconfraternity. In the mid-eighteenth century, the archconfraternity fought for and won exclusive rights to its printed material in order to gain income to maintain its shrine in Mexico City. Few other confraternities had this kind of official propaganda machine.

Only the Confraternities of the Holy Sacrament and Souls in Purgatory were more popular than the Confraternity of the Rosary in New Spain.

The advocation of the rosary was also one of the most popular confraternities within Mexico City itself. One-quarter of seventeenth-century testators who mentioned confraternity membership at all belonged to the archconfraternity of the rosary, while about 10 percent of testators who donated to confraternities at their death gave donations to the same. Only the Confraternity of the Holy Sacrament enjoyed greater popularity in the viceregal capital. Africans and mulattos who led and joined confraternities dedicated to the rosary were clearly part of a larger and popular trend in expressions of piety.

Although it is possible that advocations were encouraged or imposed by outside forces, they reveal some aspects of Afromexican confraternal piety in the seventeenth century. Whether members chose advocations or not, advocations of confraternities with black and mulatto leadership and membership demonstrate an emphasis on penitence and humility, African identity, and the importance of women members. As we will see, even an emphasis on submission could foster a distinct kind of Afromexican baroque religiosity. The approval of these advocations by friars or other authorities effectively sanctioned this kind of piety, and within the bounds of the church Afromexicans created their own distinctive space.

Baroque Catholicism valued humility and emphasized infliction of suffering on the self, frequently in the form of flagellation, which was practiced side by side with the lavish processions and sensual religious celebrations of the time.[34] The narratives that describe processions in confraternal documents help create an image of how Afromexican confraternities embraced ritualized self-inflicted discipline during Holy Week processions. Voluntary flagellation appears particularly paradoxical or ironic in light of the pain already present in the daily life of the poor and enslaved: why would the humblest people in New Spanish society choose to increase their physical suffering?

Some scholars have attempted to explain this kind of phenomena in other historical contexts. The focus is often on internal or psychological forces. In the case of Africans in New Spain, public ritual flagellation transformed society by enacting subjugation, going beyond what colonial authorities imposed, in the context of participating in Christianity. By subjugating themselves, Afromexicans gained power and position, moving beyond the dichotomies of assimilation or integration. Their ritual subjugation expressed and displayed a clear identification with the Passion of Christ, and this gave them a new and important public role and changed religious expressions in general.

Flagellation has been said to carry out specific roles and functions in several different settings since the early medieval era. For example, public displays of penitence often represented a way for less wealthy or less powerful groups in society to express solidarity with all levels of society and take part in communal life. Timothy Mitchell contends that modern-day hardship and social stagnation contribute to the continuing existence of penitent brotherhoods in Seville.[35] He suggests that when groups in society gained access to some facet of official power, they sometimes discarded penitential practices.

Ironically, flagellation often flourished in hard times, not in easier times, when it might be argued that Christians might feel a need to remind themselves of more humble ideals or punish themselves for overly materialistic values. Instead, in times of trouble, penitent displays exhibited both communal strength and personal sacrifice. During sixteenth-century public crises in Florence, only penitent confraternities marched, emphasizing solidarity and charity.[36] The first outbreaks of plague in the fourteenth century caused mass panic, which led to "flagellant movements of frenzied half-naked men and women."[37] Some historians interpret these penitent movements as factors that strengthened communities by bringing together even the most marginal members to work toward a common cause. Flagellant movements could be organized within brotherhoods with clearly delineated rules, as spontaneous, unpremeditated displays in public processions, or as private group exercises in darkened church rooms. Flagellant brotherhoods typically formed under the close supervision and approval of the clergy. On the other hand, they could also be secret and illegal.

Although penitent practices may have been popular in Spain from the fourth century, mendicant orders brought these practices into greater public view and popularity in 1233.[38] In the 1260s, responding to a recent plague, a dramatic Franciscan preacher inspired some of the earliest documented flagellant processions in Europe.[39] Up to 10,000 people joined this movement, which extended from France to Poland, and promised to make processions and flagellate for thirty-three days.[40] Informal and spontaneous flagellant groups formed throughout Europe in response to drought, war, and (especially) plague for the next 300 years.

This period also saw great organization of flagellant brotherhoods in Italy. Scholars of Italian history argue that flagellation served a social function; they suggest that fifteenth- and sixteenth-century Florentine penitent confraternities may have helped citizens integrate into urban society.[41] Ronald Weissman argues that the "agonistic character of Florentine social relations" meant that men perceived that their honor was in constant danger of betrayal by those they considered friends. Competition was harsh because of the idea that society had a limited quantity of honor and riches. Weissman suggests that although some aspects of confraternal rituals mirrored republican political structures, the experience of most Florentines in confraternities gave them a sense of *communitas* that was very different from their cutthroat daily lives. Confraternal rituals emphasized stripping a person of symbols of status, such as clothing and jewelry, creating a

> sensation of belonging to an undifferentiated humanity, a sensation that may permit spontaneous, unstructured human relations to develop, relations temporarily purged of the complex ties and obligations of the social order.[42]

During flagellation rituals, brothers suffered for the sins they had committed as functioning members of a competitive society. Confraternities also brought together people who would otherwise have no ties outside their neighborhoods. Confraternal statutes tended to emphasize punishment of crimes that threatened the social order. Joining flagellant confraternities represented one step toward becoming an active adult member of the community.[43]

Sixteenth-century Florentine flagellant confraternities used their self-punishment to make impressive public statements. In an era of increasing public ritual, *laudesi* [singing] confraternities began to concentrate on spectacular professional processions that deemphasized "their personal role in performance, which originally had been the main attraction of *laudesi* confraternities."[44] In contrast, the *disciplinati* [flagellant brotherhoods] "did take part in the processional life of the city [but] their devotion led them to impress contemporaries with their self-scourging rather than the splendid floats and sacred representations of the *laudesi*."[45] Although these confraternities had patrician members, the robes of the members stressed anonymity and equality within the brotherhood.

The history of long-term organized flagellant confraternities in Spain and the propagation of such confraternities in the New World begins with the Dominican saint and popular preacher Saint Vincent Ferrer, who inspired a revival of flagellation in Spain in the late fourteenth century.[46] Although he also incited violence against Jews, Saint Vincent encouraged imitation of the sufferings of Christ and personally organized constitutions for *cofradías de disciplina*. The flagellant brotherhoods of Italy and Spain differed from the flagellant movements of the thirteenth and fourteenth centuries in that they had a "formally constituted internal hierarchical organization, [and] the codification of their aims in official Rule Books or statutes."[47]

Just as they did throughout New Spain 200 years later, Spanish flagellants gathered every year on Holy Thursday, heard an inspirational sermon, and organized a procession of "light and blood," meaning candles and penitence, that passed by the town's churches.[48] Both Franciscans and Dominicans led the foundation of penitent confraternities. Maureen Flynn argues that plebeians were the most devoted and frequent members of *cofradías de disciplina*. Other marginalized people, including recent converts from Judaism, also formed flagellant brotherhoods. According to Flynn, flagellation gave lower-class workers and recent converts a more direct experience of religion and helped incorporate them into society. This theory has been used to explain the existence of numerous flagellant African and Indian confraternities in New Spain. Of course, the presence and leadership of Mendicants, especially Franciscans, who viewed pageantry and participation as an excellent way to draw indigenous converts, also contributed to the popularity of flagellation among the poor of New Spain.[49]

Women participated in Spanish flagellant processions, although not as flagellators. Their participation continued among Afromexican flagellant confraternities in the 1600s after Spanish authorities forbade it in the mother country. Before 1600, women in Spain walked as symbols of mercy, carrying torches and candles, helping the brothers through the streets, and wiping flagellators' faces. They performed these activities with faces hidden, which led Phillip II to forbid their participation, believing female anonymity would lead to immorality or loose morals because public reputations were not at stake. From then on women were permitted only to view processions, not take part in them.[50]

Some scholars argue that organized self-inflicted punishment perhaps enjoyed such long-lasting popularity among underprivileged populations because the lack of any official religious hierarchy in poor areas created a desire for self-discipline. For example, flagellant practices endured well beyond the era of missionary or any other clerical presence in the incredibly harsh life of the nineteenth-century Brazilian backlands.[51] Conditions in Brazil resemble those in New Mexico, where brotherhoods of *penitentes* still exist and have meaning as a form of Catholicism within the Hispano community in an area with a sometimes-limited ecclesiastical presence.[52]

Robert Levine expresses this view in his work on 1890s Brazil, where he attempts to explain why already miserable people would choose to punish themselves:

> All but the strictest flagellant sects were not so much masochistic . . . as manifestations of backland Catholicism's deep-rooted belief that life, a vale of tears, needed to be spent in self-purification. Backland families felt they had little control over life-altering events. Sacrifice symbolized at least a demonstration of control over one's self. Harsh conditions led to martyr-like submission in some but created the strength for martyrdom in others. Self-sacrifice taken to an extreme separated one from one's peers, creating a sense of moral superiority and impecunious nobility for the practitioner.[53]

Levine's words can also apply to New Spain, where flagellant practices were not censured by authorities until the eighteenth century. It is difficult to determine if flagellant brotherhoods increased or decreased their activities as life became easier or harder for their members. While the lives of all slaves seem harsh, flagellant brotherhoods seemed to flourish in areas such as San Luis Potosí, where slaves were wealthier and experienced a natural increase. Perhaps flagellant brotherhoods in these areas distinguished their members from common slaves or laborers and were perceived to indicate superiority.

Flagellation is a typically baroque practice that connects emotion and physicality to religious experience. People who joined flagellant confraternities may have been motivated by a desire to appear more humble or to show off their wealth and cohesiveness to their community. Flagellation also served as an outlet for tensions within a group or a locale, as a way to inflict self-punishment as retribution for supposed wrongs that stemmed from a sense of undeserved success, or as a way to express feelings of guilt.

The practice of self-inflicted flagellation in Mexico had both Spanish and indigenous roots. Both Diego Durán and José de Acosta, early commentators on America, reported self-mutilation as a part of religious rituals at Aztec temples honoring Huitzilopochtli and Tezcatlipoca.[54] This cultural practice may have contributed to the popularity of blood brotherhoods (*cofradías de sangre*) among colonial Indians, a custom encouraged by early Franciscan missionaries. By the end of the sixteenth century, Indians in Mexico City were taking part in huge penitent processions in brotherhoods dedicated to the solitude, Saint Joseph, Saint Nicolás, the cord of Saint Francisco, and the belt of Saint Augustine.[55] Archeological remains reveal that the indigenous practice of cutting the back with obsidian knives before a flagellant display continued even after the conquest.[56] Although the popularity of flagellation among indigenous people is not the focus of this work, it is interesting to observe that this population also punished themselves in times of crisis: the colonial Indians of Mexico at this time experienced pestilence similar to the plagues that set off widespread flagellation in fourteenth-century Europe. Africans probably learned about flagellation from both Indians and Spaniards in New Spain, and the practice began to define their baroque public piety.

Like any other activity during a public procession, flagellation was intended to create a reaction among observers. It is possible to re-create the activities of flagellant confraternities through their constitutions and expenses, but it is difficult to know the reactions these spectacles caused in the viceregal era. In a very late example, the reforming clergy of the Fourth Mexican Provincial Council in 1771 expressed concern over the practice of discipline in Holy Week processions: "The penitences that should be agreeable to God are a cause of mockery and laughter because certain vicious *castas* and drunks whip themselves with *pelotillas* [balls of wax studded with shards of glass], gird themselves with swords and do other acts of mortification that are more a proof of their barbarity than of devotion."[57] The council advised penitents to march with a rope around their necks, a crown on their heads, and a candle in their hands and practice flagellation in private.

Larkin argues that the council's use of the term "*casta*" was a general way of referring to people on the margins of society—undesirables—who were distinct from the ecclesiastical leaders who made the observations.[58] Perhaps the use of the term "*casta*" in this quote reflects not only a cleric's opinion but also a clear observation of the processions of the time and the common prejudices of clergymen who advised archbishops. To go even further, perhaps the enthusiasm Africans and Indians showed toward flagellation in the late sixteenth and seventeenth centuries led to generalizations and perceptions of *castas* as the stereotypical participants in public penitence, a vision that the penitents themselves encouraged because it gave them a place in the hierarchies of baroque religiosity and a ritually important self-defined public role. Non-Spaniards could also be perceived as the least rational members of society who clung to outdated displays of piety that had become unfashionable among the capital's elite by the eighteenth century.

Some historians have suggested that public flagellation had a practical purpose, such as the notion that it was a public and communal expression of piety and "all the emotions accompanying religious thought" that brought people together as participants and at the same time provided a kind of social control.[59] Others have suggested that perhaps flagellants interpreted Christ's words regarding remembrance at the Last Supper as going beyond memory to representation and reenactment. According to this argument, public presentations of reenactments of the Passion from the medieval period seemed to stimulate memory, especially emotional memory of suffering. Thus, "They acted out redemption scenes to preserve the memory of the original Messianic moment and revitalize it in the minds of actors and spectators."[60] Another interpretation argues that public Passion displays served to teach and reinforce Catholic beliefs to the illiterate, a way to teach through emotions. Observers who were concentrating on a narration or enactment of Christ's suffering were meant to become emotional, and "agony was found to be the surer avenue toward ecstasy." Some historians even see publicly cathartic moments as a "particularly powerful method of meditation."[61] But none of these explanations clarifies the ritual power and transformation that took place during black penitential processions.

Even if no other confraternity records, such as account books or membership lists, exist the names of confraternities in appendix 1 reveal the penitential nature of many of them. Any confraternity that used a name referring to an aspect of the Passion would have had a penitential function. Originally only confraternities dedicated to the true cross were penitent, but the popularity of discipline meant that variations on advocations that alluded to the Passion developed.[62] "Narrative" brotherhoods were "devoted to a specific moment in the Passion of Christ: thus each advocation was based on a narrative text: the gospel passages of the Passion." Other confraternities did not represent a part of the Passion narrative and were dedicated instead to the Eucharist, specific saints, or advocations of the Virgin.[63] Several confraternities stand out as expressing aspects of the Passion, although other confraternities had penitential functions. The Confraternity of the Exaltation of the Cross in Mexico and Veracruz (both founded in Franciscan convent churches), the Confraternity of Saint Nicolás of Mount Calvary in Mexico (Augustinian), the Confraternity of the Blood of Christ in Oaxaca, the Confraternity of the Humility and Passion of Christ in San Luis Potosí, the Confraternity of the Holy Burial of Christ in Ocotlan, and the Confraternity of the Expiration of Christ in Mexico City (Dominican) all have names that refer to aspects of the Passion. The Confraternity of Saint John of the Penitence, a Zacatecas brotherhood, also clearly had a penitential function. Although this study focuses on Afromexican blood brothers, called "hermanos de sangre" in confraternity record books, both indigenous and European confraternities included elements of the Passion in their practices. Lists of confraternity names found in records of pastoral visits show many confraternities with a variety of membership bases dedicated to the blood of Christ.[64]

Although several confraternities mention Passion processions in their constitutions, very little evidence has survived that documents exact practices. Inventories and accounts list objects owned by the confraternities that were used in processions, and this evidence provides one of the ways to create a vision of the activities of a so-called blood brotherhood. Accounts also show that money was spent on other aspects of the fiesta days, such as food, wine, music, fireworks, and wax.

In the seventeenth century, a lowly station in life and poverty represented one kind of holiness that Christians in New Spain honored. Confraternity flagellation was a European tradition that had more to do with penance and the pain suffered by Christ than with the economic institution of slavery. When flagellation became popular in New Spain, a greater symbolic connection was made between the humble ideals of Christianity and the more notable presence of the humblest possible social entity, slaves. New World slavery influenced the language and practice of religion in the seventeenth century, and the humble symbol of the slave, who was on display in flagellant processions, strengthened colonial hierarchies. At the same time, this very humility gave a special place and identity to Afromexicans and their confraternities. Within the Spanish system, Afromexicans forged a new form of pious ritual expression.

Repartimientos de insignias, lists that divide or assign responsibility among confraternity members for carrying the physical manifestations of various symbolic aspects of the Passion of Christ in confraternity processions, are the best source for the material side of penitent processions. Such lists exist for the two Afromexican confraternities in Zacatecas: the black Confraternity of the Immaculate Conception and Saint Anne and the Confraternity of Saint John of the Penitence, which was founded and led by mulattos. Leaders of Immaculate Conception confraternity regularly met to divide [*repartir*] the objects that would be carried in processions in the late seventeenth and early eighteenth centuries.[65] This meeting would take place before the procession, the focus of the confraternal year, and included other business such as checking accounts and electing officers. Often the members who were assigned to carry various insignias were also those who were elected as officers. This confraternity's insignias included a small bell, a banner [*guión*], a crucifix, an image of the Virgin, a well (or fountain) of flowing water, a mirror, a rose, a rosary, a door, a rainbow, an image of Saint Anne, a banner with an image of Saint Benedict, a star, and a (miniature) golden house. The inventory included other items that may have been used in the procession, such as a half-moon and several nails.

The mulatto Confraternity of Saint John of the Penitence also recorded detailed *repartimientos de insignias* starting from 1652.[66] The confraternity's 1635 founding document mentioned the goal of the processions: "We wish to have a blood procession to make penitence for our sins, to serve God and to commemorate his Passion and death." Members carried out this vow on Holy Tuesday every year. The confraternity's first books, which date from 1650, detail expenses relating to its Passion insignias. This confraternity must have had ornate and complex processions, judging by its long inventories, which included several standards and banners, a head of Saint John with a diadem displayed in a curtained box, a platform to carry Saint John and the hardware needed to carry it, bells, some kind of sign [called a *rotulo*], a silver machete, an iron cross, and a crown of thorns. The division of insignias became more complex around 1671; after that year, the following processional accoutrements were mentioned: a small bell, a knife, a lamb made "of wood with a diadem of silver," a shell, a skin (perhaps representing the clothes of Saint John), a *zepo*,[67] a hair shirt, shackles or handcuffs [*esposas*], a representation of the river Jordan, a cross, grills, a crown, an image of Saint John, a palm, a reliquary, a basin, and an angel. The yearly *repartimiento de insignia* continued with varying levels of elaboration until the confraternity's records ended in 1742.

The lists of processional accoutrements could be said to constitute a group of strange and unconnected items, but to the confraternity members these insignias held a cohesive symbolic importance tied to sensual, physical, and re-creative baroque religious practice. This symbolism related to the confraternities' advocations and remembrance of the events of the Passion. Various seemingly disparate articles have been used symbolically to represent the Passion in religious art since the fourteenth century.[68] A more complete set of symbols of the Passion, as seen on churches in Europe and Mexico, would include thirty pieces of silver, a lantern, a club or mace, a cock, a crown of thorns, a reed scepter, scourges, a basin and ewer, a lance or spear, a sponge, nails, hammer, dice, a vat of vinegar, pincers, and a ladder.[69] The Confraternity of Saint John of the Penitence had some articles relating to the Passion of Christ, but it also carried several symbols of the life of Saint John the Baptist, such as a natural skin. An Indian confraternity in Quecholac, in the modern Mexican state of Puebla, listed a fuller complement of these accoutrements for its elaborate 1666 procession.[70] This elaborate procession included each one of the items listed above as well as an image of Saint Veronica. Those who participated in the roles of centurions and soldiers may have made Quecholac's procession more of a passion play. The Confraternity of the Holy Burial in Taxco also embraced all the accoutrements of the Passion; the brotherhood was founded in 1602 by miners and other residents.[71] By carrying these objects through the town during a flagellant procession, members around the Hispanic world made a physical connection to the suffering of Christ and displayed this sympathy to their town, inviting the entire community to experience the Passion. In mining towns such as Zacatecas, blacks and mulattos were important participants in this experience.

The Confraternity of Saint John in Zacatecas had concerns about other aspects of its procession beyond what members carried. It added to its dignity in 1667 by paying some university-educated clerics to carry its cross in its procession. Saint John's constitution required members to wear a white tunic and a colored insignia and forbade them to march nude in processions, suggesting that some members did not wear enough clothes to be considered decent while flagellating. The constitution also established a set order and route for the procession, which began with those who carried bells, standards, and banners, followed by those who carried the crucifix, pennants, candles, and various insignias. Then came the image of Saint John, which was carried before the representation of his head in a box. What were called *ángeles de bien* marched at this point, perhaps children dressed as angels. The confraternity sisters followed with twelve lighted candles and the insignia of the confraternity. At the end was a holy relic, carried by a priest under a canopy. Brothers of light (non-flagellating members who carried candles) also participated in the procession, along with at least four more clerics.[72] The members hired an Indian to play the trumpet during the procession.

The route of the procession marked out the sacred geography of the town, starting at the front entrance of the cathedral (or the parish church, as it was called at this time) and moving up a narrow steep street to the Church of Santo Domingo. The confraternity then passed the other religious institutions in town, first the hospital of Saint John of God, then the convent of Saint Augustine and the house of the Company of Jesus, and finally the Franciscan church on the outskirts of town, before it returned to the cathedral. By carrying their images and insignias on this route, the confraternity members publicly associated themselves with each place of sacred importance in the town, reinforcing the importance of their uniquely humble penitent role in local society.

Flagellation in seventeenth-century New Spain was practiced within the strict parameters of societal approval. The appearance of participants in flagellant processions concerned not only confraternity leadership, as seen above in the constitution of the Confraternity of Saint John in Zacatecas, but also ecclesiastical authorities. Both groups wanted to maintain decorum: the former to preserve the dignity and reputation of their brotherhood and the latter to ensure that the procession retained its didactic function and maintained social order in spite of what must have been an exuberant public display.

A key element of an orderly appearance was dress. The flowing colored, white, or black robes and peaked hoods worn by penitents are jarring to viewers today because of associations of such a costume with the Ku Klux Klan, but the function of the robes cloaked identity for reasons other than hiding the identities of perpetrators of racially motivated hate crimes. Scholars debate about the origins of penitential garb; some see them as mourning weeds and others as baptismal robes that signify rebirth through redemption. The most convincing interpretation is that these robes "concealed social distinctions and expressed ideals of brotherhood and spiritual equality . . . erased personal identity and made [flagellants] unrecognizable to the public."[73] Losing a degree of public identity created a space for freedom and a chance to move beyond social enslavement to a more empowering ritual identity.

Late-eighteenth-century ecclesiastical authorities did not see the value in flagellant demonstrations and worried about participants' clothes and behavior. These concerns were expressed in a 1768 declaration by the Bishop of Michoacán:

> Many who participate in Holy Week processions wear a tunic and hood with little reverence for religion and no fear of ecclesiastical or secular justice, only disdain, because they go out with covered faces, and feel confident that they will not be recognized, insulting people, randomly striking people, and making other indecent demonstrations which disturb the peace and piety of the people. With regard to this issue, the most convenient remedy is: for the present I command that all people (of whatever quality or condition) who take part in these processions and attend them, do so with the modesty and devotion that is required for the edification of the people. I also command that each procession meet at the customary location to dress in their tunics, and each devotee will march in their respective processions with a covered face and hood, but when this ends, they must take off their hood . . . and leave them and the tunics in the church, and not cover their face at any other time.[74]

This decree was for the diocese in general but was sent specifically to San Luis Potosí and may have been directed at the activities of the Confraternity of the Humility and Patience of Christ. In the past, sisters in this confraternity had caused conflict with their flamboyant appearance. Another example of processional garb that hid raucous activity took place in 1753, when a Zacatecas procession became rowdy and a member of the porters' guild was thrown into a drainage ditch.[75] The Confraternity of Most Holy Trinity in Valladolid also experienced conflict while dressing for Holy Week processions—certain members refused to take off their robes in the sacristy after the procession, as was customary, which led to some heated words and complaints to the bishop. Some brothers even seemed to be carrying knives in the belts of their robes.[76]

Processions represented key moments for Afromexicans to express both definitions of self and corporate unity. Thus, brothers sometimes set their own rules for a dignified presentation during flagellant processions, highlighting the legitimacy of their contribution to public ritual. The Confraternity of the Immaculate Conception and the Patience of Christ, founded in 1659 in the Mercedarian church in Veracruz, was connected to a local mulatto militia, and members clearly wanted to impress bystanders with their respectable behavior in processions.[77] Some rules in the confraternity's constitution suggest that those who participated in flagellant processions were motivated by a desire to appear dignified and to increase or reinforce local mulattos' position in society. As militiamen and confraternity brothers, the members of the Immaculate Conception and Patience of Christ (a well-chosen name that alluded to both purity and patience) formed an elite among mulattos in Veracruz. Among all the confraternities described in this book, this one most strictly limited its membership to mulattos. Members were proud of both this fact and their religious devotion and sought reward for both corporate unity and religiosity.[78] The constitution emphasized that the confraternity needed to display the "most brilliant" procession on the Day of the Immaculate Conception and laid down strict rules instructing majordomos how to finance this celebration. Several rules addressed the issue of the confraternity's Holy Week procession. To avoid overlapping with any other confraternity, Immaculate Conception had to leave its church between six and seven in the evening on Holy Tuesday. All officials and members had to be on time. The procession had many elements, beginning with a purple standard with a white cross on it and ending with the friars from the Mercedarian convent and a procession of confraternity sisters carrying an image of the Virgin. Founders of the confraternity (one could become a founder at any time by paying ten pesos rather than the two pesos required to join) were often chosen to carry the standard, a decision that had to be obeyed. Both male and female members who participated in the procession were strictly instructed to maintain "modesty, devotion, silence, composure, and decency." Any infraction would lead to immediate expulsion from the procession and the confraternity.

This desire for decent public behavior was in line with Immaculate Conception's efforts to control female participation and thereby increase members' respectability, a subject explored in more depth in the next chapter. This group and their procession mark a transition from emphasizing distinctly Afromexican practices to a desire to assimilate to Hispanic patriarchal norms. Confraternity sisters carried a candle in the procession and had to remain separate from the members. Members were also forbidden from participating in processions with any "indecency in their person or tunics. . . . [They must march] silently in their hoods, without swords or any kind of profanity, but with humility and patience." Their lives in general should be lived as a model of humility, and the constitution also called for expulsion for any "bad examples or fighting." Their pride in themselves and the display they put on during Holy Week coincided with a strong desire for modesty, and the constitution ended with the members calling themselves "humble sons and slaves." This combination of pride and modesty, summed up in use of the word "slave," characterizes the tension and contradiction inherent in confraternities with African, enslaved, or mulatto membership.[79]

One of the crucial aspects of flagellation was its public nature and the effect this public display had on observers. This effect was both didactic and social; the goal was that observers would experience the sacred through both physical and emotional immersion in the suffering of Christ. Socially, flagellation could emphasize the strength of a community as a whole or the existence of internal divisions and separations. But Hispanic society did not perceive its divisions as weaknesses. The strength of the colonial social hierarchy, emphasized by the humble examples of a saintly African such as Saint Benedict, was especially important in confraternal life in New Spain.

Slavery and saintliness were often symbolically connected through their shared association with deprivation and physical suffering, as in Lope de Vega's play about Saint Benedict. Suffering brought people closer to holiness, and even African slaves could be saints, because "the function of a saint . . . is to attract the physical and mental pain of others in order to liberate them."[80] Confraternities of both free and enslaved Africans increased their members' physical suffering with their enthusiasm for flagellation. Because of their belief in physically experiencing the transcendent, each member thought that his or her suffering brought them closer to Christ and saintliness. Society in general approved of the connection between slavery and saintliness. Africans and their confraternities in New Spain were acceptable and even enviable because of their humble enslaved membership, which led wealthy Spanish testators to support and even join Afromexican confraternities. But this celebration of the humble was a double-edged sword. At the same time that it showed the humble to be holy and close to God, the spectacle of processions of flagellating brotherhoods, which Africans and mulattos took part in with pride, reinforced the social hierarchy by promising status in the afterlife rather than in the present.

The African nun Juana Esperanza de San Alberto provides a striking example of a humble piety that was more revered than sacrifices made by those of higher social status.[81] Esperanza was a slave in the Carmelite convent in Puebla in the seventeenth century who was "raised by the grace of God to spiritual perfection[;] despite being a poor, black woman, *bozal*, ignorant and rustic, it seems that the Lord destined her to be exemplary in such a holy community."[82] While Joan Bristol interprets Esperanza's race and ignorance as further challenges to her sanctity, I see them instead as further justifications, especially her act of refusing to become a nun until she lay on her deathbed. Esperanza showed that she was aware of her humble place in society, and her hagiographer used this awareness as another example of her saintly nature. While she was judged as saintly because of her habits of fasting, ignoring taunts, remaining silent, and quietly caring for the sick, Esperanza was also an excellent slave. She was saintly not in spite of her race and her slave status but because of them. Esperanza's actions were not so different from the way blacks and mulattos publicly flagellated themselves: it allowed them to revel in and take advantage of their humble status to give them a special place in society. In baroque Catholicism, submission empowered a subjected people by bringing them closer to Christ.

The term "*esclavo*" was often used to refer to special devotion to the Eucharist or the Virgin. Having pure Spanish blood and lacking any taint of a slave ancestry may have been one ideal in New Spain, but joining a confraternity sometimes meant accepting the label "slave of the Virgin," "slave of the holy Sacrament" or "slave of the Rosary." This terminology was not pervasive in confraternity documentation, and only some members chose to become symbolic slaves as a pious act. For example, the constitution of a Texcoco confraternity in 1713 describes members as "slaves of the Holy Sacrament." It stated that "mulatos, chinos, mestizos, indios y coyotes" could join, but only *españoles* could hold offices.[83] In this confraternity, slavery to the Eucharist meant a symbolic devotion; more tangible manifestations took the form of paying for masses and flagellation. People who were closer to the status of slave in the legal and economic sense were humbler members of the confraternity than the Spanish members, the true slaves in this case. But on the other hand, in a unique rule, the Texcoco confraternity mentioned that its processions had been led in the past by *morenos*, perhaps flagellating themselves. Because there were no longer enough *morenos* in the town, "mestizo, chinos y coyotes" could perform this role. The fact that there was a set place for *castas* in the procession suggests not only their role in the colonial racial hierarchy but also that they provided a special kind of sacred humility in the confraternity's public display.

Other confraternities included *castas* in their processions, especially flagellant processions. Two towns in the Diocese of Michoacán, Leon and San Miguel el Grande, had a constitution for confraternities dedicated to Our Lady of Solitude.[84] This 1584 constitution followed a model for a *cofradía de disciplina* constitution, perhaps imitating a Mexico City Confraternity of the Solitude, a practice similar to the adoption of a standard Rosary constitution throughout New Spain. The Confraternity of the Solitude of the Virgin claimed that it had been founded in 1593, so it is difficult to determine where the 1584 constitution came from or who used it.[85] The constitution is of interest because it mentions that blacks and Indians were to lead the flagellant procession, in front of the standard with the insignia of the confraternity or its image of the solitude of the Virgin. The constitution also emphasized the meaning of suffering and discipline:

> We command memory and remembrance that in the time of the passion of our Lord Jesus Christ, when his Majesty endured so much agony for our sins . . . with his holy mother Mary in his company. . . . In the pains of Purgatory we have to pass for our sins and for the burden and relief of our consciences we agree that on Holy Friday at four PM every year of our lives we will be obligated to make a procession of all the members and brothers of this confraternity . . . [wearing tunics] so we will not be known. . . . The blood brothers [hermanos de sangre] will go in pairs, disciplining themselves with a cross in front of them to remind them of their sins and our Lord Jesus Christ and the brothers of the cross will march praying and in their devotion, without hoods or shoes.[86]

This quote sums up the idea of a public display of emotion that evoked memory and pious reenactment and put the symbols of humility, in the form of Africans and Indians, at the head of the representation.

Many confraternities in New Spain used the term "*esclavo*" in a symbolic way, regardless of the social status or racial designations of the members. Symbolic slavery to the holy sacrament or the Virgin could be fulfilled with the promise of prayer and donations. The practice of discipline was also a possible requirement; the Church of the Holy Trinity in Mexico City had a confraternity called Slaves of the Holy Sacrament.[87] In the constitution of the Rosary confraternity in Orizaba, the words "*esclavo*" and "*cofrade*" seem interchangeable. Members were listed as "slaves of the Virgin," although the nearly 700 members included some of the more prestigious people in local society.[88] In 1639, a confraternity of Slavery to the Holy Sacrament was founded in Zapotlan that was made up of Indians, slaves, and some Spaniards.[89]

Confraternities that were described as advocating enslavement to the Virgin or the Rosary usually appeared in the eighteenth century, well after the peak of economic slavery in New Spain. The 1734 constitution of another Rosary confraternity in Apatzingan specifies that slavery to the Virgin meant a weekly rosary and donation of two pesos for a mass.[90] In 1739, a confraternity in a pueblo near Celaya was founded under the name of the Slavery to the Holy Sacrament.[91] The founders were the town leaders and the indigenous people of the pueblo. Those who wanted to join gave a small entrance fee, but those who wanted to be "slaves" had to pray five Hail Marys and five Our Fathers every day and think about Christ's life, passion, and death. They marched in procession every week. The thirty-three founders of the confraternity pledged to take part in this "slavery."

The idea of a sacred form of slavery was so pervasive that even people who were legally enslaved united in a group called Slaves of the Virgin in seventeenth-century Puebla, symbolically doubling their slave status. The patents of the Puebla Congregación de la Esclavitud de la Annunziata de los Morenos [Congregation of Slavery to the Annunciation of Morenos] made specific reference to slavery, advocating that members symbolically prostrate themselves at the feet of the Virgin and swear to serve her eternally.[92] The Virgin was also described as being a slave to the Lord because of her ardent love. While their name referred to slavery in a symbolic religious sense, the members of this Jesuit-sponsored congregation could have been slaves in their daily lives. The name of their confraternity was presumably not a further justification of legal slavery but rather an appropriation of the language that exulted in bondage and equated it with an elevated kind of piety.

Through participation in the confraternity, members actually became better slaves. According to the nineteenth-century Jesuit chronicler Francisco Javier Alegre, Poblano Jesuits at first needed to convince the enslaved members' masters to let them take part in the confraternity's activities. However, "soon this was not necessary, because the masters themselves saw the benefit in the faithful and prompt service, the peaceful family life and the instruction and reform of their servants."[93] The members were instructed in terms that befitted their "coarseness" and performed charitable works such as visiting hospitals and jails.

They also encouraged other local slaves to leave their concubines, reject other bad habits, and join the congregation, which led to "sincere manifestations of penitence."

Both symbolically and practically, slaves were viewed as special cases when it came to actual penitent practice. At least some of the spiritual leaders of New Spain recognized the conditions of actual slavery and how these conditions influenced pious practice. This issue was addressed by a Carmelite friar in a book published in 1610 as a guide to confraternal devotion to Our Lady of Carmen.[94] This book aimed to explain in simple laymen's terms the expectations and rewards of membership in a confraternity dedicated to Our Lady of Carmen. The most basic rules of devotion included praying at the canonical hours, not eating meat on Wednesday and Saturday, guarding chastity, and wearing a scapular with an image of Our Lady of Carmen. This friendly guide specified that the meaning of the prohibition on eating meat on certain days was open to interpretation and really meant avoiding "*grosera* [gluttony]" in general. Both wives and slaves were given leeway in the interpretation of this rule. Women whose husbands disliked rules about meat-eating and slaves "who had nothing else to eat" could ignore dietary rules with no threat to the indulgences granted to members of the Confraternity of Our Lady of Mount Carmel.[95]

Although slaves frequently served as officers in confraternities, constitutions often had to make special rules to accommodate enslaved members. The 1700 constitution of Antequera's Confraternity of Our Lady of the Snow allowed slaves to be elected as officials only with the permission of their masters.[96] This rule existed in spite of the fact that African slaves founded the confraternity sometime around 1600.

The condition of slavery, which was associated in the Hispanic world with people of African heritage, had a complex symbolic meaning in the seventeenth century, which intertwined the importance of social hierarchy with an idea that ignorant humble people of low station might have had a special closeness to the sacred that somehow put them on a higher spiritual plane even though it did not elevate their social status. Confraternities with African or indigenous members could draw attention to this poverty and humility as their personal and unique connection to the sacred. The physical and emotional experiences associated with baroque religiosity also meant that it was considered valuable to emulate the suffering of Christ, and who knew physical suffering more than a slave?

Hispanic traditions and the missions of the secular and regular clergy in New Spain created an opportunity to develop confraternities that carried a distinct social and spiritual importance. African confraternities, especially those founded in parish churches, emphasized the humble status of their members by embracing the flagellant element of confraternal piety. Their celebration of their own social lowliness inspired devotion from people of higher social standing, as shown in their pious bequests. In the seventeenth century, flagellation, humility, an emphasis on social and racial hierarchies, and female-led confraternities devoted to African saints combined to create an Afromexican baroque piety that flourished in several areas of New Spain.

2

Sisters

Women in Confraternities

Early in their history, Afromexican confraternities needed women's organizational skills and resources to fulfill charitable goals. Women served important symbolic and actual functions in black and mulatto confraternities in the seventeenth and eighteenth centuries. In a social context in which life expectancy for slaves was very low, African women were able to provide other slaves with much-needed charity. The confraternities of slaves and Africans in the seventeenth century provided the precious benefits of health care and burial, and women helped fund and lead these confraternity activities. Baptism records suggest that these women were sometimes single mothers who were struggling to survive their work environment. Black and *mulata* women must have made a strong public statement as they successfully drew in alms to give to confraternities.

Spanish women, in contrast, expressed their piety in a more private way. Wills of wealthier women in seventeenth-century Mexico City, who were generally Spanish, show a high level of devotion to confraternities, although men were always the founders, leaders, procession participants, or alms-collectors in confraternities founded by people of European descent. The women who appear with the least frequency in confraternity records are the poorer women of Spanish descent. While there were many such women in New Spain, they did not have the funds to make large donations or the freedom to lead or participate publicly in confraternities. The mores of Hispanic culture and the patriarchy of Spanish confraternities did not allow the Spanish women to fulfill the roles available to black and *mulata* sisters.

Wealthier women did have one option that could lead to a position of authority in a religious organization: becoming a nun was one road to a kind of independence with opportunities for leadership, if a woman was so inclined. In following this path, a wealthier woman could lead other women in religious activities. Spanish women's religious authority did not come from the public participation seen in Afromexican confraternities; instead, it came from their wealth and family connections. Afromexican and Indian women, by contrast, did not have access to material resources that could be converted into religious authority. They relied on their labor in confraternities to provide them with respect and authority in life and tangible benefits for their survivors after their death.

Confraternity membership could make even an Afromexican woman on trial by the Inquisition appear respectable. In 1778, in a village outside of Pinzándaro in the Diocese of Michoacán, Magdalena Bolanos, described as a free *mulata*, was accused of making a pact with the devil.[1] The accusation came from a self-described gambler called Orejel, a 40-year-old day laborer of Spanish heritage. Orejel claimed that Magdalena had tempted him three times with the promise of success at games if he took a certain stone in her possession to a secret place and lit a candle to the devil. He said that Magdalena described herself as a good friend of the devil. After he carried out the spell with the special rock painted with a bird and a candle in the shape of a serpent, he became petrified with fear and decided that denouncing Magdalena was in his best interest. However, a local Inquisition commissary who knew Magdalena very well testified that Magdalena was more sad and dignified than satanic and evil. Her husband violently abused her and openly carried on with another woman. This treatment led Magdalena to religiosity rather than vice; she confessed and took communion every year, as was the normal custom. Magdalena was so devoted that she regularly decorated a local chapel in Pinzándaro with roses. For two years, her son served as majordomo of the confraternity of this chapel, leading the procession in Holy Week. Magdalena also took part in the confraternity as a *madre mayor*, or "head mother," and the commissary had seen her publicly participating in processions and attending Holy Week sermons. Because of her good reputation, which was based on this evidence of her participation in and leadership of a confraternity, inquisitors decided that Orejel's denunciation was false and calumnious, especially because he confessed that he cheated at gambling.

Despite the fact that Orejel was a Spaniard and Magdalena was a *mulata*, Inquisition officials did not consider him morally superior. On the contrary, Magdalena and her son were among the town's reputable people, in large part because of their participation in a confraternity and its public activities, particularly the Holy Week procession, where they made a yearly public statement of their piety and positive presence in the community. Magdalena's case defies assumptions that the Inquisition would have declared her guilty simply because of her race and gender. In her story, a Spanish man is immoral and a black woman is respectable and upstanding.

A large body of work deals with the topic of Spanish, African, and Indian women in Mexico; such scholarship tends to emphasize the early modern desire to separate women from men in order to avoid their corrupting influence.[2] In Spanish primary sources as well, misogyny and separation, not participation and leadership, are the dominant themes; such sources include confession manuals, prescriptive literature, and Spanish law. These sources reveal that the official policy toward women in both the New and Old Worlds emphasized separation based on the idea that women were seductive and sinful by nature, an idea that derived from the belief that Eve was a corrupter and the cause of original sin.[3]

But when we look beyond the ideal and scrutinize the daily lives of women, we find that laywomen of all classes in New Spain were involved in socially acceptable day-to-day associations with the church. Many women participated in confraternity life through their donations and others gave heavily to convents, although only a tiny percentage of New Spain's society was able to show devotion in this form. Wealthy Spanish laywomen took part in a spiritual economy by donating to convents,[4] but it is difficult to trace non-conventual female religiosity.[5] Black and mulatto women were not able to make the large pious donations we find in the wills of the Spanish elite. They worked for confraternities in other ways, by nursing, collecting alms, and carrying images in processions. The women this chapter examines interacted daily with the world in a public way; their work in the streets and plazas of colonial towns was highly visible.[6]

It could be argued that the prominent and public role African women played in seventeenth-century Afromexican confraternities is one of the most African characteristics of seventeenth-century Afromexican baroque piety. Sisters or *cofradas* [female confraternity members] such as Magdalena led confraternities in Veracruz, San Luis Potosí, Zacatecas, and other mining towns. All of these towns had large black and mulatto populations that enjoyed at least a small disposable income or access to alms. The highly visible participation of confraternity sisters is an illustration of the ways Afromexicans negotiated with colonial authorities to maintain a distinctive spiritual space in New Spain. Ecclesiastical and secular authorities had a tolerant attitude toward the opulent confraternity fiestas put on by these African slaves and free people of color; they even encouraged their sometimes-rowdy street parties because they felt that they offered spiritual benefits and fell under the rubric of the exuberant practices of baroque Catholicism. Women took part in processions, gathered alms, decorated churches for celebrations, and were even among confraternity founders.

However, when mulatto men began to strive toward assimilation in the eighteenth century, the place of women in confraternities was one of the first things to change. Confraternities in general became more businesslike, focusing more on providing dependable funeral benefits for all members through steady incomes based on rent. They also began to spend less on fiestas and flagellant processions. By the 1700s, mulatto men had taken over women's leadership roles and made their confraternities increasingly similar to male-dominated Spanish brotherhoods. As men sought Spanish-defined respectability in the 1700s, they deemphasized women's public participation.[7] In the later viceregal period, women continued to dominate the brotherhoods numerically and take advantage of confraternity benefits, but they no longer led the organizations. Confraternities lost their unique and perhaps African-influenced practices, exchanging agency through marginality for advantage through inclusion in Hispanic society.

Confraternities in New Spain had always welcomed women as members, referring to female members as *cofradas*, *hermanas*, or *madres* (sisters or mothers). Confraternity records indicate that Indian, black, and mulatto women played a more active role in day-to-day confraternity activities than Spanish women. While better-off Spanish women were able to give more land and property to confraternities, they limited their participation in routine activities. There is very little evidence of a strong female role in Spanish confraternities or in any position of religious leadership outside convents. Spanish confraternities were male-dominated organizations.[8] In contrast, women of African birth were active sisters. The leadership roles black and mulatto women held, mainly in seventeenth-century mining towns, linked them to the traditions of rural Indian confraternities and perhaps to gender roles in Africa.

Women were religious leaders in both Africa and pre-Hispanic Mexico; African traditions and indigenous practices may have had a strong influence on the ways women expressed their piety in New Spain. It is likely that the chaotic experience of surviving the Middle Passage compelled Africans who arrived in New Spain in the 1600s to accept the leadership of whoever could manage to rise above their intolerable situation to work toward community-building, and oftentimes these leaders were women. But Africans also saw the example of Indian women's involvement in and leadership of confraternities that drew upon pre-colonial indigenous traditions.[9] The activities of Indian confraternities were observable in many cities, towns, and rural villages, and rural and urban Indians often had some degree of interaction with *castas*. These groups may have had shared visions of how a confraternity should be organized.

Because female religious leadership reached a peak in seventeenth-century confraternities and faded as the number of slaves that arrived in New Spain decreased, it is tempting to propose an African origin for this kind of organization. But scant historical evidence exists to support the argument that sixteenth- and seventeenth-century slaves continued to practice an unchanged and complete body of African religion in New Spain. Historians have found that rituals and concerns surrounding death, female spiritual leadership, and the concept of brotherhoods perhaps best represent African religious practice in New Spain.[10] Catholicism may have dominated, but women's leadership of Afromexican confraternities suggests African influence.

Tracing African influences is a challenge because records do not always specify slaves' exact place of origin. Most Africans who arrived in New Spain in the 1600s came from Angola and the Congo, which were characterized by a matrilineal kinship system and public leadership roles for women. [11] Women in late-seventeenth-century Congo were priestesses and holy visionaries.[12] In Brazil, Angolan slaves had begun to develop unique confraternity traditions in which women held offices and royal titles by the seventeenth century.[13] A long line of priestesses dominated Afro-Brazilian religion, especially the Yoruban religion of Candomblé that was practiced in Bahía, where male participation was not common until well into the twentieth century.[14] Although black and *mulata* involvement in confraternities developed in the particular colonial setting of New Spain, it is possible that these structures had African roots.

Some European confraternities also included women, although not without struggle and compromise for both men and women. Women participated in medieval confraternities that focused on prayer and songs that praised the Virgin, but the rise of flagellant confraternities in the sixteenth and seventeenth centuries was a threat to female participation.[15] The penitential practices of these groups separated the sexes because discipline took place at night in darkened rooms, which was considered an inappropriate setting for women. This change led women in Bologna around 1500 to protest the conversion of a confraternity to a flagellant organization, because the change would limit their participation and force them to pray privately at home while the men practiced their discipline as a group. The sisters protested with an embarrassing public display that shamed the men and the town. As a result, they were permitted to form their own branch of the confraternity.[16] Perhaps authorities made this concession to maintain religious peace and preserve the community. This kind of public shaming and grudging male accommodation was not uncommon in confraternities in

New Spain, where women of African descent walked in flagellant processions (although we do not know whether they actively disciplined themselves) and acted boldly and dressed flamboyantly in confraternity funerals.

The Catholic church tolerated lay female groups when they served a charitable purpose, and charity was often an important aspect of the leadership roles of black and *mulata* sisters in New Spain. Although the Council of Trent had decreed that religious women had to live enclosed lives, historians have found that charitable organizations were open to laywomen. The seventeenth-century French Daughters of Charity worked within acceptable social norms, using unmarried working-class women to carry out nursing and educational roles that were funded by noblewomen.[17] This arrangement did not challenge the post-Tridentine church. In some ways, the French practice of having lower-class women care for the poor was not unlike the nursing functions confraternity mothers in New Spain carried out for their peers, although, and this was more problematic for authorities, female participation did not always stop at nursing.

The typical member of a confraternity in New Spain was a woman. Women, especially poorer women, dominated the membership lists, although not as leaders, of almost every one of the hundreds of confraternity record books available in parish and diocesan archives.[18] Four kinds of confraternity sisters emerge from documents such as wills, confraternity records, and ecclesiastical court cases: the rural Indian woman, for whom confraternity membership was woven into the fiber of village life; the successful urban black mestiza or *mulata* woman, who joined and sometimes led confraternities and succeeded in increasing her status and profile in her locale; the poorer town-dwelling black, *mulata*, mestiza, or Indian woman, who joined a confraternity to protect her soul and guarantee that she would receive a good burial; and the wealthy (usually Spanish) woman who donated money, goods, and membership fees to several confraternities. The presence or absence of these four kinds of women varied a great deal throughout urban and rural New Spain.

Confraternities were a rare opportunity for poor non-Spanish women to participate in communal piety because, with few exceptions, women who lacked *limpieza de sangre* could not become nuns. The convent represented a much more restricted expression of religiosity. A few convents and *beaterias* [houses where pious women lived without taking vows] catered to women who were descended from pre-colonial lords but forbade entrance to *castas*, especially those categorized by authorities as having African heritage.[19] For example, Gertrudis Joseph tried to enter the convent of Saint Catherine of Siena in Valladolid in

1708.[20] Difficulties arose because she wanted to take the "white veil," reserved for those who could claim *limpieza de sangre*. Gertrudis's mother was identified as *mulata* and her father was described as Spanish, and "public knowledge" of her African antecedents prevented her from taking her vows. Her sister also wanted to enter the convent; both women hoped to take advantage of their musical abilities, which were demand in Valladolid at the time.[21] The convent needed musicians, and the sisters wanted access to the convent despite official race-based restrictions. It is significant that these two women were called *moriscas*, the racial label that indicated the smallest amount of notable African ancestry, less than people called black or mulatto.

It is more likely that women of African descent lived in convents as servants or slaves than as nuns. In 1600, the abbess of the Convent of the Encarnation in Mexico City requested permission to hire six "free *mulatas* to serve in this convent."[22] Two percent of the wills sampled for Mexico City in the 1600s mentioned donations of slaves to male convents, including the convents of Saint Augustine and Saint Francis and the Jesuit house; a wide range of female convents also received legacies of slaves. These donations showed the testator's piety and possibly an interest in the slave's spiritual well-being. But most likely such bequests were made because of a desire to help a relative, especially a child dedicated to the religious life. The practice of donating slaves to religious institutions led to conflicts that were often sparked by lay family members who felt neglected and resented the benefits received by the convent and the nun or friar living in it.

In 1653, one of these slaves rejected the enclosed life of the convent. In a 1625 will, a female owner bequeathed the three-year-old *mulata* slave Martina de San Diego to the Convent of the Conception in the viceregal capital. Martina moved into the convent at the age of five and faced a lifetime of serving the nuns. Twenty-five years later, 30-year-old Martina could not stand another day enclosed in the convent walls. Although she had served the nuns faithfully for more than a quarter of a century, Martina said that she felt "grave despondency and such a lack of health that I feel like dying every day."[23] She complained to the guardian of the convent, who took the case to the Archbishop of Mexico. Although the religious authorities involved in the case sympathized with Martina, they were careful to attend to the financial side of this issue and sought the archbishop's permission to change the will and sell Martina to an owner outside the convent.

Confraternities led by elite Spanish women existed only in the contexts of the convent and master-servant relationships. Around 1659, the Dominican nuns of the San Bernardo convent in Mexico City established a confraternity dedicated to the rosary. Founded in imitation of the distinguished Confraternity of the Rosary in the convent of Dominican friars, this confraternity survived at least until 1809.[24] The nuns had two altars to serve the Virgin of the Rosary, one for themselves and another "for the servants of said convent," the enslaved women who came to the convent as gifts to nuns who were making their professions or as legacies to relatives. More than 200 women joined the confraternity under the title "serving girls" or "maids" between 1659 and 1809. *Niñas*, girls who lived as students in the convent and were addressed with the title of "Doña," could also join. No members of this confraternity lived outside the convent, a situation that offered a rare opportunity for elite women to lead a confraternity. Nuns held all the offices. Every year they elected two female majordomos and six deputies. These well-educated women managed to maintain their group at a very high level of organization, much higher than normally seen in the poorer and more disorderly lay groups. Elections were held every year, and candidates and office holders were listed in the books precisely and neatly. This cloistered confraternity carried out many of the normal activities of public confraternities. There were masses on the fiesta of the Nativity of the Virgin in October and on the first Sunday of every month and alms processions were held within the convent. Like confraternities in the outside world, this conventual confraternity held memorial masses for members.

Outside the convent, throughout Latin America, women who worked in public places typically were of African or indigenous descent. But poorer women's lives were not always about selling merchandise or the flamboyance described by observers such as Thomas Gage. In many parts of New Spain, non-Spanish women participated publicly in confraternal celebration and routine. These women also had some economic power, at least among their peers.

It is possible that the leadership roles of women in Afromexican confraternities were consistent with or carried over to other aspects of social life. Women of African heritage appear prominently in property transactions in the notarial records of some towns, such as Valladolid.[25] Women with racial labels such as black or *mulata* or with very simple names (without the title "Doña"—a significant omission that could mean non-Spanish status)[26] bought and sold property throughout the colonial period.[27] Wills made by *mulata* or black women also show that they owned houses, such as the 1697 will of Ursula de los Angeles, a free *mulata* woman from Valladolid, who owned a house and two stores.[28] A woman called Beatriz, described as a *negra jolofe* [black woman of the Wolof ethnic group], was a slaveholder in Valladolid in 1632.[29] In 1734, Pascuala de Ochoa, a free *mulata* woman who owned a house and *solar* [plot of land], carefully mentioned she was a "single women, free of *patria potestad* [paternal authority]."[30] The will of Francisco Mondragón, a black man involved in confraternities in Valladolid, gave his wife María Teresa credit for earning all the money necessary to build their house through her "personal labor."[31] Women of African descent have often been viewed only in the context of their deviant activities or as exotic figures; how they behaved in socially acceptable situations or how they may have influenced the accepted norms of society has been less studied.[32] The average black or *mulata* woman was not a seller of love potions or a seductress, although historians have written much about these exceptional characters. Less-documented but more-numerous women owned property and small amounts of wealth and participated in confraternities. The Valladolid examples illustrate that the ability of women to buy and sell property did not decline during the eighteenth century, when women lost power in their roles in confraternities.

Black, *mulata*, mestiza, Indian, and Spanish women all had options about how they could express their piety, depending on where they lived and how much wealth they had access to. Although women often held undocumented behind-the-scenes power, their control of property throughout the colonial period suggests that the leadership roles and authority they held in confraternities may have not been purely symbolic. For a short time, confraternity leadership was one of the most powerful roles women of African descent could hold in society in New Spain.

Sisters of African birth or heritage who lived in areas with a large population of African descent, such as the town of Veracruz and mining and agricultural towns, helped define a unique form of confraternal piety. Confraternities offered a variety of levels of participation to women. At the top were the founders and *mayordomas*; at the bottom were *madres mayores*, who held nursing and caretaking duties. The leadership roles for black and *mulata* women resembled those in Indian confraternal structures. These women seemed to have achieved some limited prosperity, dominating at least one confraternity, sometimes with substantial funds.

Many Afromexican confraternities were founded in the seventeenth century. Founding documents, especially constitutions and documents directed to ecclesiastical authorities, show how women negotiated the transition from implicit leadership to official positions of authority in confraternities. The term "founding" was used to describe a confraternity's move from an informal institution to an organization that was officially part of the church structure and was documented and approved by a bishop or an ecclesiastical court judge. Confraternity founding documents list both women and men among those who provided the impetus for establishing the confraternity. A list of founders frequently was included in a confraternity's constitution, a document that was usually preserved and/or copied into the confraternity record book. Lists of founders often provide information on the race and sex of the founders.

Confraternities with female founders included the Cofradía de la Humildad y Paciencia de Christo Nuestro Redentor [Confraternity of the Humility and Patience of Christ Our Redeemer], founded in 1657 in the parish church of San Luis Potosí.[33] This town became a center for mining not long after silver was discovered there in 1583. Because there was no large indigenous population in the area, Afromexicans constituted the bulk of the labor force.[34] The list of founders of the confraternity included six mestizos, fourteen mulatto men, and ten "founding sisters." These women were listed as follows: "Juana de la Concepción, free *mulata*, Luisa Flores, mestiza, María *mulata*, Tomasa de los Reyes *mulata*, Juana Lopez, *mulata*, Polonia de Guzmán *mulata*, Magdalena de la Cruz, *negra*."[35] Most of these women had surnames that were common among slaves, such as de la Cruz. One name, María *mulata*, was probably the most common name given to women of African descent in the seventeenth century. Only one woman was labeled as free, and the other names give the impression that the women were slaves or children of slaves. Despite their lack of status in Hispanic society, these women were leaders among their peers.

Another confraternity with female founders was the Confraternity of the Coronation and Saint Benedict of Palermo in the Franciscan convent in the city of Nueva Veracruz.[36] This confraternity was founded in 1636 by "negros y mulatos"—seven men and eighty-five women. Other than one woman who was listed with the last name "Biafara" (a reference to a West African nation or ethnicity), the specific race or nationality of these founders was not listed.

Women had authority within this confraternity. Founders of the confraternity produced a constitution that granted extraordinary privileges based on seniority. Because women were the overwhelming majority of the founding members, they probably had a say in the rules of the constitution. Both male and female founders of this confraternity had special status and obligations. During Lent, male and female founding members were responsible for decorating Saint Benedict's chapel on Wednesdays, and confraternity officers called mothers did this job on Fridays. The confraternity's constitution encouraged founders and mothers to make the altar look as respectable and "decent" as possible.

Like most confraternities, the confraternity of Saint Benedict had a box with three keys in which it guarded its alms, books, and other possessions of value. Women's donations were often crucial to the finances of confraternities, but generally women were not officially recognized as the financial leaders of the group. That position was nearly always entrusted to men, a reflection of men's roles as the financial leaders of society as a whole. Women's wealth was usually put under men's care to carry out pious ends. In most cases, a priest, the majordomo, and the rector or another high official controlled these keys, but in this confraternity, one key was given to the "the oldest male founder, another to the confraternity's rector and another to the oldest female founder."[37] The constitution also made very clear that each of these three people had to be present at any opening of the *caja fuerte* [strongbox] and that each of them had a say in how the confraternity spent money, a rare example of officially mandated female control over confraternity finances.

Both male and female founders passed their higher status in the confraternity of Saint Benedict on to their children. As stated in the constitution:

> If a male or female founder dies and leaves children, these can succeed in the same place as their parents and with the same status [antiguëdad] that their parents had, without preference to the child of the oldest founder over the more recent founder. Founders which currently number seven can name others up to twelve so that these and the founders can enjoy all the privileges . . . and prerogatives conceded to founders.[38]

Hispanic society did not grant social status to people of African descent, but confraternities may have been one place where Afromexicans could establish their own hierarchies or carry on those that they knew from their life before enslavement in New Spain. African hierarchies may have had a longer life in Veracruz, where most slaves disembarked.[39] Just as it could in Angola, *antiguëdad* could be passed down through the maternal line in some confraternities in New Spain. This confraternity's constitution is unique in its concern for succession and for maintaining a specific ruling group. Perhaps the founders of the confraternity of Saint Benedict chose some of their own values when they established the traditions of this mulatto organization.

Indian and Afromexican confraternities were both similar and different in the roles they offered to women. Like Afromexican women, Indian women provided the impetus to found confraternities that were funded by their donations of property. They also held the title of *mayordoma*. But confraternities led by blacks and mulattos developed in larger towns, where economic conditions drew in slaves (as in Veracruz) or free workers (as in mining areas that also had a slave labor force). In contrast, Indian confraternities were most common in smaller villages, and their funding was usually based on money raised from selling agricultural products such as pulque and cattle. Indian sisters did not have the opportunity their Afromexican counterparts did to collect alms in an urban setting, an activity that was much more suitable in larger, wealthier towns. Instead, Indian men collected alms by traveling from village to village within a certain region.[40] Although some Indian women led confraternities, their status was probably based more on a village hierarchy or the inherited wealth they could give to confraternities. In contrast, slaves or freed slaves were often newcomers to a boomtown and had no lineage ties or long-term settlement patterns.

In one important respect, black, *mulata*, and Indian women shared the same experience. By the middle of the eighteenth century, the ability of all three groups of women to fill leadership roles in confraternities was fading. One example of Indian women's loss of power illustrates the point. In early-eighteenth-century Orizaba, María Vásquez donated a house to the Confraternity of the Good Path, located in the parish church of San Miguel.[41] In exchange for the donation, María asked to be buried near the altar "*de los naturales* [native-born, i.e. Indians]." The Confraternity of the Good Path included male members but was led by a *cabildo*, or council, made up of "*hermanas indias doncellas* [maiden Indian sisters]." The confraternity focused on paying for regular masses and a Passion procession and providing all the necessary altar decorations, clothes, and insignias. A 1722 inventory of worked silver and rich damask cloth demonstrated the confraternity's wealth.[42] María Vásquez served as *mayordoma* for many years. Other officers included "*diputadas maiores y menores* [female major and minor deputies]," who controlled confraternity finances until around the 1740s. In that decade, the position of an officer with the title of "administrator" emerged. In one case, this officer was named Juan Vásquez; his position, which took real authority away from the members of the female council, could have been connected to a relationship to María Vásquez and a responsibility to care for her donation.[43] By the 1740s, men dominated this organization and female officers were no longer mentioned, and by the 1780s this confraternity was simply described as made up of "brothers of the native republic of this town." The confraternity in San Miguel transferred from female to male domination during the eighteenth century.

Other kinds of religious organizations developed later that offered leadership to women; for example, a prayer group made up entirely of Indian women in the parish of the Holy Angel in Analco, an Indian village near Puebla de los

Angeles. At the end of the eighteenth century, an organization called the School of Christ of the Holy Sepulcher of Mount Calvary was led by women who served as sisters, porters, secretaries, and nurses.[44]

Although people in power did not always view Indian women as religious leaders, they did recognize their piety and devotion to confraternities, and the humble Indian sister became a stereotype in New Spain. The guardian of the Franciscan convent in Celaya showed this attitude in his written support of a 1670 petition that eighty Indians made to the Bishop of Michoacán asking that he allow them to found a Confraternity of the Cord of Saint Francis:

> The devotion to our father Saint Francis and his cord is innate in these Indians, so much so that the poorest little Indian sister gives her alms happily when they are requested. [Es innata en estos naturales la devoción a nuestro padre San Francisco y a su cuerda y como tales la más pobrecita india hermana da su limosna de muy buena gana cuando se la piden].[45]

The guardian described the devotion of this founding group as regular and organized in supporting masses and burials, and he suggested that the brotherhood become an official confraternity because otherwise majordomos would spend the pitiful alms on their own whims. One senses a patronizing attitude here toward what is assumed to be natural and meek devotion, especially on the part of the women who gave their small but hard-earned donations.

Indian women held offices or titles in confraternities, such as *mayordoma*, mother, head mother, and head sister, although most women were simply sisters [*cofradas*] and had no special privileges or prestige. The vast majority of constitutions stated that anyone could join, specifying "both sexes." Sisters enjoyed all the benefits of membership in confraternities with the same burial privileges as those accorded to men, an important benefit of confraternity membership.

The scant evidence that refers to *mayordomas* tends to come from primarily Indian confraternities. Their male counterparts, majordomos, oversaw all financial decisions and religious arrangements with the priests or friars who hosted the confraternity's altar in their church. The majordomo had to pay any confraternity debts before he left office, a substantial cost that was best met by those with organizational and leadership abilities (i.e., the ability to avoid debt in the first place by securing an income for the confraternity), good connections and patronage networks, and personal wealth. Confraternities could have more than one majordomo. This was a position of great respect and responsibility. Some men held on to the position for decades, and others served only a short term. Because of these responsibilities and the need for majordomos to liaison with ecclesiastical authority, women rarely served as majordomos. A few examples of this title appear in ecclesiastical court cases that came before the Bishop of Michoacán. In 1770, a case was brought up by "Gertrudis Michaela Pícaro *mayordoma* of the Confraternity of the Most Holy Sacrament of Our Lord in the parish church of the pueblo of Maravatío."[46] She complained to the ecclesiastical judge about an Indian village that normally gave money every year for wine for masses and had recently failed to do so. Gertrudis wrote the petition and signed it. This confraternity was made up of Indians, as was the general population of the town.[47] The Confraternity of the Crucified Lord of Mercy in the Church of San Juan de Dios in the city of Celaya also had a *mayordoma*: Juana de Alimansa, who went to Valladolid in 1730 to ask permission from the bishop to beg for alms outside the city.[48] Juana followed the customary manner for asking this permission, stating that the Confraternity of the Crucified Lord was poor and lacked the rent to pay for its annual celebrations and maintain the "divine cult." Although this was a standard and commonplace request, it was unusual for a woman to be sent to do this important job.

The title of mother also implied a higher level of leadership than sister or *cofrada*, but mothers had caretaking or nursing duties and lacked the rank of majordomos. Confraternities of people of African or indigenous descent often elected several mothers a year. Indian confraternities commonly elected numerous female officers called *cihuateopisquis* (which was spelled in various ways). Before the conquest, the *cihuatepixque* were female "officials in charge of women" who fulfilled duties in the indigenous government of Nahua towns. In the 1500s, Fray Diego Durán found that this title was used for older Indian women who had been appointed as "guardians of women," in local government structures.[49] The title continued to be used in Indian confraternities, showing their connection to local government structures. Two confraternities in the late colonial period in outlying parishes of Taxco were dominated by female officers, including *cihuatpisquis*, head mothers, rectors, and a *mayordoma* "of the small Christ," a title implying that this officer cared for and/or carried this image in processions.[50]

Mothers in Afromexican confraternities had various duties connected to their care for the sick. These confraternity *madres* became mothers in a larger sense for their fellow members through their rudimentary nursing skills. Slaves and poor brothers and sisters depended on confraternity charity for care in times of sickness. For example, in the Confraternity of the Coronation and Saint Benedict in Veracruz, founders and members elected a head mother every year.[51] This head mother chose five "female companions" to do "all necessary for the augmentation and devotion of this confraternity" who also had "the duty to visit all brothers and sisters who fell ill." The head mother determined who was in need and gave them two pesos in alms from the funds of the confraternity. A sister was also appointed by the Confraternity of Saint Benedict to help care for the sick.

Another Confraternity of Saint Benedict of Palermo, which was officially founded and approved by the Bishop of Michoacán in 1646, had leadership roles for female members and an overarching symbolic connection to motherhood. This confraternity, based in the Franciscan convent in San Miguel el Grande (now San Miguel Allende), had founders who were described as *morenos*.[52] One of its record books displayed a large and detailed drawing of Saint Benedict of Palermo with an inscription stating that he was the special patron of pregnant women. The picture is a tantalizing image of an African-looking saint, but there is no way of knowing if Saint Benedict inspired the dedication of the members because of this connection to women and fertility, because of his dark-skinned iconography, or because of his ties to the Franciscan Order. Saint Benedict's confraternity in San Miguel endured in a variety of forms until the mid-nineteenth century. Benefits of membership included care in sickness (probably by female members) and burial compensation. The most important yearly activity was a procession on Wednesday of Holy Week, when members carried candles, the insignias of Christ's Passion, and the standard of the confraternity. Head mothers as well as second and third mothers were elected every year and the members determined who would carry the various standards and insignias of the Passion. Some of the mothers, including one named María Josepha, served in the role of head mother over several years. This simple name, which has no surname, indicates that María Josepha was not considered an important person outside the confraternity, despite her leadership within the organization.

The position of head mother for this confraternity indicated specific processional roles; elections often refer to a "madre mayor de Santa Efigenia" and "madre mayor de la virgen," suggesting that these women either cared for or carried these images in processions. In 1718, two women were appointed or elected to serve "por el paso [procession] de San Benito," another "por el paso de Nuestra Señora," and three more "por el paso de Santa Efigenia." Thus, these sisters played an active and public role in Saint Benedict's confraternity and their duties were intertwined with an overall association with motherhood.

Women supported the Confraternity of Saint Benedict in San Miguel in two ways that typify the methods women used to finance confraternities. First, they used the more elite form of giving expensive donations in a will; for example, one sister gave "gold to help gild the altarpiece."[53] Second, women worked to collect alms publicly. Alms collection by female members played an important role in Saint Benedict's finances until the end of the eighteenth century. The mothers who collected alms were often given a meal in return for their efforts. Because mothers supported this confraternity in several ways, it is not surprising that they were publicly presented as confraternity leaders in processions.

Black and *mulata* sisters in Valladolid also left evidence of leadership in the seventeenth century, especially in caretaking roles. Although few records survive from the long-lasting Confraternity of the Incarnation and Saint Blaise based in the cathedral in Valladolid, one remaining document records the 1664 election.[54] This group divided elected officials by race with male and female officers described as blacks, mulattos, and Indians. In 1664, eight *morena* mothers and sixteen *mulata* mothers were elected to help care for the sick. The name of the *mulata* head mother gives us a picture of her personality: Catalina Galvan "la machina." Another women had the interesting nickname "Orejita." These nicknames identify some unique aspect of their personality, although it is hard to interpret nicknames that signify "the machine" (or little macho?) or "little ear." These names were not assigned at the baptismal font and offer a suggestive glimpse into a more personal world hardly ever seen.

Although these roles were most prominent in mining towns, sisters led confraternities in other urban areas of New Spain. The Jesuit supervisors of the confraternity called the Humilde Congregación de la Annunziata de Morenos y Pardos de la Esclavitud de Nuestra Señora [Humble Congregation of the Annunciation of Morenos and Pardos of the Slavery of Our Lady] openly approved the election of female officers in eighteenth-century Puebla de los Angeles.[55] This very Catholic and Spanish city had a large population of African descent that often came to the attention of the colonial authorities in the early 1600s. Jesuits rarely sponsored Afromexican confraternities but were very active in promoting this Congregation of the Annunciation, which was dedicated to charitable activities and Christian education for members. The Jesuits provided a precise format for the notation of elections held by this congregation. Around 1700, a Jesuit scribe left a blank form delineating the offices to be elected in the yearly election. These included offices such as protector, advocate, secretary, and procurator. The scribe provided blank spaces to be filled by names and filled in titles such as "Don," "Doctor," or "Señor." The scribe included offices for male and female members of the Congregation of the Annunciation such as prefect, substitute for the prefect, and nurse. Every office, as indicated on the form, was to be filled by either a *pardo* or a *moreno*. As they were in other confraternities, women were caretakers and nurses. The unanswerable question is, who decided that women would hold official leadership positions? Did the Jesuits simply codify a tacitly accepted confraternity practice? An educated guess might be that the Jesuits, who were not known for their encouragement of female power, were responding to a norm organized by the members of the group.

The congregation carried out the directions provided by the blank election form: male officers were elected every year and the offices of prefect and substitute alternated between men described as *pardo* or *moreno*.[56] This exchange of offices ended in 1730, when a Jesuit padre decided that neither age nor color should have any bearing on office-holding. Female officers did not alternate between *parda* and *morena* and were elected from 1723 to 1766, shortly before Jesuit expulsion. A *parda* and *morena* prefect and substitute were elected every year, as were female advisors, leaders, assistants, nurses, and sacristans. The labels of *parda* and *morena* continued until the final days of the congregation, and confraternity membership and leadership remained African, as suggested by the name of one of the nurses appointed in 1751: Juana la conga.

These fragmentary glimpses of the leading roles black, *mulata*, and Indian women held in several confraternities throughout New Spain hint at a world of unrecorded female authority that possibly derived from African and indigenous cultures, one that continued non-Hispanic values in the context of colonialism or enslavement. Although confraternities had an active place in the towns of Valladolid, San Miguel, and Veracruz, seventeenth-century mining towns provided the setting for the most exuberant confraternal life for Africans and their descendants, and women were at the center of this life.

Women supported confraternities as founders, nurses, alms-collectors, and patrons in the seventeenth century. They accepted these duties with independence, confidence, and personality. Even the driest confraternity account books bring to life the enthusiastic participation of women in Afromexican confraternities, especially in the turbulent ambience of boom-and-bust mining towns. Black confraternity sisters in seventeenth-century Taxco, Zacatecas, and San Luis Potosí found their greatest expression of public religiosity in the colonial period.

In the early and trying times of seventeenth-century slavery, confraternities and Afromexicans in general depended on female support. The Hispanic and Catholic society tolerated and even supported women's public participation and leadership. But gradually men began to reject these humble, less-Hispanic forms of religiosity. Early hints of this transformation and transfer of authority can be seen in 1687 in San Luis Potosí. Officers of the Confraternity of the

Humility and Patience of Christ, which was founded by mulatto men and women, wanted to disassociate themselves from female behavior they considered unsuitable. These unseemly actions were perpetrated by women who were prominent in the public processions of the Confraternity of Our Lady of the Solitude, a confraternity of *morenos* that was also located in San Luis Potosí. The mulatto confraternity did not want to associate itself publicly with the apparently darker and more-African group, although Our Lady of Solitude was much older than the Confraternity of the Humility and Patience of Christ; it had been officially recognized as a confraternity in 1606 and was more than fifty years old when the mulatto-led confraternity organized.

Processions were among the most public activities of the confraternity and an opportunity to mold the town's opinion of the confraternity and of Afromexicans in general. Only three decades after they organized the Confraternity of the Humility and Patience of Christ, Pedro de Aguilar and Diego Pérez, along with other members of the confraternity council, decided that it was in the organization's best interest to limit female participation in confraternity processions

> because the women in the processions of the confraternity of Our Lady of Solitude act in an indecent manner, which is of grave concern to us. To avoid this occurring the said Diego Pérez and Pedro de Aguilar and other brothers have considered this matter and decided that they are obligated to continue to carry out the procession of the Virgin for all the days of their life, with tunics, wax, and all the rest that is necessary for the "lucimiento [lighting]" of the said procession but the said mothers will not go out in this procession which is understood by all members of the council. In said procession only three of the founding mothers will go out every year and these will be elected by the council and will consist of a head mother and two helpers.[57]

Diego Pérez, Pedro de Aguilar, and the other mulatto councilmen did not approve of the possibly scandalous behavior of female members, although it was normal for black and *mulata* sisters to participate in processions by carrying certain insignia or statues. Women were a driving force in the San Luis Potosí confraternities, but men believed a confraternity's decency was compromised when women made public processions. While Pérez and Aguilar led the approval of a new rule and tradition in the confraternity that downplayed female participation in processions, they compromised by allowing three of the most important sisters to participate. When women begin to dominate groups in patriarchal society this type of negotiation is not uncommon—it also occurred in the Bolognese example described above. This example from San Luis Potosí shows one method for moving away from female domination of confraternities as male authority began to coalesce.

In contrast, the Confraternity of the Solitude in San Luis Potosí, which was also described as having indecent processions dominated by women, had female leadership, flagellant processions, and a very African membership.[58] Dominated by African slaves until the mid-seventeenth century, Solitude had existed as a flagellant brotherhood since 1598 under various names.[59] The leaders were Africans of the Zape, Bran, Angola, and Congo nations. This more-slave-based membership may have motivated some of the disdain the mulatto confraternity exhibited toward the Solitude confraternity in San Luis Potosí. It is no surprise that Solitude had lost its autonomy by 1708 and merged with other confraternities in San Luis Potosí while the Humility and Patience confraternity, which aimed for more-Hispanic confraternal norms, survived and prospered at least until 1828.[60]

Even though the Solitude confraternity brothers tried to control their sister members in their 1606 constitution, women emerged early in positions of power. The first rule tried to ensure that confraternity mothers would be chosen from the women who were listed in the membership book. Many of the women who joined and even served as mothers were slaves. The names listed for 1614 indicate this; they included María Conga, *esclava*; Clara, *esclava*, and María, *esclava*. Funerals had a set hierarchy that involved members with titles of queen and empress [*reina* and *emperadora*]. At funerals, majordomos provided the wax given to the queen. All members were required to attend funerals of other members, but the mothers had to sit "in their place as indicated by the majordomos" in a seat located near "the queen and other longtime sisters." *Madres* who disobeyed this rule would be fined two pounds of wax; they would be expelled from the confraternity for a second offense. What the position of "queen" entailed was not clarified (although she had something to do with the wax used at funerals) and the constitution does not explain anything more about funeral customs, but these rules suggest that some African-controlled confraternities practiced unique funeral customs with prominent roles for women.

Solitude brothers tried to impose some order on their female members in their 1606 constitution, and sisters' dress was a point of contention. Mothers were punished if they came to the funerals "dressed in a gaudy manner, not wearing their shawls in a decent way appropriate to a funeral."[61] Apparently women did not cover their heads or bodies enough for the occasion and did not dress modestly or soberly, as was considered appropriate for the occasion and their social class. Confraternity rules also dictated members' dress more generally. Brothers would be punished for collecting alms without wearing the tunic and official scapular of the confraternity and had to wear the tunic and hood of the confraternity in penitential processions. Although this was a confraternity of African slaves, early in its history the male members began to take a role in determining the dress of sisters, usually the prerogative of the colonial power.[62] Before they had even lost their status as slaves, African men sought to emulate Hispanic dictates regarding dress and argued against women dressing above their rank.

Thomas Gage's famous description of the decadent apparel of both slaves and free women offers a vision of what these women considered festive dress and why they caused offense.[63] Gage wrote that in seventeenth-century Mexico City, chains, pearl bracelets, and earrings with "considerable jewels" were not uncommon among black and *mulata* women. They wore dresses covered in silver and gold lace with belts studded with pearls and "knots of gold." Their sleeves were made from colored Chinese silk, "hanging down almost unto the ground." Their headgear was of silk with a ribbon crossing the forehead, "commonly worked out in letters some light and foolish love posy." Even shoes were often covered in silver plate. While this description applies to Mexico City, quick riches earned in mining may have permitted this kind of ostentation in San Luis Potosí as well.

The tendency toward luxurious dress led to sumptuary laws, designed to clarify publicly and visually that only those who truly did sit at the top of the social pyramid could dress in an elite fashion. In 1612, in direct reaction to a recent rebellion, but also to control these inappropriate displays in general, the Mexican high court and the king agreed that

> No black or mulata woman, free or in captivity, can wear gold or silver jewelry, pearls or clothes of Castilian silk, silk mantels, or sleeves with gold or silver borders, on pain of 100 lashes and the confiscation of their clothes, jewelry, pearls and the rest.[64]

It is unlikely that this threat was carried out. However, the example of the Confraternity of the Solitude in San Luis Potosí demonstrates that both Africans and Spanish authorities disliked or felt ambiguous about the boldness of black and *mulata* women. Their ostentatious dress and lack of deference did not mesh with Hispanic ideals of proper dress for the occasion and for their racial category, but women's authority and usefulness within the confraternity made it difficult to completely suppress them until the men achieved a more stable and prosperous status in society.

Confraternal life in seventeenth-century San Luis Potosí involved uniquely African funerals, alms collection, care for the sick, and processions. All of these important aspects of Solitude's activities included women in leadership positions. While their behavior and dress caused some concern and led to stricter rules, confraternity accounts show that women, especially slaves, benefited from the fact that the confraternity provided for their funerals. Because of all the rules surrounding this ritual, funerals must have been lively events, perhaps with some input determined by the members, both male and female, many of whom were born in Africa.

People of African birth or heritage also founded confraternities in Zacatecas, another mining town that reached a pinnacle of prosperity in the seventeenth century. Founded in the sixteenth century after silver was discovered there in 1546, Zacatecas had a population of 25,000, which included 3,000 African slaves, by 1601. Far from the center of the colony, Zacatecas was located 360 miles north of Mexico City (requiring approximately three weeks' travel time) and 120 miles northwest of San Luis Potosí.[65] As the largest and most prosperous mining town in seventeenth-century New Spain, Zacatecas provided the setting for lavish confraternity processions and fiestas. Women played a prominent role in both the mulatto Confraternity of Saint John of the Penitence and the *moreno* Confraternity of the Immaculate Conception and Saint Ann. While brothers tried to control the confraternity from within in San Luis Potosí, more-official powers regulated confraternal life in Zacatecas.

In Zacatecas, sisters carried the image of the Virgin or another female saint and helped collect large amounts of alms, an important job in poorer confraternities. Saint John, founded in 1635, took advantage of the sisters' aggressive alms-collecting, and from 1651, confraternity mothers or sisters who begged for alms for this confraternity showed great enthusiasm and devotion to this work.[66] The male officers conscientiously asked for alms on a monthly basis but rarely managed to get together more than five pesos each time they went out. However, when the women went out "begging [*pidiendo*]," they enjoyed greater success, and their collections normally made up from one-third to two-thirds of the confraternity's annual yearly budget of approximately 100 pesos. Men went onto the streets to beg alms on their own, but women went in pairs. After 1667, the Confraternity of Saint John began an opulent era that was funded by the large amounts of alms sisters collected during Lent. In that year, the men only managed a peso or two when they were on the job, but women, including Angela de Aguilar, María de la O, and Nicolása Pérez, collected an average of twenty pesos each time they begged for alms for a total of eighty pesos, which brought the total yearly intake to over 200 pesos. These women may have been more than volunteers, because the confraternity spent two pesos on a meal for them every time they went out to ask for alms. Collecting money for the confraternity in a sense became their part-time job.

Although some of this money would be used to help sick sisters, the wine-soaked fiestas were the major expense for the Confraternity of Saint John at the end of the seventeenth century. Fiestas may have become raucous; the Confraternity of Saint John consumed ten to fifty pesos' worth of wine on fiesta days, an expense certainly considered superfluous by the ecclesiastical hierarchy of the time. Alcohol consumption posed a potential threat to public safety. In fact, the Bishop of Nueva Galicia forbade the fiestas in 1673 and claimed that these activities caused spiritual and "temporal" damage.[67] However, it is not clear that fiestas led to drunkenness; the large amount of wine may have indicated a large membership or a street party.

Women were not documented as official leaders in the Confraternity of Saint John in Zacatecas until the election of head mothers in 1703, but they did participate in processions in the seventeenth century. As a penitent confraternity, the occasion of the procession of *sangre* or *disciplina* [blood or discipline] was the focus of the year's activities. Saint John's 1635 constitution, which was put forward for approval by "free and enslaved mulattos," described the procession in great detail. Twelve sisters walked in procession carrying candles and wearing the insignia of the confraternity. This must have been a very impressive display; in its late-seventeenth-century heyday, the confraternity spent up to 100 pesos on wax for its fiesta.[68]

Elections in discipline or blood confraternities involved the *repartimiento*, or division of assignments for carrying the numerous insignias of Christ's Passion. Women were not involved in this *repartimiento* until 1742, well after the best years of the Confraternity of Saint John. In this confraternity, women seemed to play an equally public or prominent role in the eighteenth century as in the seventeenth, although by the later era, this was a confraternity (and an entire town) in decline. Even when the town and confraternity began to decline, women retained visible public roles. Sisters carried images of Saint John and Saint Efigenia and participated actively in the procession. These sisters were longtime members with status in the confraternity, and each individual held on to her processional function for several years.

The emphasis in 1742 on the *repartimiento* was new and in fact an attempt to resuscitate the confraternity, which had begun to neglect even the all-important yearly flagellant processions in the 1730s. Once again women played a leading role in maintaining the strength of confraternal traditions, although their role in processions was to carry images or candles and not to flagellate. Unfortunately, we have no records of this confraternity beyond the mid-eighteenth century, so there is no way of knowing if the confraternity did in fact embrace male control and respectability as defined by the Hispanic norm. By the eighteenth century, lack of finances prevented the lavish fiestas the confraternity had enjoyed in the 1600s. The fortunes of Saint John of the Penitence were tied to the fortunes of the mines of Zacatecas.

The *moreno* Confraternity of the Immaculate Conception and Saint Ann in Zacatecas also depended on alms and had lavish processions in which women participated. Immaculate Conception did well in collecting alms, which funded its inventory of images, crosses, and silver jewelry encrusted with jewels. In the 1720s three sisters donated property to the confraternity and it was able to change the basis of its income from alms to rent. After the 1720s, the confraternity more consistently paid for frequent masses, especially for Saint Ann, according to the testamentary requests of female patrons. A new constitution was made that emphasized the obligation to say these masses. (Unfortunately, the old constitution is not available.) By the late 1730s, the confraternity was led not by blacks but by men with titles that included "general" and "captain," obviously Spaniards. Even membership lists recorded people with the titles of "Don" and "Doña," forms of address almost never allowed for people of known African heritage in the colonial period. The fate of the Confraternity of the Immaculate Conception illustrates that *moreno* confraternities were assumed to be poor, dependent on alms, and unfit for controlling the large, dependable rent incomes designated for masses. Even when *morena* sisters made the donation, Spanish authorities found a way to control it.[69]

Like the confraternities in San Luis Potosí and Zacatecas, the Confraternity of Saint Nicolás Tolentino in Taxco, which was founded and led by mulatto men and women, depended on women for the collection of alms.[70] Taxco, located 100 miles southwest of Mexico City in the modern state of Guerrero, had mines in "full production" by 1552 and a large, racially mixed population of miners by the 1570s.[71] The confraternity dated back as far as 1644, and confraternity mothers collected alms from that year until well into the eighteenth century. Like the confraternity mothers in Zacatecas, sometimes these mothers seemed to have more success at alms-collecting than the male members of the confraternity. Head mothers and assistants to the head mother were elected regularly.

Women in this confraternity knew they could rely on the head mother and her assistant to provide care when they fell ill.

The accounts of this confraternity, which include details about flowers, rich fabrics, paper, and other decorative items for the fiesta, suggest that women participated in many aspects of confraternal life. The accounts specifically mention paying a confraternity mother for the "adornment of the church door."[72] Flowers were extensively used in every fiesta. Mothers clearly played a role in maintaining banners and decorating altars, but they were also involved in buying, selling, and organizing the decorative aspects of confraternal life, and this would have also involved female market women, also probably of African descent. The Confraternity of Saint Nicolás Tolentino in Taxco regularly baked what they called "buns for the brothers." Here women were involved in the transactions and process of providing the buns to the confraternity. In Taxco, women probably contributed to the highly decorated fiestas both directly as sisters and indirectly as sellers of material.

In the seventeenth century in mining towns such as Zacatecas, San Luis Potosí, and Taxco, women made distinct contributions to a thriving confraternal life that included organizing fiestas, participating in dramatic processions, collecting alms, and playing specific roles at funerals. Women often founded confraternities or strengthened them by providing health care and financial support. Yet these roles did not often sustain high status over time; as early as the seventeenth century, authorities within and outside the confraternities began to restrict women's bolder displays, especially regarding dress at funerals and decorum during processions. Confraternities continued to be founded, but they began a slow decline in popularity in the eighteenth century, and they stopped being founded by women of African descent. Women would not occupy leadership roles in confraternities again until the mid-nineteenth century. Nevertheless, women of all backgrounds continued to join confraternities in large numbers even after they lost official positions of authority toward the end of the seventeenth century. Instead of leading, *mulata* women became confraternity beneficiaries.

In the eighteenth century, a more-individualized form of confraternal participation superseded the sumptuous baroque ceremonies. Eighteenth-century wills show an increasing concern with the monetary value of the funeral benefits the confraternities provided.[73] Confraternity membership provided something similar to life insurance. By this time members preferred to receive a monetary payout rather than an actual burial surrounded by confraternity brothers. This emphasis on personal monetary gain was certainly a dramatic change from the processions and fiestas at the heart of confraternity ceremonies in the seventeenth century. For their part, ecclesiastical authorities wanted piety to be more interior and less sensual in the eighteenth century, and confraternal piety did become more private and concerned with the individual.[74]

By the eighteenth century, *casta* women living in towns such as Valladolid had come to depend on confraternity membership contracts as burial insurance and a promise of help in purgatory. From the 1500s, wealthy Spanish women had expressed concern for the fate of their souls and had purchased confidence in salvation by joining several confraternities; through these they could pay for any elaborate burial they desired and even secure entombment in holy places such as convents (thought to offer direct access to heaven), while subsidizing myriad masses to be said for their souls. In the seventeenth century, testators demonstrated a great concern for the fate of their souls in the afterlife with detailed requests for large funerals and many masses for their souls. In the eighteenth century, wills of the wealthy referred less frequently to confraternity membership or donations.[75] This decrease in confraternity memberships among better-off testators does not necessarily equate to an overall decrease in confraternity membership among the poor. Because less-affluent individuals could not afford to draw up legally notarized wills, confraternity membership served as their last will and testament. The poor could feel more secure that they would receive a decent burial and at least one mass would be said for their souls, along with prayers from fellow members. Often poor people could afford membership in only one confraternity, but the choice to join was an important one. It guaranteed that an individual's burial would be organized in the proper Christian way. Women may have had special fears in this regard, especially if they were widows and did not trust children or more distant relatives to provide them with a funeral or pay for masses for their souls. Confraternities could give poorer women, those who could not pay a notary to draw up a will, more confidence in their eternal fate. Economic instability may have also played a role in an increasing concern for a monetary return on investment in confraternity membership.[76]

Although a number of aspects of confraternity life changed over time in the seventeenth and eighteenth centuries, one thing stayed the same. In the historical record of confraternities that survives, women of all races and social classes seem to dominate as members, especially in the eighteenth century. In confraternity record books from rural and urban areas of New Spain, women's names generally appear at least twice as often as men's names.[77] Moreover, women often automatically joined with their husbands without being listed in the records.

Late-eighteenth- and early-nineteenth-century confraternity membership contracts called patents provide insights into when and why women joined confraternities. Patents for earlier periods are rarely extant, perhaps because this bureaucratic side of confraternity life was less established and less organized in the 1600s. The mere fact of a more organized form of record-keeping is evidence that the benefits confraternities gave their members in the 1700s were more stable. The increasing concern for better records suggests that eighteenth-century confraternities focused more on individual benefits: people did not want to lose out on their investment in a confraternity, whether it came in the form of cash for survivors or a good Christian burial for the deceased member. The patents that have survived from eighteenth-century confraternities indicate a change in function, away from lavish festivals and dramatic flagellant processions—public activities that gave a church, a town, or a certain saint local prominence—to a more self-centered concern for burial insurance and the fate of one's soul.

Surviving confraternity patents give a sense of what confraternity membership meant and what benefits it conferred. Table 2.1 shows the names of all confraternity sisters who had patents issued and returned them to the Confraternity of Saint Nicolás Tolentino in Valladolid in the late eighteenth century.[78] This confraternity, which was founded in the church of the Convent of Saint Augustine in 1657, was led by Indian and mulatto men in the eighteenth century. The information in the table was taken from patents issued when these women entered the confraternity. The patents were printed or handwritten documents that described devotion to Saint Nicolás Tolentino; they often included a picture of the saint. The new member received a patent when he or she paid an entrance fee of two reales—a very small amount for some, but a day's wage for a laborer[79] and the patent remained valid if the member continued to pay a half-real every week in dues for at least four months and attended the mass on Saint Nicolás's fiesta and the anniversary mass for the souls of living and dead members. The patents of people who kept up their end of the bargain would be returned to the majordomo upon the member's death so that benefits could be disbursed, and for this reason, patents have been preserved in ecclesiastical archives. The member received several benefits in return for keeping up with his or her membership dues. These included extreme unction when gravely ill, which took place in the presence of fellow brothers carrying candles. When the member died, the confraternity would provide a shroud, a requiem mass with bells and members in attendance with candles, and burial or eight pesos in cash. This amount was equal to one month's wage for a laborer. The burial shroud was worth around six pesos. Table 2.1, which shows all available patents

Table 2.1. Eighteenth-century patents for the Saint Nicolás confraternity in Valladolid

Names	Entered	Died	Benefit received	Years of confraternity membership
Women				
Juana Claudia Calletana	1767	1798	12 pesos	32 years
María Dominga Ramirez	1772	1792	12 pesos	20 years
María Joseph Candelaria Olivos	1772	1795	12 pesos	23 years
Isabel Jusepe Hurtado	1778	1794	Habit, 6 pesos	16 years
Guadalupe Hores	1778	1794	12 pesos	16 years
María Micela de la Paz	1778	unknown	unknown	unknown
María Joseph Abalos	1778	1794	11 pesos 4 reales	16 years
María José Sagreda	1778	1796	12 pesos	18 years
María Teresa Edugige	1779	1795	12 pesos	15 years
María Clara	1779	unknown	unknown	unknown
María Felipe Ortiz	1779	unknown	unknown	unknown
María Nicolasa Miranda	1779	1797	12 pesos	18 years
María Fabiana Vargas	1782	1793	12 pesos	11 years
María Salvadora Linares	1782	1794	12 pesos	12 years
María Salvadora Soto	1786	unknown	unknown	unknown
María Santos	1786	unknown	unknown	unknown
María Joseph Pena	1786	1791	unknown	5 years
María Felipe de la Cruz	1786	1792	12 pesos	6 years
María Geralda Andrada	1786	1796	12 pesos 4 reales	10 years
María Francisca Navarette	1786	1797	12 pesos	11 years
Ana Joseph Barena	1790	unknown	unknown	unknown
María Cirilia Gutíerrez	1790	unknown	unknown	unknown
Isabel Guevara	1790	1792	12 pesos	2 years
Francisca Barria	1790	unknown	na	unknown
María Joseph Hernández	1790	unknown	unknown	unknown
María Camargo	1790	1797	12 pesos	7 years
María Gertrud Castro	1790	1792	12 pesos	2 years
María García	1790	1797	12 pesos	7 years
María Manuela Mendoza	1790	1798	12 pesos	8 years
Juana María Marquez	1791	1796	12 pesos	5 years
María Magdalena Zamora	1791	1794	11 pesos 4 reales	3 years
María Joseph Jiménez	1791	1794	12 pesos	3 years
María Teresa Hernándes	1791	1791	12 pesos	0 years
María Bartola de la Cruz	1792	unknown	unknown	unknown
Ana la Paz	1792	1793	11 pesos 4 reales	1 year
María Ana Bustillo	1792	1798	12 pesos 4 reales	6 years
Joséph María Ildelfonso	1793	unknown	unknown	unknown
María Guadalupe Abiles	1794	1798	12 pesos	4 years
María del Carmen Díaz	1796	1798	12 pesos	2 years

Table 2.1—continued

Names	Entered	Died	Benefit received	Years of confraternity membership
Men				
Ignacio Domingo	1777	1791	12 pesos	14 years
José Pio Quinto	1778	1795	unknown	17 years
Anselmo Morales	1778	1793	11 pesos 2 reales	15 years
Joséph Andres Ruiz	1778	unknown	unknown	unknown
Joaquím Palomares	1779	1795	12 pesos	16 years
José Luardo	1782	unknown	unknown	unknown
Don Lorenzo Sendejas	1782	1796	10 pesos	14 years
Juan Andrés Taverna	1785	unknown	unknown	unknown
Antonio Quintero	1790	unknown	unknown	unknown
José Antonio Marquez	1792	1793	12 pesos	1 year
José Silbero Sagas	1792	1793	unknown	1 year
Ricardo Antonio Villaseñor	1792	1793	10 pesos 4 reales	1 year
Josef García de León	1792	1794	11 pesos 4 reales	2 years

Source: "Patentes de la Cofradía de San Nicolás Tolentino, Morelia, 1767–1798," Casa de Morelos, Caja 1265, leg. 2, sf.

from 1791 to 1798, shows that most heirs preferred to receive the entire amount in cash from the majordomo or the treasurer.

The evidence that survives from the 1790s shows that three times as many women as men took out patents with confraternities. None of these women had wills recorded in Valladolid's notarial records during these years. Perhaps the only confraternity member who had a will was Lorenzo Sendejas, who was called "Don" on his patent. This man was prominent in Valladolid and was associated with several confraternities, including mulatto confraternities such as Saint Nicolás Tolentino. He made wills in 1762 and 1791, asking to be buried in the habit of the Third Order of Saint Francis in the Carmelite church.[80] Both the fact that he was a member of the more elite Third Order and his title of "Don" indicates that Sendejas was either of European descent or had succeeded in shedding a lower-status racial designation. But Don Lorenzo was a very unusual case, and he made an extra effort to prepare for the afterlife. The other confraternity members listed in table 2.1 could only depend on their patents.

Both men and women joined the confraternity of Saint Nicolás Tolentino an average of nine years before death. Most men signed on from one to seventeen years before death. Women may have joined much earlier in life, spending twenty or up to thirty years as members before they died. Some men joined when they felt pressure to think about the afterlife; some women made a long-term commitment and perhaps were more involved in the regular confraternity activities.

While table 2.1 shows that *casta* women in the late eighteenth century took advantage of the funeral benefits confraternities offered, their roles as leaders had declined. They were no longer described as founders or mothers with important alms-collecting or processional duties. In fact, bishops expressly forbade female alms-collecting from the late 1600s, considering it a cause of "great inconveniences."[81] In the late eighteenth century, an advisor to Viceroy Revillagigedo decried the "indecent" way Indian women accompanied men who were traveling to collect alms, although Indian men actually supported this activity.[82] Indian men's continuing desire to involve women in their confraternities stands in contrast to the attitude of men in mulatto confraternities. In Valladolid, the town with the most surviving evidence of Afromexican confraternity life, the male leadership became firmly entrenched. The prominence of women leaders that was so characteristic in Indian and Afromexican confraternities in the seventeenth century may not have provided upwardly mobile men with the public presentation they sought. As they became leaders themselves, they rejected female leadership, perhaps because it made their organizations look very different from confraternities led by their social betters of European descent. From the early eighteenth century to the end of the colonial period, men were the leaders in confraternities.

The mining sector in northern New Spain declined economically in the eighteenth century, which contributed to the decline of the wealthy confraternities in these towns and the women whose behavior challenged men's attempts to achieve Hispanic-defined respectability. Guanajuato, a prosperous mining town in eighteenth-century New Spain, does not have records for the kind of confraternities we find in seventeenth-century Taxco, San Luis Potosí, Zacatecas, or Parral. Guanajuato, which reached its peak in mineral wealth after 1740, missed out on the pinnacle of confraternal piety, an important part of public life in seventeenth-century mining towns.

Women did not again lead religious organizations until the mid-nineteenth century, the time of huge growth of organizations of the *vela perpetua*, or an eternal flame lit near the Eucharist in churches.[83] Under official ecclesiastical approval, these organizations spread rapidly in the 1840s in the towns around Morelia. In the 1830s, men belong to the *velas*, but by the 1850s, they had become exclusively female organizations. Although women led and dominated *velas*, they never regained their former prominence in the viceregal-style confraternities that were still in existence after independence. The *velas* were less independent groups than colonial confraternities; they had standardized constitutions regulated by the bishop. Bishops may have been recruiting more women to the church at this time and priests might have also tried to encourage piety and care for local images, or perhaps nineteenth-century women felt that the colonial-style confraternities had lost their vibrancy and were no longer desirable sites where they could hold leadership roles.[84]

In the eighteenth century, women of African descent held on to hard-earned prosperity over the centuries through control of property and businesses. They may have also controlled confraternities behind the scenes through their access to rent and urban real estate, but they had lost their publicly recognized authority and disappeared as overt leaders. Although confraternity sisters could not define confraternal practice throughout the colonial period, they continued to take advantage of the benefits and respectability gained by confraternity membership. When mulatto men became more prosperous in the eighteenth century, their confraternities could begin to aid women rather than depending on them for help. With the help of early sisters, slaves and free people of color constructed a charitable confraternal infrastructure that survived, albeit precariously. The decline in women's leadership positions in confraternities is an important part of a trend in which men of African descent adopted patriarchal values whenever possible. This, in turn, reflects a shift in how confraternities functioned. They moved from being instruments of accommodation *with* to instruments of assimilation *into* Hispanic colonial society.

3

Africans in Mexico City

From Rebellion to Religious Conformity

On the eve of the largest and most destructive rebellion in Mexico City's colonial history, Sor Juana Inez de la Cruz (1651–1695) created African characters living in New Spain's capital who were simple, pious, and a source of comic relief during religious fiestas. This great colonial poet wrote light-hearted *villancicos* [poetic songs sung during church holidays] for the 1679 and 1685 celebrations of the Assumption of the Virgin that took place in Mexico City's cathedral.[1] In one poem, two slaves, Cristina and Blasina, discuss the possibility of abandoning their job of selling chickpeas and *camotes* [literally sweet potatoes, but also a word for fool] and enjoying the fiesta instead. But they think better of this and decide to attend mass, singing praises to God and the Virgin.[2] In the muddled language typically ascribed to Africans in Spanish literature, the jovial slave woman sings:[3]

> Esa sí qui se nombraba
> escrava con devoción,
> e cun turo culazón
> a mi Dioso serviaba:
> y polo sel buena Ecrava
> le dieron la libertá.
>
> [This is what they call a devoted slave, and I serve God with all my heart: for being a good slave, I will be freed.][4]

Sor Juana closely followed Spanish models that portrayed Africans as non-threatening and childlike. This vision extended to sixteenth-century Spanish religious fiestas, where *negrillos* [black children] danced and provided comic relief.[5]

Combining conventional literary models with portrayals of the diversity of her surroundings, Sor Juana used several languages in her poetry, including Nahuatl, Latin, and Portuguese. In this *villancico,* she interweaves the slaves' songs with other verses sung by indigenous faithful in Nahuatl and a clergyman character who signs perhaps equally humorously and incomprehensibly in Latin.

Through these entertaining, popular, and vital, if stereotyped, local characters, Sor Juana emphasizes how Christianity can bring together the various residents of the capital. Religion tames the slave in the poem; her faith pushes her to strive for personal improvement. Sor Juana's poems also acknowledge an African presence in the capital, even on the part of a cloistered nun: Sor Juana would have encountered black and *mulata* servants and slaves in her convent. In contrast to the fear colonial authorities felt toward Africans in the sixteenth and seventeenth centuries, Sor Juana views Africans as harmless, jolly, pious, and humble.

But the reality for Africans and their children and grandchildren was much more complex, and the roles they played in Mexico City's public and private worlds were always in flux. New Spain's capital was a place of extremes for Afromexicans: Mexico City was the crucible for violent statements of African identity at one extreme and assimilation to the norms of successful Spanish life at the other. This chapter cannot easily resolve these contradictory currents. The evidence does not support a simple analysis that chooses one of these extremes as dominant. A sense of this contradictory perspective existed even within the elite Spanish rulers and observers: Sor Juana's poetry showing a happy-go-lucky slave was a local favorite at festival time, but viceregal decrees demonstrated fear of Africans.

Afromexicans immersed themselves in the religious ambiance of the viceregal capital by joining confraternities, institutions that could display conformity to a colonial culture in formation. This chapter situates confraternities, especially confraternities led by people of African descent, within a society preoccupied with Spanish conventions and beliefs regarding death and salvation. Funerals publicly displayed the deceased persons' confraternal connections. A broad spectrum of society celebrated holidays with elaborate processions and public flagellation. Confraternities peaked in popularity in the seventeenth century, especially among wealthier Mexico City residents.

But while Spanish culture, wealth, and power in the New World was concentrated in capitals such as Mexico City, this power was not always strong or stable. Ironically, while religious and civil authorities encouraged this form of group organization by example, they remained concerned about rebellion among lower-class confraternity participants. Rebellious conspiracies, confraternities, and efforts to provide charity to the broad community existed simultaneously, as Africans and their descendants sought a place in Mexico City society, both on their own terms and according to the Spanish norms. For at least the first half of the seventeenth century, individuals of African descent made social connections through church-sanctioned confraternities, but they also occasionally took part in rebellious activities against authority. At the same time, they helped put down rebellions of other Africans, leading troops and gaining prestige through military positions.[6] Despite threats of rebellious conspiracies and the resulting backlash, Mexico City was not unlike Seville, a great Spanish city that also offered blacks and mulattos opportunities to play an active role in religious life. Some of these individuals even achieved success and fame in the seventeenth century, most notably the well-known baroque painter and free *pardo* Juan Correa.

More Africans lived in New Spain in the seventeenth century than at any other time. Emigrants from China, the Philippines, Africa, Portugal, India, and even Japan also resided in the seat of the viceroyalty in the 1600s along with rich and poor Spaniards and Indians.[7] Historians disagree about the demographics of this population. Lourdes Mondragón Barrios estimates that 11,736 Africans, blacks, and mulattos lived in the capital in 1570 as compared to only 2,794 Spaniards.[8] Douglas Cope writes that 8,000 slaves lived in Mexico City in the 1570s along with 18,000 Spaniards.[9] Probably there were large numbers of Africans and creole blacks in sixteenth-century Mexico City, but 8,000 seems too high a number for the enslaved population, although Cope is probably more correct in his estimate of the number of Spaniards. Colin Palmer also perhaps overestimates the number of slaves and free people of color, estimating that by 1612, 50,000 Africans and people of African descent, 15,000 Spaniards, and 80,000 Indians lived in the capital. Probably there were more Spaniards by the 1600s and a roughly equal number of enslaved and free Afromexicans. Palmer also cites Gemelli Careri, who observed a large black and mulatto population in 1698, when he offered his estimate of a total of 100,000 residents in the city.[10] Maybe one-half to two-thirds of Mexico City's residents would still have been Indian at this time, with the rest divided between Spanish and *castas*, including mestizos, Africans, and people of African descent. The accuracy of all these statements is compromised by the fact that racial labels were probably already being manipulated at this time. Regardless of how precise the numbers are, it is clear that slaves and their descendants made up a large part of the population of the central city and had a notable presence there until at least the early eighteenth century.

Documents that relate the history of Africans in the capital come from many voices: viceregal authorities present pronouncements from the top, while wills show the final wishes of the small number of people of African descent who were able to achieve a modicum of prosperity. Some aspects of Afromexican religious life emerge through surviving confraternity documents. Some of these voices depict Africans and their descendants as threatening and others as an inherent part of the public ceremonial life of the city.

This chapter will present a chronology of the 1608 and 1612 slave conspiracies in Mexico City and describe the less-threatening side of African organization, especially confraternities, and the success stories of a few wealthy Africans and *pardo* residents. Much of this history is lost to researchers because of the dearth of confraternity records for Mexico City. Although the Archivo General de la Nación houses some scattered documents relating to confraternities in the capital, no complete list of members, election results, or even account books covering a period of time have come to light for a confraternity designated as black or mulatto. Mexico City's parish records have suffered exceptional damage since the end of the colonial period, more than some other areas of the country such as Orizaba or Morelia, where comprehensive histories of confraternities can be constructed using full series of record books. Perhaps partially due to the incomplete sources, historians have analyzed wealthy confraternities in the capital in detail but have mentioned non-elite organizations only in passing.[11]

However, testaments from the seventeenth century compensate for the few and scattered institutional records and present a more complete picture of confraternity life in the capital. These wills show confraternal devotion in a context that is more personal. Statistical analysis of wills illustrates the predominance of membership in a confraternity as a way to address concerns about salvation. The very few wills Africans and their descendants made reveal that although they shared these concerns, they had a slightly different approach to confraternities. The wills and documents further illustrate that prosperity was possible for only a limited number of people of African descent in the seventeenth century. By detailing the ways that Africans and their progeny participated in both rebellions and confraternal life, this chapter will present two opposing forces in their life in the seventeenth century: a desire for Hispanicization and integration and an impulse to preserve African identity and autonomy through violence. Confraternities had the potential to bridge these conflicting aims.

Rebellions were an early manifestation of African organization, and some occurred before people of African descent formed more peaceable confraternal and charitable groups. In the seventeenth century, rebellions and conspiracies were based around African culture, autonomy, rituals, and, ultimately, confraternities. Black and mulatto confraternities at first focused on a distinct, possibly African religiosity that emphasized the very humble position of their members. Rebellious activities and the harsh response of authorities contrast dramatically with these peaceful confraternities.

The fact that the threat of violence seethed underneath the façade of Mexico City's society complicates our understanding of the benign portrait Sor Juana's Assumption Day *villancico* offers. Spanish authorities perceived Africans in a variety of ways. By the 1500s, Africans had long been a part of Spanish life. Spaniards were accustomed to the presence of African slaves, at least those Spaniards familiar with cosmopolitan, slave-trading cities such as Seville. However, in New Spain, at least in the eyes of colonial authorities, Africans lost the reputation for joviality assigned to them in Spain.[12] One of the greatest fears of early colonial authorities was that African slaves and indigenous people would cooperate to foment rebellion. Early rebellions in 1537 and 1608 increased these fears and led to legislation that further limited the lives of the black population and their ability to interact with Indians. Despite the harsh punishments and restrictions African slaves suffered in the early colonial era, they continued to organize in confraternities. Some men of African descent chose another path; they chose to participate in militias that put down slave rebellions and achieved a degree of prestige for their service. Conformity to colonial authority could trump race in a quest to become a successful member of Hispanic society.[13] Viceregal authorities, whose priorities were loyal subjects and a non-threatening workforce, clashed with those Africans who occasionally displayed a more organized and threatening solidarity through the opposite poles of rebellions and confraternities.

While "Black Spaniards" such as the six slaves who came with Cortés during the conquest of Tenochtitlan helped bring Castilian culture and domination to Mexico, this peaceful collusion between Spanish masters and African slaves ended abruptly in 1536 with the first slave rebellion in Mexico City.[14] The 1537 Codex Telleriano-Remensis illustrates the harsh punishments meted out to these rebels, who apparently wanted to set up their own kingdom. Viceroy Mendoza executed the African king who led the rebellion and asked Charles V to limit the entrance of slaves. The king made the first laws to control Africans in New Spain.[15] Royal decrees forbade holiday gatherings (and gatherings on normal workdays) in the plaza and street because the authorities believed the dancing and festivities would lead to injuries, theft, and even death. The authorities described slaves as aggressive and threatening to their masters.[16] The perceived threat of rebellion in the 1540s led to the passage of laws that also sought to limit the independent housing and business undertakings of the apparently belligerent Africans.

Other official sources illustrate aspects of government anxiety toward Africans and people of mixed parentage. In 1590, Viceroy Villamanrique was careful to advise his successor Luis de Velasco about the growing threat of rebellion. Villamanrique provided Velasco with both a description of the situation and a possible solution, which I quote here at length because these words helped create the long-enduring myth of the violent African vagabond:

> In this land there are great numbers of dangerous and pernicious free Africans and mulattos, as your Lordship knows. They are only capable of living as vagabonds, robbing and causing violence. Although they owe tribute to his Majesty, the majority avoids it by not registering as I commanded for all on pain of death. I sent an order to the alcaldes mayores and corregidores to register the free Africans and mulattos in their districts. They will also be punished if they absent themselves from the districts where they are registered. This order serves two purposes. First, his Majesty collects the tribute that must be paid to him. The other intent, more central to the security and well-being of the country, is to command them to gather together for registration and then to apportion each one among all the mines, so they can serve there with miners, who will pay them. Others will be apportioned into labor gangs subject to an alcalde mayor and not permitted to leave their assigned district or contract without a registered license. This will protect the country from these vagabonds at large and their violence and robberies. The miners will benefit greatly from having these servants to relieve most of the Indians from service. The Africans and mulattos themselves also benefit by earning a steady wage making them more dependable. Their sons will be raised in this life, will enjoy and continue it. I did not have the time to carry out this plan. In the government records, your Lordship will find the order, which you can carry out as you see fit.[17]

This advice reveals the desire of Spanish authorities to confine Africans and Mexican-born blacks almost completely to work camps and thereby achieve greater control over their lives. Failure to act on the more extreme aspects of this advice grew from a desire to make these colonial subjects more productive workers, a goal that was finally achieved, but only after centuries of colonial rule.

The authorities had reason to fear organizations and unrest in the center of the viceroyalty of New Spain. In 1608, rumors circulated that Africans were meeting and crowning kings and organizing a court at their banquets.[18] Viceroy Velasco heard about a possible African conspiracy planned for the Día de los Reyes (January 6). Several slaves were publicly punished to counter fears that the conspiracy would be realized. During this period, concerns about the rebel slave holdouts in the countryside, especially those near the Veracruz–Mexico City road, ran strong. A *palenque* had existed in Yanga, not far from Córdoba, since around 1570. In 1609, a renewed outburst of attacks on haciendas in the region prompted an expedition that included mulatto militiamen against the settlement. The rebels demanded freedom from the mistreatment they experienced as slaves and wanted to be governed by Yanga, an escaped slave who had become their king and for whom the community was named. Eventually, in 1635, this settlement of runaway slaves, after negotiation with Spanish authorities, was granted status as an official town and given the name of San Lorenzo de los Negros.[19]

The most serious threat of African rebellion in the viceregal capital surfaced in 1612 and, just as authorities had feared, it was connected to a confraternity.[20] The 1611 death of a slave woman, which Mexico City slaves attributed to her master's cruelty, sparked a demonstration in the city. A majordomo of a confraternity in the church of Our Lady of Mercy organized a procession to carry her body to the church for burial. This unnamed confraternity was one of the two African confraternities in this church, either the Confraternity of Saint Joseph or the Confraternity of Saint Efigenia, which also had its own chapel in the church.[21] A group of 1,500 black and mulatto confraternity brothers and sisters accompanied the body, shouting in the streets and presenting their grievances publicly before the archbishop's palace and Inquisition headquarters.[22] The rebels began to throw stones at the official buildings, and the authorities drove away the crowd with arms. The first majordomo was beaten publicly for his display of the dead slave's body. Shortly afterward, another majordomo, a slave from Angola, took control. This leader and his wife declared themselves monarchs.

When this newly declared king died of unknown causes, his funeral was surrounded by pomp, ceremony, and dances that the Mercedarian friars could not control. Although rebel leadership was in flux, around the time of the funeral the brothers planned their uprising for Holy Week. Funding for weapons was organized through the confraternity. The cauldron-maker who succeeded the dead slave king was meant to marry the widowed queen. Other slaves sought to gain support among their brothers and angled for leadership in the confraternity and the title of monarch. Most of these leaders were slaves of prominent Spaniards, including a *regidor* [local official] and an *alcalde* [mayor] of the court. During Lent of 1612, some Portuguese slave traders discovered the slave leaders' plans. The traders claimed to understand the talk of conspiracy in the Angolan language and reported to Spanish authorities that the slaves promised death to all Spaniards.[23]

These reports, along with warnings from Mercedarians, caused the high court to crack down on Holy Week celebrations with several decrees in April of 1612. Black confraternities were prohibited from gathering because their meetings in plazas, streets, and markets caused "harm, disturbed the peace and were inconvenient to residents."[24] No group of more than three Africans could congregate. Disobedience carried a sentence of 200 lashes, and priors of convents were encouraged to strictly enforce these rules and forbid blacks and mulattos from entering their churches. The flagellant processions for all confraternities were prohibited, with the order that

> no blood brotherhoods [cofradías de sangre] will march in the Holy Week processions, nor will anyone be permitted to flagellate any other person. . . . In this city under no circumstances will discipline nor any kind of procession be permitted, neither in the day time nor at night.[25]

Churches were closed on Holy Thursday, both in the capital and in Puebla. The majordomos of all the African confraternities in the capital were arrested and imprisoned. (Unfortunately the names of these confraternities were not documented.) Africans in Mexico City visited the imprisoned leaders, creating a festive and communal atmosphere in the jail. However, the mood changed when King Phillip III's wife, Doña Margarita of Austria, died. Non-African confraternities held mourning processions, breeding resentment among the imprisoned leaders because they could not participate. This resentment spread to their visitors and helped foment rebellion conspiracies. Rumors spread of plans to set up another king, free the prisoners, and possibly to poison the city's water supply. To this point, the only evidence against the rebels was rumor of conspiracy. But when authorities discovered some weapons, they meted out harsh punishments.[26]

Various sources provide different estimates for the number of Africans who were punished after this rumored revolt. From thirty to thirty-five people were hung in one day, and from three to fourteen of these were women. This punishment was made very public to discourage further thoughts of rebellion. Reports say that the bodies were left in the nooses for a day. Some heads remained on display and some bodies were quartered. Other individuals (the exact number is not mentioned in the contemporary account) were banished.[27]

This reaction reflects the anxiety authorities harbored regarding their slaves and free Africans. It was a much harsher reaction than the response to another revolt later in the century, in 1692.[28] In that uprising, which was actually carried out and resulted in the burning of the viceregal palace as well as looting, most of the culprits were sentenced to corporal punishment (a severe sentence of 100 to 200 lashes) and hard labor. Only fifteen people—eleven Indians, a Spaniard, and three *castas*—were executed, this time by a gunshot to the head.[29] The responses to the two revolts indicate that a greater fear of African revolt existed at the beginning of the century, when an unrealized conspiracy led to summary hangings. Perhaps authorities in the early 1600s believed that the African population might grow so much that they could no longer control their labor. This would have caused serious problems for the dominant class; the incipient revolt took place at a time when the Indian population continued to suffer from epidemic disease. This preoccupation with cooperation between the subject races suggests that authorities were insecure about their control of the many different groups that came into contact with each other daily, especially in a city the size of the viceregal capital.

The trials after the 1692 revolt were quite organized and were based on evidence of looting. By contrast, the 1612 trials were based more on rumor and devolved into a kind of witch hunt. Douglas Cope argues that "as long as the lower classes . . . lacked group consciousness and were not mobilized in a class war or a struggle against Spanish rule," punishments were lenient.[30] Apparently in 1612, authorities viewed the African conspirators as a more serious and organized political threat, whereas in 1692, having seen the lack of organization and the clear goal of personal gain in a time of want, a consummated revolt seemed somewhat less frightening. African confraternities were perceived as especially dangerous early in the century since they clearly gave Africans an opportunity to organize and elect leaders, and authorities seemed especially chagrined when seeming conformity to a Spanish religious institution masked rebellion. However, confraternities flourished openly for the entire seventeenth century, despite the fact that they had been outlawed twice since the mid-1500s. Perhaps, over the course of the 1600s, the Spanish government came to feel that Africans had gradually succumbed to colonial social and religious control and were no longer a threat. After all, African military leaders helped put down the 1692 revolt.[31]

In the early 1600s, Thomas Gage sensed an atmosphere of alarm and of African strength during his 1625 visit to the viceregal capital.[32] After describing the flamboyant dress worn by African and mulatto women, Gage turned to more serious subjects, connecting this dress to the rebellious nature of Africans in general:

> Most of these are or have been slaves, though love has set them loose, at liberty to enslave souls to sin and Satan. And there are so many of this kind, both men and women, grown to a height of pride and vanity, that many times the Spaniards have feared they would rise up and mutiny against them. The looseness of their lives and public scandals committed by them and the better sort of the Spaniards were such that I have heard those who have professed more religion and fear of God say often they verily thought God would destroy that city, and give up the country into the power of some other nation.

Gage penned these impressions thirteen years after the 1612 plot, but his words help explain the extreme punishment meted out to the supposed conspirators. The perceived disorder of colonial society, where freed slaves seemed to have more power than their masters, might lead to chaos and destruction, as a judgment from God.

In 1612, Viceroy Luis de Velasco cited numerical superiority and the threat of collaboration with Indians as the most menacing aspects of the African presence in New Spain. The Viceroy's *relación* [account] expressed the way in which Spanish authorities came to fear the growing presence of Africans and their strong expressions of cohesion:

> The great number of free and enslaved blacks and mulattos in the kingdom, in villages, farms, ranches and especially in Mexico City is increasing with those born here as well as those brought from Guinea in slaves ships. . . . They live with great liberty and license because of the rewards and good treatment they receive. [They also have] expensive dresses and suits, dances, marriages, confraternities, funerals and live freely due to their daring and vicious nature; whether free or enslaved, they are not servile because they dominate over Indians. . . . And seeing so many who are so powerful in the Spanish houses, where Indians fear and obey them, they try to revolt, kill their masters, rob and dominate the land. If these people were not so barbarous and inclined to liberty, atrocities and crimes, we would not need to fear them.[33]

The account goes on to mention the Yanga rebellion. The viceroy viewed Africans as increasingly threatening, especially in light of the toleration of their developing separate ceremonial life. Velasco also worried that Africans would lead Indians to overthrow the Spanish and that failure to control their behavior would only increase their already-substantial power. However, by 1692, this threat had receded in the minds of colonial leaders. By that time a poor class of *castas* was more numerically dominant than Africans, and this urban mass did not seem able to cooperate with Indians in an effective and focused rebellion. Colonial racial divisions had become more diffuse over the course of the 1600s.

The viceroy's words also suggest that before 1612, in spite of laws made in response to rebellions, a policy of leniency and even self-rule existed toward Africans and their descendants. This leniency led to the emergence of African leaders and the preservation of African culture, at least in confraternity, marriage, and funeral ceremonies. The practice of electing African kings and queens before the 1612 rebellion suggests a form of limited ceremonial self-rule. Appointing African monarchs, a practice with both African and Spanish origins, was also tolerated in other Iberian colonies such as Brazil and Cuba.

From the time of King Enrique III in fifteenth-century Castile, Africans living in Spain chose their official leaders, who were approved by the monarchs. These leaders functioned as justices of the peace and intermediaries with the other sectors of society.[34] Although colonial authorities knew that the existence of an office of king meant a nucleus for plans of rebellion, they did not forbid this tradition and even celebrated the figurehead ruler. In 1539, less than two years after Viceroy Mendoza had executed an African king for rebellion, Bernal Díaz del Castillo witnessed a fiesta called "The Battle of the Wild Men and the Blacks," during which fifty richly attired and bejeweled African men and women marched ceremonially with their king and queen.[35] From the 1500s, including so-called African monarchs in post-conquest displays showed the unity, strength, and benevolent tolerance of the empire.[36] Apparently these ceremonies had an effect on New Spain's Indian subjects, who began to incorporate *negrillos* [little black boys] into their own fiestas not long after.[37] The viceroyalty made concessions to African leaders of the Yanga palenque, so they may have also allowed self-rule in confraternities for a time.

At the time of the 1612 rebellion, the African population in Mexico City and other areas of New Spain seemed to be increasing. Around 1600, Mexico City had a large and vital African population that more closely resembled the population of colonial Cuba or Brazil than is generally assumed. American-born blacks did not outnumber Africans in New Spain until after the mid-1600s, when the Indian population finally recovered from decimating plagues and the number of slaves imported began to decrease. When Africans, rather than Hispanicized blacks, made up the majority of the population of African descent in the vice-regal capital, authorities feared rebellion and chaos. And their fears were not always unfounded. Spanish laws encapsulated the ambivalent attitudes authorities held toward Africans: the courts harshly punished an unrealized conspiracy that revealed African slaves shared common goals, yet tolerated confraternities that brought blacks together in honor of Spanish religion.

Confraternities in the capital fulfilled several valuable social and charitable functions for their African and creole black members. Some early African confraternities in the capital resembled immigrants' organizations and brought together a group of individuals from a particular region in Africa. Health care was the motivating factor for the founding of several confraternities. Afromexicans tried to found a hospital as early as the sixteenth century. The participation of Africans in public religious demonstrations also played an important ceremonial role from the earliest years of the Spanish conquest.

Confraternities with mulatto or black membership and leadership flourished for a short period from the late 1500s to the late 1600s. African organizations may have been less popular because plebeian, class-based ties seem to have become more important than race-based social ties, to the point that in Mexico City, unlike in other areas of New Spain, many late-seventeenth-century confraternities had stopped specifying their racial designation. Africans and their descendants in the capital city lost the opportunity to organize in confraternities organized by race or place of origin. Other groups in Mexico City also joined confraternities less frequently, a trend that took place from the mid-1600s to the independence period. However, this trend did not happen in provincial cities such as Valladolid, where a mulatto confraternity grew stronger as the eighteenth century progressed. Throughout the small towns of New Spain, race was an important factor that drove plebeian confraternities well into the 1700s.

The little evidence that can be found of Afromexican confraternity activity in the seventeenth century indicates that these groups flourished in the capital during this period, when a focus of activity was displaying their wealth and devotion through processions. Table 3.1 lists the names of all documented confraternities designated as led by blacks or mulattos in Mexico City. Although a total of nine are listed, these may have not existed simultaneously. Some have a very elusive history; they disappeared too quickly to leave any record of their existence. Isidoro Sarinara, a parish priest of the Santa Veracruz church, described the spectacle of a 1666 confraternal procession, probably made to recognize the death of Phillip IV in 1665. The morose black standards and clothes

Table 3.1. Afromexican confraternities founded in Mexico City, 1600–1706

Confraternity	Order/Church	Date of founding
Exaltation of the Cross and the Tears of Saint Peter	Parish church of Santa Veracruz	No record
Holy Christ of the Expiration and the Holy Burial	Dominican	1602
Our Lady of Sorrows	San Juanino	1706
Our Lady of the Conception	Hospital of the Marquis of the Valley	1600
Precious Blood of Christ	Parish church of Santa Catalina Mártir	1665
Saint Benedict and the Coronation of Christ	Franciscan/Santa María Redonda	1600
Saint Efigenia	Mercedarian	No record
Saint Joseph	Mercedarian	1706
Saint Nicolás of Mount Calvary	Augustinian	1668

Source: "Memorial de todas las cofradías de españoles, mulatos e indios, Mexico City, 1706," AGN, Bienes Nacionales, vol. 574, Exp. 2, sf.

worn by participants prefigured the demise of the Hapsburg dynasty. Sixteen confraternities "of blacks, mulattos, *chinos* and Tarascan Indians" marched in order of seniority.[38] The confraternities were divided by their standards, which were covered in embroidery and images of their advocations.

Black confraternities in Mexico City came and went, and only the richest enjoyed the luxury of longevity. In some cases, confraternities were labeled as having Afromexican members and leaders at one time in their history, but we do not find this designation in documentation from another time period. Freedmen living in the capital may have rejected associations with an African or enslaved past earlier than confraternity brothers in provincial towns such as Valladolid. Tracing the history is challenging because some confraternities in Mexico City, unlike in many other towns, failed to preserve their earliest documents, including constitutions that stated the date of founding. This is the case for the confraternities dedicated to Saint Efigenia and the Expiration of Christ. In the absence of confraternal records that stretch over decades, we must rely on anecdotal evidence for insights into confraternal piety at its peak.

In 1706, all convents, churches, and hospitals in Mexico City made a list of their confraternities.[39] This survey indicates which of the confraternities listed in table 3.1 survived into the eighteenth century. The 1706 list is only a snapshot; it does not list all confraternities ever in existence in Mexico City. Only two confraternities listed in 1706 were identified as "*de negros o mulatos*": the Confraternity of the Precious Blood of Christ in the parish church of Santa Catalina Martir (which was linked to a Spanish confraternity of the same name) and the

Confraternity of Saint Joseph in the Mercedarian church. The remaining confraternities listed in table 3.1 had either disappeared or were no longer considered Afromexican organizations by 1706. Black confraternities apparently did not exist alongside elite confraternities or in side chapels built by members' donations in the cathedral.

As table 3.1 shows, only two confraternities led by individuals of African descent were founded in Mexico City parish churches. These two parishes, Santa Catalina and Santa Veracruz, were founded in response to the expansion of non-Indian residents of Mexico City beyond the central *traza* [city center] into the formerly indigenous barrios.[40] Originally non-Indians attended mass in the cathedral and Indians were served by the outlying churches of Santa María Redonda, San Sebastián, San Pablo, and San Juan Bautista. After 1550, ecclesiastical divisions were made in response to the change in settlement patterns and the parish churches of Santa Catalina and Santa Veracruz were created. The Franciscan Order maintained these churches, and by 1600, Santa María Redonda was hosting a *moreno* Confraternity of Saint Benedict that was supported by proselytizing friars.

Before Africans and their descendants took part in founding and leading confraternities, they worked to develop other charitable structures in the capital, beginning in 1568 with a request by the "mulatto residents, born in New Spain [vecinos mulatos naturales de Nueva España]" for the king's permission to build a hospital to serve them.[41] The mulatto petitioners complained that neither treatment nor last rites were available to them, since the existing hospitals admitted only Spaniards, mestizos, and Indians. The petitioners proposed a site near the San Hipólito church for a new hospital. Concerns about health care and burial motivated almost every example of black group cooperation for much of the colonial era.

In the petition, the mulatto tailor Juan Bautista claimed that many of the 6,000 mulattos living in the capital were poor and in need of charity. In a revealing summary of their heritage, the petitioners described themselves as "sons of black men and Indians or black women and Spanish men that live in this land in service of Spaniards and practitioners of all crafts"; they also worked "as cow herders." Juan Bautista mentioned that a mulatto servant had helped organize sixty men to guard the city in the "time of rebellion," although he did not give specific details of this rebellion. Perhaps he was referring to the 1536 slave rebellion documented in the Codex Telleriano-Remensis. Witnesses to the petition described these guards as diligent and careful men and those who wanted to found the hospital as educated in the Catholic religion and virtuous. Although all witnesses agreed about Juan Bautista's good character and the need for a hospital, no action was taken in response to this petition. In 1582, a doctor named Pedro López successfully petitioned for the creation of a hospital to serve blacks and mestizos, which led to the founding of the Royal Hospital of the Epiphany or Nuestra Señora de los Desamparados [Our Lady of the Orphans].[42]

After this early failure to independently found a hospital, Africans and their descendants began to organize other charitable organizations. Confraternities with African membership were probably being organized by the end of the sixteenth century, although not without conflict with authorities. In 1601, a group of enslaved and free mulattos and blacks were denounced by the archbishop's secretary for

> meeting and congregating in the monastery of Saint Augustine and founding, by their own authority, a penitential confraternity to go out on Holy Thursday afternoon, with a procession of many mulattos carrying a standard, trumpets, bell and a paso [effigy carried in procession] of the passion and marching in procession before the confraternity of the Holy Name of Jesus. . . . This confraternity does not have a license and has committed an offense deserving punishment which was noted and talked about amongst the people there.[43]

The problem with the confraternity seemed to be the lack of a license, which broke a 1585 law that prohibited blacks from organizing confraternities. Perhaps it was also problematic that the mulattos marched ahead of another confraternity. Evidence suggests that this confraternity was actually founded in the Dominican church and went to San Agustín simply to organize their procession and hand out the tunics worn in the procession, which was led by a free mulatto majordomo. They did not have a real standard, only a green cross. The archbishop denied their petition for an official license. Although no punishment was recorded, the men were declared guilty of an unlicensed meeting and an illegal procession. The fate of this confraternity cannot be traced, but a confraternity described as "de mulatos" did continue to exist in a chapel in the Dominican convent in Mexico City; in 1682, a wealthy Castilian woman left four pesos to a confraternity called "the Expiration of Christ in the chapel of the mulattos in Santo Domingo."[44]

Because so few records have survived for Mexico City, many confraternities with Afromexican leadership appear in the historical record only when they are involved in a conflict. Only fragments of information survive for several confraternities, including Saint Benedict, Saint Nicolás, the Precious Blood of Christ, and Our Lady of the Conception. However, even in this incomplete history of confraternities in the capital, Afromexican identity, communal care, and public reputation emerge as fundamental motivations for their existence.

The African rebellions in the viceregal capital described in this chapter suggest that slaves and freed slaves worked together and discussed the possibility of improving their situation. The descriptions of the activities surrounding the 1608 conspiracy demonstrate that African culture was not completely destroyed when Africans arrived in the New World. Like rebellions, confraternities brought together people with African heritage, although in this case for peaceful ends or perhaps out of pride and a desire to gain social status. Not unlike other immigrants, people of African descent in New Spain sought connections with people who shared their cultural background as a step in the process of adapting to life in a new setting. Spanish immigrants to New Spain also tried to protect the exclusivity of their confraternities. The famous Basque confraternity dedicated to the Virgin of Aránzazu was founded in 1671 and had strict rules regarding benefits for Basques only. A similarly exclusive confraternity founded by Spanish from the Montanes region also existed in the seventeenth century.[45]

At least one confraternity was founded by individuals of a specific African language or cultural group living in the viceregal capital: free people and slaves from the Zape *nación* (the term used in the colonial era to designate African ethnicities) led a brotherhood based in the Hospital of the Immaculate Conception. The confraternity's patron was the Marquis of the Valley of Oaxaca, the hereditary title of nobility granted to the descendants of Hernán Cortes.[46] The Zapes were brought to New Spain mainly in the sixteenth century from coastal Sierra Leone in West Africa. Their enslavement was a result of the breakdown of the Mandinga empire in this region.[47]

The number of Zapes who were brought to New Spain decreased after the Portuguese united with the Spanish crown in 1580 and Spain gained access to Portuguese Central African slave traders. The Portuguese had had a presence in the region of Congo and Angola since the mid-1400s, and the result of Portugal's union with Spain was that more Congo and Angolan slaves than any other group were sold in seventeenth-century New Spain.[48] Zape slaves arrived in the Hispanic world much earlier than Angolan slaves and were sold in Mexico City from the 1560s to the 1580s.[49] Zapes also lived in Spain: Golden Age poets and dramatists used the word "Zape" to refer to Africans, as did Quevedo's 1607 play about Saint Benedict of Palermo.[50]

By around 1600, Zapes in Mexico City had attained their freedom and had sufficient social status and wealth to found their own confraternity. Perhaps they felt motivated to do so because many of them, who would have been elderly in the early 1600s, felt superior to the newly arrived Angolans and wanted to make sure that they retained a distinct identity among Africans in the capital. Ironically, Zapes' strong sense of identity was intertwined with their long-term residence and relative success in the Hispanic world of Mexico City. This confraternity may have helped maintain links between enslaved Zapes and freedmen, helping the slaves improve their situation and the freedmen maintain connections to African roots.

In the 1600s, the Zapes struggled through financial fluctuations to maintain the autonomy of their confraternity's finances and leadership. The Confraternity of the Immaculate Conception was far from wealthy and petitioned to be relieved of a twelve-peso fee they had to pay a priest for permission to have their fiesta in 1600.[51] When a prosperous founder of the confraternity, Juan Roque, died in 1629, he endowed the group with a property in the San Hipólito barrio worth sixty pesos.[52] This was probably a modest one-story house, but it offered the confraternity a small yearly income, which might have been enough to pay for perhaps one or two masses to be said in honor of the members' souls. However, this legacy did not come to the confraternity uncontested. Although witnesses stated that Juan Roque's wishes were common knowledge among the Zape community, for some reason a priest named Joseph de Peñafiel had taken direct control of the rental income of the house (which added up to twenty-four pesos for four years after Juan Roque died; a Spanish woman was the tenant) and the majordomo and deputies wanted this money, along with control of the house. Perhaps the brothers doubted that the priest was actually carrying out Roque's bequest because they appealed to Juan Roque's heir, his daughter Ana María, described as a free black woman who had married a mulatto tailor. When the case came before the ecclesiastical court in 1634, Ana María had also died, leaving no heirs. A few weeks before her death, she asked the members of the Zape confraternity to carry out her father's wishes regarding his house. Several Zapes represented the confraternity and claimed that Ana María had told them that her father meant to give the house to the confraternity to pay for pious works the confraternity could do for his soul. The case ended in their favor, with the help of the official in charge of chaplains and pious works.

Despite their status as slaves, these Zapes led their peers and, to a limited degree, Spanish authorities, who were willing to officially recognize their confraternity as an independent organization of Africans from the Zape nation. Because most Zapes came to New Spain before 1600, Juan Roque and the other leaders of the confraternity had probably spent thirty years of their adult lives in Mexico, during which time they had gained freedom and some prosperity. In 1634, the ages of the Zape witnesses were given as forty-six, fifty, sixty, and seventy; they were certainly old enough to be confraternity leaders and respected members of a community. The Zapes' longevity attested to a decent standard of living. They may have become leaders because their descendants and peers thought that those who had survived the Middle Passage and slavery deserved honor. Perhaps these Zapes had held positions of importance in Africa. Court scribes described the witnesses in the case as fluent in the Spanish language, indicating they were Hispanized Africans rather than *bozales* (recently enslaved Africans; the word literally means wild or untamed). The fact that Juan Roque's daughter was free indicates that either he arranged for her freedom or that she was born free because her mother was not enslaved. The Zape confraternity in at least one case contributed money for a member's letter of manumission. However, this is the only example of this practice in New Spain, although it was common in other areas. This confraternity was a respected, if humble, institution, and was led by well-regarded individuals.

The Zapes controlled their confraternity for as long as possible. In all documentation generated in the dispute over Roque's property, the confraternity was referred to with the words "of *morenos* of the Zape nation." At least ten individuals were mentioned in this case, although oddly one of these officials was named Juan Bautista Xolofo, a reference to another African ethnic group that was frequently taken to New Spain. This small group of Zapes led the confraternity based in their modest and numerically small community. Although Juan Roque's daughter Ana María married a mulatto, not a Zape, she defended her Zape connections and allegedly refused to sell the house even when her husband asked her to.[53]

A decade later, in 1644, another conflict arose over who owned the house that was meant to be perpetually in the care of Zapes. A faction of the confraternity emerged that was led by the Xolof Juan Bautista, who controlled the administration of the house. Confraternity members requested Bautista's resignation in 1644. The older brothers of the group wanted to maintain its Zape identity, and Xolof Juan Bautista apparently posed a threat to that goal. Nine Zape men and four Zape women defended the ethnic exclusivity of the confraternity.[54]

Juan Bautista, not surprisingly, reacted negatively to the revocation of his power and issued a statement against those who had demanded he relinquish his office. In this statement, which was not considered valid by the court, Juan

Bautista said that he was not the only confraternity official who was not Zape; others were Biafaras or were from other unnamed African regions. He alleged that one of the officials should not be allowed to lead the confraternity because he had been prosecuted as a thief, for which he had received 200 lashes and had his earlobes cut off, a very public sign of disgrace. He also pointed out that one of the petitioners was supposedly a slave, not free as claimed, and held no official position in the confraternity. Juan Bautista's testimony attempted to discredit his enemies and undermine their arguments, and in the process it provides a rare glimpse of what a seventeenth-century African considered undistinguished behavior for another African living in New Spain.

The Zapes were not able to maintain their control of this confraternity. A constitution from a confraternity of the same name dating from 1674 shows no evidence of Zape leadership.[55] This new constitution was modeled after a congregation of the Crucified Christ in Seville and seemed to be led by clergy and perhaps by less-wealthy Spaniards. It is likely that this group took over from the Zapes some time after the mid-seventeenth century. Conflicts over leadership, the aging of the Zape population, and intermarriage probably hastened the decline of this African brotherhood.

Another early confraternity, which was founded by *morenos* and promoted by Franciscans in the church of Santa María Redonda, was dedicated to Saint Benedict and the Coronation of Christ with the goals of providing medical care. Saint Benedict was a favorite advocation of confraternities in Veracruz, San Miguel el Grande, and Querétaro (see appendix 1). In a 1599 papal bull, Clement VIII granted the *moreno* brothers three plenary indulgences, which were given on the day of joining, the day of death, and the fiesta of the coronation of Christ.[56] The Franciscan Agustín de Vetancur, writing in 1697 in his *Crónica de la provincia del santo evangelio de México* (36), noted that the Saint Benedict confraternity was moved to the Franciscan convent church in 1633. A 1688 patent described some of the confraternity's functions.[57] Members were obligated to give two reales for an entrance fee, a half-real every week, and four reales for wax during Lent. In return, the confraternity provided medical services, including a surgeon and pharmacist. When they died, members received ten pesos and wax at their funeral. The group made a procession on Holy Wednesday.

This confraternity was one of the few that was mentioned in the will of an African living in Mexico.[58] In 1651, Juan Congo, a free slave who described himself as "*casta mengala*" (referring to an African language or region), was relatively well off; he owned a modest house, cattle, and other material goods. He attended the church of Santa Veracruz and asked for a funeral with attendance by his brothers in Saint Benedict and the Confraternity of Christ in the Santa Clara monastery.

Little else is known of this confraternity's activities. By 1765, the confraternity's peak had long passed and all of its images and paintings had been sold or destroyed.[59] In 1788, the Confraternity of Saint Benedict, with extinction threatening, merged with the Confraternities of Saint Efigenia and Christ of the Expiration, the two other confraternities originally founded by *morenos* or *pardos*.[60] Like Saint Benedict, these two brotherhoods were struggling to survive by the end of the eighteenth century.

The fact that many black confraternities in New Spain were connected to a hospital or dispensary reinforces the sense that health care was a primary concern among sixteenth- and seventeenth-century people of African descent. Two confraternities in the capital were located in hospitals: the Zape Confraternity of the Immaculate Conception in the hospital of the Marquis of the Valley and the Confraternity of the Virgin of the Sorrows in the hospital of San Juan de Dios. The confraternities dedicated to Saint Efigenia, Saint Benedict, and the Precious Blood of Christ also had medical functions. Slaves and their progeny clearly understood that they had to take the initiative when it came to their health care.

Only a few details are known about the confraternity founded in the Mercedarian chapel of Saint Efigenia.[61] The only record of this organization is in the sources that document the 1788 reorganization of the capital's confraternities.[62] In that year, Saint Efigenia's majordomo had possession of the original founding documents, although unfortunately they were not copied into the record. Pope Clement VIII (1592–1605) had approved this founding in the peak era of confraternal organization. The goals of Saint Efigenia were similar to those of several other confraternities in the capital: to help "free *pardos* and *morenos* of the court [capital city] with the obligation to give succor in times of sickness, to administer medical care, medicine and a surgeon and give ten pesos, funeral and burial at their death."[63] The confraternity was still functioning on a very small scale at the end of the eighteenth century. The majordomo and their doctor had possession of members' patents, and the organization had an income of around forty pesos a month, including rent from a small property worth 1,000 pesos and income from the interest on a loan. However, the confraternity owed several hundred pesos to pharmacists and doctors and had not been paying off all its patents. Members could barely afford the wax needed for their fiestas and had not had a meeting for more than five years because every member of the governing body was deceased. Saint Efigenia's reasons for merging with Saint Benedict and Holy Christ are very clear.

A final confraternity with a known goal of aiding the sick was the Confraternity of the Precious Blood of Christ, founded in the parish of Santa Catalina Martir. This confraternity was divided by race; a Spanish branch was founded around 1605 and a mulatto branch was founded some time before 1680.[64] Their image of Christ of the Column achieved fame in the seventeenth and eighteenth centuries, and clerics dedicated at least two novenas, or prayer cycles, to it in the 1780s and 1790s.[65] A few fragments of the accounts from the 1720s show that the confraternity spent more than 200 pesos a year on medicine.[66] Precious Blood of Christ was still an organization of *morenos* and *pardos* in the eighteenth century.

Other Afromexican confraternities had problems with the authorities and remained under the shadow of suspicions of rebellion long after the harsh reaction to the 1612 conspiracy. The confraternity of Saint Nicolás Tolentino of Mount Calvary, which was founded by mulattos some time around 1668, appears in the historical record only because of authorities' fears that the brotherhood would cause a disturbance.[67] In 1668, the officials of this confraternity, three free mulattos who were in their forties, started a shouting match with the group's rector. Apparently, the officials working on the confraternity accounts in the San Pablo barrio house of Juan Galindo had discovered discrepancies in the records of the alms spent on wax. One year later, another commotion, described as a "noisy disturbance or riot," occurred as the brothers left the cathedral for a procession. A free mulatto named Juan de Medina did not want to be accused of involvement in the uproar and, in seeking absolution, called witnesses to testify that he was not present. The witness Miguel Burgos Rendon, a royal treasury official, did not prove very helpful to Medina's case. Rendon declared that "with all the mulattos present, he could not distinguish each individual nor know their names." The confraternity also experienced conflict over the 1672 election of Juan Galindo as majordomo. Finances were again the source of trouble, as the founders of the confraternity, Nicolás Gallego and Francisco Maldonado, decided that Galindo did not have the wherewithal to carry the heavy financial burden of leadership. Galindo argued that he was capable since he had been able to contribute sixty pesos for masses when he served as *mandatario* [leader] of the confraternity.

Disturbances and threats of violence were still present in the later 1600s and occurred both in barrios such as San Pablo and in the center city outside the doors of the cathedral. Disorders at this time represent significant precursors to the larger 1692 rebellion. These cases also intimate the dignity and status brothers of African descent sought to achieve with their participation in these organizations: Juan Galindo strove to demonstrate his financial solvency and Juan de Medina fought to clear himself of charges of disturbing the peace.

The last known Afromexican confraternity to organize in the capital was the Confraternity of Our Lady of Sorrows; it was founded in the early years of the eighteenth century in the hospital of San Juan de Dios.[68] To counteract the rowdy and even rebellious reputation some seventeenth-century black confraternities had earned, the founders of the confraternity dedicated to Dolores emphasized their peaceful and precise nature in their constitution and promised to expel any members who acted otherwise. The constitution explicitly mentioned a desire for order and good organization and a decent and clean presentation of the confraternity's image of the Virgin of the Sorrows. In a nod to confraternity tradition, thirty-three official founders initiated the confraternity and were obligated to pay nine reales upon entrance and one real every month, in addition to a four-real payment for their fiesta. If any member failed to fulfill this financial obligation, thereafter "they had no right to ask anything of the confraternity." The founders and their wives were promised lavish funerals worth twenty-five pesos. Besides caring for their own needs, the founders promised to care for and pray for the poor in the Hospital de San Juan de Dios. This constitution demonstrates the desire of Afromexicans who created confraternities in the eighteenth century to reinforce the social status and reputation of their members, a shift from the conflicts and disruptive behavior that characterized some seventeenth-century confraternities.

Even with the scarce documentation of seventeenth-century black confraternity brothers in the capital, hints of Afromexican confraternity values emerge. Once they founded confraternities for themselves, however marginal, blacks provided themselves with health care and burial rights. As Sandoval wrote, these were services that Africans sorely needed. And in the eighteenth century, the Sorrows confraternity aimed to achieve and solidify respectability, as did other Afromexican confraternities in that century.

Detailed wills of wealthy Spaniards reveal the model of Hispanic piety to which upwardly mobile blacks aspired. Spanish traditions regarded elaborate bequests and devotion to confraternities as routes to salvation. Perhaps more than residents in any other city in America, Spaniards living in the capital of New Spain sought to continue Spain's public religious traditions, which included the large funeral processions that were so popular in sixteenth-century Madrid. People of African heritage shared their masters' hope for communal routes to salvation and emulated this kind of devotion whenever possible. Only a few people of African descent could hope to imitate even the simplest pious bequests made by the elite of the viceregal capital. However, Africans and their descendants did try to imitate lavish baroque death rituals, which included the presence of confraternity brothers.[69]

Only the wealthy elite could afford wills, but confraternity membership may have functioned as a last testament for the poor. It provided a measure of security, burial, masses, and communal prayers. In a sense, confraternity members had already sufficiently demonstrated their loyalty to the church with their contributions to their confraternity or confraternities. Perhaps they felt they did not need a will to guarantee a donation they had made in life, especially if they had consistently paid their confraternity membership dues.

Spaniards brought their devotion to confraternities with them to the New World in the sixteenth and early seventeenth centuries, and their children and grandchildren carried on this tradition until the end of the 1600s. The most dense population of Spanish government officials and members of the religious hierarchy lived in the viceregal capital. In Mexico City, at least one-third of seventeenth-century testators who declared membership in five or more confraternities claimed that either they or their parents had been born in Spain. Elite interest in confraternities in these two capitals of the empire reached its peak in the late 1500s and early 1600s, but by the third quarter of the seventeenth century, the popularity of confraternities among testators was declining. Confraternities survived part of the eighteenth century but had virtually disappeared from wills by the early nineteenth century.

Confraternal piety among the wealthy had declined precipitously by the mid-eighteenth century, as their wills demonstrate. In 1696, 25 percent of testators mentioned confraternities. In 1737, 20 percent were confraternity members; in 1779, it was 10 percent, and by 1813 only 5 percent of those who left wills mentioned confraternity membership.[70] The practice of joining more than one confraternity peaked before the end of the first half of the seventeenth century; only two wills in Mexico City mention five or more confraternities after 1650. The testators who listed nine or more confraternities all made their wills before 1621.

The several hundred seventeenth-century wills that survive from Mexico City represent the last wishes of a broad range of the property-owning class in the viceregal capital, mainly people of Spanish ancestry. Testators in a random sample of these wills were almost equally divided between men and women (213 women, 227 men). These people were born in a variety of places, from Africa to Brittany to Malaga to Santo Domingo to Peru. In this sample, 156 testators (36 percent) were born in Spain and 16 (3 percent) were born in other areas of the Old World, especially Portugal. Just under 50 percent, or 212, were born in New Spain, and 4 were born in other areas of the Americas, such as Peru or Cuba. Although less than half of the wills mention a profession or any other description of life activities, those that do list a profession reveal that testators came from a wide variety of occupational backgrounds and social classes, ranging from the heir to an entailed estate to a dealer in pigs.

Many women left bequests to confraternities, but they did not directly declare confraternity membership in their wills. Among these female patrons, 46 percent either belonged to confraternities or bequeathed money, images, jewels, paintings, silver lamps, or other belongings. For example, the 1672 will of Doña Juana de la Mancha does not state that she was a member in any confraternity. However, she asked to be buried in the Dominican convent and have 200 masses said for her soul, and she also gave a gold cross and jewelry to the Dominican Confraternity of the Rosary.[71] Wealthy women such as Juana de la Mancha also donated slaves, silver plate, jewelry, and large amounts of money to convents and paintings and *retablos* [painted altarpieces] to chapels.[72] These substantial donations testify to the popularity of confraternities among financially secure, independent Spanish women who were unable to hold offices in the brotherhoods they joined.

"Spiritual accounting," a popular trend at the time, demonstrated an exuberant hope that one could gain salvation through high numbers: when individuals had many participants in their funeral procession, many requests for masses for their soul, and joined many confraternities, they believed that they increased their chances of salvation.[73] Among the 440 wills analyzed for the seventeenth century, 36 percent mentioned membership in one or more confraternities. The number of memberships for each individual ranged from one to twelve, and some confraternity enthusiasts, after listing a few of their confraternity affiliations, requested that their desks be checked for confraternity patents because they could not list them all.[74]

People who were interested in confraternities had many to choose from in seventeenth-century Mexico City, as illustrated in table 3.2, a list of all confraternities mentioned in seventeenth-century wills in the capital and the number of testators that belonged to each. Many of the advocations mentioned in seventeenth-century wills had been popular in Spain in the sixteenth century. In the late decades of century, new chapels were founded in Spain dedicated to

Table 3.2. Confraternity advocations in seventeenth-century Mexico City testaments

Confraternity	Testator members	Percent
Holy Sacrament	60	38
Third Order	54	34
Our Lady of the Rosary	38	24
Precious Blood of Christ	28	18
Holy Trinity	28	18
Souls in Purgatory	14	9
Our Lady of Montserrat	11	7
Holy Burial	12	7
Our Lady of Carmen	11	7
Our Lady of Guidance	9	6
Our Lady of Mercy	9	6
Our Lady of the Solitude	6	4
Congregation of the Savior	4	3
Four Evangelists	4	3
Guardian Angel	4	3
Our Lady of Charity	4	3
Holy Name of Christ	4	3
Our Lady of Atocha	4	3
Saint Michael	3	2
Saint Anthony	3	2
True Cross	3	2
Saint Francis Xavier	3	2
Guadalupe	2	1
Saint Sebastián	2	1
Remedies	2	1
Saint Crispín and Crispiniano	1	less than 1
Saint Cosmé and Saint Damián	1	less than 1
Jesus Nazarene	1	less than 1

Source: Archivo General de Notarías, Mexico City.

the Rosary and the True Cross,[75] and the popularity of Our Lady of Montserrat was a New World manifestation of loyalty to this Catalonian shrine to the Virgin. The image of the Virgin of Atocha and the Virgin of Soledad had popular shrines in Madrid in the late sixteenth century. Images of Jesus the Nazarene and Our Lady of Charity also emerged as revered regional saints at this time.[76] William Christian found that during the sixteenth and seventeenth centuries, people lost interest in obscure local saints and devotion to Christ and images of Mary associated with the Passion became more popular.[77] Table 3.2 shows that less-well-known local saints who were honored in Spanish rural villages did not become foci for confraternities in seventeenth-century Mexico City. Residents of New Spain preferred more universal advocations such as the rosary.

Analysis of testaments made by well-off Spaniards in Mexico City reveals that seventeenth-century African slaves and free people of color were surrounded by enthusiastic confraternity members and were influenced by the popularity of this institution among their masters and religious authorities. Most Afromexican confraternities were founded before 1650, before confraternal piety among elite testators began to decline. The confraternities that survived carried on the institution after it had fallen from favor among the rich.

Only ten of the seventeenth-century wills that have been found in Mexico City were clearly made by testators of African descent, although possibly more Afromexicans made wills; not all wills mention the race of the testator. People of African descent were more likely to appear in wills as slaves who were given small inheritances by their masters or who were donated to a relative as property. Some black and mulatto testators made no pious bequests. A very wealthy *pardo* confraternity leader named Mateo de Aguilar expressed a desire for limited clerical involvement in the planning of his funeral. This was a very different situation from that of the *mulata* Catalina de los Angeles (her will is dated April 8, 1683), who was fully involved in Hispanic confraternities. The 1651 will of Juan Congo asked that his brothers in Saint Benedict and the Confraternity of Christ in the Santa Clara monastery attend his funeral. Juan Roque was obviously another enthusiastic member of confraternities; he spent a large sum on masses in 1629. Both Marcos Pérez, a *pardo* fruit dealer who made a will in 1645, and Dionisio de Pina, a *mulata* servant who made a will in 1653, made no mention of confraternity membership and left only the common donation of two reales to free captives in Jerusalem and beatify Gregorio López.[78] A free black woman named Valentina de Morales also listed no confraternity affiliations in her testament made in 1654, but she made the customary donations, in this case to the holy places in Jerusalem and the Virgin of the Remedies; she also asked for a novena and a sung requiem mass in the Santa Veracruz church.[79] These testators may have held more widely varying conceptions of confraternal membership and what it meant to their salvation than the wealthier Spanish testators they sought to emulate.

The remaining three Afromexican testators used their wills to make a final declaration of their dedication to their local religious organizations and institutions. Although their small pious bequests stand in stark contrast to the requests for opulent masses in the wills of Spanish testators, these small donations of money or property probably meant a great deal to those who gave them. One example comes from the 1692 will of Agustín de Dueñas, a free *pardo* and master bricklayer.[80] Dueñas wanted to be buried in the Carmelite convent. He gave the convent a house and named the Carmelite friars his universal heirs so they would celebrate a mass in his name on the fiestas of Easter and Saint Nicolás Tolentino. This last saint is an interesting choice of advocations because of Saint Nicolás's popularity as the advocation of several black confraternities, although Agustín's will does not say he was a member of a Confraternity of Saint Nicolás. Agustín also gave a donation of eight reales to the beatification of Gregorio López and said that he was a member of the Confraternity of the Misericordia, which may have been located at the convent of Saint Catherine of Siena.[81]

José de Valle was also a devotee of Nicolás Tolentino, in this case through the saint's official local confraternity. In 1693, he asked to be buried in the chapel of San Nicolás of the *pardos* as a deputy of the brotherhood.[82] Valle was also a member of the Confraternity of the Name of Jesus in the convent church of San Agustín and asked that all his goods go to the "rector and deputies of this confraternity to spend as they deem fit on the divine cult and adornment of the chapel of this confraternity" in the event of the death of his universal heir, his mother. José de Valle was also wealthy enough to request 100 masses for his soul and give the customary donations to captives and Gregorio López.

Judging from his will, Juan Roque was a prosperous man; he was able to afford several other pious bequests beyond giving his house to the Immaculate Conception confraternity.[83] His 1629 testament is one of the more detailed accounts available of personal piety by an African living in New Spain. Juan wanted to be buried in the church of the Immaculate Conception hospital, where he was a member of the confraternity. His will also offered the option of burial in the Santa Veracruz church, where he was a parishioner. Roque requested that along with his fellow confraternity brothers, twelve people accompany his body in his funeral procession. He also asked that members of the Confraternity of the Holy Sacrament from the Santa Veracruz church join his funeral entourage, and he allotted twenty pesos in alms for their attendance. Although Juan Roque was a free African, his funeral appears very elaborate and elegant. The mass fit the normal pattern for wealthy Spaniards in Mexico City in this era: a sung requiem mass with a deacon and subdeacon present and the offering of communion. Juan Roque also asked for a full complement of masses for his soul, although he did not request, and probably could not afford, the thousands of masses an elite Spaniard would have asked for. Roque asked that ten masses be said at altars of indulgence, twenty masses in the Carmelite convent, ten masses in the hospital of the Immaculate Conception, four masses in the Espíritu Santo hospital, ten masses in the Royal Indian Hospital, and twenty masses generally for the souls in purgatory and the soul of his wife, a *morena* named Isabel de Pereira. Many Spaniards' wills did not include such extensive pious bequests.

Juan Roque, who probably had come to Mexico as a slave no more than fifty years before his death, left no evidence of how he was able to pay for all of these pious requests . How did he move from slave status to having the wealth to pay for such an impressive number of bequests? Patronage from a Spaniard, probably the master who freed him, might have financed his prosperity. The elaborate procession and mass suggests that Juan Roque may have been viewed as a more prominent man than most other Africans living in the capital, at least by those who took part in the ceremony. Perhaps he was known as an important person before he left Africa or emerged as a Zape leader after spending time as a slave in Mexico. It is important to remember that Juan Roque requested this stately ceremony surrounding his funeral only seventeen years after the harsh reaction to the slave rebellion of 1612. Juan was not a typical freedman, but his will suggests that at least a few Africans achieved wealth and status in seventeenth-century Mexico City.

We do know that a few extremely successful men and women of African descent with strong social connections to powerful individuals existed in the seventeenth and eighteenth centuries. These fortunate people included Mateo de Aguilar; Pascuala de Santoyo, the mother of the painter Juan Correa; and of course Juan Correa himself. Their lives reveal that prosperity was possible for Afromexicans if they were fortunate enough to be born to parents with useful family ties, patronage, and talent. Juan Correa's parents provided him with the connections, wealth, and training he needed to rise to prominence as a painter in the late seventeenth century. Juan Correa's father, also called Juan Correa, was a mulatto born in Spain.[84] The father spent years proving his *limpieza de sangre* so that he could serve as a barber and surgeon in the jails of the Inquisition in Mexico City in the 1640s; he described his parents as Spaniards from La Mancha and Cádiz.[85] Juan Correa senior was not wealthy but he worked hard, performing hundreds of tasks as a barber and surgeon in the jail, and he complained of the loss of his independent barbershop due to these extra jobs.

The painter's mother, Pascuala, had money, ties to government officials, and property that probably helped the Correas in their social and financial challenges. The couple may have been brought together through his work for the Inquisition and her ties to the Spanish government: it is possible that the treasury official Alonso de Santoyo, who acted as a patron to the family, was also Pascuala's grandfather or her mother's lover. In her 1677 will, Pascuala described herself as the daughter of María de Santoyo and Bartolomé (she did not know his last name), blacks, probably two slaves of the treasurer.[86] When Alonso de Santoyo died in 1630, he left Pascuala, her mother, her brother, and her four illegitimate children the rent from a sugar hacienda worth 6,000 pesos. Pascuala's illegitimate children were all given the last name Santoyo; one was a Franciscan friar, another a nun in the Santa Isabel convent, where Pascuala was buried. She also had two legitimate children with Juan Correa senior: Juan junior, the famous painter, and Joseph Correa, also a painter. Amazingly, considering the Correas' social connections, Joseph Correa married a slave and his son was born in slavery. Despite these social differences, Juan, Joseph, and Pascuala's daughter, the nun, worked together as trustees of her will and inherited the large income from rent the treasurer had left their mother. It is unfortunate that Pascuala did not stipulate the details of her funeral in her will, but her children said that the ceremony, masses, and other expenses added up to 363 pesos, or around 6 percent of the value of her sugar hacienda.[87]

Juan Correa's connections to Spanish elites were extensive, judging from his numerous commissioned paintings, but he also associated with some wealthy people of African descent, including his son-in-law Cristóbal de Castillo, a rich muleteer who received 2,200 pesos in dowry when he married Juan's daughter, and Mateo de Aguilar, an affluent dealer in jewels. Correa had financial connections with several other wealthy men described as mulattos, including a merchant in Zacatecas, a miner from Pachuca, apprentices, tradesmen of African descent in Mexico City, and his own slaves.[88] Despite all of these connections, Correa was labeled *mulato* in documents dating up to 1678; after this he was simply called *maestro*, but he was never addressed as "Don."

Correa maintained ties to the painters' guild and was a confraternity devotee throughout his life. As an inspector in his guild, Correa exercised considerable power over other members; Spanish painters probably disliked the fact that such authority was held by a man who was referred to as a mulatto. During his lifetime, the guild's regulations were changed to allow Indians, blacks, and *castas* to join, perhaps in response to his influence.[89] Unfortunately, Correa left little testamentary evidence of his time as an active member of the painters' guild or of his confraternity membership. In an early will from 1669, he mentioned membership in the brotherhood of the Holy Burial, located in a Franciscan church, and requested burial there. In his final will of 1716, Correa wrote "I am a brother of several confraternities, according to the patents in my power. I demand that after I die, these confraternities be advised and carry out their obligations as I have carried out mine."[90]

Mateo de Aguilar was a very well-off man who was labeled mulatto and achieved his wealth and status through a Spanish parent and his connections to the Taxco silver mines. His 1705 will reveals a fiercely independent approach to confraternity life. Aguilar was born in Taxco, the legitimate son of a Spaniard from Toledo and a free *parda*.[91] He married a free *parda* and described his occupation as a "jewel runner [*corredor de joyas*]," which probably meant he was involved in the buying and selling of jewels.[92] How Correa and Aguilar knew each other is unknown, but Correa spent several years carrying out Aguilar's bequests, organizing Aguilar's accounts, and arranging the dowries of Aguilar's daughters.[93] An inventory of Aguilar's property valued it at 8,420 pesos. He left dowries worth several thousand pesos to each of his daughters. The sources that document these dowries list some of Aguilar's family possessions, which included hundreds of pesos' worth of silver and gold; several paintings (perhaps by Correa); clothes made with European fabrics; furniture; extensive jewelry that included pearls, diamonds, emeralds, and coral; and religious images and statues.[94] His daughters were called free *pardas* and married men of the same racial designation. One son-in-law was a merchant, another a master shoemaker. Even though their dowries were extensive, the daughters did not marry Spaniards. Marrying a master shoemaker might have been considered a step down by those of Aguilar's social standing. The Afromexican elite in the capital, even the wealthy Aguilar and the well-respected Correa, did not have a hold on status and prosperity that could be passed to the next generation, which suggests that race remained a powerful divider in society into the eighteenth century.

Aguilar's unusual wealth distinguished him from other people of African descent in Mexico City, and this unusual position may have led to his desire for a religious life tailored to his personal demands. Unlike the members of the Confraternity of Our Lady of the Sorrows described above, Aguilar did not need to associate with confraternities to improve his social status and reputation. The lengthy testaments that wealthy devout Spaniards left demonstrate that the rich often worked hard to solidify and personalize their routes to salvation, and Aguilar had the wealth to imitate these models through distinctive personal bequests. As the founder and treasurer of a confraternity dedicated to the "burial of Christ and the Cross of Caravaca" in the monastery of Santa Isabel,[95] Aguilar made that sure all unfinished confraternity business was left in the hands of other officials and his trustees. Although he left no details and asked that it be arranged in secret, he left one-fifth of his wealth to provide for his burial and funeral. Aguilar requested that only his trustees, not "ecclesiastical [or] secular judges," be involved in the disposal of his wealth and last requests.

Like Pascuala de Santoya's will, the 1683 will of the pious and seemingly prosperous free *mulata* Catalina de los Angeles shows that being a servant to powerful Spaniards could lead to prosperity and associations with elite confraternities.[96] Although she was not as wealthy as Juan Correa's mother Pascuala, Catalina had a stock of religious images and pictures that included

> An image of the Conception with marble hands, a baby Jesus, a statue of Saint Joseph, two crucifixes, four imprints of Saint Peter Martyr, a painting of Saint Anthony, a statue of Our Lady of Guadalupe one vara in height with a gilt frame, a painting of Our Lady of Angels, two varas in height, another painting of Our Lady of Zopotlan, and [a] print of Saint Catherine.[97]

These possessions were gifts from Catalina's employer, a deceased cathedral prebendary. Catalina's will demonstrates that some masters influenced and cared about the religious practices of their servants or slaves. Her membership in the Confraternity of the Holy Sacrament in the cathedral may also have been the result of the prebendary's patronage. Catalina probably lived in the very center of the capital and had at least indirect connections with elite Spaniards and *castas* in a similar position to her own. She gave some of her goods to two other free mulatto servants because she had no children. One of them served a chaplain in the cathedral and the other served a member of the high court. In addition to these links to the upper echelons of society, she was a member of two elite confraternities and was a sister of the Confraternity of the Holy Christ "*de los chinos*" founded in the Santa Catalina monastery. This organization, possibly made up of people from the Philippine Islands, is an intriguing but mysterious group, another fleeting glimpse into the wide variety of options for expressions of confraternal piety in seventeenth-century Mexico City. Catalina made arrangements for a funeral that fit her requirements by joining the Confraternity in the Church of the Trinity, which permitted burial in its chapel. She was also a member of the prestigious Confraternity of the Holy Sacrament in the cathedral. She prepared for the afterlife by asking for a sung funeral mass and twelve more masses for her soul.

Catalina was obviously deemed a respectable *mulata* by her master and the members of the elite confraternities who allowed her to join and be buried in their chapel. This patronage enabled Catalina to hope that she could achieve salvation. Almost 20 percent of seventeenth-century testators in Mexico City mentioned owning slaves, which leads us to wonder whether other servants and slaves observed and participated in the religious practices of the Spaniards they served. Master-slave relationships were one possible way to bring Spanish confraternal devotion to people of African descent; other ways included the promotion efforts of the official religious hierarchy and the distribution of charity.

The wills described here also illustrate how Africans and Mexican-born blacks created their own religious milieu in Mexico City by supporting particular advocations that did not always coincide with those that were popular in wills European-born and Creole Spaniards made. Analysis of hundreds of testators from the seventeenth century reveals that a significant number of people mentioned the Confraternities of the holy Sacrament, the Rosary, or the Third Order in their wills. Other very popular confraternities carried the names Precious Blood of Christ, Tránsito, and the Holy Burial. Only one *mulata* testator, Catalina de los Angeles, belonged to these popular Spanish devotions. Other non-Spanish testators instead favored advocations with which they had a closer personal connection; the Indian Petronila María and the *pardo* José de Valle mentioned the Saint Nicolás Tolentino confraternity. None of the wills made by Spaniards mentioned this brotherhood.[98] Juan Congo's will was the only one to mention the Saint Benedict confraternity and only Mateo de Aguilar referred to the Confraternity of the Cross of Caravaca.[99] Juan Roque was the only testator interested in the Confraternity of the Immaculate Conception, which was founded and funded by Zapes. None of these non-Spanish testators mentioned Rosary, Holy Burial, Holy Sacrament, or any other popular confraternities in their wills. Catalina de los Angeles, who was surrounded by high-ranking clergy and government officials, was the only testator with African heritage who belonged to the elite confraternities of Mexico City, including Holy Sacrament and Holy Trinity, but she also included the obscure Confraternity of Christ of the Chinos in her will. Only one Spanish will mentioned a black confraternity: María de Saravia, a wealthy Castilian women, left four pesos to the confraternity of "the Expiration of Christ in the mulatto chapel in Santo Domingo" in 1682.[100] Mexico City was a large and rich city and had enough churches and convents to allow for a diverse range of organizations.

Although the authorities feared that confraternal organization among slaves could lead to rebellions, as it did in 1608, the popular institution of the confraternity spread to residents of African heritage. Mexico City was influenced by trends in confraternal piety that came directly from Spain, and the wealthy of the capital embraced confraternities with enthusiasm before 1600. However, this enthusiasm had ebbed by the end of the seventeenth century.

Several patterns of generational change emerge from the anecdotal evidence presented here. First- or second-generation mulattos in New Spain petitioned for a hospital in 1568, displaying a very early desire for access to charity. Juan Bautista told authorities that he and his fellow petitioners were descended from unions between Indian women and African men or Spanish men and African women and that these unions led to children who resembled American-born Spaniards in language, religion, clothes, and customs if not in appearance, wealth, and social position. Juan Roque, a Zape slave who arrived in New Spain around 1590, represents another line of descent. Roque gained his freedom, and his daughter, Ana María, was also free. Although Ana María tried to carry out her father's wishes regarding support for a Zape confraternity, she married a mulatto tailor and her children probably felt no connection to their Zape heritage, especially since this group of people and their confraternity had disappeared from existence by 1674. Descendants of Juan Roque, Juan Congo, and Juan Bautista probably had a great deal in common by the late seventeenth and early eighteenth centuries; they represented the third, fourth or fifth generations of their families in New Spain. If they were very successful, they could have made wills such as those José de Valle, Catalina de los Angeles, or Marcos Pérez made, each of whom showed a different degree of interest in confraternities. If they had moderately prosperous lives, mulatto descendants could have joined respectable mulatto confraternities such as those dedicated to Saint Nicolás or the Virgin of the Sorrows. Mulattos also achieved success in the Hispanic world if they were recognized as legitimate sons of a Spanish father and had strong connections to Spanish wealth, the story of the lives of Juan Correa and Mateo de Aguilar.

It should not be forgotten that the seventeenth century began and ended with severely punished racially articulated rebellions; all of the individuals described in this chapter may have been affected by or participated in the 1692 revolt. But the effects of the 1612 conspiracy do not seem to have stood in the way of the organizing efforts of later generations of people of African heritage or hindered limited prosperity and upward mobility for blacks and mulattos. In the sixteenth, seventeenth, and eighteenth centuries, Africans and their descendants were more likely to organize confraternities than to rebel against viceregal authorities. A peaceful embrace of the elaborate model of confraternal life presented to them by Spaniards born in Europe and America must have seemed both more compelling and more rewarding than violently rejecting Hispanic society and its institutions.

4

Confraternities in Valladolid

In the seventeenth century, the leaders of the confraternity labeled *de los morenos* in Valladolid were generally slaves or children of slaves, but by the eighteenth century, they had achieved success and prominence as respected craftsmen on Hispanic terms and in Hispanic society. This change opened up the possibility for changes in their confraternities. Seventeenth-century Afromexicans were poor and enslaved, and they depended on alms and pious bequests to maintain their confraternities. But when they were no longer the poorest members of society, they sought financial independence and prominence for their confraternities within Hispanic society.

At least three confraternities with Afromexican membership or leadership existed in Valladolid. These include the mulatto Confraternity of Our Lady of the Rosary, founded in the Franciscan convent church in 1586; the Confraternity of Our Lady of the Incarnation and Saint Blaise, founded in 1610 in the cathedral; and the Confraternity of Saint Nicolás Tolentino, founded in the Augustinian convent church in 1617. All three confraternities had turbulent histories yet endured into the nineteenth century. Against the barriers of colonial-era racial distinctions and hierarchies, their members formed a group of local leaders who worked together and passed down their status through generations and linked leaders' families across confraternities and across time.

This chapter will focus on two confraternities, the Confraternities of the Rosary and the Incarnation and Saint Blaise.[1] These confraternities achieved their popularity and financial success at different times, and their leaders came from distinct social and racial categories. At the peak of the Confraternity of the Incarnation and Saint Blaise in the seventeenth century, many of its leaders were enslaved. In contrast, Rosary's members tended to be free mulattos who worked in various trades. In the eighteenth century, mulatto master architect Diego Durán brought the mulatto Rosary group into greater wealth and prominence. In contrast, at this time, the Incarnation group had to be saved from extinction by a concerned government official.

Testifying to the continuing importance of racial labels, the Rosary confraternity, willingly or not, held on to its mulatto or *pardo* label for the entire colonial era. Did this label hinder its success? The history of confraternities in New Spain shows that sometimes, especially in the seventeenth century, a claim to more humble status gave a group a certain special connection to the sacred and attracted the more powerful members of society. This chapter will examine the Incarnation confraternity, a confraternity of enslaved and free blacks, as an example of a very humble group that generated support and bequests from wealthy Spaniards. The members of Rosary did not need such bequests; its mulatto and mestizo leadership achieved some degree of upward mobility. Rosary's leading members deemphasized alms-collecting, penitence, and strong female participation in their brotherhood, the very characteristics that made Incarnation a particularly Afromexican yet respected confraternity in the seventeenth century.

These two prominent confraternities led by people of African descent in Valladolid had very different histories. Incarnation and Saint Blaise was led by Africans and slaves born in New Spain and was funded by alms and pious bequests. Incarnation and Saint Blaise was perhaps able to achieve the prominence it did in part because there was no Spanish counterpart to overshadow it; the Afromexican Rosary confraternity contended with the presence of a more powerful Spanish Rosary confraternity. Rosary was led by mulatto and mestizo craftsmen and supported itself through rental income and interest income from loans. The two Afromexican groups finally joined forces late in the eighteenth century.

One way of judging the public perception and local renown of a confraternity is to study available wills, usually made by wealthy property owners, for references to membership or pious bequests. Using this methodology, Incarnation and Saint Blaise stands out in the seventeenth century, while the mulatto Rosary does not make an impression. Incarnation tapped into the devotion baroque-era testators felt toward humble organizations with enslaved African members. In contrast, when Rosary was mentioned in a will in the eighteenth century, it was usually for economic reasons, such as the finalization of a rental agreement.

Only a few people in seventeenth-century Valladolid mentioned confraternities in their wills. Compared to Mexico City at this time, Valladolid residents had very little interest in making pious bequests or giving instructions regarding their funerals in their wills. However, in the 1630s, testators, who were almost always of Spanish descent, seemed more aware of local confraternities and took care to mention and make donations to the ones they had joined. This is an exception; for the rest of the century, no will mentioned confraternities. The concern for communal support through prayers, processions, and funeral attendance seen in sixteenth-century Madrid and seventeenth-century Mexico City was not as evident in Valladolid, perhaps because its leading citizens were not as wealthy as the elite in these capitals or because it did not have as many royal officials and nobles in residence.

Pious bequests to confraternities in wills demonstrate the importance of racial distinctions as an aspect of confraternal piety. In 1632, Rosary unofficially divided into two groups. However, it was not until 1681 that the members wrote a new constitution and the group officially divided itself into two separate *gremios* [guilds], one designated for Spaniards and the other made up of mestizos, Indians, and mulattos. By 1632, some, but not all, testators were acknowledging racial distinctions among confraternities, which indicates that some testators were concerned about the racial composition of the confraternities they mentioned while others remained oblivious to these distinctions.

An example of the concern about race in pious bequests can be found in the will of a merchant of Castilian descent named Pedro de Millan, who died in 1631. Millan was careful to associate himself only with confraternities that represented his Spanish heritage.[2] This pious man requested 1,000 masses for himself and his family and 200 for the souls of Indians he had dealt with in life, a common bequest that perhaps tells us something about the conscience of testators. Moreover, he left 200 pesos to help buy clothes for Franciscan friars in Valladolid and requested burial in their church. His only request regarding confraternities was:

> I command that every confraternity of Spaniards in this city be given six pesos in alms so they charitably allow me to join as a brother in order to gain the indulgences as suffrages like any brother and I ask that they accompany my body on the day of my burial.

This merchant wanted to be helped in the afterlife only by confraternities of Spaniards, thus avoiding association with the confraternity dedicated to the Incarnation and Saint Blaise.

While several other wills in this decade mention small donations to every confraternity in the city but do not make distinctions based on race, other 1630s testators expressed concern about racial distinctions in confraternities. In 1633, Doña Gerónima de Boróquez listed several confraternities to which she belonged, asking that the majordomos be advised of her death and come to her burial. She mentioned the Spanish Rosary and the Confraternities of the Holy Sacrament, the Immaculate Conception, Our Lady of Solitude, the True Cross, and the Incarnation and Saint Blaise. Doña Geronima wanted to be associated with the Spanish Rosary confraternity yet she also associated herself with Incarnation, a confraternity of slaves.

Other testaments made by people of European descent made pious bequests to Incarnation and Saint Blaise and asked that the confraternity participate in their funeral processions. This final request openly displayed a testator's association with a black confraternity, so the testators must have perceived such a request as positive and of benefit to his or her earthly reputation and quest for salvation. A will from 1631 made by Gabriel López, a store owner whose parents came from Toledo, asked for burial in the Franciscan church, fifty masses for the souls of Indians in purgatory, and a donation to the infirmary of the Franciscan convent.[3] López was a member of the confraternities of the Rosary, the True Cross, the Holy Sacrament, Solitude, Tránsito and "the Incarnation of the *morenos*." He gave six pesos to each of these confraternities, reminding them to come to his burial with wax, "as is customary." In 1632, Alonso Núñez de Villavicencio asked to be buried in the Franciscan church and gave one peso each to the confraternities of the Rosary, the True Cross, Incarnation, Solitude, Tránsito, and the Holy Sacrament.[4] Another will from this era was made by Doña Geronima de Cisneros, a widow who wanted to be buried near her parents in the Tránsito chapel in the Augustinian church. She donated two pesos to the Confraternities of the Holy Sacrament, Rosary, Immaculate Conception, the True Cross, Tránsito, and Incarnation.[5] The Portuguese testator Enrique de Miranda made similar requests in his 1634 will.[6] He asked to be buried in the cathedral and gave six pesos each to Holy Sacrament, Rosary, Immaculate Conception, the True Cross, Tránsito, and Saint Blaise, "so that all the brothers [of these confraternities] will accompany my body carrying candles." A Castilian, Juan Martínez, was another very devoted confraternity member who belonged to the Third Order of Saint Francis and "every other confraternity in this city."[7] He lists these confraternities, mentioning Rosary (without mentioning race) and "Incarnation of the *morenos*." He requested that members of Incarnation attend his burial and give him the customary masses; he was the only seventeenth-century testator to mention this obligation. A will made in 1635 by a Valladolid government official and his wife, who certainly were both of European extraction, also mentioned membership in every confraternity in the city, but at the same time made a special request to join Incarnation and Saint Blaise after their deaths, giving whatever alms were customary for membership.[8]

These bequests to Incarnation and Saint Blaise, a confraternity known to be led by slaves and free blacks, testify to the special devotion some people felt toward more humble displays of public piety, which was seen commonly in Valladolid when members of Incarnation begged for alms or marched in flagellant processions accompanied by the confraternity's mothers. Bequests created a good income for the confraternity. Wealthier people in society affiliated themselves through important death rituals with the lowest-status people in their society, including slaves and close descendants of slaves. As will be shown in the next chapter, the parish records and records of slave sales prove that during this time, people of African descent living in Valladolid were the among most humble on the social hierarchy. This was the only time testators gave to Incarnation, and the confraternity seems to have had a specific role in funeral displays because of the humility of the confraternity and its members.

None of the thirteen additional wills made in the 1630s in Valladolid mentioned any membership in confraternities, a trend that continued after this decade. This makes it difficult to assess the popularity of confraternities among Spaniards in Valladolid. While both confraternities continued to be very active in the seventeenth century, people who were able to make wills showed no interest in confraternities whatsoever, suggesting that to some in seventeenth-century Valladolid, baroque funeral ceremonies were not very important. Or it may be the case that notaries carelessly neglected to note confraternal bequests.

Spanish and Portuguese residents of Valladolid may have been aware of the prominent and respected black confraternities in Iberia. The fact that they joined Incarnation and Saint Blaise illustrates that it was neither an embarrassment nor a cause of public shame. The confraternity's physical presence at a funeral gave the event a more complete representation of a hierarchical society, a public display that included members of both low and high status. Even Gerónima de Boróquez, the testator careful to show her connection to the Spanish branch of the Rosary confraternity, associated herself with Incarnation. Although little is known about the activities of Incarnation, the confraternity must have somehow earned the respect of the successful and prestigious members of Valladolid society, despite the fact that it was led by slaves.

Rosary was mentioned in all of the aforementioned wills, but not every testator indicated if he or she referred to the Spanish or mulatto branch. The wills from the 1630s were made fifty years before Rosary was officially separated into two groups based on race, but this was a time when mulattos, Indians, and mestizos already had unofficial separate constitutions. It appears that the separation of the confraternity was not widely known by non-members in the 1630s, so Miranda and Doña Gerónima de Cisneros simply made their bequests to the organization without making the racial distinction that more-informed members, which included Doña Gerónima de Boróquez, were careful to make. Others, such as Juan Martínez, clearly knew that Incarnation was led by *morenos* and perhaps did not care whether their wills referred to the Spanish or the mulatto section of the confraternity. These differences show that not all testators were equally worried about race, especially when it came to their fate in the afterlife. Perhaps their attitude reflected a belief that it was more important to have several communities to attend one's funeral and pray for one's soul than it was to worry about racial divisions between people. Incarnation and Saint Blaise fit well into this social and spiritual hierarchy.

Incarnation and Saint Blaise had many traits that were typical of seventeenth-century confraternities led by Africans, slaves, or free blacks in New Spain: scattered evidence suggests that Incarnation was a confraternity with lively and public activities, one that was oriented toward the broader Valladolid community and was somewhat ostentatious even though it was poor. Its alms-collecting put the confraternity in the public eye, which led to testamentary bequests. People would be willing to give to a confraternity only if it had a public place and played a role in civic piety. In the seventeenth century, Incarnation was a respected institution for its humble and distinct piety, which involved begging, the public presence of women, and flagellant processions.

Incarnation and Saint Blaise was always on the margins of Valladolid's religious landscape. The earliest records for this organization, the only confraternity in Valladolid officially labeled "de los morenos," date to 1654,[9] although the confraternity was actually founded in 1610 in the church of the Mercedarian Order, one of the less-wealthy religious orders in Valladolid, or possibly in the cathedral.[10] The confraternity moved from Merced to the cathedral (or vice versa—its early history is lost), then to the church of San José, finally settling in the Santa Veracruz church. The confraternity's saint, Saint Blaise, was an early Christian bishop and a popular saint in sixteenth- and seventeenth-century rural Castile. A few Spanish towns claimed relics and visions of the saint, who was known for his miraculous cures of humans and animals. Perhaps a Spanish friar, cleric, or layman encouraged devotion to this advocation to help people during plagues.[11] And perhaps Blaise's association with the day-to-day concerns of disease and animal husbandry appealed to early members.

Incarnation and Saint Blaise's original constitution was probably lost in the seventeenth century. The earliest surviving constitution dates from 1726 and gives a sense of its charitable goals, piety, and public displays.[12] The rules stated that the confraternity had to elect a majordomo and four deputies and make an inventory of confraternity property every year. At this time, the confraternity owned 150 pesos' worth of houses. The income from this property was not enough to support confraternity activities, and members had to ask for alms inside and outside the city. It had yearly fiestas on the days of both of its advocations and a celebration on Holy Wednesday. Brothers and sisters joined in the Corpus Christi procession, walking with their standard and candles in hand. Every eight days, the majordomo was supposed to lead the other brothers in saying the Rosary aloud in the Santa Veracruz church. One rule involved care for the sick: all the members were to meet to visit sick members and give them "two reales for a chicken." At death, brothers and sisters were honored with a nighttime prayer vigil, and all members processed at the funeral with candles, led by a brother ringing a small bell.

Alms-collecting funded nearly all of Incarnation and Saint Blaise's activities and was part of the confraternity's public profile from the 1650s; confraternity mothers were prominent in this activity. Some members of the confraternity, both male and female, managed to collect nearly one peso every Sunday, Wednesday, and Holy Thursday. The same kind of alms-collecting was recorded for 1684, but by that time the brothers and mothers had extended their territory to the barrios that surrounded central Valladolid.[13] Mothers served as public representatives, and the confraternity elected *morena* and *mulata* mothers from its founding until the end of the seventeenth century.[14]

From 1663 (and possibly earlier), Incarnation and Saint Blaise sent out licensed alms-collectors to other towns and rural areas throughout the Diocese of Michoacán to collect money to pay for their Corpus Christi dances, for wax to illuminate the church on Sundays and holidays, for charity for the sick, and for regular masses.[15] The license permitted the confraternity's representatives to collect alms in the areas around Pátzcuaro and Pinzándaro for a six-month period. By the 1660s, the prominence of the women in the confraternity seems to have become unwelcome, at least in some circumstances, because the bishop would grant the license only on the condition that women would not be permitted to collect alms outside Valladolid under any circumstances, because of the "great inconveniences" this caused. The confraternity continued to ask for these licenses until the end of the eighteenth century.[16]

Incarnation and Saint Blaise had a special departure and welcoming ceremony for their alms-collectors. According to its constitution, when the "pilgrim" who was sent out to ask for alms was leaving the city, the majordomo and all the brothers had to go with him to the "exit [*salida*]" of the city, carrying their standard and lighted candles, accompanied by the music of trumpets, drums, and *truenos* ["a thundering noise" that probably came from fireworks].[17] When the pilgrim returned, the brothers received him on the outskirts of the city with the same ritual.

When majordomo Antonio Romero died in 1724, the confraternity's inventory for that year was listed in his will. The inventory illustrates the challenges of long-distance alms-collecting.[18] Besides an extensive list of all the jewelry and clothes connected to the image of the Incarnation of the Virgin, Romero also stored an image of Our Lady with a special silver hat, which the inventory stated was used only for the begging for alms in the "*tierra caliente* [hot lands]" of the Diocese of Michoacán. The journey to distant regions called for the use of the confraternity's two horses; one of the two saddles the brotherhood owned was for use in "hot lands." Although a record book was mentioned in Romero's will, it has not survived; indeed, none of the record books of this kind of alms-collecting have survived. The officials of the confraternity needed to have special trust in the person they sent long distances to beg. He had to care for valuable and venerated items day and night. In 1680, their emissary absconded with the money he had collected for the confraternity, stealing 100 pesos.[19] Confraternity officials described this thief as a prominent Spaniard in Valladolid.

In the eighteenth century, Incarnation and Saint Blaise's reputation deteriorated, while the mulatto Rosary confraternity forged ahead, increasing its wealth and prestige. Incarnation and Saint Blaise lacked strong leaders such as Diego Durán and Joseph de Sosa, respected mulattos who perhaps purposefully chose not to connect themselves with such a poorly led confraternity or one with an embarrassing reputation. By the 1700s, Incarnation and Saint Blaise probably looked pathetic in their eyes, a throwback to a kind of slave-led confraternity that depended on charity, the type of organization that they wished to move away from as prosperous tradesmen. The leaders of Incarnation and Saint Blaise in the mid-eighteenth century certainly were not impressive: in 1739 correspondence written by officials of the Confraternity of Our Lady of Mount Carmel, Incarnation's majordomo was described as "*rústica* [uncouth or rustic]."[20] Ten years later, the bishop requested that "an intelligent person" assess the state of the confraternity.[21] This witness, a man named Silvestre Ruiz, described Incarnation as decadent and in ruin and without funds to make their Holy Week procession. Confraternity members requested the election of a new majordomo to resolve their problems. The bishop was forced to donate six pesos and goods such as tunics, candles, and other necessities so they could make their procession.

Its decline continued until 1764, when the confraternity faced new and more serious problems.[22] Majordomo Joseph de Aguilar, rector Juan Pardo, and deputies Manuel Vaca and Francisco Mondragón faced the bishop's disdain for their apparently inept handling of confraternity business. Their lack of care was to blame for the confraternity's declining reputation, according to the priest of Santa Veracruz. They had not made much effort to pay for masses or celebrate their fiesta, despite the fact that the confraternity had rental income from some small houses it owned. Saint Blaise did not have the wherewithal to decorate and honor its sacred image, the pride of most confraternities, something that was usually maintained under stringent watch and with great care. This neglect was a clear sign of the confraternity's deterioration. At this time, the confraternity possessed only an old standard, a silver cross, and some candleholders, far less inventory than Romero had mentioned in his 1742 testament. The ecclesiastical authorities did not accuse anyone of stealing, but the priest in the church where the confraternity was located believed that

> it would be better to erase them from the records and expel these useless majordomos and find someone who would serve the confraternity with love, disinterest and devotion. They were founded by blacks. If they do things badly, Spaniards or anyone else who can do better should take over.[23]

This priest's words illustrate a shift in values: from the pious devotion to humility and holiness of the seventeenth century to the privileging of property and stability that characterized the eighteenth century. At the same time, the priest expressed concern about the loss of more than a century's worth of tradition and history because of bad leadership. Although his comments were moderate compared to the accusations leveled against other confraternities led by people of African descent, his suggestion that black leadership be removed was carried out, at least temporarily. Don Fernando Bustillos, a town council member, decided, out of "special devotion," to help the confraternity of Incarnation and Saint Blaise avoid extinction. His help came in the form of service as majordomo; he organized the confraternity's goods until "mulattos and blacks" or any other person could take over as elected majordomos and serve the confraternity efficiently.[24]

Although Incarnation was no longer important in Valladolid's confraternal landscape in the eighteenth century, it participated in late-eighteenth-century citywide petitions to increase the rights of confraternities and majordomos. The confraternity did return to Afromexican control after the interlude of Don Fernando's service, and documents testify that Incarnation and Saint Blaise celebrated yearly fiestas at least to 1841 and still maintained a large membership in 1876.[25]

The Confraternity of Our Lady of the Rosary was the longest lasting and, for three centuries, the most prominent confraternity in Valladolid and later Morelia. The history of the mulatto branch of the Rosary mirrors the increasing prominence of mulattos in eighteenth-century Valladolid and parallels the ascent of people of African descent in Hispanic society from slave status to members of a plebeian class of tradesmen and even skilled professionals. Rosary's leaders included Diego Durán and other men who were respected as master craftsmen and family men with connections to elite society.

The advocation of the Rosary was one of the most popular in New Spain. Although the Dominican Order usually sponsored devotion to the Rosary, convents of other orders and parish churches throughout Mexico often served as headquarters for Rosary confraternities, which were founded in imitation of the original in the Dominican convent in Mexico City. Valladolid did not have a Dominican convent, but at some time in the sixteenth century institutionalized devotion to the Rosary began there. It is unknown if this devotion was sponsored by a layperson or a religious, probably someone from Mexico City or Spain who brought his dedication to the Rosary with him.

The early years of the mulatto Rosary in Valladolid are somewhat shrouded in mystery, although, unlike Incarnation and Saint Blaise, Rosary always had a permanent location in the Franciscan church and a connection with a prominent Spanish confraternity. The earliest historical record of Rosary appears in a 1681 confraternity book that establishes that the confraternity was founded in 1586 in the convent of Saint Francis.[26] In 1681, the members decided they needed to separate the confraternities of Spaniards, Indians, and mulattos. The decision to divide the Rosary into two *gremios*, in this case meaning corporate groups, made a long-standing unofficial division explicit. Instead of sharing an altar with Indians and mulattos, Spaniards began to worship Our Lady of the Rosary at the altar that

> is in the main chapel of this church on the right side next to the priest's seats. The altar of Our Lady of the Rosary that is in the body of the church immediately to the right of the main chapel is designated for the guild of mulattos, mestizos and Indians.[27]

If, previous to 1681, the entire confraternity worshiped the Rosary at one altar, the division between the two branches of the Rosary stressed different positions in the church depending on race. The Spanish branch had a superior position in the main chapel due to their higher position in the colonial racial hierarchy and the fact that they could afford to build and maintain this chapel. As the confraternity became more prominent and more wealthy, Spanish members wanted to preserve a more elite membership, even though and perhaps because, the many non-Spanish members were very active in the church.

The rules for the Spanish section of the confraternity were clearly presented in their record book in 1681 and follow the norms for a wealthy confraternity. They stated that Spaniards had sufficient rental income and properties to pay for the masses and wax that expressed their devotion to the Rosary. The confraternity could afford to spend 200 pesos a year on masses alone, which meant that it owned property worth approximately 10,000 pesos, since the typical return on investments connected to the church was around 5 percent. The confraternity owned a great deal of property all over the Diocese of Michoacán, probably as a result of a combination of members' bequests, contributions, and good financial management. Perhaps the wealthier members decided that because the poorer group, which also happened to be the Afromexican group, did not contribute enough to the financial well-being of the confraternity, it did not deserve to benefit from the large number of masses sponsored by the Spanish members. In this case, the elite did not want a religious organization with universal membership.

With its large annual income, the Spanish Rosary confraternity was able to sponsor masses every Saturday that included "songs with bell-ringing for deceased members" after every mass.[28] Rosary also had a procession on the first Sunday of every month, when a special mass was said for the souls of living and dead brothers. The confraternity celebrated all four of the feast days of the Virgin and the feast of Saint Joseph with vespers and a solemn mass. Instead of a yearly remembrance mass, which was the norm for many poorer confraternities, the Spanish Rosary confraternity had four anniversaries every year in honor of their deceased brothers. Despite its large rental income, this confraternity had the bishop's permission to collect alms in the city of Valladolid on Saturday. Perhaps it felt it needed this source of income because it did not require an initial donation as a condition of membership. A voluntary contribution of two pesos was suggested; in return, the members gained the spiritual benefits of all the masses mentioned above and indulgences for saying the Rosary every week and on the four feast days of the Virgin.

Throughout the seventeenth and eighteenth centuries, the Spanish Rosary confraternity grew in wealth but decreased in numbers. Members continued to be Spaniards who focused on cementing the confraternity's close relationship with the Franciscan convent where the statue of Our Lady of the Rosary was located. In the late seventeenth century, the Spaniards gave 300 pesos to the convent each year for masses and helped illuminate the church with the immense sum of 2,000 pesos for 1,300 pounds of wax, which certainly would have made a brilliant display.[29] They contributed to the upkeep of the Franciscan convent with a donation of 1,900 pesos for velvet seat covers and silver decorations. They also maintained the shrine to the Virgin of the Rosary, buying expensive clothing and jewelry for the image of the saint. In the 1690s, the brothers spent 60 pesos each on a new cloak of wool from Naples, Italy, and a silver crown.

In 1710, the Franciscan guardian assessed the contributions of several confraternities based in the convent church.[30] The Spanish Rosary confraternity exceeded all in wealth and donations and was the most "blessed with indulgences." The friars received 200 pesos a year to sing eighty-seven masses for the confraternity. In a generous gesture, the brothers (this confraternity had no female leaders) gave the Franciscans 150 more pesos out of their income. Clearly the problem was not lack of funds. And leadership was stable as well: rectors and deputies held their offices in perpetuity, while majordomos were elected regularly. Nevertheless, the Franciscan guardian observed that Rosary's membership list was nearly empty because people were not aware of its existence. The Franciscans were motivated to change this situation "for the greater good of their souls and the service to Our Lady" and suggested that the majordomo take Rosary's membership list to Sunday mass, which the confraternity paid for. This would lead to "new members amongst all the faithful who wish to join, as long as they are Spanish."[31] The guardian predicted that within seven months, all the Spanish people in the city would be members of the confraternity.

But the group's lavish support of local fiestas with fireworks, music, and masses did not lead to larger membership. The members of the more elite confraternity had separated themselves from their lower-status members. Their financial domination did not lead to popularity or spiritual solace for the general populace. In fact, they functioned more as a behind-the-scenes investment partnership than as a confraternity. The wealthy Spanish group owned extensive urban properties and rural haciendas and made money from rent and agricultural production. Only a few members managed these investments, operating more like a modern board of directors than a festive religious brotherhood.

The development of the mulatto Rosary confraternity took a very different path. Members needed almost a century to attain even a somewhat stable income in rents and tried various schemes to make money when they faced financial difficulties. It took ambitious men such as Joseph de Sosa and Diego Durán to generate income and status for the confraternity; individuals such as these two helped it survive the independence period. The rest of this chapter will trace the rise in fortunes for the confraternity known as Rosary of the Mulattos.

A 1733 copy of the original 1633 constitution of the mulatto branch of the Rosary confraternity established its long traditions and showed that the mulatto Rosary was similar to other humble black confraternities formed in the seventeenth century.[32] In this document, Rosary brothers explained their version of their history. The 1633 officials, including Bartolome Pérez and Juan Biafara (whose name points to an African ethnicity), asserted that the confraternity had been founded fifty years before, referring to its 1586 foundation date. The racial labels used to describe the 1633 officials indicate that blacks, mulattos, and mestizos led the brotherhood. The constitution claimed inspiration from that of the Rosary confraternity in Mexico City. In 1633, the confraternity had no rental income and depended entirely on alms, with the bishop's consent. The constitution suggested that new members made some kind of donation, probably whatever they could manage. The masses paid for by the mulatto Rosary were much less impressive than those of their Spanish counterpart. The constitution said that Rosary had to give the Franciscan convent one peso each week for a Sunday mass and twenty pesos for the celebrations on each of the Virgin's four feast days. The confraternity also celebrated the fiesta of the Rosary with solemn vespers and a sung mass, with a total worth of twelve pesos. The constitution promised a mass for every dead brother or sister, at which attendance by members was mandatory, and a weekly procession.

From the beginning, the mulatto Rosary confraternity struggled to maintain itself with an adequate inventory of goods.[33] In the seventeenth century, it owned items such as a cross, silk mantles, silver crowns for the Virgin and the baby Jesus, and a standard with silver embroidery. Other items in its inventory, however, showed that it was still a poor confraternity. Its candlesticks and plate for collecting alms were not silver, which was the norm for many confraternities.

Like officials in other confraternities in the Diocese of Michoacán, Rosary officials emphasized the poverty and humility of the mulatto confraternity when they approached the Bishop of Michoacán to ask permission to gather alms outside Valladolid. They petitioned the bishop for this permission in 1664 and 1667.[34] Each petition described various aspects of and causes for their poverty: the absence of rental income, the inability to pay for expenses, the absence of inventory, a lack of alms. A 1679 petition went even farther:

> This confraternity always has been sustained by alms, which members beg for outside this jurisdiction, with the permission of the bishops and the most illustrious council. Within the city and the jurisdiction they cannot collect sufficient alms for the ornaments and wax of the most holy Virgin, nor for her masses, nor the anniversaries said for the souls of the poor slaves our fathers. We also pay to succor the sick and for the wax at the funerals of the poor that we attend punctually and devotedly.[35]

This petition not only presented the group's piety, charitable activities, and poverty; it also sought pity from the bishop for the souls of their "poor slave fathers." In reality the early leaders of the confraternity were mostly free mulattos, blacks, and mestizos, although there were a few slaves. While charitable concerns would certainly have interested the bishop, an emphasis on humble slaves reminded him of the connection between low social status and charitable piety. On the other hand, the late-seventeenth-century Rosary members emphasized the fact that their *fathers*, not they themselves, were slaves.

Starting around 1643, Rosary began to maintain its own modest accounts, which included alms collected by confraternity sisters.[36] Begging for alms was competitive in Valladolid, perhaps because the wealthy Spanish Rosary still sent members out to ask for money. Rosary sisters did not have the success commonly experienced by their Afromexican sisters who collected alms in mining towns or even the other local female alms-collectors of the Incarnation and Saint Blaise confraternity. For instance, on Holy Tuesday in 1685, eighteen confraternity mothers together only managed to take in fourteen pesos. That year, Rosary's income was just over 100 pesos a year. However, the confraternity celebrated impressive fiestas, paying for entertainment such as fireworks, flowers, clarinets, singers, streamers, and wax for candles to illuminate the church and processions. At the end of the seventeenth century, they could afford only ten pounds of wax a year as compared to the 1,300 pounds the Spanish Rosary supplied. While the Spanish confraternity paid to illuminate the church brightly for the entire year, the non-Spanish branch could light the church only during a few special masses.

Antonio de Sosa and Joseph de Aguilar, who were majordomos in the 1680s, worked on developing a different—and perhaps what they considered more dignified and stable—approach to Rosary finances than depending on begging for handouts. Borrowing an idea from rural, typically indigenous, confraternities, the brotherhood began to care for herds of cattle and attempted to make an income from selling cheese. Surviving accounts show that confraternity leaders began spending money on the ingredients and containers needed to make cheese in the 1680s and by 1684 had arranged for the care of Rosary's 160 milk cows and several horses and donkeys.[37] Although the confraternity was spending more than 100 pesos a year on expenses connected to their livestock, accounts do not show a great income from this cheese business, and it had disappeared from the records by 1700. From that point on, the confraternity depended more on alms-collecting and a small, but increasing, income from its properties.

Joseph de Sosa, son of Antonio de Sosa, the seventeenth-century majordomo who started the cheese business, saved Rosary from the disintegration Incarnation and Saint Blaise faced in the eighteenth century. Joseph may have been an officer in the Rosary from the early 1700s, and perhaps his office was in some way inherited from his father Antonio. The differences between the two Afromexican confraternities in Valladolid demonstrate the importance of strong leadership for a confraternity's survival. Family ties and lineage intertwined and coexisted with merit gained from help given to the confraternity when a confraternity elected its officials. In 1733, Joseph de Sosa assumed leadership of the confraternity and ushered in an era of financial success and social prominence. Sosa served as majordomo until 1747. His guidance helped the confraternity remain strong, avoid disintegration, and increase yearly income from 100 pesos a year to close to 1,000 pesos.[38] Greater attention to rent and alms and a large dues-paying membership led to this larger income. In his 1736 reelection, brothers described Sosa as "careful, vigilant and prudent in the accounts and growth of this confraternity" and stated that "without him it would have been in total decline."[39]

As Sosa aged, the confraternity appointed helpers, including his son Miguel, who served as an official assistant to the majordomo because of his father's ill health in 1746. At this time, Sosa was more than sixty years old. Rosary officials were upset by Sosa's decline and reelected him in 1747 even though the clerical inspector of their elections said that

> he was very old, near death and unable to govern this confraternity and keep his accounts in order, so someone else, more able and suited to this burden should be elected, but the brothers present say that Sosa restored this confraternity and helped it grow to this point despite his age, and they fear that if now they take away his job he will be filled with grief and this may cost his life, so the election of Sosa is approved, under the con-

> ditions that he has several helpers, that he not effect any business except in the presence of his helpers and when he can no longer serve, another election must take place.[40]

Sosa's son Miguel, the grandson of the seventeenth-century majordomo Antonio de Sosa, took his place, but the confraternity began to lose money and Miguel soon lost power. He served as majordomo in 1748 and as deputy in 1749, but then he disappeared, along with the name Sosa, from the ranks of Rosary's leadership, ending the century-long domination of the confraternity by the Sosa family. It seems that voters realized that merit would help them more than inherited rank, although the Sosas remained a prominent family even when they no longer controlled the confraternity.[41]

The power vacuum caused by Sosa's decline was filled in short order by the second effective and ambitious leader, Diego Durán, an architect and builder. His contact with the confraternity leadership began in 1743, when his uncle, Juan Durán, served as a deputy. Diego Durán began holding office in 1746, when he was twenty-five. By 1750, he had worked his way up from deputy to fiscal to majordomo. Several men served with Diego Durán as his supporters, including Thomas Huerta (another builder), Onofre Martínez, Sebastián Cortes, and Nicolás Rangel. These men, all skilled craftsmen like Durán, had important family connections with each other: for example, Martínez was a witness at Durán's third and fourth marriages.[42] Upon being elected majordomo, Durán immediately tripled the income of the confraternity, bringing it close once more to 1,000 pesos annually, with ambitious property development (including purchasing and renovating houses) and alms-collecting projects. Durán spent this money on improving Rosary's status among other local confraternities through a more munificent display of wealth and pious devotion. He also emphasized unity with other non-Spanish confraternities.

Durán clearly viewed Rosary as on par with the most prestigious confraternities in Valladolid, and his pride in the brotherhood seemed to be an extension of his own sense of status. Both shared a mulatto label that would not disappear: until after the end of the colonial era, Rosary was labeled *de los pardos* or mulattos. Durán's own life showed the success possible for a man designated as mulatto in eighteenth-century Valladolid, but he was never addressed as "Don" or even "Señor," a testament to the limits of his rise.[43] His plans for Rosary also faced limitations that were not overcome until after independence.

Durán's ambitious plans became clear soon after he took power over the Rosary confraternity. In 1753, he attempted to move the altar of the confraternity to a better location in the Franciscan church.[44] Since 1681, the mulatto branch of the Rosary had been relegated to a small, "extremely uncomfortable" area on the side of the church. Durán and other confraternity leaders hoped that the Franciscans would allow them to expand and bury members in a new chapel. Durán claimed that expansion and a more lavish chapel would lead to greater veneration of their image of the Virgin. Because the area where Durán wanted to expand was a chapel that already sheltered the permanent illumination of the holy sacrament, he suggested that the confraternity assume this cost, which he put at fifty pesos annually, another obligation that would bring glory to the confraternity. The Franciscans approved the new location for Rosary's chapel but scoffed at the suggestion that it could pay for the oil for the lamp, noting that this serious undertaking could not be given to a confraternity that did not have access to secure principal worth more than 1,000 pesos. The friar observed that although the mulatto confraternity was taking in more and more alms, he wondered what the future would bring. Obviously he did not think that this confraternity was as financially stable as Spanish brotherhoods. But Durán continued to push the issue and produced evidence that Rosary owned several properties. This presumption irritated the friar, and he decided that the altar should not be moved because it involved the disruption of graves. But Durán had already started the building and complained that he now had to pay 300 pesos of his own money for the work. This manipulation enabled Durán to achieve his goals of a new chapel and responsibility for the illumination of the host. Durán's other suggested reforms included a 1754 idea that the confraternity, in the presence of two friars, should have a monthly illuminated procession around the convent as it recited the Rosary.

Durán's ambitions created some enemies, although he led the Rosary confraternity from 1750 to 1775. In 1775, Durán presented his accounts after many years of service.[45] They showed that Rosary owned property worth 1,550 pesos, although the confraternity did not take in much rent. Its income came from alms and membership dues, which it collected regularly. For a few years in the late 1770s, the composition of the confraternity council changed and Durán's followers no longer served. But by 1780, Nicolás Rangel and Durán, now called "the retired master architect," returned and shared the office of first brother until at least 1784, when election records end.

In the late eighteenth century, the confraternity experienced a series of conflicts. These disagreements, divisive as they were, may also indicate that the confraternity still had meaning to its active leaders, even if their own egos shifted the focus away from the general good. After Durán's first long term as majordomo ended in 1775, a new faction, led by longtime secretary Juan de Dios Mercado, took over and continued efforts to bring Rosary to a more elevated position in Valladolid confraternal life. Mercado is an enigmatic figure who is very present in Rosary records, often in the important position of secretary. No proof exists that he was not Spanish, but if he was Spanish, then how do we explain his lifelong involvement in a mulatto confraternity? Mercado's presence might be one indication of the confraternity's reach into the higher ranks of society; he sometimes used the surname "Betancurt," a name associated with one of the wealthiest families in Valladolid at this time.[46]

One of Mercado's first acts as secretary is characteristic of a new focus of confraternity life in the eighteenth century. He petitioned the bishop for permission to display the wealth of Rosary, which largely consisted of unset jewels, in a more visible way. The petition claimed, as most confraternity petitions did, that the changes it suggested would lead to "greater decency, worship, and adornment" of the Virgin, Mercado and his followers requested permission to fashion a new crown for their image and to buy a new banner for the confraternity.[47] The brothers told the bishop that their saint had many jewels, clothes, and ornaments, but her crown was made of an unsuitable cheap material. They wanted a new crown of gold and silver that was inlaid with the several jewels in their possession. The confraternity owned 380 pesos' worth of gold, emeralds, pearls, and rubies, a respectable inventory for a *casta* confraternity, all of which probably came from the income generated during the tenures of Durán and Sosa earlier in the century. The bishop approved the request, and Rosary purchased a crown worth around fifty-eight pesos. This new accoutrement openly and clearly represented the wealth and success of the Rosary.

The mulatto branch of the Rosary survived the independence struggles from 1810 to 1824 as well as the early national period and lasted at least until the 1850s. Rosary was displaying renewed vigor in the 1830s, despite the great expense of funerals for the members who died in "disastrous epidemics," which forced them to sell some of their goods.[48] Perhaps the confraternity remained popular because it demonstrated good faith by continuing to provide funeral benefits to members even under difficult circumstances. In the 1840s, the confraternity had only twenty-one members, yet it continued to pay twelve pesos to survivors and give each member three masses when they died.[49] The evidence that exists of this confraternity's survival into the mid-nineteenth century includes numerous patents (proof that the brotherhood was paying members their promised burial insurance), invitations to the bishop to attend their yearly fiesta in the 1840s, and accounts showing around 100 pesos of yearly income from membership dues.[50]

In contrast to the mulatto Rosary, the Spanish Rosary did not keep its members through the era of insurgency. Throughout the eighteenth century, this confraternity continued to increase its wealth in goods and property.[51] In 1730, the Spanish Rosary united with the Confraternity of the True Cross, which was also located in the Franciscan church. The confraternities shared a majordomo, although Rosary had an income of around ten times that of the Confraternity of the True Cross. Famous historical figures from Valladolid society were members of Rosary, including Garcia Obeso and Isidro Huarte.[52] By coincidence, the two long-separated branches of Rosary happened to be located in the church at the same time in 1752. A suggestion, probably by the always-ambitious Diego Durán, was made to reunite them, but it was quickly rejected as "inconvenient," perhaps euphemistic language from members of the Spanish division. Perhaps this reunification would have led to a longer life for the Spanish branch of the centuries-old confraternity. During the years of the independence struggle and after, the Spanish Rosary survived as a property-owning corporation, but it had lost all members by 1811. Even so, it maintained an income of 400 pesos a year and owned haciendas in 1837.[53] The confraternity managed to collect income from rent (presumably collected by the Franciscan convent) to 1829, but by 1840, it was among the many "extinguished" colonial confraternities.

The Spanish confraternity was so exclusive in its membership that most people of Spanish descent in Valladolid did not belong. In contrast, the mulatto Rosary confraternity always had a wide membership, and the family connections that maintained it through other difficult eras continued to exist through the era of insurgency: an 1835 majordomo of the confraternity was a descendant of Juan de Dios Mercado, the eighteenth-century leader.[54] Perhaps members and leaders of the less elite Rosary had a greater interest in confraternities in the national period. Rosary *de españoles* had more to lose during the 1804 consolidation of *vales reales* [royal loans], which required confraternities to call in outstanding loans, and when haciendas were sacked during the independence struggles that began in 1810. Whatever the reason, this case shows that wealth and powerful members were not the only factors that determined whether or not a confraternity would enjoy long-term success. Despite the hierarchical economic structure and opulent baroque values of the colonial church, poor and humble organizations sometimes attracted the most devotion. By the eighteenth century, the Spanish Rosary's status in Valladolid society was tenuous.

After the 1820s, the racial labels of the colonial period were abolished, and overt racial barriers to prominence ceased to exist for Rosary and other Afromexican colonial confraternities.

This change was summed up elegantly by a Franciscan friar after independence; his words also permit a kind of long-delayed financial justice for the mulatto Rosary. In 1833, the friar mentioned that there was once, "in remote times," a division between two *gremios* of the confraternity dedicated to Our Lady of the Rosary, one of Spaniards and the other of *pardos*.[55] The friar continued:

> The latter is currently functioning and satisfactorily meeting all its obligations while the former is long gone and permanently abolished, along with this odious [racial] distinction, because there was another confraternity for the faithful to completely satisfy their piety. . . . All that belongs to the former should legally revert to the current confraternity designated as of pardos.[56]

While post-independence Rosary and its members could never completely shed the burdens of the caste system, the confraternity's leaders worked to improve its status and give it a higher profile in Valladolid's Hispanic social order. After the official end of racial hierarchies, people who had previously been labeled mulatto were ready to take up positions of leadership that had been impossible in the colonial period, and the friar's words show they succeeded in assuming these roles within their confraternity. The centuries-long process of Hispanicization of African slaves had reached its final stage in Valladolid. The next chapter looks more closely at the personal lives of *casta* confraternity leaders and examines how they extended their influence and interests to other confraternities in Valladolid and became leaders in a broader late-colonial plebeian society.

5

Moving toward Freedom in Valladolid

In the seventeenth century, most children born to African and creole black mothers were enslaved and lacked recognized fathers. Many were also orphans. Statistics culled from baptism records indicate that, by the eighteenth century, family structures had changed and that a primarily mulatto population had embraced the patriarchal values of the paterfamilias. By the eighteenth century, people of African descent had shed their status as slaves and had become a class of urban workers, many of whom, like Diego Durán, profited from Bourbon public works projects. These developments parallel the changes in their confraternities. Chapter two revealed the many important roles held by female confraternity members. By the eighteenth century, men dominated the Rosary, which had become almost bourgeois, and had a stronger role as fathers in their families. This chapter will use statistical analysis to examine these demographic changes in Vallalodid's population

Throughout the colonial period, members of Valladolid's Afromexican confraternities were prominent leaders of their own social group. This chapter will show that the men who led the Rosary confraternity struggled to improve its profile among other confraternities in Valladolid. These leaders worked within the framework of an organization that was officially labeled and generally referred to as the Rosary confraternity "de los mulatos," or, as it was labeled in the eighteenth century, "de los pardos." Despite their long history, they were labeled in a way that surely reminded them of the racial divisions of colonial society and their own supposed inferiority. How did those who achieved some upward economic mobility fit into the racial hierarchy of New Spain's caste system? Does the story of the Rosary "de los mulatos" ultimately argue against the continuing presence and influence of this structure?

Some historians argue that the caste system may have become more open and flexible in New Spain in the late eighteenth century, especially for successful people of color. A few people of African heritage even received a royal decree elevating them to "official" Spanish status.[1] The king was more ready to agree to this label if the petitioner was already successful enough to associate on more or less equal terms with local Spaniards. In general, people with darker skin were no longer officially labeled *mulato* or mestizo if they had achieved some degree of social status, and notaries used these racial identifiers far less consistently in the mid-eighteenth century than they had in the seventeenth century, when the labels were always used.[2] Socioeconomic factors had become more important than race in determining rank by the end of the eighteenth century. For these reasons, people labeled *mulatos* were able to improve their social position in the late eighteenth century and possibly even fill leadership roles after independence. The history of the Rosary confraternity shows the brotherhood taking tentative steps toward increasing respectability for Valladolid's mulattos, both as a group and individually.

Race was a more crucial and immutable factor in defining social status at the very top and very bottom of society; people in these two groups would find it very difficult to move into a higher social group or out of a lower group, whether through marriage or changes in economic status. A successful mulatto often had only a tiny portion of the wealth that high-ranking Spaniards had, and because they posed no threat to the economic elite, perhaps this kind of person served as a social middleman who helped expand but also maintain the hierarchy through successful example.[3] The confraternity members explored in this chapter and the next undoubtedly fit into a middle group, the most dynamic and upwardly mobile urban group. The argument that an embryonic middle class existed in colonial Mexico, especially one made up of mulattos, may seem untenable. However, the long-term success, stability, and professional careers of men who led confraternities in Valladolid do make them possible candidates for the label of middle class. In the eighteenth century, membership in confraternities, a more stable family life, and access to professional careers all increased the social status of mulattos.

Valladolid's status as a provincial town may have given its mulatto residents a better chance for upward mobility than people of color had in the capital. Certainly the careers of Juan Correa and Mateo de Aguilar show that mulattos, through strong connections to Spanish society and wealth, could achieve prosperity in seventeenth-century Mexico City. But well-off *castas* in seventeenth-century Mexico City may have enjoyed only fragile success.[4] Miguel Hernández was a mulatto who achieved prosperity and respect in Querétaro in the late sixteenth century.[5] Hernández' move from the viceregal capital may have increased his chances for improving his life. Towns that were farther away from the center of Hispanic economic and political power may have had more opportunities for social mobility. Yet size seems to have mattered. Perhaps Valladolid was a big enough city to foster diverse occupations, especially relatively high-status crafts and trades, while smaller towns could hold back social advancement because of a limited number of opportunities.[6]

Membership in and public devotion to confraternities helped emphasize personal achievements and express personal interpretations of religious piety. Miguel Hernández was a member of a *mulato* confraternity and the Spanish-dominated Confraternity of the Holy Sacrament, which was generally the most prestigious confraternity in any town. He had a steady career, owned property, was addressed as "Señor," and had close personal connections to the local Franciscan monastery. Overall, the status of people of African descent in Valladolid improved from the seventeenth to the nineteenth centuries: their leadership roles in prominent confraternities may have been both a cause and an effect of this development.

But those Afromexicans who did not achieve a degree of prosperity are nearly lost to the historical record. Individuals of African descent appear infrequently in documentation, and when they do, their names are often recorded imprecisely or inaccurately. This makes it difficult to trace their lives and suggests that their individuality was not crucial to Hispanic observers and the authorities who created the written record. For example, blacks and mulattos, whether slave or free, were identified without surnames by the priests who baptized them. The closest many entries in official documents come to surnames are labels such as "free *mulata*" or the substitution of an African ethnic identity for a family name—that is, unless individuals were called by the name of their owner or the family name of the house where they served. At best, many were given generic last names such as "de la Cruz," a name that appeared frequently in the parish records of both Valladolid and Mexico City in the seventeenth century.[7] In contrast, throughout the colonial period, every confraternity leader, male or female, provided a last name for the records of the Confraternities of the Rosary and the Incarnation and Saint Blaise. This indicates that these leading members were already from an "elite" that was known by more the common names "Juan" or "Joseph" or, most common of all, "María." Perhaps many people had surnames or nicknames that were not recorded.

Cope's study of naming practices led him to the conclusions that *casta* surnames were often important only in bureaucratic settings and that "lineage was not central to self-definition."[8] I would argue that concern for lineage based on male parentage—as recorded through the use of last names—was rarely possible for people of African descent in the seventeenth century, but perhaps they had undocumented internal hierarchies that are unknown to historians. In the eighteenth century, Hispanic concepts of paternal lineage became increasingly important, especially among mulattos. However, the last names of prominent members of Valladolid's Afromexican confraternities in the eighteenth century may reflect the names of prominent seventeenth-century masters, such as Rangel and Vetancur.

The following analysis comes from the Latter Day Saint's microfilm rolls for *casta* baptisms in Valladolid's cathedral, recording baptisms from 1597 to 1789. The books of *casta* baptisms also included mestizos, but I eliminated these from my statistical analysis, focusing on baptisms that involved people with some degree of African descent. Because the numbers of baptisms were small until the 1700s, it is possible for the solo researcher to record and statistically analyze many more years of records in the 1600s. For the late sixteenth and seventeenth century, I recorded all *casta* baptisms from 1597 to 1620, 1636 to 1641, 1643 to 1646, 1652 to 1670, and 1690 to 1694. This spread and choice of years will not satisfy a statistician, but is instead determined by available baptism books and the years covered within them. Because the baptisms increased in number in the 1700s, I was able to record all baptisms for only a few sets of years to get very general trends: 1709 to 1713, 1733 to 1737, 1758 to 1762, and 1785 to 1789.

Africans and their children were not given official last names, and their circumstances may have made it impossible to assign them a paternal lineage. Accurate population statistics are hard to find for the colonial period, but according to one population estimate, there were forty male Spaniards and fifty male and female slaves in Valladolid in 1570.[9] Baptism records for the town do not go back that far; the first available book of *casta* baptisms covers the years 1598 to 1620, the era in which the future founders of the Rosary and Incarnation confraternities would have been born. Seventy-four of the ninety-eight Afromexican babies recorded in this first book did not have a father present.[10] In baptism records, this condition was described as "*de padre desconocido* [of an unknown father]." Only three of the mothers were described as the legitimate wife of the man present. Seven of the known fathers were slaves. Forty-two of the mothers were described as slaves, and only six of these women had a spouse present, sometimes a fellow slave who was serving the same master. Perhaps fathers could not be recognized because of their servile or enslaved position in a family house or the violent circumstances of the conception, especially for the six mulatto children with unknown fathers of women described as black slaves.[11]

Whether they conceived under duress or willingly, it is impossible to believe that almost three-quarters of mothers of African birth or heritage did not know

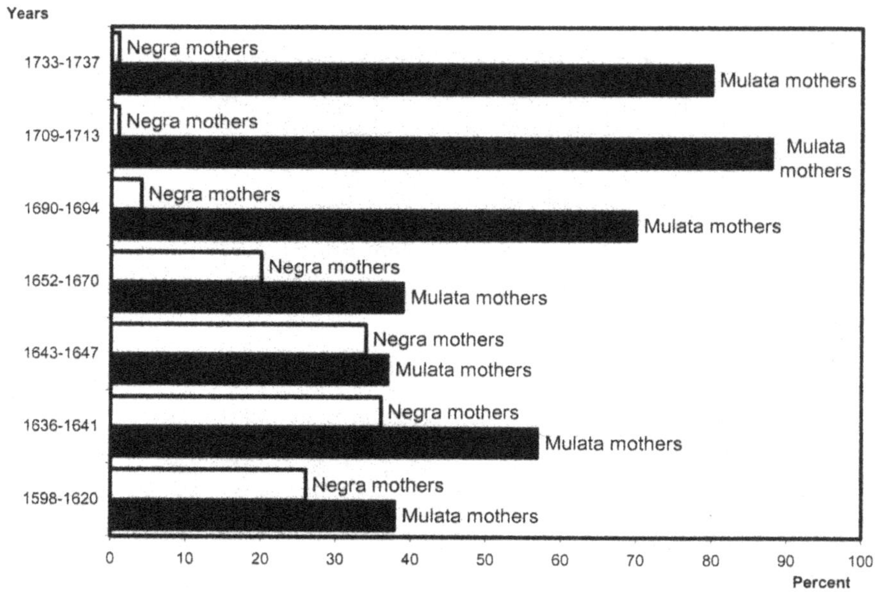

Graph 5.1. Race of Afromexican mothers in Valladolid baptism records, sample years 1598–1737. *Source*: Libros de bautismos, Morelia, 1598–1786, LDS rolls 644686, 644687, 644688, 644689, 644850, 644852.

the fathers of their children. There must be another unknown, violent, or secret explanation for the absence of fathers at baptisms. In general, when servants or slaves had their children baptized without a father present, the priest referred to their situations with euphemistic language: "of unknown father" probably designated a illicit conception within their masters' households.[12] Because this label was used so often, it cannot mean that the father was simply indisposed or out of town. Instead, a powerful reason must have prevented men from acknowledging their children at baptism. Likely, the majority of these children were the illegitimate result of sexual relationships between women and their masters or with their peers. Both kinds of fathers chose not to grant their child official paternal protection from birth; they chose not to fulfill an obligation that was a source of personal honor and a fundamental value in the Hispanic world. The phenomenon of "unknown fathers" does not necessarily mean that children were not cared for; instead, it represents the sexual and familial dynamics of men and women in Valladolid's lower-class society.[13]

The frequency with which specific racial labels were used also changed in the 200 years of baptism records analyzed here. The use of the racial designation *negro* declined after the early seventeenth century, and even in that period, blacks did not account for a majority of Valladolid's *casta* baptism records. From 1598 to 1620, 38 percent of mothers were called *mulatas* and 27 percent were called *negra* or *morena* (see graph 5.1 for demographic change over time in the racial groups mothers belonged to; the graph combines *negra* and *morena* mothers). These figures indicate that Valladolid's population of African descent, even in the early 1600s, was primarily mulatto. Thus, many women in Valladolid had already had children with Spaniards by the end of the sixteenth century, or perhaps the *mulata* label was a cultural category that indicated a Hispanized black woman, a woman who spoke Spanish and dressed in a Spanish manner.

Other mothers of children who were baptized in the early seventeenth century were not labeled by race; they were simply called slaves. Among the twenty-two total men that appear as fathers, six were called mulatto, nine were labeled black or *moreno*, and a few were called slaves. In the early decades of the seventeenth century, only ten free blacks and mulattos appeared at the baptisms of their legitimate children. Only one of these men was married to a slave, in this case a *china esclava*, or a Philippine slave, and two free men were married to Indians. Even this early in Valladolid's history, we see a move away from African slavery to a free mixed-race *casta* population. Table 5.1 indicates that during the period 1598 to 1737, most black and mulatto babies who were baptized did not have named fathers. Further, table 5.2 demonstrates that in the 1630s, of those fathers that were identified, a high percentage were slaves.

From the late 1520s, slaves were brought to the Valladolid area to work first in mines, then on haciendas surrounding the city or in *obrajes* in the city.[14] Others worked as domestics in these settings. Indians also performed this labor, but their

Table 5.1. Afromexican babies baptized in Valladolid whose fathers were unknown, 1597–1789 (selected periods)

Period	Number unknown fathers	Total Afromexican babies baptized	Percent unknown fathers
1597–1620	75	98	76.5
1636–1641	90	121	74.3
1643–1646	83	113	73.4
1652–1670	337	449	75.0
1690–1694	80	133	60.0
1709–1713	231	489	47.2
1733–1737	315	813	38.7
1758–1762	331	1,087	30.4
1785–1789	281	986	28.5

Source: "Libros de bautismos, Morelia, 1598–1786," LDS rolls 644686, 644688, 644850, and 644852.

Table 5.2. Afromexican babies baptized in Valladolid whose fathers were slaves, 1597–1789 (selected periods)

Period	Number slave fathers	Total Afromexican babies baptized	Percent slave fathers of known fathers
1597–1620	9	98	39
1636–1641	21	121	67.7
1643–1646	14	113	46.6
1652–1670	26	449	23
1690–1694	7	133	13.2
1709–1713	9	489	3.8
1733–1737	49	813	6.0
1758–1762	0	1,087	0.0
1785–1789	1	986	less than 1

Source: Libros de bautismos, Morelia, 1598–1786, LDS rolls 644686, 644688, 644850, and 644852.

population was decreasing rapidly and Africans were highly prized as workers; masters preferred them if they could afford them. Slave sales in the 1600s show a decrease in the number of Africans sold as slaves; Africans were quickly replaced by large numbers of mulatto slaves. As was the case in many areas of New Spain, Africans and their language, culture, and religion were most dominant in Valladolid before 1650. The Confraternity of the Incarnation and Saint Blaise shows an especially strong membership of slaves and Africans at this time.

Chávez Carbajal found 348 documented slave sales for Valladolid between 1590 and 1650. The following discussion draws on 238 slave sales, all the sales documents I could find in Valladolid's notarial records between 1630 and 1789. Before 1640, the majority of slaves sold in Valladolid were born in Africa. These Africans, most of whom were men, almost always came from Angola or Mozambique, although a few came from Congo or Biafara. Chávez Carbajal also found sales of slaves from the Bran, Zape, Wolof and Cape Verde regions. These slaves probably came to the New World before Spain's union with Portugal in 1580. After 1580, Angolan slaves dominated imports. In terms of race, 81 percent of the slaves sold before 1640 were described as black (see table 5.3), either born in Africa or in the Americas. By the 1680s, creole blacks still constituted a large part of the slaves sold, but the number of Africans had decreased. This decrease intensified after 1640, when Portugal regained its independence from Spain and Spain no longer had direct access to the slave trade originating in Angola and Congo.[15] By the end of the seventeenth century, mulattos accounted for most of the slaves sold in New Spain. Slave buyers no longer needed to de-

Table 5.3. Race of slaves sold in Valladolid, 1630–1789[a]

Time Period	Racial group								Total slaves sold
	Black[b]		Mulatto		Creole black		Other[c]		
	n	%	n	%	n	%	n	%	
1630–1639	16	31	9	17	26	50	1	2	52
1640–1649	0	0	0	0	0	0	0	0	0
1650–1659	0	0	0	0	0	0	0	0	0
1660–1669	19	51	17	46	0	0	1	3	37
1670–1679	0	0	0	0	0	0	0	0	0
1680–1689	10	32	16	52	4	13	1	3	31
1690–1699	2	5	31	84	2	5	2	5	37
1700–1709	2	11	17	89	0	0	0	0	19
1710–1719	0	0	0	0	0	0	0	0	0
1720–1729	0	0	0	0	0	0	0	0	0
1730–1739	6	32	13	68	0	0	0	0	19
1740–1749	0	0	6	100	0	0	0	0	6
1750–1759	0	0	0	0	0	0	0	0	0
1760–1769	0	0	10	83	0	0	2	17	12
1770–1779	0	0	8	89	0	0	1	11	9
1780–1789	0	0	16	100	0	0	0	0	16

Source: Libros de Notarias, Morelia, 1630–1780, Archivo Histórico de Notarías, Morelia.
[a]Because of rounding, the percentages in some rows may not total 100.
[b]Not born in New Spain
[c]Includes blanco, loba, morisco, and morisco blanco

pend on Africans as a source of labor, because the population of African descent in New Spain was reproducing itself and mixing with other groups in society.[16] Of course this meant an increase in slaves only if mothers were enslaved, since children born to male slaves and free women were born free.

Slaves were considered a valuable commodity in Valladolid in the 1600s. More often than not, slaves sold in Valladolid until 1699 were men described as black (see table 5.4). The average price for male slaves was always above 300 pesos (graph 5.2). The price of slaves of both genders under twenty years old was far less than the selling price of men in their prime working years of age eighteen to twenty-four, which brought down the average price per slave. There were some exceptions to the correlation between price and age. In 1680, Teresa, a fifteen-year-old black girl born in New Spain, was purchased for 425 pesos. Fourteen-year-old Anton, a creole black, was purchased for 450 pesos in 1630. The highest price paid for a single slave in the samples taken was for Antonio, a 22-year-old Angolan, who sold for 550 pesos in 1635. These prices are similar to

Table 5.4. Male and female slaves sold in Valladolid by decade, 1630–1789

	Male		Female	
Decade	n	%	n	%
1630–1639	35	67	17	33
1640–1649	0	0	0	0
1650–1659	0	0	0	0
1660–1669	20	54	17	46
1670–1679	0	0	0	0
1680–1689	16	52	15	48
1690–1699	20	54	17	46
1700–1799	9	47	10	53
1710–1719	0	0	0	0
1720–1729	0	0	0	0
1730–1739	9	47	10	53
1740–1749	2	33	4	67
1750–1759	0	0	0	0
1760–1769	2	17	10	83
1770–1779	3	33	6	67
1780–1789	3	19	13	81

Source: Libros de Notarias, Morelia, 1630–1780, Archivo Histórico de Notarías, Morelia.

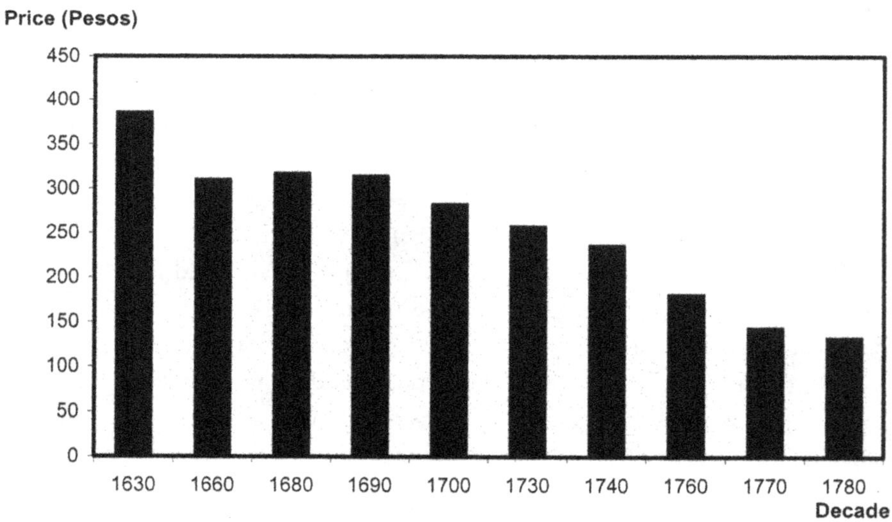

Graph 5.2. Price of slaves in Valladolid by decade, 1630–1780. *Source*: Libros de Notarias, Morelia, 1630–1780, AHNM.

Table 5.5. Afromexican orphans baptized in Valladolid, 1597 to 1789 (selected years)

Period	Number of Afromexican orphans	Total Afromexican baptisms	Percent orphans
1597–1620	2	98	2.0
1636–1641	0	121	0.0
1643–1646	40	113	35.4
1652–1670	181	449	40.3
1690–1694	24	133	18.0
1709–1713	57	489	11.6
1733–1737	24	813	3.0
1758–1762	0	1,087	0.0
1785–1789	47	989	4.7

Source: Libros de bautismos, Morelia, 1598–1786, LDS Rolls 644686, 644687, 644688, 644689, 644850, and 644852.

those in the sugar-growing areas of New Spain (although African slaves skilled in sugar refining could cost up to 600 pesos).[17]

African slaves were a luxury item and must have had great value for their masters, whether as status symbols, as a source of income, or simply as workers in their own enterprises. Even though the slave trade ended around 1640, slaves were sold in Valladolid until the 1780s.[18] After 1690, newly purchased slaves were usually American-born mulattos. Historian Frank Proctor argues that the proportionally larger number of female slave sales indicates a population capable of reproducing naturally and establishing a normal sex ratio, and my sample shows that beginning in 1700, more women than men were sold as slaves in Valladolid (see table 5.4).[19]

Baptism records from the seventeenth century reveal the impact of slavery on family life. Table 5.5 shows that a substantial percentage of children born in the mid-seventeenth century did not have a recognized father *or* a recognized mother present at their baptisms. All of these children were left at the church or, even more mysteriously, found at the house of the person who brought them to be baptized. Perhaps mothers in bad domestic situations, especially servants or slaves with illegitimate children, abandoned their babies at the doorsteps of trusted families.

A number of factors may have contributed to a high number of legal orphans: very high maternal mortality, the shame of illegitimate births, or the danger of acknowledging illegitimate children. Perhaps some mothers were willing to make this extreme sacrifice because they knew that an abandoned child was assumed to be free. Abandoning a child may have given him or her an adoptive family (if he or she survived the first crucial five years of life). More than one-third of the babies baptized in Valladolid from the 1640s to at least 1670 were officially orphans. This apparent lack of blood relations may have had the effect that Valladolid's Afromexican community placed greater importance on adoptive families and connections that went beyond nuclear family groups. Individuals who were "orphans" at their baptisms may have seen confraternities as their family group and relied on them for care when they were sick and depended on their remembrance and prayers after death.

Yet the number of orphans had declined precipitously by the turn of the eighteenth century. In the period 1652 to 1670, four in every ten Afromexican babies who were baptized—nearly half—had neither biological parent present for the ceremony. By the period 1709 to 1713, the proportion had declined to just over 10 percent, and three decades later, the proportion was tiny—only 3 percent. During a roughly eighty-year period, the Afromexican family stabilized to the point that most children had at least one parent present in their lives when they were baptized.

A decline in the rates of infant mortality and abandonment in the eighteenth century took place in the context of a stronger Hispanic-style paternalism among the more well-off mulattos and the few remaining men described as black. The next section will look at confraternity leaders, men who played the role of paterfamilias, and men who had several children with a legitimate wife, a very rare arrangement for the 1600s. These were men who were present at the baptisms of at least some of their children, although they may have fathered illegitimate children as well.

Baptism figures in the late seventeenth century indicate the first sign of changes in family life. During the period 1690 to 1694, approximately twenty-seven Afromexican children were baptized each year in Valladolid. If 60 percent of these babies did not have fathers present, as table 5.1 shows, the other 40 percent did. This was a significant increase from the 1650s and 1660s, when only approximately 25 percent of such children had fathers present.[20] This increase signifies an important change. The greater presence of husbands and fathers at the baptismal font may have meant less personal independence for mothers, but the tradeoff was that they were more likely to be in settled relationships and have a more stable home life.[21]

Baptism data indicate that by the end of the seventeenth century, Valladolid had a growing free population with African, indigenous, and European heritage, a population that was generally labeled mulatto. As table 5.2 shows, only 13 percent of fathers who were present at baptisms were slaves in the 1690s, a

Table 5.6. Afromexican babies baptized in Valladolid whose mothers were slaves, 1597–1789 (selected years)

Period	Number slave mothers	Total Afromexican babies baptized	Percent slave mothers
1597–1620	34	98	34.7
1636–1641	74	121	61.1
1643–1646	56	113	49.5
1652–1670	262	449	58.3
1690–1694	30	133	22.5
1709–1713	62	489	12.3
1733–1737	73	813	9.0
1758–1762	56	1,087	5.1
1785–1789	6	986	less than 1

Source: Libros de bautismos, Morelia, 1598–1786, LDS rolls 644686, 644687, 644688, 644689, 644850, and 644852.

decrease from a high point of 67 percent in the period 1636 to 1641, the period when the slave trade to New Spain was coming to a close. The percentage of orphans halved, dropping from a high of 40 percent of Afromexican children who were baptized in the period 1652 to 1670 to 18 percent in the period 1690 to 1694 (see table 5.6). The number of baptized Afromexican children who were born to slave mothers also decreased: from 58 percent in the period 1652 to 1670 to 23 percent in the period 1690 to 1694 (see table 5.6). Less than 10 percent of mothers were labeled black after 1690, another sign that fewer slaves from Africa or their direct descendants were living in Valladolid. These statistics reflect the overall decrease in the slave population in Valladolid that began in the early 1700s, a trend also seen in the declining slave sales. As the number of slaves and women of more direct African heritage decreased after 1690, the number of women called *mulatas* rose to 70 percent of the mothers; many of them were called free *mulatas*.

It is clear that family stability increased for Afromexicans from the late seventeenth century to the end of the eighteenth century. A snapshot from the period 1709 to 1713 illustrates the trends very clearly. It seems likely that more children survived beyond the first few days of life, although we do not know whether this was due to an increase in the birth rate or better record-keeping. In contrast to the average of twenty-seven Afromexican babies baptized annually in the early 1690s, more than 100 Afromexicans were baptized yearly in Valladolid by 1709.[22] The vast majority of these babies had at least one parent present at the baptism; only 11 percent of them were baptized with no recognized parents present. Thirty-seven percent of the children baptized during this period had a father present, a change from the higher rate of illegitimacy in the early seventeenth century. Slavery also continued to decline: only 3.8 percent of the babies baptized had enslaved fathers, although 12 percent of the babies baptized for this period were born into slavery through their birth to slave mothers. Very few mothers were described as black in the early eighteenth century, when labels such as *coyote* (a mix of African and Indian heritage) and *morisca* became more common. The vast majority of mothers present at baptisms during this period carried the racial label *mulata*; more than 80 percent of the mothers were described in this way.

The baptism data from Valladolid enable us to make several generalizations. In the seventeenth century, Afromexicans in Valladolid were more likely to be slaves and be born outside marriage. In the eighteenth century, most Afromexicans were free mulattos or were given other labels that indicated indigenous and African ancestors, and they were more likely than not to have an officially acknowledged father. This trend accelerated during the century; in the period 1709 to 1713, almost four of every ten babies baptized had named fathers. By the period 1785 to 1788, that statistic had increased to over seven in every ten babies baptized. The general population's composition was changing, and these changes affected aspects of life. A large population of free *castas* was forming.

Of the 1,000 Afromexican and mestizo babies who were baptized during the period 1733 to 1737, more than 150 each year were mulattos.[23] The baptism book for *castas* in the these years also includes many mestizos. Seventy-eight percent of the mothers of these babies were given labels that indicated some African heritage, such as *morisca, mulata*, and *negra*, and 84 percent of the fathers were labeled in a similar way. Fewer baptisms of children with unknown fathers were performed. In the 1730s, only 38.7 percent of the babies had fathers who were considered "unknown," indicating that the majority of these children had a recognized father (legitimate or illegitimate) present at their baptism, and perhaps in their lives. Unknown mothers also became very rare; only about 3 percent of these children were abandoned. In the eighteenth century, children were more likely to live with their birth parents in nuclear family groups. A far smaller percentage of children carried the stigma of illegitimacy, and they had a stronger paternal lineage, which was highly valued in Hispanic society, even if they were not of 100 percent European descent. In addition, most of the parents of these babies were free; by the 1730s, only 6 percent of the known fathers were slaves, and only 9 percent of the mothers passed on their captivity (see tables 5.2 and 5.6). Slavery was slowly decreasing in Valladolid. Society was also becoming more racially mixed and less African. In the 1730s, out of 813 baptisms, only five fathers and eight mothers were labeled *negro*. More parents were labeled *lobo* or *loba* instead; this label, which was used to indicate Indian and African ancestry, was new to the baptism records in the 1730s.

A decreasing number of slave sales meant an increase in the number of slaves with mixed racial heritage in Valladolid. By 1740, all slaves were called mulattos, *moriscos*, or *lobos*: thus all slaves sold in Valladolid at this time were American-born and had some indigenous or European ancestry. By the late 1700s, the monetary value assigned to slaves had decreased to less than half of the seventeenth-century prices. By the end of the century, the average price of a slave was less than 150 pesos. It was also much more common to sell female slaves in the eighteenth century, a sign that slaves were reproducing without African trade.[24] People who were not in their prime working years—those under age twenty or over age forty—account for more than half of the slave sales in the sample. The large number of sales of children and elderly slaves suggests that people were purchased for paternalistic reasons; these individuals did not have the work capacity of slaves in their twenties and thirties. For example the purchase of two-year-old Teresa in 1760 for 100 pesos hardly seems like a good investment; it was more likely a whim or perhaps a charitable gesture. At the other extreme, 40-year-old Francisca changed owners for only 50 pesos in 1780. Statistics show that by the end of the eighteenth century, the slave trade was not of great economic importance in Valladolid.

Other sources show that the number of *castas* in Valladolid continued to grow in the colonial period. Around 4,000 non-Indian families lived in Valladolid in 1745.[25] If about 200 *castas* were born each year, this population was a significant part of Valladolid society. While we do not know the death rate, *casta* births represented a significant increase in Valladolid's non-Indian population.

The trends seen in the early eighteenth century continue in a sample of almost 1,087 Afromexican baptisms from 1758 to 1762. During this period, a new development emerged: more parents labeled Spanish appeared at the baptisms of mulatto children.[26] As the Afromexican birthrate increased, so did its rate of legitimate births: the fathers of 65 percent of the children in this sample were present when they were baptized. All of these men were free; the number of enslaved fathers dropped to zero. About 5 percent of the mothers were still slaves, but this figure was dropping gradually, as was the percentage of parents described as black. By the mid-eighteenth century, only a few parents were given the label of slave. But in a significant new trend, twenty-three fathers and thirty-one mothers were identified as Spanish. A handful of these labels were qualified when the priest wrote "*dijeron ser* [they were said to be]" before the label "*español*." This suggests that parents themselves had a say in what label was assigned to them, at least in this era, and they may have exaggerated their European heritage. Although priests showed their doubts with the qualifier "*dijeron ser*," they also showed their toleration for looser labels. This could be a sign that the "racial norm" was beginning to take on a darker appearance. Either people of European (or presumed European) descent were marrying into the *casta* population or were recognizing their children by attending their baptisms or more people of mixed racial background were calling themselves Spanish. The large number of unknown fathers and orphans from the seventeenth century might indicate that European men always had children with women of different racial labels but denied responsibility for these children, at least at their baptisms.

As shown in the last chapter, by the end of the eighteenth century, several confraternities with Afromexican leadership and membership were well established in Valladolid, and the information collected at baptisms demonstrates a similar stability for family life.[27] Notarial records testify to the fact that most eighteenth-century confraternity leaders were property owners, and some evidence exists that demonstrates their occupational success. During the late 1700s when the Rosary confraternity was flourishing and its members sought to lead and gain respect from their fellow residents in Valladolid, two-thirds of Afromexican children could name their fathers. In the 1780s, almost 70 percent had a father present at their baptism (see table 5.1). Around twelve children a year among the Afromexican population still had to seek homes as orphans; but this phenomena occurred among all groups in Valladolid. Only seven children were born into slavery in the late 1780s.

The tendency in eighteenth-century Valladolid baptism records was toward using the term "*mulato*" to refer to the vast majority of *castas*. In contrast to the many permutations of race we see in *casta* paintings of the late 1700s, racial labels did not get more complex as time went by. The tendency to use the term "mulatto" to describe all people with African heritage indicates that mulattos were a defined group in society with a specific economic role and status.[28] In the late eighteenth century, mulatto men were working as craftsmen, and there were more eligible free *mulata* women for ambitious spouse-seekers. This combination inevitably led to more families with trades to hand down to their sons.

All of these changes were set down in the records of baptisms and changed the lives of people of African descent living in Valladolid over a period of 200 years. In contrast to children born in the seventeenth century, children born in the eighteenth century could more likely depend on the care of two parents, although they may have always had a network of relatives to raise them. The presence of a paterfamilias in most homes may have meant that women had less economic independence, although women continued to control property transactions in Valladolid's notarial records. It seems likely that life was less precarious with two parents raising children together. The decrease in the rate of illegitimacy shows that Valladolid Afromexicans gradually complied with the value Hispanic society placed on paternal lineage. Baptism records suggest that once men began carrying out these expected roles in the eighteenth century, *mulata* women were less subject to sexual violence and the involuntary pregnancies that led to illegitimate births. Even though baptism records leave many questions unanswered, they illustrate an overall change in life for individuals of African ancestry. This change played a role in the lives of individual confraternity leaders and the development of these confraternities in general.

Leaders of the Afromexican Incarnation and Saint Blaise and Rosary confraternities stood out from their peers. Early on, this upwardly mobile group began to carry out the patriarchal family values honored in Hispanic society. They were in the vanguard of the process of Hispanicization of people of African descent from the seventeenth century forward. Family connections between confraternity brothers over several generations reveal a tight-knit society among these prominent Afromexicans. Confraternity leadership became a family tradition for a select few families, and offices came to be dominated by certain families even if these roles were not formally inherited. Here we will not deal with the rank-and-file members, who left very little evidence in the historical record—most did not even leave their names. The focus will instead be on confraternity leaders, who were listed frequently in records of confraternity elections and in petitions to the authorities. In their function as majordomos, deputies, or other confraternity officials, including confraternity mothers, these people stood out as leaders of their community in Valladolid, and their prominence continued to increase to the end of the eighteenth century. While these leaders led the trend toward stable family life, the lives of rank-and-file members had also radically changed by the eighteenth century, and it is possible that confraternity leaders represented models for this broader transformation in family life.

By the eighteenth century, almost everyone, except slaves, received a surname in sacramental records, an indication that officials recognized the individuality of people of African descent. Although the seventeenth-century leaders of the Incarnation and Saint Blaise and Rosary confraternities came from the almost-anonymous underclass of Valladolid, their family histories can be traced because they were assigned first and last names in the written record. This suggests that they had some kind of status, if only in their own social group. For whatever reason, at their marriages and deaths and at the baptisms of their children, they presented themselves in such a way as to appear respectable enough for the cleric to add a last name to the record. This may have happened because confraternity leaders assumed Hispanic styles of self-presentation, such as dress, manner of speaking, or carrying themselves, despite the fact that they were not Europeans or were enslaved. By Hispanic standards, these men began to appear more individualized and less anonymous to authorities. Last names were not just given to those who appeared a little whiter and were given the label *morisco.* Some men described as black, as will be seen below, had last names and always used them in confraternity documentation. Thus, the names, the personal identity, and the individuality of these men were to a minimal degree recognized by colonial authorities with whom they came into contact, regardless of the color of their skin.

One difficulty in tracking down members of confraternities in the seventeenth century comes from the mutability of names. Many people, especially the wives of confraternity leaders, appear with several different names and racial designations.[29] Like illegitimacy, these ever-changing and simple names testify to a weaker connection to the values of Hispanic society in the seventeenth century; their lives did not comply with the norms of a society concerned with patriarchy and lineage. By the eighteenth century, their connection to this society had strengthened, as illustrated by the fact surnames for mulattos had become the norm rather than the exception.

It is possible to trace the lives of the leaders of Rosary from 1634, the date of the first record of the *mulato* branch of this confraternity, two years after their division from the Spanish branch of the confraternity. From this time, free blacks, mulattos, and mestizos dominated Rosary's membership; there are signs of connections and cooperation among free *castas.* The first officers of the *mulato* Rosary are listed and described in the confraternity records as Pedro Hurtado mulatto, Francisco Magdaleno free black, Francisco Sánchez mestizo, Cristobal Vargas, and Alonso Agustín de Contreras. The majordomo, Bartolome Pérez, is the only member from this early period whose family history can be elaborated. In the same year the confraternity was founded, 1634, Pérez, described as a free mulatto, baptized his son Diego. The mother of this child was the Indian woman María de la Cruz; she is not specifically referred to as his legitimate wife in the baptism record. Pérez may have died in 1641 and left his property and garden to the confraternity to fulfill a debt.[30] His son Diego maintained connections throughout his life to members of the Rosary confraternity.

Fortunately, much more can be recovered about Luis de la Serna, the first majordomo of Incarnation and Saint Blaise for whom we can trace a history; Serna served the confraternity in the 1660s. Serna, who was always described as a black slave, was an exceptional man for his time. Baptismal records show that Serna and his wife, Magdalena de Sandoval, had at least six children. Serna's name does not come up in any other baptism records of the era, but since around three-quarters of these children have no fathers listed, it is certainly possible that he also fathered illegitimate or unrecognized children. In the baptism records for their children, Magdalena was occasionally described as his legitimate wife. She was also labeled either mestiza or Indian, so Luis's children were all born free; none inherited their father's slave status from birth. We cannot know what factors Serna was considering when he chose his wife, but the fact remains that through this choice his children were born into freedom. In that single life choice, he ensured that the legal status of his children would be better than his own status. Despite their African and Indian parentage, Serna's children were sometimes called *mulatos*, a term usually used to indicate African and European heritage. The children were usually referred to as *lobos*, a term indicating Indian and African ancestry. Serna's legitimate children were exceptional among the children of slave fathers in the baptism records for the period 1650 to 1670. Luis and Magdalena had their first child in 1653 and their sixth in 1670. In these eighteen years, 451 *casta* baptisms were recorded in Valladolid. Of these, only 25 percent mention fathers, and of that group with fathers, almost 1 in 4 was born to a slave mother. So Luis and Magdalena's family represented about 5 percent of all the legitimate children born from 1652 to 1670 and 25 percent of the legitimate births to slave men.

Luis was one of the many Afromexican confraternity leaders who lived a far longer life than other non-elites in New Spain, a testimony to his high standard of living. At his death in 1680, Luis, who was still a slave, was survived by his wife.[31] If Luis was mature enough to have his first child in 1653 and serve as a majordomo in 1663, he was probably born in the 1630s or earlier. This means he died at approximately age fifty. His wife, who had survived the births of at least six children, was probably in her mid-40s when he died. The survival rate of their children, if we could know that, would tell more about the success of this family, but the fact that a woman lived ten years after the birth of her sixth child testifies to the general health and well-being Luis de la Serna's household maintained.

No proof exists that Luis's children held positions of authority in Incarnation and Saint Blaise. Perhaps because they were free and only half African, they wanted to disassociate themselves from a confraternity led by slaves. Even though he did not pass the office of majordomo to any of his sons, Luis would have been a public figure as a confraternity leader and perhaps an inspiration to his peers.

The stability of Luis's family life can also be found in the lives of some of the other men and women whose names we find in the records of the Incarnation and Saint Blaise election in 1664, although others who were mentioned had life patterns that were more typical for people of African birth or descent.[32] The 1664 election record lists officials by gender, using the designations *morenos* and *mulatos*. A few of these confraternity brothers and sisters left behind other records of their existence. For example, the majordomo in the list of *moreno* members, Joseph de Gudino, had a family life that perhaps resembled that of Luis de la Serna.[33] Gudino was a slave in the 1660s, although he may have been freed later. In 1661, he had a daughter, Anna, whose mother was also referred to as a black slave. Probably the same Joseph de Gudino, who in the 1680s was called a free mulatto, had two children with a mestiza. If this is the same Joseph, his life went through several changes, from enslaved to free status, from marriage to a slave to marriage to a free woman.

Three other Incarnation officials show an improvement in status over their lifetimes. In 1664, two deputies sat on the *mesa*, or governing body: Juan de Barrio el Viejo and Juan Barrio el Mozo. (Their nicknames mean "the old man" and "the boy.") The elder Juan de Barrio was a slave in 1637 when he married a free *mulata*.[34] By 1662, he was freed by a legacy left at the death of his master.[35] However, his son, Juan, who was about fifteen or sixteen years old that year, was mortgaged in the amount of 140 pesos, meaning that he was not free but had been used as collateral for a loan. It is unknown whether or not Juan de Barrio el Mozo had succeeded in gaining his freedom by the time he served as a deputy on the Incarnation governing body several years later, when he was at most eighteen years old. At a time when 75 percent of Afromexican babies had no father present at their baptism and 40 percent were officially abandoned by their mothers, these two Juan de Barrios seem to have had a close bond, especially as they served together as confraternity leaders. The third black Incarnation officer in 1664 who moved from enslavement to freedom was Pedro de la Cruz, "el Congo," the assistant to the treasurer. This Pedro may have been the same Pedro el Congo who was granted his freedom in 1662, at the approximate age of fifty. He was married to Ana Gertrudis, an Indian woman.[36]

In 1664, Incarnation and Saint Blaise elected several mulatto officers, some of whom were prominent family men. All we know of one of these men, Nicolás de Tinoco, was that he was a free *mulato* married to an Indian woman and that he died in 1686, more than twenty years later.[37] Another mulatto officer, Augustín de Arizaga, a slave of the prominent *alferez* [local official], Augustín de Elejalde y Arizaga, married María de la Cruz, a *morisca* slave, in 1662 in the presence of several witnesses.[38] This couple baptized their children in 1665, 1666, and 1670.[39] Augustín's wife's name was given in various forms: María de Cervantes (who was called his wife and was referred to as a slave), then María de Gallardo (who was described as a "*mulata*, his woman"), and finally simply María de Gallardo with no racial label. All of these names likely represent the same woman, Augustín's legitimate wife María. Their children, Blasa, María, and Bernardo, were all described as mulattos.

Incarnation and Saint Blaise also elected several enslaved black and *mulata cofradía* mothers in 1664, but most of them have disappeared into anonymity. Some probably bore illegitimate children, possibly fathered by their masters. Their unique names, such as Teresa la Catorce, Catalina Galvan la Machina, and Francisca Sánchez Orejita, were never used in sacramental documents, so their histories cannot be traced in church-generated documents. One mother, Francisca de Villalobos, who was described as a black slave, may have been the mother of a "María *mulata*," who was born in 1662 with an unknown or unavailable father.[40] Even though Francisca fit the statistical norm for seventeenth-century enslaved women in Valladolid by having an illegitimate child with a person of European descent, her peers considered her to be a good choice as a leader of their confraternity. Although men and women both led the confraternity, seventeenth-century men, such as Luis de la Serna and Augustín de Arizaga, were more likely than women to generate large, stable families.

Another black confraternity mother might have had a slightly different life experience in Valladolid. In 1661, María de Virela was sold by the Jesuit administrator of a sugar mill in Uripitio for 350 pesos.[41] Only three years later she was serving as a confraternity mother. María de Virela's experience shows that the slave community in Valladolid quickly incorporated new residents. It was possible to form connections with or even lead peers.

Evidence of close connections in the community of *castas* in seventeenth-century Valladolid begins to emerge more clearly when we trace the lives of the leaders of the Rosary confraternity.[42] The Rosary majordomos from the 1660s to the 1690s included Blas Gómez, a mulatto slave, Salvador de Pineda, a mestizo, and Joseph de Aguilar and Antonio de Sosa, both free mulattos. Certain families, especially the Sosas, began their century-long domination of the Rosary at this time.

Salvador de Pineda was a *casta* with indigenous and European ancestry. Born in 1656, he married a free *mulata*, Juliana de Contreras, in 1679. In 1689, their son, also called Salvador, was born. Salvador senior served as majordomo in 1690 at age thirty-four. He later married Juliana Rangel—a relative of many mestizo members of a family that was prominent in Valladolid confraternities—and had two more children in 1709 and 1711. He died the year his last child was born, at the age of fifty-five, which was elderly for the time, and was buried in the Church of Our Lady of Mount Carmel—a significant honor and expense. His son Salvador maintained connections with the Rangel family, serving as a witness at the 1720 wedding of Antonio Rangel, a deputy of the Rosary confraternity.[43]

Blas Gómez, who served as an official and deputy in the 1660s, was the first prominent Rosary leader. Like Salvador de Pineda, Gómez was a successful family man despite his slave status. Gómez's birth is hard to trace: a few babies described as mulattos that were named Blas were born in Valladolid in the 1630s and 1640s, one to a *mulata* slave, one to unknown parents, and one to a woman simply designated *morena*. Any one of these babies, none of whom had father present at their baptism, could have been Blas Gómez. Blas appears in the records as the paternal head of a family over a long period of time, and his marriage to a free woman meant that his children were not slaves. From 1663 to 1675, he had three children, all with a woman named Isabel.[44] Blas Gómez was always described as a mulatto slave in these records, but his wife's racial label changed over the years. She was called Isabel Magdalena, free *mulata*; Isabel de los Reyes, mestiza; and simply "Isabel, his woman." Blas's children also had flexible racial identities: one was called *morisco*, while the others were described as mulattos.[45]

Antonio de Sosa, who was active in the Rosary confraternity in the 1690s, was another family man, in this case one who started a dynasty of confraternity leadership in Valladolid and had extensive personal connections with other confraternity leaders and well-off mulatto families. Antonio, a free mulatto, was called "the Portuguese" in the record of his 1674 marriage to Josepha Alvarez, a woman described both as mestiza and *mulata*. Because Sosa was a Portuguese name, historian María Elena Díaz speculates that one of Antonio's ancestors "may have [been] baptized in Angola even before enslavement or conversely [been] enslaved to a Portuguese man by the same surname."[46] Two Portuguese slaves were sold in Valladolid in the seventeenth century; perhaps they were related to Antonio.[47] Antonio had three children with his first wife, who died around 1678.[48] In 1679, he married again, to Leonor de Ibarra, a free *mulata* who was the daughter of Joseph Tafoya and Juana de Pedraza.[49] This Juana may have been related to or served in the same house as María de Peraza, a leading black mother in the Incarnation confraternity. The last name Tafoya designated a prominent family that was occasionally involved in property sales recorded in the Valladolid notarial records.[50] Antonio had four children with Leonor during the period 1686 to 1690. Joseph de Aguilar, another Rosary official, was present at the baptism of one of these children, Salvador, as his godfather. Antonio's sons Joseph and Salvador both married, and the records of their marriages indicate that Antonio had died by around 1700 and his wife had died by 1710.[51] Antonio de Alvarado, a Rosary board member, was a witness at Joseph's wedding in 1711. Another Joseph de Sosa, possibly a brother of Antonio, was an official of the Rosary in the late seventeenth century, but it was Antonio's son Joseph, born in the 1680s, who regenerated Rosary in the mid-eighteenth century. Antonio de Sosa's son, Miguel, led the Rosary confraternity in the early 1700s, and other Sosas figured prominently in this confraternity in the eighteenth century.

The life of Antonio de Sosa is a fragment of a larger picture of an emerging, interconnected, and prosperous mulatto community in Valladolid that would grow stronger during the last century of the colonial period. By the eighteenth century, it was common for fathers to be present at the baptism of their children. Women were more likely to have stable relationships and were less subject to the sexual violence inherent in the slave system. The lives of people of African descent changed in significant ways over the course of the seventeenth and eighteenth centuries; the lives of majordomos such as Luis de la Serna, Augustín de Arizaga, Blas Gomez, and Antonio de Sosa illustrate these changes, and they may have been the vanguard of such change.

Some men who were prominent as leaders of the eighteenth-century Rosary gradually acquired property in the eighteenth century. A variety of circumstances contributed to their increasing financial success. For example, Antonio Parra served as a deputy in the early eighteenth century, when he was around fifty years old. As a young man, he had received a donation of a house from a cleric named Gregorio Sánchez.[52] Sánchez showed generosity to the Parra family because Antonio's mother, a free *mulata*, had cared for him while he was seriously ill. Another deputy from 1711, Antonio Pardo, who was described both as a free black and a mulatto, purchased property located near the Augustinian church for thirty pesos in 1704.[53] These two transactions are the beginning of documented property ownership for Afromexicans in Valladolid. Testaments also show evidence of their gradually increasing wealth.

In Vallodolid's notarial records during the period 1630 to 1795, testators described as Spanish were usually the ones to make wills, although some non-Spaniards were involved in property transactions. More *castas* owned enough property to make wills in the eighteenth century, but because of the fact that racial labels were used less often by notaries during this period, it is impossible to determine a testator's race unless he or she was given a label in another context, such as confraternal documents or sacramental records. Sometimes members of confraternities were referred to in wills of other people: these references are very useful in uncovering the complex net of social connections and relations in Valladolid. Although they were not confraternity leaders in the eighteenth century, women of African descent appear more frequently in property transactions during this period, especially those involving people of lesser status, people not given the titles "Don" or "Doña." If we could know the names of the wives, mothers, and sisters of every confraternity leader, larger and more complex webs of property ownership and networks of wealth would doubtless emerge.

Only five to ten wills appear in any given year in the notarial records for Valladolid, and in that small number, very few document enormous wealth. In these wills, the concern for masses and pious bequests was tiny compared to the number of wills that requested these religious rites in Mexico City, where seventeenth- and eighteenth-century wills have pages of provisions for mass requests and document the fact that some testators were members of up to a dozen confraternities. Because Valladolid had several confraternities in the seventeenth and eighteenth centuries that were characterized by non-Spanish membership, the poor who could afford a few pesos a year were able to provide for their needs in the afterlife without resorting to a will. Even the simplest wills always indicate at least minimal property ownership and a few small debts, both of which were signs of stability and prosperity in society. Those people who did not own a house and a lot probably had very little to bequeath other than the most basic items of daily use. Very few people of African descent possessed more than what was needed for subsistence, but a small number had a foothold in the dominant group in society, despite the fact that they were assigned the racial labels of black or mulatto. While these people are very difficult to trace, their wills show that they had some access to wealth and the pious demonstrations that wealth allowed.

Juana de Bustos was the first leading member of a black confraternity known to have left a will, and her seventeenth-century testament provides a glimpse of how a wealthy black woman might have expressed her pious bequests. A woman by this name was one of the confraternity mothers in Incarnation and Saint Blaise in 1664, and in 1663 a woman of this name made a will. No racial label was mentioned in this testament, and the testator was described as the wife of a merchant, but this may be the same Juana who was a confraternity mother.[54] Her bequest of a dress to Incarnation supports this conjecture, although nothing else is known about her life, other than that she also left a "toca con puntas grandes de flandes [embroidered cloth imported from Flanders]" to the Tránsito confraternity in the Augustinian church and that she wanted to be buried in the cathedral. Whether Juana was the confraternity mother or a Spanish woman of the same name, these pious bequests and her marriage to a Spanish man of property made it necessary for her to make a will. Almost every other non-Spanish woman in Valladolid was in a different situation. The only way they could have a say in how they were buried and how many masses were said for their salvation was through membership in a confraternity.

A few other seventeenth-century wills of fairly well-to-do people of African descent exist, and, like wills in the capital, they show a varying amount of interest in pious bequests and variety of paths to success. Francisco de Arrellano, a "resident of brown color" who made a will in 1665, was a "son of the church," an abandoned child in the same situation as many other Afromexicans of his era. He grew up to become a property-owning muleteer with debts and close connections to Spanish society through his marriage to a Spanish woman.[55] He made no pious bequests. Ursula de los Angeles, another seventeenth-century testator, left her house and two stores located in the barrio of San José to an *exposito*, a child abandoned at the church who was her adopted heir. Her pious requests were limited to the standard donations for the beatification of Gregorio López and the Casa Santa in Jerusalem. Juana de Ayala, a devout ex-slave and the widow of a slave, left the Rosary confraternity pearl and silver necklaces, clothing, and forty pesos in 1681.[56] Another free black woman called Francisca de Estrada made a will in 1699 that showed strong connections to the religious sphere; she made a Franciscan friar her trustee and asked for burial in the Franciscan church and 100 masses for her soul.[57] Francisca was relatively prosperous; she asked for far more masses than the average testator in Valladolid. She was born legitimate in Mexico City but only gives the first names of her parents, so they may have been slaves at one time. These four individuals were unusually successful, and they were the only definitively non-Spanish testators recorded in Valladolid in the seventeenth century.

Unfortunately (from the perspective of the historian), the use of racial labels in wills declined in the eighteenth century, when it was more likely that an Afromexican would be able to make a will. However, early in that century, some testators were given racial labels, including Felipe de Brisbescas, a free mulatto.[58] His will shows an interesting series of three marriages to women who each had a different racial label. It could be said that Felipe progressed up the social scale by first marrying an Indian woman, then a free *mulata*, then a mestiza. Perhaps he did not consider the race of his chosen spouses to be important and his marriage choices were based more on the social proximity of all three racial communities, as Cope would argue. However, the fact that Felipe made a will at all indicates that he was not as desperately poor as many other free people of color. He was wealthy enough to pay for his request for fifty masses to be said for his soul. He must have been considered a good investment, because he had several debts, and his house, worth 157 pesos, was mortgaged to the Rosary confraternity. This mortgage is one of the first signs of the slow and gradual rise of this confraternity from complete poverty and marginality to prominence in Valladolid society. It marks the beginning of Rosary's transition from an income based entirely on alms to an income that was largely based on interest on loans and rent, the standard way rich Spanish confraternities made money.

Another will from the early eighteenth century supports the argument that a slow and tentative economic rise had begun among people of African heritage in Valladolid. Although Juan de Villaseñor Cisneros, a free black, did not mention confraternities in his will, he had enough surplus wealth to request that ten masses be said for his soul and to specify that two reales be spent on the beatification of Bishop Juan de Palafox y Mendoza.[59] Juan owned a house that had a separate room that served as the kitchen; he also owned six silver spoons, which he left to his wife. His property was large enough to include a corral. This man reached a level of material comfort that was quite unusual among people labeled black.

Because only Afromexicans who lived on the often-tenuous margin of financial success could make wills, confraternity majordomos were among those most likely to become testators; they were the financial, social, and (perhaps in some senses) political leaders of their peers. The twelve wills made by individuals of African descent in the eighteenth century include two made by majordomos of the Incarnation and Saint Blaise confraternity: Antonio Romero in

1742 and Francisco Mondragón in 1763. Francisco Mondragón was called a free black.[60] Antonio Romero's will does not specify his race, but his membership in the Incarnation and Saint Blaise confraternity suggests that he carried the same racial label as Romero.[61]

Diego Durán, who was the most influential mulatto in Valladolid in the late 1700s, made a will in 1795. Durán was a master architect who was known for his contributions to the repair of his city's aqueduct and work on its cathedral. He buttressed his status through confraternity leadership, skill at a trade (in this case one that carried a high level of prestige), and connections with the Hispanic world. Only a few people labeled mulatto in colonial Mexico are remembered now; this small group includes artists such as Juan Correa, who took a different route to fame and success in the late-seventeenth-century viceregal capital. Diego Durán was called *mulato* throughout his life, but he was so famous that after his death he was falsely given credit for work on the ornate Church of Santa Prisca in Taxco.[62]

Despite Diego's racial label, the Durán family actually had Indian heritage.[63] Genealogy was obviously not the crucial factor in this label. Perhaps the label mulatto seemed the appropriate one for a family of urban builders such as the Duráns. Diego Durán's maternal grandfather, Lucas Durán, lived in the Indian barrio of San José in Valladolid in the late seventeenth century. Lucas and Diego's maternal uncle, Juan, were both reputable architects. We do not know whether these titles were official or were given out of respect, but we do know that a trip to Mexico City would have been necessary to pass an examination to become a master architect. Both Lucas Durán and Diego Durán are credited as the leading architects for the Valladolid cathedral, on which they worked from 1704 to around 1744.[64] Diego Durán helped maintain Valladolid's beautiful aqueduct and the hospital of San Juan de Dios and other buildings in and around the city.[65] Diego's mother, María Nicolása Durán, who was described as an Indian, married his father, a free mulatto from Penjamo, in 1717. When Diego was born in 1721, his parents were both called free mulattos. Diego took the name of his mother and his highly esteemed grandfather, and he received his inheritance and status through his mother's relatives. Male-based family life was a relatively rare phenomenon before the early eighteenth century, and Diego was lucky to know several generations of his mother's family and to have their background in building to give him both a family trade and training, a foundation for his success.

During his lifetime, Diego Durán was widowed three times; he married in 1745, 1749, 1764, and 1765. Some of his wives helped increase his wealth, especially through their ownership of valuable pieces of urban property. His first two wives were called *mulatas*, the third was called Spanish, and the fourth was called mestiza. Durán's family did not reproduce because of the mortality of the mothers of his children, a danger even for a well-off person in the eighteenth century. After the death of his third wife, Durán was left with only one daughter. He adopted another girl, who some viewed as his illegitimate child. Durán seemed to be rather stingy with this adopted daughter, who married a prestigious Spaniard but received only a mortgaged house as her dowry from her adoptive father.[66] With his fourth wife, Durán had six living children. This wife was the only one to bring him a significant dowry, which consisted of three large houses.[67] It was common for affluent men of African descent (and perhaps other men in New Spain) to marry several times: Durán's longevity and wealth made him desirable as a husband. His repeated marriages suggest that he was looking for inheritors. The continuation of his legacy may have been an important motivating factor for Durán, who had only one living child from his first three marriages and nine children, with six survivors, from his last marriage.

Through his family profession, his marriage, and his ambitions, Durán became a wealthy man. In his later life, he lived in a substantial house worth more than 4,000 pesos. He worked among all social groups and races in Valladolid to acquire more property and influence throughout his life. His connections, which he established throughout his long lifetime and gained through his skilled profession and ownership of land, were complex. Durán appears regularly in property transactions and loans after the mid-eighteenth century, especially in the 1770s, when he worked hard to increase the status of the Rosary confraternity. In his role as an architect, Durán frequently assessed properties that were donated to confraternities or were being purchased by his peers. For example, in 1782, Nicolás Julian and Justo Pineda sold a house to the Confraternity of Saint Joseph and asked Durán to assess its value.[68] (The Pinedas were the mestizo family mentioned above that was also involved in the Rosary.) Durán also held positions such as trustee of the 1764 will of Doña Margarita del Valle, a *doncella* daughter of parents with the titles of "Don" and "Doña."[69] Through real estate and the Rosary confraternity, Durán made connections to this higher, most likely Spanish, segment of society. Margarita had no other heirs; and she left all her worldly goods to the Rosary confraternity Durán led; she was forced to leave the brotherhood her house because she owed it forty pesos on a loan with the house as a guarantee. Onofre Martínez was a witness to Margarita's testament and frequently served with Durán as a Rosary official; he also was a witness to Durán's third and fourth marriages.[70]

Durán was an ambitious man who made enemies over his lifetime, but he defended his integrity to the end. In the year of his death, 1795, Rosary confraternity officers formed factions and challenged some of his accounting practices, claiming that he owed money to the confraternity.[71] Although the officials were careful to begin their petition to the bishop with respectful words for Durán, mentioning his integrity and long-term concern for confraternity interests, their claims that Durán owed fifty pesos in rent to the confraternity led to protests from an opposing faction. Those who opposed the petition included two of Durán's sons from his fourth marriage, Toribio and Maríano Durán, and the guardian of the Franciscan convent where the Rosary confraternity was located. The aged Durán also responded to these accusations. At the end of his life, Durán's voice speaks loud and clear in this petition:

> The facility with which the [originator of the petition] and his accomplices throw suspicion on my conduct is reprehensible and inexcusable. It is well known in this city that for more than 25 years, since 1776, I have led this confraternity as majordomo, taking care of all expenses from the past and present. After so many years, I left my successor 1,000 pesos, incontestable proof of my great care and the pains I took in conserving this confraternity and adding to its alms and rents.[72]

Durán said that the Franciscan guardian supported his claims and blamed Juan de Dios Mercado, the other majordomo, for the loss of the confraternity's property. The case resulted in the bishop's review of Rosary's accounts, but Durán died a few months later without producing them.

After Durán's death, the dispute over Rosary accounts continued and became even more vituperative.[73] The petitioners seemed to blame all their problems on Durán. Factions clearly formed around the Mercado and Durán families; the Durán faction was led by Diego Durán's fourth wife and their daughter, his main heirs. One of the first complaints was that Durán made the confraternity pay thirteen pesos for the funeral of his adopted daughter even though she had never paid confraternity dues. Confusion and conflict mounted because Durán owed the confraternity on a loan he borrowed from them using his house as collateral. Durán's shaky handwriting in his final accounts shows he did some confraternity work during his final illness, and his heirs said it was done conscientiously; they claimed that the estate owed Rosary only eighty pesos of the 150 originally demanded.

These cases reveal that even though Durán was a trusted leader with two generations of family success behind him, he still faced challenges to the honor of his reputation. Without his strong leadership, Rosary broke down quickly into factions that threatened to tear apart all the confraternity had achieved in the eighteenth century. Durán's leadership had helped make Rosary strong enough to last through the eighteenth and early nineteenth centuries, a time when many other confraternities were falling apart, and when his leadership was gone, the stability of Rosary disappeared as well.

Although people of African descent were able to improve their lives in Valladolid in the eighteenth century, such advancements were fragile, and those of designated African heritage definitely faced checks to their social and professional ascent. Despite his prestige as an architect, Durán was never called "Don," although his adopted daughter was addressed as "Doña."[74] Durán associated and did business with people called "Don," but never broke through this titular barrier himself.

However, a custom existed in eighteenth-century Valladolid of addressing prominent *castas* with the title of *maestro*. This title was a concession to their respectability, which they achieved through the route of skilled workmanship, not through great wealth or lineage. Most of Rosary's leaders could claim this title. One of the earliest maestros was master tailor Salvador de Pineda, who was a deputy in the Rosary from 1690 to his death in 1711.[75] Durán was always referred to as a master architect or master builder. Thomas de la Huerta was another master architect or builder who led the confraternity.[76] Luis Ruíz, a master tailor, was majordomo of the Rosary in 1776 and 1781. The memberships of Pineda and Ruíz demonstrate that Rosary was not just a guild of builders, as Moisés Guzmán Pérez has suggested. [77] It is more likely the case that the builders that were members were a few of Durán's professional colleagues that he had attracted to the confraternity. [78] The Incarnation and Saint Blaise confraternity also had at least one *maestro* as a leader: Nicolás Pérez, majordomo in 1781, who was a *maestro* singer.[79] Nicolás Rangel was referred to as a master architect in notarial records and in the Rosary confraternity elections in the 1780s.

The records of these elections show that confraternity members greatly valued the title of *maestro*; it was used constantly to refer to Durán, Rangel, and Ruíz. Perhaps the title was emphasized in the context of confraternity business to enhance the brothers' respectability and in the hope that this honor would continue into other spheres of society. The title may well have compensated for the fact that the brothers would never achieve the status the label "Don" carried. The great attention to titles reveals that these men wanted to generate some kind of deference and had internalized the Spanish obsession with hierarchy. Through their leadership of a confraternity, these men were at the summit of at least one hierarchy. At the same time, because Rosary was a mulatto confraternity that maintained this racial designation at least until the end of the eighteenth century, these men could not deny the racial group to which they had been assigned from birth.

Under the colonial system, non-Spaniards of all kinds faced limitations in autonomy at the end of the eighteenth century. After 200 years of effort to integrate into Hispanic society and at the same time create identities through racially designated confraternities, Valladolid's mulattos, even those with renown, property, and wealth, faced impassable social barriers and could not rise above the social level of a very skilled craftsman, regardless of the amount of wealth they managed to amass.

Gradually over the course of the seventeenth and eighteenth centuries, mulattos began to appear in official documents as property owners and testators; they began to achieve success in the wider sphere of Spanish life. These documents illustrate the meaning of success for mulattos, which developed from simply maintaining a large, legitimate family, as did Luis de la Serna, to reaching a position among Valladolid's leading artisans. These changes led to greater status and wealth for the Rosary confraternity and a decline in the Incarnation confraternity.

Douglas Cope's *The Limits of Racial Domination* traces the change from a race-based to a class-based society in Mexico City in the seventeenth century. He posits that in Mexico City around 1700, social connections went beyond people who shared racial labels and extended to economic ties within the city's less wealthy underclass. He argues that this kind of connection strengthened as patronage relationships broke down between the poor and the *gente decente* [respectable people]. In a provincial town such as Valladolid, hints of this change occurred throughout the eighteenth century. From the 1720s to the end of the eighteenth century, mulatto and Indian confraternities occasionally united to work toward common goals, demonstrating a sense of plebeian community that extended beyond confraternity ties.

In Valladolid, social connections were formed through confraternities, family ties, property deals, and occupational ties. Data from Cope's work and my analysis of baptism and marriage records from Valladolid suggest that marriage was not always racially endogamous and that marriage choices did not always indicate a desire to ascend to a higher racial designation. Other kinds of social connections may have had more value. Long workdays and labor-related travel probably meant that social networks formed in the workplace were just as important as marriage alliances in colonial-era racial identity.[80] Men gathered in confraternities with other men who shared similar occupations.

Cooperation among various confraternities in Valladolid helped create a sense of common purpose and unity, even when this solidarity conflicted with Hispanic authority. In 1725, the majordomos of the Confraternities of Saint Roque, Incarnation, the Blood of Christ, Tránsito, Saint Nicolás, and Rosary united to petition the bishop to distribute the costs of Corpus Christi more fairly.[81] Each of these confraternities—whose members were generally poor Indians, mestizos, or mulattos—had to pay fifty pesos for wax in the cathedral during this fiesta. Because they all depended on alms and lacked property or rental income, this payment was a hardship that forced some confraternity leaders to risk loans secured by their inventory, especially their silver. In their petition, the majordomos stated that their priority was to pay for masses for the dead, not for wax. They suggested that the bishop order the Confraternities of Our Lady of Mount Carmel, Mercy, Christ of the Misericordia, and the Column of Saint John to share this payment so that each confraternity would only have to pay five pesos each. The latter confraternities were founded after the first six, and they already participated with their standards in the fiesta and took part in the dances. In this case, six non-Hispanic confraternities came together to challenge four other confraternities whose membership was not specifically characterized as *mulato*, *negro*, or Indian. Unfortunately, it is difficult to assess the success of this union. The result of the petition was a drawn-out conflict between the Carmelite convent and the bishop. The officials of the Confraternity of Our Lady of Carmel refused to pay this new fee, although the bishop pointed out that even the ancient Rosary confraternity—founded with all possible privileges under the auspices of the Franciscans—had to obey the bishop.

In 1781, the poorer, less prestigious Valladolid confraternities demonstrated unity once again. In that year, *casta* majordomos organized a unified front to guarantee that they would receive what they considered to be proper status and respect after death. This group included José Luis Ruíz of the Rosary; José Ramos of the Precious Blood of Christ, located in the convent of Saint Catherine of Sienna; Nicolás Pérez, leader of the confraternity of the Incarnation and Saint Blaise; Bernardo Chávez, majordomo of the confraternity of the Trinity in the Mercedarian church; José Joaquín Durán from the Confraternity of the Sacred Heart, also in the Mercedarian church; and Nicolás Xaramillo, majordomo of the Confraternity of Saint Nicolás in the Augustinian church.[82] Majordomos of the Confraternity of the Cord of Saint Francis, the Confraternity of Tránsito in the church of the Augustinian convent, the Confraternity of Our Lady of Mount Carmel, the Confraternity of Saint Joseph, the Confraternity of Our Lady of Mercy, and the Confraternity of Saint Roque also participated in the agreement. The majordomos promised to attend each other's funerals, contribute wax, and ensure that they received a decent and respectable burial. They promised that this larger group would participate in funeral rituals for any and all deceased majordomos. They also promised these burial rites for parents and wives of majordomos and all members of confraternity councils.

Another case reveals how confraternities as a group viewed themselves, their history, and their status vis-à-vis other local confraternities. A conflict among Afromexican confraternities began in 1796 over the issue of which confraternity should lead and which should follow in processions.[83] The majordomos of the Confraternities of Our Lady of Tránsito, the Precious Blood of Christ, Incarnation, Our Lady of Mercy, Holy Trinity, Saint Joseph, Sacred Heart of Jesus, Saint Nicolás, and Saint Roque told the bishop that the Corpus Christi procession had always been organized according to a confraternity's date of founding. All of the members who testified in this case carried the labels *mulato* or mestizo. This petition did not discuss Spanish confraternities; these confraternities probably had their own procession with a well-established hierarchy that was completely separate from that of the petitioning confraternities. In the procession of non-Spanish confraternities in this debate, the oldest confraternities were placed at the end. Rosary's sixteenth-century founding date was not mentioned; it was assumed that Rosary would end the procession. For some reason, the Confraternity of Our Lady of Mount Carmel had decided to participate in the procession with the Confraternity of the Rosary, carrying their insignias among those of the oldest group, even though they were one of the more recently founded confraternities. The majordomos explained this presumption as "caprice or a dominant spirit." The only acceptable time a confraternity could join with another in the procession, according to the majordomos, was when a confraternity had no insignias of its own. According to this logic, it would have been best for Mount Carmel to walk with Saint Roque, because these two confraternities were closer in seniority. Although the Mount Carmel confraternity had been seen carrying an insignia in weekly processions, its majordomo claimed they did not have an insignia and had to borrow one from the Carmelite convent. But he presented a different reason for his confraternity's position in the procession; he argued that it was customary for Mount Carmel and Rosary to walk together because their memberships overlapped.

In response, the other majordomos presented their earliest documents to prove the age of their groups. The Confraternity of Tránsito was founded around 1600, Saint Nicolás was founded in 1617, Precious Blood of Christ was founded in 1644, Saint Roque was founded in 1682, and Trinity was founded in 1743. The majordomo of the Confraternity of the Sacred Heart admitted that they had been founded only in 1759, but he used their "quiet and peaceful" manner and reputation to argue for the right to walk near Rosary. This comment reveals that antiquity really had little to do with a confraternity's position in a procession; founding dates were simply chosen as a good weapon to use against the aggressive Mount Carmel confraternity. The good reputation of a confraternity was a more important indicator of where it should be placed in the procession. Also, no one was sure whether Mount Carmel was founded in 1680 or much later. The bishop decided that Mount Carmel could only walk behind the Confraternity of the Trinity and of the Sacred Heart, since these were the only confraternities that were definitely younger than Mount Carmel. This decision rationalized the procession, making it truly based on age rather than on privilege, tradition, demeanor, or favoritism.

In another case of cross-confraternity cooperation, leaders of all the confraternities based in the Franciscan church joined together in 1798 and succeeded in obtaining the bishop's permission to build an organ for the benefit of the friars and the confraternities.[84] The Rosary majordomo, along with majordomos from the Confraternity of the Cord of Saint Francis and Saint Roque, which was a poor Indian confraternity, spoke on the part of their governing councils and members, arguing that a new organ would improve their fiestas. While Saint Roque could give only sixty pesos to the cause, the other majordomos gave 100 pesos each. This example illustrates the ability of Rosary to influence other Afromexican confraternities in the late eighteenth century.

In 1766, a group of men led by Diego Durán fomented a movement that can only be described as both political and plebeian; it involved a group of 150 men with a variety of racial backgrounds who were unified by their status as members of the working class. This group sought to influence the viceroy in the appointment of the *alcalde mayor* of the province.[85] It is possible that filing this type of petition was as politically active as Afromexicans could be in the colonial era. More than a few of the petitioners were also leaders or members of the Rosary. These include Diego Durán, Tomás Huerta, Antonio Durán, Joseph de Aguilar, Sebastián Cortes, Joseph de Sosa, Diego Rangel, and Luis Ruíz. The surnames of many others who signed suggest that their fathers or other relatives were among the prominent Rosary members, including men with last names such as Parra, Serna, Vásquez, Arisaga, Pineda, and Magaña. All of these family names appear often in the records of the Rosary. This document strongly suggests that membership in a confraternity extended beyond religious, occupational, or social ties and into the political realm. It is not clear how to analyze the role of Rosary in this case. One could say that personal and family ties led men to join a confraternity that provided a path to political action. One could also say that men with similar backgrounds as craftsmen joined confraternities and were motivated by similar political interests.

The petitioners, calling themselves the "plebe" of Valladolid, asked the viceroy for the continuation of Don Luis Velez de la Cueva in the office of *alcalde mayor* of the province and presented several justifications for their request. Cueva displayed special care for the poor, orphans, and Indians, they said. His decisions were fair and were not influenced by wealth or power. He relented on various "emoluments" that were usually charged to the poor. His just and benign term of office had led to prosperity for the area. Only Diego Durán and Florenziano Cardona signed the document (the other men's names were listed in the head of the document). Perhaps Durán believed that the conditions of Velez's term had helped his own rise and that of his peers. This petition and the unification of purpose among men who were also the members of the same confraternity suggests that poorer members of Valladolid's local society had begun to sense their common interests by the end of the colonial period. One wonders if Miguel Hidalgo y Costilla, who was born, like Durán's ancestors, near Penjamo in 1753 and educated in Valladolid, and José María Morelos y Pavon, who was of African descent and was born in Valladolid in 1765, heard anything about this *casta* political movement as they were growing up. Certainly the demographic changes we see in Valladolid's *casta* population had some role in shaping the ideas and actions of these future national heroes of Mexico.

In the seventeenth century, Africans, blacks, and mulattos were often enslaved, poor, illegitimate, or even abandoned as children. Mothers, for reasons we do not know, abandoned their children, who were then raised by a neighbor or the church in the hope that perhaps their sacrifice would enable their children to achieve freedom. Many women had sole responsibility for raising their children, and it is likely that a significant number of these children were conceived under violent circumstances. Knowing that they could not count on charity for health care or burial, seventeenth-century slaves and free people of color organized confraternities to provide for their social needs; these groups were often led by the women who raised money and nursed the sick. The Confraternity of the Incarnation and Saint Blaise was associated with an especially sacred symbolism because of the very humble nature of its members, leadership, and financial status. Some of the wealthier local residents joined this confraternity posthumously, a practice that was rarely seen even in the much more extensive record of Mexico City wills from the same era. Despite their poverty and slavery, some people succeeded in maintaining their families, achieving financial stability, and leading confraternities.

In the eighteenth century, some Afromexicans in Valladolid would no longer consider slavery or even a heritage of enslavement the central facet of their self-definition. Their identity came from family ties and skilled work, which helped them raise their standard of living. Men rather than women filled leadership roles in confraternities. The Rosary confraternity no longer needed to depend on alms or pious bequests, and it rejected female leadership that derived from alms-collecting and the public displays associated with that practice. Men such as Diego Durán and his fellow master craftsmen left servitude and humility behind and interacted with the Hispanic world on an increasingly equal footing. These men did what they could to further their own interests within the limitations of the colonial hierarchies and the caste system. Yet barriers to elite status remained, and no Afromexican was able to cross them.

6

Patronage and the *Pardo* Confraternity in Parral

Parral's *pardo* Confraternity of the Immaculate Conception was barely tolerated for much of its history. It was not considered an acceptable part of Parral's public life until the late eighteenth century, when *castas* accounted for the majority of Parral's population and the town's days of prosperity had long passed. No Afro-mexicans in Parral achieved the success Diego Durán and his peers experienced in Valladolid, nor was their confraternity as well respected as Valladolid's Rosary, but Parral's *pardos* did move up the social scale from slaves to urban craftsmen. Poverty, disease, drought, and hunger meant that Parral's *pardo* confraternity achieved only limited stability and far less opulence than the boisterous Afro-mexican confraternities in successful mining towns in the seventeenth century. However, over the course of the seventeenth and eighteenth centuries, the confraternity of *pardos* became one of Parral's most enduring and popular religious institutions.

San José de Parral (now Hidalgo del Parral in the state of Chihuahua) was founded in 1629 and experienced one of the late silver bonanzas in New Spain. The town's religious institutions were not founded until the 1640s, well after the founding date of many confraternities, convents, and churches in other parts of colonial Mexico.[1] Because of an ongoing threat of Indian raids and a nearly constant state of war, fluctuating population numbers, and a bonanza that ended by 1700, Parral's public ceremonial life was very simple.[2] Nevertheless, the citizens of Parral, including the clergy, attempted to found and maintain confraternities similar to those in more important cities, towns, and villages.

This chapter presents a social history of the slaves who became members of Parral's laboring classes in the eighteenth century and the story of their confraternity and the many challenges to its existence.[3] Many leading local figures emerge in this story because the confraternity depended on the patronage and support of elite Spanish residents from the time of its founding at the silver refining hacienda of Cristóbal Montaño de la Cueva to the eighteenth century, when the brotherhood finally became an accepted local institution. Although men of African descent in both Parral and Valladolid were generally tradesmen in the eighteenth century, Parral's plebeians were less likely to achieve social and financial success. Parral did not experience the economic boom Valladolid did, although the town was affected by the military aspect of Bourbon reform and eighteenth-century authorities put much effort into organizing and supplying the local troops.

The terms "*casta*" and "*pardo*" will be used here more often than in previous chapters because these terms give a greater sense of the development of racial and social divisions in Parral's society. In eighteenth-century Parral, Immaculate Conception was always referred to as a confraternity of *pardos*, although membership and census records show that the confraternity's leadership came from a more generally plebeian group of mestizos, Indians, and mulattos. The literal meaning of *pardo*, "brown," makes sense as a description of this group of people. "*Casta*" is also used to refer to anyone who was not considered Spanish because of darker appearance, lower social status, and a low-prestige occupation.

In Parral's remote location, power and wealth were concentrated in a few hands: Montaño de la Cueva and his descendants were members of a small powerful group in Parral that controlled the town's military, civil, economic, and ecclesiastical hierarchies in the seventeenth century.[4] This was typical of northern New Spain, where one man or one family often had power over several facets of town life. The Confraternity of the Immaculate Conception could not survive without patrons who were members of the powerful elite, even though such individuals frequently hindered confraternity activities with religious and civil sanctions or used their power as slave owners to control their slaves.

Silver was mined in the region of Parral from 1567, but Parral's population remained minuscule until 1632, when the population mushroomed to 300 men, their servants and slaves, and a few wives.[5] Most people came to Parral from the formerly great mining center of Zacatecas (about 400 miles to the southeast) to seek a new source of mineral wealth. Parral may have been the next best hope for the people who migrated there, but it never reached the levels of wealth Zacatecas had enjoyed in its heyday.

From the beginning, slaves, Indians, and free blacks came to Parral with the official residents of the town, or *vecinos*, although the names of these servants and slaves were not recorded in public documents. Almost immediately new slaves were imported to the fledgling mining town: miner Francisco Montaño de la Cueva purchased one of the first slaves sold in Parral in 1632.[6] In the first decade of Parral's existence, local residents purchased 350 slaves. The population of Spaniards also grew, reaching 800 by 1640 and 1,200 by 1650.[7]

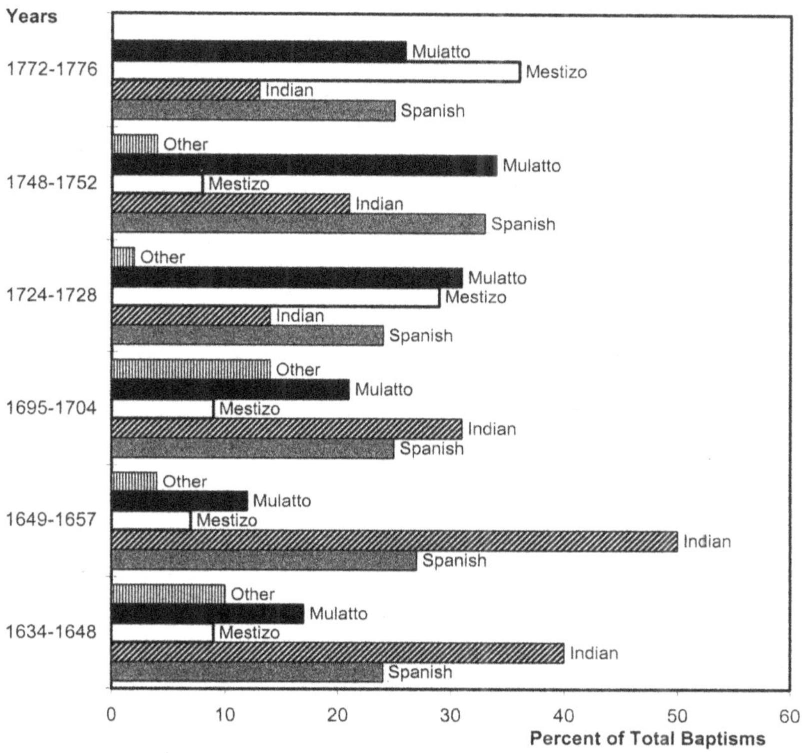

Graph 6.1. Parral baptisms recorded by racial labels, 1634–1776 (selected years). *Source*: Libros de Bautismos, Parral, 1695–1776, LDS rolls 162529, 162530, 162531.

Parral was surrounded by what were considered wild Indians, indigenous people who had not been completely conquered by the Spanish. Indians made up a significant proportion of Parral's population for the entire colonial period. Priests and friars immediately set out to bring this warlike population under their control; half of all baptismal records for the first forty years of Parral's history were for Indians, and recently converted adults accounted for some of these baptisms.[8] In the seventeenth century, the Indians baptized in Parral were from outlying areas. After 1660, fewer Indians were baptized than were buried, and their number was already decreasing relative to the other groups in the population (see graph 6.1). Many local Indians were assigned a label at the baptismal font that designated their cultural and language group, such as Apache, Concho, or Yaqui.

Parral was always a town with a large *casta* population. There was never a time in Parral's history when people who claimed pure European descent dominated numerically. In the seventeenth century, people described as Spaniards probably made up less than one-third of the population, and Afromexicans, *chinos*, and mestizos made up one-quarter to one-third of baptized infants.[9] The majority of the population was Indian until the eighteenth century, when mestizos and mulattos began to dominate numerically. Spaniards wanted to hold on to their authority in the seventeenth century, which meant controlling a group of Indians and African slaves and their children that was much larger than their own group. Their response was to create strict racial, social, and political hierarchies. Later, when the Spanish population and the wealth of the town decreased, this domination loosened, *casta* residents were allowed more autonomy, and racial lines began to blur. By the eighteenth century, there was simply not enough at stake in Parral for authorities to concern themselves with restricting the lives and the confraternity of local *castas*.

Even though there are no dependable population statistics until the second half of the eighteenth century, the number of baptisms each year in Parral provides a sense of when the town was growing or declining. From 1634 to 1657, around 1,000 children were baptized in the town, at a rate of about forty per year. As the town grew toward the end of the century, when the mines were still producing, the birthrate more than doubled. Mulattos and mestizos gradually made up a more substantial percentage of infants baptized than they had before 1704. Parral's birthrate and fortunes reached their eighteenth-century low from the 1720s to the 1750s. Its population was clearly decreasing during these decades because of economic hardship; as mining became less viable, people left Parral or moved to ranches outside the town. The Spanish population decreased slightly during much of this period, while the indigenous population decreased sharply, if the number of baptisms is a reliable indicator. But during this nadir of the town's fortunes, mulattos made up the largest percentage of total baptisms.

The group that constituted the "other" category in graph 6.1 disappears in the 1770s. In the seventeenth century, most of this group was made up of slaves described as black. Occasionally the slaves baptized in Parral were adults who had come directly from Africa. After 1650, no new African slaves arrived and no one called *negro* was baptized. In the period 1720 to 1760, the "other" group was made up of members of the racial groups referred to with the new terms "*lobo*" and "*coyote*." But these terms did not last for long; by the end of the colonial era, only the more general racial labels of Indian, mestizo, mulatto, and Spaniard persisted, each label signifying specific social and economic roles in the town. Of course, the racial labels used in Parral's baptism records may have been manipulated. It was common for authorities to use the labels mestizo and mulatto interchangeably, but even, or perhaps especially, in a remote town such as Parral, the Spanish elite had a firm position that could not be assumed

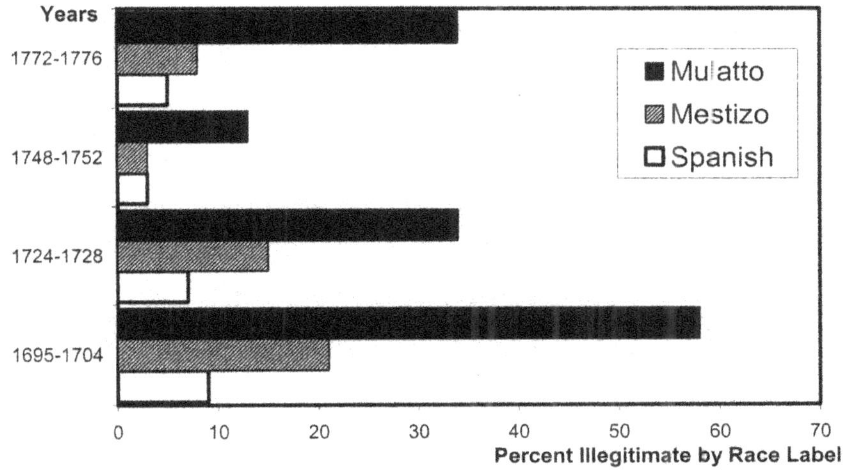

Graph 6.2. Baptisms of children with no father present, Parral, 1695–1776. *Source*: Libros de Bautismos, Parral, 1695–1776, LDS rolls 162529, 162530, 162531.

by people who lacked *limpieza de sangre*. Graph 6.1 shows the gradual rise of a mestizo population; in the seventeenth century, this group was very small, but by the 1770s, it accounted for the largest group among baptisms. Perhaps the label mestizo was applied in the 1770s to people who had been called mulatto in the 1740s and 1750s. As these mulattos or so-called mestizos became more prominent in town life, local priests might have allowed them a more prestigious racial label at baptism.[10]

The trend in illegitimacy rates for Parral resembles the trend in Valladolid, although in Parral it is easier to compare illegitimacy across racial labels because the town's priests always recorded all baptisms in one book. Among Afromexicans, Spaniards, and Indians, blacks and mulattos were most likely to bear illegitimate children in the seventeenth century; the incidence of illegitimacy in these two groups decreased in the eighteenth century. Babies born into slavery almost never had a recognized father at their baptisms. Slaves were born in Parral into the 1770s, and that group contributed to a continuing high rate of illegitimacy at this time. The percentage of illegitimate children decreased when the birthrate decreased. As the town's overall population decreased, the calmer economic environment, smaller community, and absence of fortune-seekers who were only temporary residents contributed to a more stable family life. In the eighteenth century, children labeled mestizo almost always were baptized with their fathers present, almost at the same rate as children born into Spanish families. Perhaps this was one reason why mestizos were viewed as a more respectable group in society than mulattos.

Parral society was highly stratified, and racial labels were used in all official documents until the end of the colonial period. It would have been very difficult for a person labeled mulatto to rise above the position of artisan or craftsman; the elite were concerned with maintaining social hierarchies and there were very few economic opportunities. No studies have been done that analyze the social role of the militia in colonial Parral, but this may have been one path to upward mobility for Afromexicans in the eighteenth century, especially if it meant moving out of the region to areas such as Alta California that were even less developed than Parral.

Parral was 250 miles, or two weeks' travel, from the nearest city of Durango and 800 miles from Mexico City, perhaps a two-month journey. Given its remoteness, its high crime rate, the uncertainty of the mining economy, and the constant menace of Indian invasions, it is surprising that the town was able to support a local religious infrastructure. However, in the seventeenth century it maintained several confraternities and eventually a convent of Franciscans, a Jesuit house, and a hospital run by the religious order of San Juan de Dios. Settlers in Parral, who came from Spain, Durango, Mexico City, or Zacatecas, quickly founded religious institutions, re-creating what they viewed as essential elements of urban life. Confraternities dedicated to the Holy Sacrament and the Souls in Purgatory had been founded by the beginning of the 1640s. An Extremaduran merchant made generous bequests to these first confraternities in 1641.[11] The town also had a confraternity dedicated to Saint Nicolás Tolentino, and the first settlers in Parral founded a hospital for Indians that began construction in 1642.[12] Local confraternity advocations in seventeenth-century Parral followed the pattern of other towns in New Spain and included the Rosary and local devotion to a miraculous image of Nuestra Señora del Rayo, Our Lady of the Lightning.

Immaculate Conception did not inspire the pious devotion other humble slave confraternities did, such as the Confraternity of the Incarnation and Saint Blaise in Valladolid. The confraternity did not receive pious bequests from other town residents until it became associated with the San Juan de Dios hospital in the 1680s. By that time, testators had begun willing property to the confraternity to support its charitable actions, but the relationship was one of patronage rather than the desire to associate spiritually with the humblest and most marginal members of society, as wealthier people did in Valladolid. Confraternal life for Afromexicans living in Parral was about patrons and clients rather than flagellation, alms-collecting, and elaborate processions. Women did not feature in the history of confraternities in Parral, and women of African descent did not have behind-the-scenes economic power based on property ownership.[13] Evidence shows that Parral's Immaculate Conception consistently faced challenges to its acceptance in the community and could not count on it for support. Its dependence on patronage reinforced the social hierarchy and did not create opportunities for increased social status through group organization.

Immaculate Conception existed because Parral was founded in the seventeenth century, when confraternities still enjoyed great popularity among elite town leaders. Parral's institutional religious life developed in a pattern that resembled that of many other mining towns that flourished in the seventeenth century. Confraternal life in Parral declined in the eighteenth century, and brotherhoods lost elite support.

The confraternity of the Immaculate Conception may have existed since the town's founding, but it was not well supported by Parral's Spanish residents in general until the confraternity undertook its hospital project in 1680. Wills in Parral commonly included donations to confraternities after the 1640s, but testators did not refer to Immaculate Conception until the 1680s. Several other confraternities, the Indian hospital, and the confraternity dedicated to Saint Nicolás Tolentino were non-elite religious organizations that benefited from pious bequests before Immaculate Conception became popular among testators.

A 1641 will made by a merchant from Extremadura exemplifies the confraternal piety local residents brought with them to Parral from Spain, Mexico City, Zacatecas, and Durango. The testator, Antonio Juan Márquez, left donations to religious institutions in his hometown in Spain and his new home in Parral.[14] His bequests show a desire to make these two worlds more similar. Márquez, who requested burial in the habit of Saint Francis, gave fifty pesos to Parral's Confraternity of the Holy Sacrament, thirty pesos to the Confraternity of the Souls in Purgatory, and 150 pesos to a convent and confraternity in his hometown. He also sent 400 pesos to Mexico City for the purchase of images of Our Lady of the Rosary and Saint Anthony for Parral. The capital was an intermediary step between Spain and Parral and helped provide the accoutrements needed to bring symbols of Hispanic piety to remote towns. Márquez's will also included a donation for the adornment of Saint Nicolás Tolentino in Parral. This will provides evidence that three confraternal devotions existed as early as a decade after the town's founding, and Márquez helped promote the Rosary, an essential confraternity in every seventeenth-century town in New Spain. By 1651, other testators had begun to show their devotion to this image of the Rosary by asking for burial near it.[15]

By 1657, wills in Parral had begun to refer to a full range of local confraternities, including the Holy Sacrament, Souls in Purgatory, the Rosary, and Saint Nicolás Tolentino.[16] Confraternities dedicated to Saint Nicolás Tolentino were common among mestizos and people of African descent, so it may have had black and mulatto members in Parral. Saint Nicolás Tolentino was also referred to as the patron of the Indian hospital in Parral, although in the 1660s the hospital was dedicated to Our Lady of the Lightning, Parral's miraculous image.[17]

The Immaculate Conception confraternity did not fit comfortably with this panorama of local religious institutions. Although its members were among the town's first residents and owners of property, the continuing existence of slavery in Parral until the eighteenth century prevented people of African descent from ascending the social ladder. Instead, the elite used the enslaved status of the brothers as a weapon against them in legal battles. Immaculate Conception was founded on a silver-refining hacienda, and it more closely resembled other hacienda confraternities than confraternities founded in mining towns such as Zacatecas. Immaculate Conception's founding on a hacienda both guaranteed patronage and support and prevented autonomy. It also strengthened a patron-client relationship between slaves, servants, and *hacendados* [estate owners]. Unlike confraternities in mining towns, which were very independent, were founded in parish churches, and supported themselves through alms-collecting, hacienda confraternities had to deal more carefully with elite patrons. Until they were completely free of ties to hacienda owners, they lacked independence, self-sufficiency, and freedom to conduct rituals and fiestas as they saw fit. Even after those ties had been shed, members were well aware of their history of dependence.

The Immaculate Conception confraternity had a well-documented connection to the silver-refining plant owned by the men of the Montaño de la Cueva family, who created a veritable dynasty in Parral through their access to various sources of power, wealth, and authority. The leaders of this family, all *hacendados*, held important local offices for the entire seventeenth century, beginning with the *maestre de campo* [field master] Don Francisco Montaño de la Cueva (d. 1647), a man who had served as a military leader in Nueva Vizcaya from 1616.[18] Francisco passed his estate on to his nephew, the presbyter Don Phelipe Montaño de la Cueva (d. 1679). Phelipe's brother, Don Cristóbal de Villamayor y Carvajal (d. 1693), and another brother, the sergeant major Don Gonzalo de Carvajal (d. 1686), carried on the dynasty almost to the end of the century, when the family's domination in Parral and over the Immaculate Conception confraternity ended. All four of these men were powerful miners and administrators in seventeenth-century Parral and were deeply involved in the fate of the Immaculate Conception.

In addition to the official military and religious titles Francisco and Phelipe held, the Montaño de la Cueva men held various other positions of power in Parral. Their mining dynasty began in 1632 when Francisco bought a mine for 1,760 pesos.[19] To add to their economic autonomy and wealth, the family owned its own silver-processing hacienda, which brought royal patronage through grants of mercury, which was used to refine silver.[20] The king held a monopoly over this essential silver-processing element. Francisco, who was referred to as *maestre de campo* in all documentation, was also a town justice and *alcalde* and held the title of general in the 1640s.[21] Phelipe had a variety of titles that illustrate the diverse functions of Parral's elite. In his 1676 will, Phelipe's full title is given as "professed friar of the order of Knights of Santiago, son of the convent of Santiago of the sword in Seville."[22] Phelipe was also referred to as *canónigo* [canon]. Whether or not Phelipe actually did any work connected to the church is unknown. Many men in Parral had clerical titles but did not perform any services for the church, instead making money as miners, *hacendados*, or ranchers.[23] Phelipe certainly had other economically viable activities, but his will mentions that he was both an Inquisition commissary and the pastor of the small mining settlement of Our Lady of Montserrat.

In contrast to this entrenched elite, Immaculate Conception brothers, as individuals and as a group, struggled for their place in Parral society. Secular and ecclesiastical court cases throughout the seventeenth century challenged their hold on power over their confraternity. At every moment in Immaculate Conception's history, when the brothers were trying to increase their local presence and activities, a leader of the confraternity faced a demoralizing criminal charge. Although Spanish and Indian residents dominate the criminal records, the occasional appearance of Immaculate Conception brothers as defendants harmed attempts to promote the confraternity.[24] While the powerful Francisco Montaño de la Cueva and his descendants often seemed to be involved in unsavory activities that included violence and theft, their honor remained intact. However, if a mulatto brother was imprisoned for debt, as Antonio Narváez (b. 1613) was in 1660, he further weakened his already-tenuous reputation.[25] In Narváez's case, owing ninety-two pesos brought charges that he was a *vago* [vagrant]. The word "vagrant" was considered a high insult at this time; a mestizo, Juan de Dios, was tried in Parral in 1672 because he used *malas palabras* [bad words] against a Spanish woman, thus defaming her reputation. Juan claimed he was only responding to her public insults; she had called him a "vagrant dog" and a "Chichimec dog."[26] Both Juan de Dios and Antonio de Narváez had to defend themselves against accusations that they were vagabonds by asserting their ties to the locale or to employers.

Antonio de Narváez, a mulatto deputy for Immaculate Conception in the 1670s when the confraternity was striving for autonomy, struggled at various times against accusations of criminal activities. In 1677, when he was sixty-four, he fought in court with Cristóbal Villamayor over who was responsible for the Immaculate Conception chapel and its contents. During this conflict, Narváez was accused of buying stolen goods. But he was able to use his *buena fama* [good reputation] to argue successfully against the accusations. Witnesses in his defense presented him as a respectable mulatto; they described him as "a man of good faith and reputation, well known in this town."[27] His public activities, which were connected to his leadership position in Immaculate Conception, and his private life attested to impressive social status for a seventeenth-century mulatto. Twice widowed during his lifetime, Narváez had made marriages with three "honest" women; at least one of these wives was lower on the colonial racial hierarchy than he was: his wife in the 1640s was called "Luisa, free black."[28] In 1644 and 1647, the couple had a daughter and a son, both of whom were described as mulatto. They also served in the important and trustworthy position of godparents for an Indian baby in 1650 and a *mulata* orphan in 1646.

His title of sergeant was probably the strongest testament to his good name. Narváez earned this title through active duty, and he may have been a leader in the mulatto militia. Military titles were very common in Parral, and citizens were frequently called upon to respond to attacks by Indians.[29] Witnesses also defended Narváez's reputation by testifying that he "was received in the government palace and in private houses for celebrations and feasts." He gave "worked silver, ornaments and jewels to the church," gifts perhaps connected to his position as deputy of the Immaculate Conception confraternity. Because of these favorable accounts, Narváez was declared innocent of the charges of buying stolen goods.

Lázaro de los Reyes, who was described as a free mulatto servant, was another prosperous leader of the Immaculate Conception confraternity. Reyes was probably a servant on the Villamayor hacienda; he was a witness to a crime committed near the Immaculate Conception chapel on the hacienda in 1681.[30] Reyes served as the rector of the confraternity in 1685 and participated in the official welcome of the Juanino friars as caretakers of the confraternity hospital.[31] Reyes died before 1692, because in that year his unmarried daughter mentioned him in her will, saying he had bequeathed her a house near the hospital of San Juan de Dios.[32] The daughter donated this house to pay for her burial in the hospital and the masses she asked the friars to say for her. She was wealthy enough to leave donations to every confraternity and religious institution in town. These fragments of information indicate that Reyes left his daughter fairly well off, with enough surplus income to make pious donations for her salvation.

Generally, disputes between Immaculate Conception confraternity brothers and powerful members of society were worked out in the ecclesiastical courts, but clashes also took place in the town's public plazas, streets, and private haciendas, leading to involvement by civil authorities. The problems confraternity brothers such as Antonio Narváez faced were intertwined with tension over confraternity conflicts. Even though the Confraternity of the Immaculate Conception was led by men with some degree of social status, the fact that it was founded in a hacienda chapel meant that these men were powerless leaders. A number of disputes arose over who officially owned the confraternity's inventory and, most important, its statue of the Virgin. Through these cases, the history of the confraternity can be pieced together from 1633 until 1795.

Information about the early days of the confraternity's history can be glimpsed only from second-hand accounts and circumstantial evidence, which includes two opposing versions of its founding taken from a dramatic 1680s ecclesiastical court case. In a dispute over access to the chapel and its contents, the confraternity's mulatto majordomo Lorenzo Albirdes claimed that the chapel and the confraternity's possessions had been officially in the hands of the members since 1633, only one year after Francisco bought the hacienda.[33] This version of the confraternity's history suggests that Francisco's workers immediately founded a religious brotherhood when they began their work in the silver refinery. This account may be correct, because the documented history of the chapel—although not the confraternity—goes back as early as 1634, when a baptism was performed there; *maestre de campo* Francisco Montaño de la Cueva served as godfather.[34]

The confraternity definitely existed in a rudimentary form by 1647, when Phelipe Montana de la Cueva began sponsoring fiestas for the Virgin in the chapel he inherited from his Uncle Francisco, although this fiesta was not specifically associated with any confraternity in the historical record. These early celebrations were often more chaotic than pious, which is not surprising in a remote mining town. In 1651, several hacienda workers were involved in an altercation that led to a murder right outside the chapel.[35] Violence was extremely common in Parral at this time; it took place wherever people gathered and involved all groups in society. In 1656, violent behavior again occurred outside the chapel, this time on the night of the fiesta dedicated to the Immaculate Conception.[36] The testimony of a victim provides a sense of the excitement at the fiesta and the wide range of people present, including many of Don Phelipe's workers:

> María, Indian servant in the work gang of the miner, Don Phelipe Montaño de la Cueva, wife of Juan Batista, Indian driller [barretero] of Don Phelipe . . . says that last night, after the moon had set, being midnight more or less, the whole work gang was there, along with many other black and mulatto men and women, and Indians from other gangs and merchants from the town. All were there celebrating the fiesta of the most holy Virgin in Don Phelipe's chapel.[37]

María and other witnesses who were described as slaves, Indian servants, and even *chino* mentioned hearing screams and noise. The chapel was clearly a social center for Parral's diverse population.

Yet no evidence has survived in the historical record that speaks of penitential processions or alms-collecting during this period; presumably it was not necessary for the confraternity to gather alms because of Don Phelipe's patronage. Although fiestas had been held at the chapel by 1676, when Don Cristóbal gave his family's version of the confraternity's history in a court proceeding, Albirdes's account of Immaculate Conception's founding in 1633 may have given the confraternity a longer heritage than it really had.

Don Cristóbal de Villamayor y Carvajal's version of the history of the confraternity of the Immaculate Conception conflicted with Albirdes's testimony but agreed with eyewitness accounts from earlier decades such as the one given by the Indian María in 1656. According to Don Cristóbal, the hacienda did not have an independent confraternity, but the *hacendado* [landowner] organized the fiestas dedicated to the Virgin as a diversion for his workers. He said that his uncle, Don Francisco, originated and funded all the early fiestas to the Virgin. The *maestre de campo* owned the chapel, and "the so-called brothers were also his, because they were his slaves and servants."[38] Don Cristóbal made the patronage relationship between Don Francisco and his workers even more clear:

> This chapel, owned by me, inherited from the Señor, maestre de campo, Don Francisco Montaño de la Cueva, my uncle, a very opulent miner in these royal mines, who had a large gang of mulatto and black slaves, and many other servants, was founded so the entire [work force of the] hacienda and mines could hear mass, especially on Holy Days. . . . The chapel

> is dedicated to the Immaculate Conception, and has an image of Our Lady and is the chapel for my mines. . . . The chapel is next to the hacienda for refining silver with mercury where all the slaves and the rest of the work gang work. The maestre de campo was very devoted to the Immaculate Conception and had the chapel decorated with all the ornaments necessary to celebrate mass. Every year, the slaves and other servants had the fiesta of the Immaculate Conception . . . and made a procession.

Immaculate Conception's existence, according to Don Cristóbal, depended on the support of Don Francisco. Don Cristóbal's words clearly describe a paternalistic *hacendado* in complete control of his workers though his generosity and public displays of piety.

Don Phelipe's 1676 will confirmed Don Francisco's lavish patronage of the chapel and the substantial wealth of the family.[39] Don Phelipe owned buildings, livestock, silver-processing materials, seven slaves, works of art, large amounts of worked and unworked silver, furniture (which included twenty-four chairs, three desks, and three Chinese trunks, among many other items), a considerable wardrobe (with at least twelve of every item, such as shirts, socks, stockings, etc., at a time when many people owned less than one complete outfit), and expensive linens, along with a significant inventory of religious artifacts in the chapel of the Immaculate Conception. Any Afromexican confraternity would have been happy to have access to the accoutrements in this chapel. The image alone was worth fifty pesos; it had a silver crown and six sets of clothing in red, purple, white damask, green, and black and one described as "for spring." The inventory included necessary confraternity paraphernalia such as a blue damask standard with a silver cross and a staff for carrying it. The chapel also had three bells and other silver items. Don Phelipe continued his patronage after his death by bequeathing the chapel twenty-five pesos for masses for his soul.

Immaculate Conception may have been founded before 1671, but before that time, the Montaño de la Cueva chapel was the only recognized religious institution of that name in Parral. Over time, the workers who congregated around that chapel and its fiestas formed a confraternity with a membership that extended beyond the boundaries of the *hacienda*. Because no official constitution for the Confraternity of the Immaculate Conception exists, its founding date, early leaders, and rules are unknown. In the 1670s and 1680s, Immaculate Conception's leaders endeavored to establish their autonomy and legitimacy as an official confraternity among Parral's other religious institutions. By asserting independence from the patronage of the Montaño de la Cueva/Villamayor clan, the brothers struggled against the racial and social hierarchies so deeply entrenched in this new town. For two decades, these workers, whether or not they served Phelipe Montaño de la Cueva and his brother, tried to forge a new place for themselves in Parral's society, out from under the thumb of *hacendados*. They did not achieve unqualified success in this effort and simply changed patrons in the process.

Scattered evidence suggests that the chapel of Our Lady of the Immaculate Conception had existed since the 1630s, but the confraternity of the Immaculate Conception was not officially documented until 1671. In this year, Julio Martín, who was described in other documents as an Indian *barretero* and a servant of Don Phelipe Montaño de la Cueva,[40] petitioned the ecclesiastical court judge for right of access to property owned by the Confraternity of the Immaculate Conception. Martín was the confraternity's majordomo. The judge declared that all inventory should be turned over to current majordomos, citing past precedents for this ruling. This case seems to indicate that it was already an officially recognized confraternity. Nevertheless, some of Parral's leading citizens did not recognize its existence and challenged its autonomy.

In 1677, Immaculate Conception strengthened its position as a confraternity by petitioning for and receiving official papal approval for its fiestas in the chapel of Don Phelipe Montaño de la Cueva.[41] Juan de Truxillo (b. 1657), a free mulatto and servant on the Montaño de la Cueva estate, was the confraternity majordomo at this time.[42] Sergeant Antonio Narváez and other brothers supported Truxillo's petition. Pope Innocent XI gave the confraternity permission to celebrate the day of the Immaculate Conception in December and during other fiestas with masses in its chapel and granted indulgences to members who attended. Truxillo, Narváez, and the other deputies successfully petitioned for permission to post the pope's response to their petition on church doors in Parral.

Even though they were successful with their appeal to the pope, they faced challenges from Parral's powerful residents. From 1676 to 1678, majordomo Antonio de Narváez and Antonio de Urrecha (1653–1698) argued about the validity of the confraternity's activities and its access to Phelipe Montaño de la Cueva's chapel, before ecclesiastical judges.[43] Urrecha used the confraternity to promote his own reputation. Despite associating himself with it, he disdained the predominantly non-Spanish membership. Urrecha became involved in this ecclesiastical court case to strengthen his control over the confraternity. He insulted its *casta* leadership and provoked conflicts, while at the same time insinuating himself into their project to found a charity hospital.

Antonio de Urrecha was a Spaniard from Durango, a servant of Don Phelipe. His status as a servant was very different from that of the *hacienda* workers and slaves: he was a member of Cueva's entourage, not a laborer, and he would later own property of his own.[44] Urrecha clearly viewed himself as superior to other servants of Don Phelipe, especially the brothers of the Immaculate Conception. It is interesting that Urrecha's opponent in this dispute, Narváez, was *not* a servant of Don Phelipe and, despite the fact that he was a mulatto, was a respected and well-off military man forty years Urrecha's senior. Perhaps Urrecha was jealous of Narváez's success. Whenever he spoke against the confraternity, Urrecha mentioned the race of the brothers. He subtly referred to a literal interpretation of *limpieza de sangre* and manipulated the idea of legitimacy, knowing that mulattos and mestizos carried this stigma. He also argued that they were unsettled, law-breaking vagabonds.

Both Urrecha and the Immaculate Conception brothers testified that their disagreement had come to a climax during a procession of the confraternity's image of the Virgin of the Conception. According to the Immaculate Conception brothers:

> On the eighth of December [1676], having celebrated the fiesta of Our Lady of the Solitude, or by another name, la Concepción, as is a yearly custom in this confraternity, we honored the Virgin with a procession of the image of Our Lady owned by Canon Don Phelipe de la Cueva Montaño, carrying it in our hands with solemnity along with the standard. A servant of Don Phelipe, Antonio de Urrecha, left the road and dropped the image, causing a scandal in the town, because of the harm that could have been done to the Queen.

The brothers' testimony made no reference to their race; they always used titles of office in the confraternity. And they did not slander Urrecha, despite the fact that his testimony against them was vituperative and vicious.

Urrecha began his testimony by stressing his race and origins: he was a Spaniard from Durango, Nueva Vizcaya. He immediately mentioned race when he noted that he was responding to a petition to the ecclesiastical authorities made by "a mulatto called Antonio de Narváez." Urrecha used the word mulatto numerous times in his testimony and implicitly pointed out that regardless of any status Narváez had attained, he remained inferior in the racial hierarchy. When Urrecha described the procession, he said that the mulattos had carried the image of the Virgin in a precarious manner. He testified that because the wind was high, he had advised "the said mulatto Narváez" and "other blacks and mulattos" not to carry the image in procession. Urrecha said that the image should be treated with reverence "in the hands of a priest" and that the mulattos and blacks had acted "indecently." It is unclear whether he pushed the image out of their hands, whether they dropped it, or whether the wind blew it over. Either way, the image suffered damage, and Urrecha's words implied the brothers were not "clean" enough to touch sacred objects.

Urrecha also challenged the confraternity's right to appear before the court, especially with Narváez as their leader. He seemed to believe that race and social status put Narváez beneath the attention of judicial institutions, saying "this mulatto is impudent to bring a case before a court as solemn as this" and "put such an incapable and naturally crude person before your prudent, discreet attention" (see note 44). This approach worked. After Urrecha's demeaning testimony, Narváez gave up on the case, saying he could not speak for the entire confraternity. (Not all of the brothers had signed the petition against Urrecha.) In his testimony, Urrecha flattered the judge and denigrated the brothers. His techniques were successful.

Scholars have claimed that "los humildes pardos [the humble brown people]" were the first to found a hospital in the territory of the modern state of Chihuahua, but in fact Parral had had an Indian hospital for several decades by 1680.[45] Unfortunately, the founding documents have been lost and it is possible to look at the founding of the Immaculate Conception hospital only through secondary sources written by authors who had access to the originals before they disappeared. In these versions, Urrecha becomes the hero of the story: in 1680, as the appointed "procurator" for the confraternity, Urrecha appealed to secular and religious authorities, describing the "sad situation of the mine workers," who died for lack of the most basic necessities.[46] Certain unnamed curates rejected the brothers as suitable founders for the hospital because of their status as lowly laborers. Despite this resistance, the bishop gave permission in March of 1681 for Immaculate Conception to found a hospital and chapel if public donations for the hospital exceeded 6,000 pesos of principal, which earned 300 pesos of yearly income, by the standard church interest rate of 5 percent. Urrecha organized a drive for donations to reach this goal. Don Gonzalo de Carbajal y Villamayor was among the miners who met early in 1682 to collect the alms to pay for the undertaking and to seek a piece of land for the new building. Carbajal y Villamayor also played a role in laying the hospital's first stone.[47] The hospital's founding and financing did not stay in the hands of the confraternity; it became a charitable undertaking led and funded by Spanish town leaders. Immaculate Conception might have broadened its pool of patrons and moved its chapel away from the *hacienda* to a location in the center of town, but it remained beholden to the wealthy and powerful members of the community.

The hospital order of San Juan de Dios arrived in Parral in 1684 and quickly established rules and thanked the town leaders for their patronage.[48] A San Juanino nurse, a pharmacist, and a chaplain would staff the hospital. The hospital rules stated that it would serve poor men and women, with the exceptions of lepers and the insane. Masters had to pay for care of their slaves. The opening of the hospital was delayed by legal struggles for another two years, but the building was finally ready in 1686, and Immaculate Conception brothers were given official ecclesiastical permission to move their chapel to the hospital and were authorized to celebrate mass. At this time the brothers performed a simple ritual: "They made the customary procession for this kind of celebration, leaving by one door of the church and entering by the other."[49]

Immaculate Conception faced its greatest challenges from 1687 to 1688, during the time Urrecha succeeded in gaining official approval to affiliate the Hospital de San Juan de Dios with the confraternity. The confraternity took its statue to this new location on January 6, 1687, and immediately Cristóbal de Villamayor y Carvajal claimed that he in fact owned the statue. He began a bitter struggle in the ecclesiastical courts with a description of the events that occurred at midnight on the night of January 2, 1687:[50]

> They opened the chapel of the Immaculate Conception, which is mine and belongs to me, and they took from me a holy image of the Most Holy Virgin of the Immaculate Conception which is located in the principal altar of the chapel, and which gives the chapel, founded by my uncle the field master Don Francisco Montaño de la Cueva, its name. They also stole a gilded chalice.[51]

Don Cristóbal described several items he said had been stolen. From the start, he asserted his social status and wealth by claiming that he owned the chapel and its contents.

As Urrecha had done in his dispute a decade earlier, Don Cristóbal unfavorably contrasted his personal identity and honor with the "illegitimacy" of the confraternity members. His petition to the ecclesiastical court made the point that Don Phelipe Montaño de la Cueva, "presbyter and my brother," had left the key to the chapel in the hands of Joseph de Rivera,

> mestizo majordomo of an Immaculate Conception brotherhood of mulattos and mestizos that is founded in said chapel, belonging to me. Without

> doubt, the said mestizo majordomo daringly and violently robbed and fearlessly plundered . . . the sacred place of sacred things. This robbery is sacrilege which demands punishment for said mestizo and the rest.

The brothers' response to Don Cristóbal demonstrated that they recognized his methods and had learned to manipulate such weapons in their favor. Apparently, they spent several months working on their defense against Don Cristóbal's accusations. In September 1687 they officially presented him with the confraternity records,[52] and a few months later, Juan de Albirdes submitted to the court a long vindication of the legitimacy of the confraternity.[53] His strategy throughout was to call for justice against the denigration of himself and the confraternity and to appeal to the court's sense of charity and compassion. He stressed the official approval that had been given to the confraternity. He wrote in a repetitive and wordy legalese in an attempt to show respect for judicial process, probably in an attempt to counter Urrecha's earlier accusation that the brothers had demonstrated disrespect for the court's authority.

More than once Albirdes accused Don Cristóbal of showing malice. He began by producing official inventories that indicated that the confraternity had purchased the items Don Cristóbal said members had stolen. He also produced evidence that the brothers had paid for the erection of the chapel. His account reveals that Don Cristóbal had confiscated the items during the January confrontation, although, according to Albirdes, they belonged neither to him "nor his ancestors."

Albirdes highlighted the brothers' pathetic circumstances by saying that Don Cristóbal wrote his malicious letter "with a powerful hand" defaming "said confraternity of poor mulattos and destitute Indians" (see note 44). He hoped that the judges would show their customary fairness in dealing with this unjust accusation. Albirdes concluded his letter by calling for justice and the return of the documented property from a usurping and false "patron or owner." The majordomo had appealed for justice that even the lowest members of society deserved.

Don Cristóbal wasted no time in responding to Albirdes's charges with a bombastic and defamatory salvo. Don Cristóbal's response countered the careful approach of Albirdes that relied on a careful examination of confraternity records by hammering away at the idea of illegitimacy, an accusation that Don Cristóbal seemed to think a powerful weapon against any official documentation the brothers might bring forward. Don Cristóbal emphasized the disparity between the illegitimate brothers and his own legitimacy throughout his response. He responded to Albirdes's attempt at a legalistic presentation with sarcasm and condescension, mocking the majordomo's attempts to use sophisticated language:

> Don Cristóbal de Villamayor y Carvajal, resident and miner in these royal mines, legitimate and universal heir of Don Gonzalo de Carvajal, my deceased brother, received a petition presented by a mulatto named Juan de Albirdes, in which he is entitled majordomo of the said confraternity dedicated to the Immaculate Conception of Our Lady. All of said petition is full of foolish blunders, sophistry and idle words without reasonable foundation or substance. . . . I cannot respond. . . . The mulatto Juan de Albirdes, with his pretext of majordomo of the said confraternity should not be allowed to testify because I do not know him as legitimate nor of a legitimate and authentic title for the foundation of the confraternity that is called de la Concepción. . . . This mulatto and the other must prove, with authentic titles, not chimerical words, . . . that they are legitimately majordomos.

Don Cristóbal hoped to remind the court of the importance of legitimacy (and deny the value of the confraternity's documents) as a determiner of position in society and of the authenticity of the confraternity. According to Don Cristóbal, without legitimacy, the confraternity did not deserve the consideration of the judicial system and the members' attempts to legally resolve the case in their favor had no value whatsoever.[54]

Albirdes responded to Don Cristóbal's testimony by again asserting the validity of the confraternity's access to its inventory. He pointed out that Don Cristóbal was the thief here; he had taken possession of the majordomo's key to the chapel. He again begged that "this poor confraternity . . . of mulattos, blacks, Indians and many Spaniards . . . receive justice." This statement countered Don Cristóbal's disparagement of the confraternity and presented it as a more diverse and possibly more respectable group than Don Cristóbal had implied. The majordomo obviously understood the power of Don Cristóbal's challenge to the brothers' legitimacy and wanted to stress that they were not just slaves and other people of the lowest social status. Albirdes pled for the return of their possessions after Don Cristóbal's "plunder."[55]

This battle continued into 1688, a year after Urrecha, with official permission, had removed the confraternity's possessions to the new location in the Hospital de San Juan de Dios. When Urrecha finally entered the fray, his testimony described these actions as entirely in line with the approved founding of the hospital. Once Urrecha became involved in the dispute, the confraternity's claims became much more official and respectable. As a Spaniard, Urrecha could not be associated with illegitimacy and was thus the confraternity's best weapon.[56]

Although the case now favored the confraternity, Don Cristóbal continued to argue on the basis of the tradition of his ancestors' patronage. His forefathers had supported the chapel and the "procession of blacks, mulattos and hacienda servants."[57] Don Cristóbal seemed to think that a frequent use of racial labels would help his case. But ultimately concern for official procedure and documentation won out over claims based on traditions that only Don Cristóbal admitted to remembering. Urrecha and Albirdes were able to legally prove their claims by presenting official licenses that permitted the confraternity's activities. However, their struggle and the type of accusations they faced indicate that Parral's elite found it difficult to accept that individuals perceived as poor "blacks, mulattos, Indians, and servants" could function as an independent entity. Even with all of the documentation the confraternity presented, only Urrecha's leadership saved the Immaculate Conception. In 1690, royal approval and patronage arrived for the hospital. This long, drawn-out process in the end achieved very little for the hospital; the Juaninos abandoned it in 1699.[58]

Although the hospital project was only partially successful, Immaculate Conception finally became part of Parral's civic consciousness through Urrecha's efforts. A few testators made generous donations to the hospital in the 1680s, and starting in 1691 they began to mention the hospital's confraternity in their wills.[59] Many testators phrased their bequests to the hospital in terms of "helping the poor" or giving to "the poor of the Hospital de San Juan de Dios." The hospital's mission always concentrated on aiding poor mine workers, especially Indians, mestizos, and mulattos. Whereas before the confraternity had depended on the direct patronage of the Montaño de la Cueva/Villamayor family, now it finally seemed to deserve the attention of a broader range of charitable donors because of the validity of the hospital project.

As these cases illustrate, the power elite of Parral barely tolerated Immaculate Conception in the seventeenth century. This organization of slaves and servants did not fit the town leaders' vision of public piety as they hoped it would be displayed and practiced in Parral. Without support from some key leaders from the town's elite for its new emphasis on charity, Immaculate Conception would not have survived.

This situation would change in significant ways in the eighteenth century. Parral's strict social hierarchy and master-slave patronage network broke down in the eighteenth century when the mining industry in Parral was in decline.

Migration to Parral had virtually stopped, especially by ambitious people of Spanish descent. It was no great honor to hold a position of authority in Parral in the eighteenth century: at times, the town did not even have a notary in residence.[60] Parral's leading residents began to have a more lenient attitude toward their social inferiors and seemed willing to let the people they now referred to as *pardos* put on fiestas with little interference. As was the case of the Rosary confraternity in Valladolid, people of African heritage in eighteenth-century Parral achieved a limited degree of status, one that at least allowed them a role in local celebrations. The confraternity began to play an active part in the public life of the town at this time, perhaps because of a decline in the fortunes of other confraternities and their members and an improvement in the social status of mulattos. But Immaculate Conception enjoyed prosperity and autonomy only for a short time.

Censuses from 1768 and 1788 give a sense of the occupations of Immaculate Conception members in the late eighteenth century. Confraternity documentation provides the names of forty-five confraternity leaders from 1739 to 1788. Of these forty-five men, twenty-three appear in the 1768 census.[61] Table 6.1 lists these men and the information the census provided about each one. The census shows none of these men were slaves. Of the twenty-three men, fifteen were described as mulattos, one was called "de color quebrado" or of broken color, a term sometimes used for *castas*. The remaining seven members were five mestizos and two Indians. Nine of the men had work connected to the mines, and ten had occupations in the skilled trades that were necessary in a small town, such as tailoring, shoemaking, and chandlery. One mulatto member was associated with the church, as a sacristan, and one Indian member worked in the margins of the labor economy as a wood collector. The ages of the members range from nineteen to eighty, and almost all lived within nuclear families, either wives and children, only the children (when the spouse had died), or a sister.

The 1788 census provides a slightly different image of the typical Immaculate Conception member. Only sixteen brothers can be found in this census. Fewer of them are Indians and mestizos and more are mulattos than in 1768. Immaculate Conception was never exclusively a mulatto confraternity, although mulattos were always the most numerous among the members and led the confraternity: from the 1600s, Immaculate Conception had a *casta* membership that included Indian, mestizo, mulatto, and black members.[62]

The occupations and family patterns of the men listed in table 6.1 and table 6.2 testify to stability and some degree of success, especially compared to the seventeenth-century brothers, who were slaves on a hacienda. Almost all of the men

Table 6.1. Immaculate Conception members mentioned in 1768 census

Name	Race	Age	Occupation	Family
Nicólas Alcala	free mulatto	unknown	mine worker	wife/children
Mariano Armendariz	free mulatto	50	driller	wife/5 children
Juan Antonio Campos	mestizo	unknown	unknown	unknown
Vicente Carrascoso	free mulatto	unknown	tailor	widower/3 children
Mariano Garcia	free mulatto	29	tailor	single
Luis Gardea	mestizo	unknown	miner	wife/children
José Garralette	free mulatto	49	master tailor	wife/2 children
Antonio Innurcio	free mulatto	33	tailor	lives w/ sister
Julian Jurado	free mulatto	unknown	sacristan at Jesuit college	wife/2 children
Gregorio Lima	free mulatto	unknown	mine worker	wife/children
Juan López	free mulatto	32	miner	wife/son
Mariano Lugo	free mulatto	19	shoemaker	wife (under 16)
José Medina	"color quebrado"	unknown	tailor	wife/3 children
Leandro Mosquedo	free mulatto	33	chandler	widower/2 children
Rumaldo de Nava	free mulatto	48	shoe maker	wife/children
Francisco Pacheco	free mulatto	80	tailor	wife/2 children
Pedro Rodriguez	free mulatto	26	tailor	wife/son
Lorenzo López	mestizo	unknown	mine worker	wife/5 children
Miguel Machuca	Indian	unknown	wood collector	
Joachim Machuco	mestizo		unknown	wife/children
Mariano Ontiveros	Indian	unknown	mine worker	
Don Félix Vedor	free mulatto	38	mine worker	wife/5 children
Domingo Villa	mestizo	unknown	miner	

Source: Padrón, Parral, 1768, Archivo Municipal del Hidalgo del Parral.

listed in table 6.1 were active members of the Immaculate Conception in the 1780s, except Francisco Xavier Pacheco, who was a majordomo in 1746 and was therefore older than the other men listed on this census. As can be seen from their ages or simply the fact that they were heads of households in 1768, these were mature men with children and perhaps grandchildren by the 1780s. Some were elderly, like Vicente Carrascoso and José Medina, who reported their ages as sixty in 1788. Their occupations also testify to their relative prosperity. The largest occupational group of Immaculate Conception members were the tailors, but there were not enough tailors to call the confraternity a guild. Mine workers naturally featured prominently, despite the downturn in Parral's mining fortunes. Many of the men, including a tailor, a miner, a shoemaker, and a sacristan, maintained the same employment for the two decades the two cen-

Table 6.2. Immaculate Conception members mentioned in 1788 census

Name	Race	Age	Job	Family
Vicente Carrascoso	"color quebrado"	60	tailor	widower/3 children
Vicente Contreras	free mulatto	38	tailor	wife/3 children
Marcelino Gamboa	free mulatto	40	bricklayer	wife/2 children
Luis Gardea	mestizo	34	patio worker	wife/children
José Pico de Grulla	free mulatto	37	tailor	wife/child
Julian Jurado	free mulatto	38	sacristan at Jesuit college	wife/2 children
Gregorio Lima	free mulatto	45	mine worker	wife/children
Juan López	free mulatto	40	unemployed	wife/2 children
Lorenzo López	free mulatto	45	mine worker	wife/children
Mariano Lugo	free mulatto	40	shoemaker	widower
José Medina	free mulatto	60	tailor	wife/3 children
Leandro Mosquedo	free mulatto	40	unknown	wife/6 children
José Antonio Muñoz	unknown	52	tailor	widower
Pedro Rodriguez	free mulatto	52	tailor	wife/3 children
José Roja	free mulatto	40	baker	wife/4 children
Domingo Villa	Indian	46	miner	wife/2 children

Source: Padrón, Parral, 1788, Archivo Municipal del Hidalgo del Parral, 1785A, Exp. G2.

suses span, although Juan López went from being a miner to a person "without occupation." The census evidence suggests that most confraternity members had stable lives.

Another type of record supports the analysis that the eighteenth century was one of increasing stability for Afromexicans in Parral. Baptism records show a trend toward legitimacy for this group during the eighteenth century. Of the 288 people called mulattos, blacks, *moriscos*, and *lobos* baptized in Parral between 1695 and 1704, more than 50 percent had unknown fathers. During the period 1724 to 1728, only 35 percent of Afromexicans who were baptized had no fathers present.[63] By the period of 1748 to 1752, only 24 percent of Afromexican babies were baptized without a father present.[64]

Occupational stability and decreasing illegitimacy were part of Parral's general economic downturn. The town had fewer short-term residents who came to take advantage of mining wealth and were likely to leave children when they left. Many unions may have been temporary in this kind of a town. People also married nonresidents: historian D. J. Robinson notes that in the late 1700s, 25 percent of all marriages "included at least one partner from outside the Parral jurisdiction. In this way, the frontier mining community was much more 'open' than elsewhere in colonial Mexico."[65]

Table 6.3. Occupations of men in Parral in 1788 census

Mine workers	702
Farmer laborers	238
Craftsmen	209
Unemployed	114
Slaves	66
Servants	54
Merchants	45
Liberal arts	26
Mine owners	18
Hacendados and administrators	12
Religious officials	9
Justices	3
Notaries	3
Royal treasury employees	3

Source: Padrón, Parral, 1788, Archivo Municipal del Hidalgo del Parral, 1785A, Exp. G2.

Parral's population decreased from 1768 to 1788, a change that led to new patterns in work life and residency that suggest a shift in power away from the Spanish elite. The population decreased from 7,500 to 5,000 residents between 1768 and 1788.[66] Fewer miners were working in Parral by 1788.[67] In 1768, according to Robinson's analysis of the census, 75 percent of the total male labor force was employed in the mines; one decade later this percentage had dropped to 52 percent and twenty years later to 47 percent.[68] Robinson found that by 1788, occupations such as tailor, baker, carpenter, and other service trades had become more common than mining. This shift can also be seen in tables 6.1 and 6.2, which show that the occupations of Immaculate Conception members moved away from mining toward trades in the service sector, which may have given them more independence and weakened ties to a single patron who was also the owner of the mine.

The census takers in 1788 analyzed the racial breakdown of male residents in Parral and found that the Spanish population of Parral was larger than it had ever been, totaling 37 percent,[69] which might indicate a "darkening" of what was considered Spanish at the end of the colonial era, especially when we consider that mulattos were the racial group most likely to marry exogenously. However, non-Spaniards still dominated Parral's population, as they did throughout the eighteenth century; 18 percent of the town's residents in 1788 were called mestizo and 34 percent were described as mulatto, *coyote*, or *lobo*. In 1788, Indians accounted for only 11 percent of Parral's residents; and these usually lived on haciendas and barrios outside the town. Despite what seems to be an increasing number of Spaniards, the 1768 census shows that the mulatto and mestizo population dominated the central district of the town; 80 percent of Parral's Spaniards lived in "barrios rather than the central township."[70] Mulattos continued to be the primary residents of the town's center in later decades. This concentrated residency might have led to greater toleration of and prominence for their confraternity as they moved in to the center from the outlying silver haciendas.

Frequent upswings and downturns characterized life for Parral's residents in the eighteenth century, and the unstable existence of the confraternity of the Immaculate Conception mirrored the uncertainty of the town's economic life. For five or six years, the population grew, then the increased population "could be, and usually was, removed within a few months by the ravages of smallpox, typhus, influenza" and the hunger caused by drought.[71] Large epidemics took place in the 1690s, the 1710s, the late 1730s, and the late 1770s. When epidemics were not occurring, mortality decreased from around 1715 to 1738 and 1741 to 1762. The eras free from widespread disease did not cause the town population to grow substantially.

Immaculate Conception struggled to survive the bad years and attempted to reorganize its structure and activities in the good times. The confraternity tried to respond to the 1690 epidemic with the newly founded hospital, but this venture did not last through the early years of the 1700s. Members attempted to recover from this decline in the period from 1718 to 1724, but Immaculate Conception barely survived the 1740s and had to reorganize once again in the 1770s.

Completely neglected after 1699 when the San Juan de Dios friars fled the hospital, the confraternity attempted its first comeback in 1718, by which time the exterior and interior of the hospital was in need of repairs and the interior furnishing needed to be replaced.[72] Members tried to raise the funds for repairs through various methods. Testators continued to donate to the confraternity and the hospital in the first decades of the eighteenth century, although neither seemed to be engaged in charitable activities or even regular fiestas.[73] In 1718, the brothers were granted permission to ask for alms in the entire Diocese of Nueva Vizcaya.[74] Later, a local widow tried to help rejuvenate the confraternity with the donation of a hacienda to help the hospital return to its charitable purpose of helping the poor. This benefactor described the hospital's condition as "ruined."[75]

One way that Immaculate Conception raised money for the confraternity was by sponsoring one of Hispanic society's most visible customs: the bullfight. Apparently the brotherhood sponsored a bullfight annually into the 1690s, although we do not know when they began this practice. We do know that they stopped the annual bullfight sometime in that decade; in 1724, Parral's mayor recalled attending the bullfight over thirty years earlier.[76] Immaculate Conception reestablished its traditional bullfight around 1718. This custom kept the confraternity alive through the eighteenth century; it provided entertainment for locals and brought in business for Parral's merchants. In 1724, the majordomos asked Parral's mayor to permit them to have bullfights on January 6. They hoped to celebrate with a mass, a sermon, plays, bulls, and a staged war between Moors and Christians.[77] These mock battles were a Spanish tradition that went back to royal practice in the fifteenth century and were gradually becoming popular in public celebrations.[78] In their request, brothers mentioned that "shortages [*cortedades*]" had prevented the celebration of the fiesta for several years.

In 1724, the mayor spoke of the problems Parral's leaders had had with the confraternity. Although he gave the confraternity a license to hold bullfights in the plaza in front of the Hospital de San Juan de Dios, he did so reluctantly. The mayor reported that, much to the disgust of local miners and other residents, the *pardos* had recently organized unofficial bullfights on their fiesta day, which caused "more harm than good." But apparently the mayor decided that the fiestas served some purpose and were not greatly detrimental to the local population, because he and other town leaders tolerated them and the bullfights grew in popularity. The authorities must have sensed the thinly disguised violence and social unrest implicit in bloody public bullfights and staged battles; it is surprising that they allowed them to continue.

In the next few decades, the confraternity became a part of local traditions and featured more prominently in the yearly calendar of major local events. By 1746, town authorities had decided that the three days of bullfights and *comedias* [plays] needed to move from the plaza in front of the Hospital de San Juan de Dios to the plaza in the center of town.[79] This move symbolized Immaculate Conception's transition from a marginal position to a fundamental part of town life. According to this case, the fiesta had become a "timeless local custom."[80] The confraternity's rise probably had more to do with the decline in power and wealth of Parral as a whole than with the upward mobility of its members. The brothers were no longer dependent on patronage to support their every move, and they no longer suffered vilification from their social superiors as they had from Cristóbal Villamayor in the seventeenth century.

Precisely at the moment when Immaculate Conception and its fiestas became a traditional event in Parral, economic pressures forced the majordomos to cancel the bullfight. In 1746, Francisco Pacheco complained that the confraternity, which had no assets, had to beg for alms from hardworking and devoted residents to pay for the bullfight. This was a financial strain in a time of "penury, dearth and poverty in these royal mines . . . especially for the *pardos* . . . who must uproot [*desarraigar*] plants from the earth to maintain and feed themselves."[81] Pacheco and the other majordomos decided that bullfights were a sacrilegious way to celebrate a sacred celebration, using papal bulls to support their opinion on the issue.[82] Decorating the church and illuminating its altars seemed a more suitable way to honor the Virgin. The authorities agreed with Pacheco, and they threatened to fine and imprison anyone who held bullfights. After this petition, the confraternity dissolved for a generation, and the town experienced further economic hardships.

Immaculate Conception experienced one more revival in the eighteenth century. This time it endured until the century ended. In 1773, a group of *pardos* decided to reorganize the confraternity and bring back the fiestas in honor of the Immaculate Conception. These men expressed great shame that their predecessors had allowed the celebration to fall into decadence, insinuating that the previous members had broken a vow to the Virgin, although no evidence indicates that earlier members had organized the fiesta to fulfill a vow. The new Immaculate Conception brothers admitted that times had been very hard, with "calamities, droughts and raids" that had especially affected "our humble class," but they asserted that the time had come to again honor the Immaculate Conception, as was customary in every other town and city. They noted that in doing so, they would also honor the king because the Virgin was the patron of Spain.[83]

An Immaculate Conception tradition of the late eighteenth century illustrates the prominence the brothers enjoyed at that time. Sometime during the eighteenth century, Immaculate Conception began to elect an annual "Grand Turk," along with Christian and Moor captains and lieutenants. The exact function of these elected military officers is not known, but they probably processed and staged a battle as part of the yearly fiesta *comedia*. Military concerns were an inherent part of life in the town; Parral's second reason for existing, after mining, was to provide an outpost of defense against the constant Indian raids. The threat of Indian invasion lived in memory, and the ceremonial battles between

Moors and Christians had a special meaning in Parral. Although most of the brothers were craftsmen, some also took part in the local militia.[84] The battles could also have hidden a criticism of the status quo, the racial hierarchy that held down men of color despite the fact that they were members of the town's largest group. (Barely disguised ceremonious rebellions returned to Parral in the twentieth century with the popular and gruesome annual reenactment of Pancho Villa's assassination.)

Late in the eighteenth century, the fiesta faced challenges once again, but an arrangement between the confraternity and town government enabled it to survive. From 1773 to 1787, the fiesta and the confraternity government continued in the usual fashion, but in 1788, Immaculate Conception leaders claimed that they lacked the funding to hold the bullfight, due to the "decadence of the mines."[85] They decided it would be best to have local residents bid to hold the bullfights, and the price of buying the rights would go to the confraternity to fund renovations of the Hospicio of San Juan de Dios, which had not served as a functioning hospital since early in the eighteenth century when the friars left. Obviously the bidder would also make money from this arrangement, perhaps by selling seats at the bullfight. Once the financial side was arranged, the brothers elected the Grand Turk and other ceremonial officers, according to their normal practice. This arrangement solidified the fiestas but separated the confraternity from the organization and funding of such events, making the celebration a secular concern that could happen at any convenient time in the year.

Immaculate Conception fought battles throughout its existence, first a literal battle for its survival and later a symbolic battle as part of an apparently innocuous ceremony. Parral's *casta* confraternity started as a barely tolerated diversion for hacienda slaves that was supported by the pious patronage of a powerful *hacendado*. When the confraternity tried to officially establish itself and become involved in a charitable hospital, the reaction of the town's elite was fierce. Paternalistic *hacendados* objected to their workers' organizing and did not want them to officially own sacred objects. This opposition continued until a reputable Spaniard became involved in the drive to create a charitable hospital for Indians. However, the hospital was not a success. The town's mine-owning elite seemed to lose interest in controlling the confraternity with a grudging approval of its fiestas in 1724.

Sixteenth- and seventeenth-century Mexico City offered a variety of paths toward increased social status for individuals of African descent and social improvement was possible in eighteenth-century Valladolid. Parral presented fewer opportunities. It was hard to sustain the basic aspects of confraternity life and its charitable activities. Parral is one town in New Spain where it is very hard to find links across generations that could lead to advantages for children; people labeled as Indian, mestizo, mulatto, or black appeared much more frequently in Parral's criminal records than they did in the notarial records. Women did not control property, and they did not leave evidence of confraternity leadership or even participation in confraternity life. In fact, a high percentage of men lived as solitary heads of households in eighteenth-century Parral, although women actually outnumbered men; the unbalanced sex ratio in favor of women was highly unusual for a mining town.[86] These women often lived as dependent servants in large households. The available documentation suggests that women were in a weak position throughout the colonial history of the town.

Ultimately Immaculate Conception was not a successful confraternity, although over a period of 150 years several individuals worked hard to make it so. Why did Immaculate Conception fail where other confraternities succeeded? First, Immaculate Conception was not in a wealthy town with a more comprehensive religious infrastructure such as existed in Valladolid or Mexico City. Although Parral's residents founded religious institutions in imitation of these cities, these institutions declined as the town became poorer after the mining bonanza ended. Second, seventeenth-century ties to the Villamayors and Antonio Urrecha hampered opportunities for independent action and development. Last, although the censuses show that *castas* constituted the largest demographic group and a limited amount of prosperity in the eighteenth century, Parral was too poor and unstable to enjoy a late fluorescence of public confraternal piety. Poverty meant that public religious festivals were limited and small, and they were more like a secular diversion than confraternity pageants in other towns. Despite the fact that Jesuits, Franciscans, and San Juaninos had at least temporary small convents and houses in the town, Parral never developed a complex religious public life. Immaculate Conception also lacked members who achieved the wealth and status of a Diego Durán. Parral's confraternity life pales in comparison to other such life in other towns in New Spain. Yet the history of the Confraternity of the Immaculate Conception illustrates how members struggled for autonomy by manipulating the colonial social order through court battles in the seventeenth century and cooperation with the town government in the eighteenth century.

7

Conflict and Accommodation in Confraternities

In 1691, Archbishop Francisco Aguiar y Seixas approved the founding of a Confraternity of Saint Nicolás Tolentino in Acapulco. This confraternity's constitution ruled that "anyone can join, including Spaniards, mulattos, and *chinos*, under the condition that *this is always a black confraternity*," meaning that blacks would always control confraternity offices and resources.[1] Confraternities in general did not last long in Acapulco because of the port's transient population and the church's lack of interest in the area; the archbishop's support for this confraternity was the exception rather than the rule. A confraternity with specifically black leadership would have had an especially tenuous existence, because in most areas of New Spain by the end of the 1600s, people called blacks made up a very small part of the population. At the close of the eighteenth century, a visiting bishop declared this confraternity to be officially extinguished.[2]

Despite their idealized purpose of bringing all colonial subjects into a Christian community, some confraternities further reinforced racial divisions. As colonial society matured, the racial heritage of individuals became more complex, but the racial labels that were commonly used in daily life were simplified to mulatto, Indian, mestizo, and Spaniard. Each of these labels signified a general position in colonial society, and the labels vary by region. Most confraternities did not begin by organizing around a plebeian identity; instead, they focused on race as the factor that determined membership and especially leadership. Many moderately prosperous mulattos who lived in small towns, many of whom worked as agricultural laborers or craftsmen, did not form organizations with other non-elite colonial subjects but instead fought for segregation within their confraternities, thereby enforcing colonial race-based hierarchies.

Mestizo and Afromexican confraternity brothers often articulated racially explicit rules regarding membership, leadership, finances, and entry fees in confraternity constitutions. Many constitutions were written in the second half of the seventeenth century, but the conflicts these racial divisions caused continued into the eighteenth century. Court cases over race-based disputes often led to the entrenchment of racial divisions within a confraternity and in the town where it was established. The cases analyzed in this chapter illustrate that confraternity rules, finances, and disagreements both expressed and perpetuated colonial racial divisions. Racial and class divisions in confraternities reflected local economic conditions, and confraternities based their rules on how different races figured into these economic and social structures. Afromexicans defended racially segregated confraternities as a way to improve their local status, a collective accommodation to a race-based social order. Afromexican confraternity brothers used their race to negotiate advantage through group solidarity.

Many confraternities in Spain and New Spain both divided people and brought them together: certain seventeenth-century confraternities in Mexico City admitted only members born in la Rioja, Galicia, Santander, the Basque lands, or the Philippines.[3] The existence of both African and mulatto confraternities in Seville suggests that even before Spaniards settled in the Americas, they viewed confraternities as racially segregated institutions. In Seville, an African brotherhood might be interpreted as yet another institution based on extralocal geographic ties, but the mulatto members had been born locally and were divided and separated from others by race. New World conditions led to an emphasis on the racially divisive side of the Spanish confraternal tradition and the purported need to use confraternities to bring Christianity to Africans and Indians.

Although Afromexicans founded and joined racially segregated confraternities, both free and enslaved Africans and mulattos lived their lives within Hispanic society in New Spain.[4] Individuals of African descent were more likely to be considered *gente de razón* ["people with reason"] than Indians were.[5] The officially mandated separation between colonial Indians and people of Spanish descent, which was based on language differences, geographic isolation, segregation laws, legal status, eligibility for military service, Inquisition jurisdiction, and taxation, was much more clear than the division between Spaniards and Africans. Although Afromexicans were subject to the tribute tax, they were under the jurisdiction of the Inquisition and could serve in the militia. Ben Vinson argues that colonial militias provided a sense of racial identity and solidarity for people of African descent and often led to upward social mobility.[6] It could be argued that confraternities similarly contributed to a sense of Afromexican identity and helped confraternity brothers play an active role in the Hispanic world.

Urban residential patterns in New Spain reveal little segregation between *castas* and Spaniards, especially because non-Spaniards lived in Spanish homes as servants. However, in many towns Indian barrios lay just outside, and Indians also lived semi-autonomously in their own villages.[7] Conflicts within confraternities often revolved around the distinction between Indians and mulattos when those individuals who identified as mulattos chose to deemphasize their association with people they considered to be less-successful colonial subjects.

However, Afromexicans and Indians both suffered legalized racism in the colonial era. They were excluded from most professions. Earlier in the colonial period, authorities attempted to keep Africans and Indians separate and control their mobility and living arrangements. Chapter 3 outlined some of the laws Spaniards established in attempts to prevent African revolt in the late sixteenth and early seventeenth centuries. If they were ever enforced, these laws seemed to have been forgotten by the eighteenth century. By that time, it was clear that any attempt by *castas* to unite with Indians to rebel against the Spanish viceregal authority would stand at odds with their desire to improve their lives according to Hispanic standards.

Thus, even though in many towns people with Indian and African heritage constituted the largest population group, they did not pose a threat to the colonial system, and separation between racial groups persisted. Some residents of every town enjoyed more social prominence because of their European heritage, and each town retained its Indian barrio. Confraternity rules and traditions, especially those made in the late seventeenth and early eighteenth centuries, illustrate the transitions that were taking place in the racial organization of towns and the reactions to these changes.

This chapter will focus on confraternities in agricultural towns in the western Diocese of Michoacán, especially in the *tierra caliente* lowlands and the Bajío region, the port city of Veracruz, and the eastern regions of Jalapa and Orizaba. The racial makeup of each of these areas changed from the seventeenth to the eighteenth centuries. In the Michoacán region, free blacks, mulattos, and mestizos formed the majority of the population by the eighteenth century. In contrast, slaves remained an important part of the working population of African descent in Veracruz, Jalapa, and Orizaba. All of these areas had once had large indigenous populations, but the decimation of the Indian population in the late 1500s created a need for a new work force. Slavery became less viable earlier in some regions than others, though, and this development affected both confraternity life and patronage based on master-slave relationships. The heritage and racial identity that confraternities that were founded on haciendas expressed differed significantly from those expressed by confraternities in urban areas. On haciendas, a past connection to enslavement sometimes led members to feel ashamed of or deny this heritage. Urban confraternity brothers were more likely to take advantage of their humble past when they argued with church authorities for confraternity concessions. While free blacks and mulattos led confraternities in small agricultural towns, only one parish, located outside Jalapa, records the confraternity life of slaves that was based around a single agricultural hacienda, despite the fact that hacienda slavery is the life pattern most often associated with the African experience in the Americas.

In smaller towns, villages, and haciendas, Afromexicans did not enjoy even the limited wealth, status, or autonomy they attained in Valladolid or in northern mining towns such as Zacatecas and San Luis Potosí. This lack of wealth, more than a lack of numbers, probably explains why small-town blacks and mulattos did not often found their own confraternities. When they did establish confraternities, their rules explicitly excluded non-Afromexicans from holding office. This defensive posture is not seen in Valladolid or mining towns, where founders seemed more confident about their continuing control. This difference may be partially explained by the fact that in smaller settlements in the late seventeenth and early eighteenth centuries, racial hierarchies were still forming. In such locations, access to power and wealth was often negotiated through confraternity rules and conflicts that were brought to ecclesiastical courts.

Even when confraternity constitutions were not segregated by race and did not include racially specific rules, racial distinctions in confraternities often led to dramatic conflicts sparked by the race of members or leaders. Controversies that mentioned the race or place of origin of members and leaders occurred in Parral, Mexico City, and Valladolid. Indian and mulatto members of Valladolid's Saint Nicolás Tolentino confraternity clashed in the eighteenth century, mainly because mulatto members wanted to distinguish themselves from Indian members. The cases presented in this chapter, most of which took place from the mid-seventeenth century to the early eighteenth century, illustrate an increasing concern over racial divisions.

In general, confraternities were meant to be open to all, to encourage all colonial subjects to join regardless of race. A sliding scale of entry fees that was determined by race was meant as a charitable gesture to encourage participation by the indigent; Spanish members almost always paid the largest membership dues and Indians the smallest. Most confraternity constitutions stipulated that anybody could join regardless of "calidad o condición, de ambos sexos [quality, condition, or sex]" if they could pay the entry fee.

However, in the seventeenth century, some confraternity constitutions began to impose criteria on members or leaders that made distinctions among individuals based on whether they were born in New Spain, Europe, or Africa. Brothers of African descent ruled against allowing mestizos, Spaniards, and Indians as members and they also instituted divisions within Afromexican confraternities. In making confraternity rules, Africans and their descendants in New Spain created affiliations based on identities formed both before and after enslavement: some confraternities characterized their members as from a specific African place of origin and others extended membership only to mulattos or blacks, making a distinction between individuals identified by these racial labels. However, the race of a confraternity's leadership was more important to brothers than general membership requirements, and confraternity founders worked hard to prevent anyone with another racial designation or place of birth from assuming leadership of their group.

One rule common to viceregal religious institutions, including confraternities, was that positions of leadership had to alternate between American-born members and Europeans. The Basque confraternity dedicated to the Virgin of Aránzazu rotated offices between Basques born in Europe and Basques born in Mexico.[8] Afromexican confraternities also adopted and adapted the practice of office rotation. In the early eighteenth century, the Jesuit-organized Confraternity of Slaves to the Virgin of the Assumption rotated offices between *moreno* and *pardo* members.[9] A confraternity on a hacienda in Zinándaro, Michoacán, rotated offices between Spaniards and "*de calidad mulato*" [of mulatto rank].[10] Another confraternity that was made up of Indians and Spaniards (the latter were described as *gente de razón* in the constitution) did not rotate offices but made sure that both groups were equally represented on its council.[11]

The detailed 1636 constitution of the Afromexican Confraternity of the Coronation and Saint Benedict, which was founded in the Franciscan convent in Veracruz, mentioned place of birth along with other very specific rules involving the rights and privileges of founders.[12] The constitution decreed that "it must be known that this confraternity was founded in the name of creoles from the beginning, and in all elections of officials, Creoles must hold the majority of offices, although other nations are also permitted to serve." In this case, "creole" does not mean American-born Spanish, a common misunderstanding of the term, but "born in" or "native to" a place. By invoking the word "creole," confraternity leaders and founders expressed their desire to have only members literally "born in" in New Spain, not in Africa. The use of the word nation [*nación*] refers to the Spanish conception of a language or cultural group in the colonial era. This constitution labeled American-born members of African descent as creoles of a different "nation" than their African-born ancestors. This constitution demonstrates that as early as 1636, blacks and mulattos were making distinctions among themselves by place of birth and, by extension, level of Hispanicization. Both creoles and people born in Africa would have been common in Veracruz because African slaves often passed through the port. Creoles, who had been born in the New World, knew that they spoke more Spanish and understood Hispanic society better than the *bozales*, or newly arriving African slaves.

This repertoire of terms resembles that used by the Zape Immaculate Conception confraternity in Mexico City in precisely the same time period. However, the desire for creole leadership on the part of the Confraternity of the Coronation and Saint Benedict offers a contrast to the Zapes' demand that their leaders be of a specific African nationality. The Mexico City Zapes had resided in New Spain's capital for decades and wanted to distinguish themselves from Congo and Angolan newcomers. Thus, whereas descendants of Africans in Veracruz valued American birth, the Zapes in Mexico City esteemed Old World "national" distinctions that had been established before they arrived in New Spain.

Color soon became another category that divided individuals of African descent in seventeenth-century Veracruz. The detailed constitution of another Veracruz confraternity demonstrates a desire to be led only by mulattos and a great preoccupation (almost forty rules' worth) with a positive public image.[13] Founded by a group of mulatto militiamen, the Confraternity of Our Lady of the Conception and the Humility and Patience of Christ uniquely combined the possibilities of racial and social distinctions both confraternities and militias offered, a rare case of the extension of militia ties into the social and charitable sphere.[14] The confraternity's constitution dates from 1659 but may have been modified before it was presented to the king in 1792. The petition to the king described the members as poor and humble *pardos* or mulattos. Perhaps because this confraternity was organized by mulatto militiamen, its rules carefully designated that only free mulattos could hold office. The writers of the constitution clearly stipulated that "only those who are legitimately mulattos and not of any other color, even if they are brothers and benefactors of our said confraternity, will have a vote in the councils." Two decades after the founding of Saint Benedict was based on distinctions between creoles and African-born blacks, mulattos had begun to describe themselves in terms of color rather than in terms of birthplace. According to their constitution, they considered the label of mulatto in some way "legitimate," a word that had a different meaning to this community than the usual way Spaniards used it. The brothers in Veracruz viewed themselves as different in appearance or color from individuals with more African ancestry and were careful to distinguish themselves from other Afromexicans.

Among the sixty documented Afromexican confraternities, very few had constitutions that specifically permitted only black or mulatto membership and/or leadership. For example, the Rosary in Valladolid was officially divided from the Spanish branch of this confraternity in 1586. The Spanish Rosary's constitution specified that members had to be of Spanish descent; another *gremio* would be formed for blacks, mulattos, Indians, and mestizos, a membership requirement to which the confraternity conformed for more than 200 years. In contrast, the racial designation of the *casta* confraternity in Parral seems to have grown from popular rather than official practice. This confraternity was not referred to as *de los pardos* in official documents until the early eighteenth century. It seems unlikely that the confraternity's lost constitution included a reference to the race of participants. Although the racial label of confraternity founders often set a precedent for future membership and leadership, sometimes confraternities would change hands and lose their racial designation. For example, the black Saint John of the Penitence confraternity in Zacatecas lost its racial exclusivity when it received a large donation.[15]

The constitution of the Confraternity of Saint Benedict in Saint Miguel el Grande also placed a strong emphasis on racial distinctions; it specified that the confraternity had to be led by blacks and would provide charity for others of what they called this "*calidad*" [quality]. *Calidad* thus represents a third way people of African descent in colonial Mexico made divisions among themselves. The confraternity's constitution, which was first written in 1646, was reapproved by the church in 1733, and the group remained active until at least 1809.[16] The constitution ruled that on the fiesta of Saint Benedict, the brothers would celebrate with vespers, mass, a procession, and a sermon. This was also the day that the brothers elected a rector, a majordomo, and three deputies, "all of whom had to be blacks and not of any other quality." The rules also mentioned that anyone could join if they paid two pesos, "under the primary condition that although Spaniards, mestizos, mulattos and Indians can enter, they cannot hold the important offices of the confraternity because these remain for blacks as the principal founders." Leaders wanted to make sure that other blacks, even if they did not reside locally, received their charity; their constitution stated that "the brothers and sisters of the confraternity are obligated to attend the burial of any black *forastero* [outsider or foreigner] who dies within this town, and to ask for alms for these burials." This rule reflects a charitable impulse to address the common needs of people of the same race, even if they were strangers.

While many confraternities made specific rules about who could lead, their constitutions do not express a similar preoccupation with the racial designations of members. In most cases, the race of both leaders and members was probably determined by custom and had to be clearly stated only in situations where conflict or challenge was a possibility. Indian confraternities, which were motivated by a need to protect wealth, land, and local autonomy, commonly stipulated in their constitutions that only other Indians could lead. One example of this rule comes from the Confraternity of Our Lady of Remedies, which was founded by Indians in 1658 in the pueblo of Santiago Tlalpuxagua. Their constitution stated:

> In said confraternity all Spaniards who are devoted and wish to take advantage of the benefits of membership can join as brothers, giving one peso in alms for their membership. Others including naturales, Indians, mestizos, blacks, and mulattos only have to give four reales, on the condition that only naturales and founders can hold offices in this confraternity to prevent dissent and litigation.[17]

The constitutions of other Indian confraternities also mentioned conflicts, litigation, and other negative results that occurred when non-Indian members tried to lead. The pueblos or the confraternities apparently felt the need to rule against further loss of property to non-Indian members.[18] Internal hierarchies also influenced leadership rules. One confraternity required that only "indios principales de buena razón [important local Indians of good reason]" could lead.[19]

Mestizo brothers also feared that Spaniards would usurp control of their confraternities. In the racially diverse region surrounding Celaya, mestizos in 1679 in the town of Apaseo founded a Confraternity of the Precious Blood of Christ.[20] Bishop Aguiar y Seixas approved the founding, and the confraternity allowed all to join but prevented Spaniards from becoming majordomos. This confraternity was funded by raising and selling livestock (as were many Indian confraternities), and perhaps the mestizo founders did not want to lose control of their investment.

These examples from Santiago Tlalpuxagua and Apaseo suggest that if a confraternity's founders did not specify leadership restrictions, a more dominant group in the town might eventually take over. Perhaps restrictions about confraternity leadership allude to local political and economic powers that non-Spanish residents struggled against in their efforts to protect a limited and fragile autonomy. This explanation is confirmed by the fact that only a few Spanish confraternities felt it necessary to state in their constitutions that only Spaniards could serve as officers. For example, the constitution of the Confraternity of the Souls in Purgatory in Tuxantla stated that "said confraternity is Spanish[,] and in the elections, under no circumstances can others who are not Spaniards be elected as majordomo, rector or deputy."[21] The members who wrote this rule perhaps feared a future challenge to their control. This fear was not unfounded: in several cases, Spaniards took legal action when *castas* gained access to leadership positions.

Later Spanish-led confraternities chose to employ more subtle distinctions than the racial labels assigned to members. For example, the constitution of the Confraternity of the Holy Sacrament in Celaya wanted to limit leadership to Spaniards. Members also expressed concerns about behavior, specifying in their 1774 constitution that "all people of whatever state, class, age, sex or condition (excluding those of scandalous habits)" could join with varying levels of membership status.[22] Only Spaniards above twenty-five years of age were allowed to govern the confraternity. All members had to donate two pesos. The constitution prefaced the confraternity's limitation of privileges with the following:

> As the Apostle Saint Paul said, there are no exceptions among people, and if any mestizo, mulatto, Indian or black wants to enter and enjoy the bread that we give them they will be received and enjoy our singular indulgences, without having the vote or a cargo [office] in the confraternity, which must be understood at the time of their entrance.

By the end of the eighteenth century, the number of *castas* in Celaya was almost equal to the number of Spaniards.[23] This confraternity's rules illustrate the desire of local Spaniards to maintain traditional hierarchies in the context of a community in which they were not the majority. At the same time, they made a nod to the more pious ideals of Saint Paul and the universality of the church.

Racially exclusive rules did not always strengthen the power of Spaniards. In many cases, in fact, they had the opposite effect; they enabled black, mulatto, Indian, or mestizo groups to establish more autonomy. By the second half of the seventeenth century, confraternity constitutions in provincial towns that were growing in size and racial diversity had begun to demonstrate an increasing concern with maintaining racial divisions. Confraternity founders created constitutions that incorporated their vision of appropriate racial divisions in their locale by controlling who could join and who could lead their brotherhoods. But constitutions could not be modified very quickly when the racial composition of a town began to change; constitutional change required unanimous approval by the governing board of the confraternity as well as official ecclesiastical approval and perhaps even a change in papal indulgences. Leaders of confraternities with no constitutional stipulations about race sometimes realized too late that the racial makeup of the members of their brotherhood had changed in a way that they did not want. These unanticipated situations often led to discord and legal action.

While disagreements about who should have access to confraternal wealth most often touched off conflicts that were expressed in racially explicit terms, ecclesiastical authorities did not always uphold conservative and racially exclusive constitutions or favor Spaniards in their decisions. Religious authorities defended petitioners of the group that had been traditionally associated with a particular confraternity, regardless of race. People who were ostensibly lower in the racial hierarchy did not always lose cases to Spaniards. In some times and places, mulattos were able to use race-based arguments to turn a case in their favor. In other times and places, mulattos and slaves were considered unacceptable as confraternity members or leaders. Most of these cases run counter to Cope's theory that late-seventeenth-century society in New Spain began to divide along class rather than race lines. The evidence shows that the situation was more complex. Even when *castas* were less well off than Spaniards in general, a shared lower economic status did not always galvanize them as a plebeian group. These cases also suggest that different races had distinct economic and social roles in each locale. In the late seventeenth and early eighteenth centuries, even though *castas* of all racial groups shared a low social status and low-paying jobs, some groups tried to exploit racial difference to improve their position in the confraternal hierarchy of power.

Confraternities dedicated to Saint Nicolás Tolentino often became involved in conflicts that were articulated in racial terms. Throughout the Diocese of Michoacán, Augustinian friars and residents alike founded a large number of confraternities dedicated to Saint Nicolás Tolentino, many of which were mulatto brotherhoods. In many of these towns, as in Valladolid and Parral, Afromexican, Indian, and Spanish populations interacted, argued with, and accommodated each other. Confraternities became involved in these interactions as groups designated by various racial labels established roles in the society of each town.

An early racially defined conflict involving Pátzcuaro's Saint Nicolás Tolentino confraternity illustrates that the specter of the *casta* vagabond loomed large in Spaniards' perceptions of people of mixed race and often stood in the way of attempts of non-Spaniards to organize independent confraternities.[24] In 1642, twelve Saint Nicolás brothers and sisters formed a separate group, calling themselves mestizo, mulatto, and *moreno* residents, and attempted to separate themselves from the Spaniards who controlled the Saint Nicolás confraternity to form their own organization dedicated to the Holy Trinity. The dissenters described themselves as "serving the confraternity with great care and precision." Spaniards saw this group differently; they emphasized that the members were either slaves or others "without houses, families, or a known neighborhood." In other words, the renegade members fit the well-known stereotype of the illegitimate *casta* vagabond. Although this group of brothers and sisters wanted to form a confraternity of their own, their opponents claimed that they did not have the established residency and stability to achieve this goal.

Much as they had in the *pardo* Confraternity of the Immaculate Conception in Parral in the 1680s, social and racial aspects of Spanish disdain for the new brothers of the Holy Trinity carried over to their attempts to deny them access to sacred rituals. In this case, Spaniards expressed concern about the days designated for processions and alms-collecting. The Spanish contingent of Saint Nicolás disliked the idea of *castas* collecting alms in a Lenten procession. They hypothesized that if these "undesirables" did not succeed in begging for alms, they were likely to steal from their masters to support the confraternity, especially because, according to Spanish testimony, all the mulattos and blacks in Pátzcuaro were slaves. The Spanish brothers believed that no free mulattos lived in Pátzcuaro, and they described each individual who wanted to form the new confraternity as an insolvent vagabond. For example, one petitioner had no wealth, and another had been absent for a year, "fleeing the city." These personal problems added to the fact that there were no free days available for alms collection. During this period, Pátzcuaro and many other towns like it were contending with how different groups would function in their local society. This struggle included the regulation of confraternity rituals such as processions and the collection of alms.

Disagreement about who should hold confraternity offices or handle confraternity property sometimes took the form of racially defined disputes or attempts to solidify racial divisions within confraternities and their locales. Election disputes in several confraternities in the racially mixed areas of the Diocese of Michoacán gave rise to conflicts that involved Spaniards, Afromexicans, mestizos, or Indians, according to which groups were trying to establish their position in local society. Election disputes played a central part in determining which group controlled a confraternity's assets. The outcomes of these conflicts often had an impact on future arrangements of power and resources.

The region surrounding Celaya, in the modern state of Guanajuato, has enjoyed agricultural prosperity and a temperate climate since the colonial period. Spaniards, including Franciscans, along with mestizos and blacks, began to settle in this region in the late sixteenth and early seventeenth centuries.[25] Salvatierra, which was founded in 1640, was a small town in the Bajío region near Celaya in the Diocese of Michoacán where local racial identities and economic divisions shaped confraternity life, which was very active. Racially motivated conflicts and racially divisive confraternity rules in Salvatierra suggest that this was a diverse town, similar to others in the region such as Querétaro, San Miguel el Grande, Celaya, Chamacuero, Acámbaro, and the Valle de Santiago; confraternities with Afromexican leadership existed in all of these towns. In the smaller towns and villages of the Bajío region, free laborers, a group that included mestizos and mulattos, made up a large percent of the population and formed groups that represented their concerns. The confraternities of these groups competed for prestige, respect, and autonomy.

Valladolid and Mexico City exerted a strong influence over the *villa* of Salvatierra with regard to trends in piety and religious organization. Many of the confraternity foundings in Salvatierra reflected popular devotions in Valladolid and in the viceregal capital. Salvatierra had a Confraternity of Our Lady of Mount Carmel founded in 1718 and long-lasting Confraternities of the Holy Sacrament, Souls in Purgatory, and Dolores, all of which were led by Spaniards.[26] Salvatierra also had five confraternities with non-Spanish membership. These included the mulatto-led Remedies confraternity, which was founded shortly after the town's official founding in 1643; the Confraternity of Tránsito, founded by free blacks around 1650 in the Hospital de San Juan de Dios; the mestizo Confraternity of the Humility and Patience of Christ, founded in 1663; the Confraternity of Saint Nicolás Tolentino, founded around 1672 by mulattos; and the Confraternity of Saint Peter, founded by mulattos and mestizos in 1677.[27] Very few other towns in New Spain left a record of confraternities that was this racially varied and vital. It is also unusual to find this many confraternity foundings characterized by such clearly defined racial exclusivity clustered in such a short time period (from about 1643 to 1677). Salvatierra, which was founded at the peak of popularity of confraternity life, was close enough to larger cities to directly imitate their elaborate public religious life and reinforce colonial hierarchies.

It is likely that the growth of Salvatierra's racially diverse population sparked fears of racial disorder and social chaos; town residents seemed to have a great need to define and separate society into groups defined by race. The racial distinctions of Salvatierra's confraternities also point to local economic divisions between hacienda laborers and urban workers. Legal disputes that centered on social, racial, and economic status in that period reflect the degree to which Salvatierra's residents resorted to ecclesiastical authorities to organize their society. Confraternity brothers found it necessary to have the official support and recognition of ecclesiastical courts to reinforce their eligibility to serve as confraternity leaders.

When the mestizo residents of Salvatierra founded a Confraternity of the Humility and Patience of Christ in 1663, they tried to consolidate their power within the brotherhood.[28] The goals of the confraternity included providing masses and prayers for its members, especially poor mulattos, blacks, mestizos, and Indians. However, the founders established that "although Spaniards, Indians, mulattos and blacks could join this Holy confraternity, they cannot vote in elections nor can they be elected as majordomos or deputies, except in the case of the rector, who has to be a Spaniard, and can vote in the elections. [With that exception], only mestizos can vote in elections and be elected majordomos and deputies."

Afromexican confraternities also protected their autonomy and access to confraternity inventory by specifying that Spaniards were not permitted to interfere in confraternity business. In 1677, Pedro Ruano, who had been defeated in an election of the Confraternity of Saint Nicolás Tolentino several years earlier, led ten other mulattos and fourteen mestizos to found a Confraternity of Saint Peter. As they explained to the Bishop of Michoacán, Salvatierra had no charitable organizations or hospitals to care for the mulattos, blacks, and Indians of the town before and after death, and a confraternity could help fill these local shortcomings. Saint Peter provided the standard benefits of prayer, especially the rosary, which was said regularly by members, and a penitential procession. The constitution ruled that

> although Spaniards can join this confraternity, they cannot be elected as majordomos, deputies, nor can they vote in elections. They can only be named as rectors, and if they are rectors, they are allowed to vote.[29]

The rector, a kind of overseer for the confraternity, was in fact often a Spaniard, usually a priest or friar in the church where a confraternity's image was located. The office of secretary, which required literacy, offered Spaniards a way to influence the activities of *casta* confraternities. Non-Spanish brothers tolerated the perhaps minimal influence Spaniards exercised through the offices of rector or secretary; perhaps they were happy to have a more socially prominent member who could serve as their advocate in the case of controversy or disputes.

A 1671 case involving the Confraternity of Our Lady of Remedies and a 1673 dispute involving the mulatto Confraternity of Saint Nicolás Tolentino show that confraternity conflicts articulated racial divisions in formation in Salvatierra. Around 1643, five women and twenty-eight men, who were described as hacienda "laborers and servants" (the group included one black slave), founded the Confraternity of Our Lady of Remedies in a chapel dedicated to the Assumption on an wheat-growing hacienda outside town.[30] The founders stated their goals as "taking care of the altar, keeping it clean and adorning it with love and care." They dedicated themselves to a procession and fiesta for the Virgin of the Remedies and carefully preserved her clothes. Sometime between 1643 and a visit from the bishop in 1668, the confraternity moved to a nearby Augustinian convent, a move that probably meant greater stability and more members. One family dominated Remedies' leadership throughout its known history from 1643 to 1714. A member of this family, Ambrosio Vásquez, led the 1671 case, which involved an election dispute.[31]

According to Ambrosio's testimony to the bishop, the brothers had begun election proceedings in their usual fashion when a friar of the convent, "with his customary zeal and prudence," gave them several suggestions for possible majordomo candidates, "exhorting" them to elect "a person of good example and care to help increase the divine cult."[32] A popular mulatto brother, Pedro de los Reyes, was not among the suggested candidates. Instead, the victory went to Francisco López, a mestizo, who accepted the responsibility even though he claimed that he was too busy to hold office. Ambrosio strongly objected to this new majordomo, who was known to be a "noisy" and disruptive person who helped foment "displeasing divisions and bands" within the confraternity. Ambrosio feared what would happen to the possessions and income of the confraternity under Francisco's care. Even more important, Ambrosio claimed that a new election was justified according to the rules of the confraternity and norms in the town:

> The new election must happen to preserve the custom of Salvatierra that stipulates that mestizo confraternities cannot be governed by mulattos nor mulatto confraternities by mestizos to prevent all kinds of problems and factions. . . . This is a mulatto confraternity and not mestizo, as the con-

> stitution says. . . . It is customary that mestizos cannot vote nor hold office in mulatto confraternities. . . . This is constitutional, observed always, convenient and makes for peaceful elections.

Several free mulatto confraternity members supported Ambrosio, a leader who was presented as very generous and concerned with promoting Remedies through the acquisition of new adornments for the Virgin.[33] Ambrosio and Pedro de los Reyes were both prosperous, respectable men. Ambrosio instituted a family tradition of leadership; he led the confraternity from the 1670s to the 1690s, when his sons took over. No clear resolution to the election dispute has survived. Yet the testimony emphasizes how important it was to the brothers that they maintain the tradition of mulatto leadership of their confraternity, even if a friar felt that a mestizo would be a better leader in a particular year.

Two years later, in 1673, the Saint Nicolás Tolentino confraternity in Salvatierra also experienced conflict over an election dispute based on racial divisions. The case shows that by this time, mulattos in Salvatierra had already achieved some degree of status and sought the same for their confraternities.[34] Unfortunately even less is known about this confraternity than we know about Remedies. Founded in a Franciscan convent, the confraternity's location suggests that the advocation was popular in Michoacán in general even beyond its presence in Augustinian convent churches. In 1673, two members of the confraternity protested the election of Pedro Ruano as majordomo in a petition to the bishop. They complained that although Ruano had been elected with twenty-four votes, nine of these were by members who had recently joined, including one Spaniard whose vote officially did not count in their mulatto confraternity, they argued. Ruano was "in debt and an upstart [*adeuado y advenedizo*]." Another candidate, who had lost the popular vote, was a more suitable majordomo because he had helped found and had worked to maintain the confraternity as majordomo for many years. The petitioners wanted to protect the confraternity's possessions and guarantee that it had a legitimate leader. They asked for a new election. This dispute, despite its racial dimension, was not exclusively a debate over race; the petitioners were concerned about protecting the reputation of Salvatierra's mulatto residents.

Salvatierra had existed as a *villa* for only three decades when these racially articulated conflicts occurred. The original town settlers, Spanish or otherwise, must have envisioned from the start that Salvatierra would function with institutionally divided races. Nearby Celaya also developed along the same lines; it had several elite Spanish confraternities, Indian confraternities, a Confraternity of the Blood of Christ founded by mestizos, and a Tránsito confraternity founded by mulattos.[35] Salvatierra also had Confraternities of the Souls in Purgatory and the Holy Sacrament, which were probably open to all local residents, but in the five confraternities described here, non-Spanish residents found opportunities to exercise leadership and control property. When these opportunities to exercise power and autonomy were threatened, members chose to strengthen racial divisions in their confraternities and, by extension, in Salvatierra as a whole.

In the late seventeenth and early eighteenth centuries, mulattos in towns in the Diocese of Michoacán were less likely to be enslaved and were moving up the social pyramid. This social and economic change led to conflicts between mulatto, Spanish, and Indian confraternity brothers in Valladolid, Pinzándaro, Zitácuaro, and San Juan Peribán. Although the latter three towns were much smaller and more rural than Valladolid, free mulatto residents experienced the same desires for autonomy in their confraternities that residents of the larger town did, and they argued for control using racially explicit language and rules.

In Valladolid, the Confraternity of Saint Nicolás Tolentino enjoyed modest prosperity throughout its two centuries of history, despite the fact that its members were not European. Like the members of its Rosary confraternity, mulatto brothers of Valladolid's Saint Nicolás Tolentino confraternity worked to create a more respectable reputation for their brotherhood in the eighteenth century. Conflicts involving the Saint Nicolás Tolentino confraternity most clearly illustrate the desire of Afromexicans to distinguish themselves from the less prosperous Indian population. The brothers argued that they, not the Indians, gave the confraternity its strong moral character.

The 1657 constitution of Saint Nicolás Tolentino did not stipulate a specific race for members or leaders, instead emphasizing the saint's decoration, confraternal celebrations, and emotional displays of unity and brotherhood. Eighteenth-century members claimed that their confraternity had been founded in the Augustinian convent in Valladolid in 1635.[36] Saint Nicolás Tolentino's constitution mentioned dances and music organized on the fiesta day, an unusual level of detail for a confraternity constitution. The confraternity held penitential processions during Lent, and in the week after Lent it honored the the fiesta of the Solitude of the Virgin by participating in a procession. Confraternity rules specified that during the procession, all the brothers had to wear clean tunics and carry wreaths of flowers and a decorated image of Saint Nicolás Tolentino.

Like members of other penitent confraternities founded in the seventeenth century, Saint Nicolás Tolentino brothers carried images in their procession other than their saint, although the details of exactly what they carried have been lost. Members displayed their communal spirit and support by paying for weekly masses for the souls of brothers "living and dead" and requiring that all members attend funerals carrying a candle. They also received some (unspecified) care when they were sick. All these benefits came from donating one peso upon entry. In addition to the right to participate in public expressions of piety, membership in the confraternity was an inexpensive way for members to receive brotherly care and protection in the afterlife. However, internal conflicts that were described in racial terms challenged this communal spirit.

By the mid-eighteenth century, members of the brotherhood, whose fortunes had now declined, claimed that they could not afford to hold their fiesta.[37] Fires, epidemics, and earthquakes had caused so many deaths among members that the confraternity had overextended itself to pay for funerals while it watched its paying membership base decrease. Unlike the Rosary, the confraternity had no income from property or other sources. In 1748, they had not even held an election for several years, which forced the Augustinians to offer to pay for their annual fiesta. Despite these financial challenges, Saint Nicolás continued to exist until the 1760s, when various groups among its membership entered into conflict with each other.

Mulatto brothers felt that they were superior to Indian members, a sense that clearly emerges in the conflict of 1766, which was led by majordomo Mathias Nicolás Duarte.[38] Duarte's opening statement in his case against the Indian brothers of Saint Nicolás reveals his racial attitude:

> The Indian brothers, having controlled the finances of this confraternity until the present, in total exclusion of ourselves, the mulattos [nosotros los mulatos], said Indians have taken advantage of these goods and alms for their private utility. For example, before they paid two pesos alms for the confraternity's masses, and today they pay four reales, with the extra twelve reales spent in their amusements and feasts [sus bureos y festines], without the slightest augmentation or benefit for the brotherhood. For this reason, and for other inconveniences that come out of this, I beg your grace to disempower said naturales of the control of these goods and the wealth of the above mentioned confraternity, commanding that the brothers of reason and not said naturales take over the accounts and the other aspects of good government.[39]

Duarte defined himself and his fellow mulatto brothers as people of reason and as sensible, sober men who knew how to spend money wisely. They were not, according to Duarte, prone to the feasts and festivities typical of Indians. His sense of moral superiority emerged in the context of the rising social status of mulattos in Valladolid. Duarte defined himself and his peers in contrast to the Indians who shared membership in Saint Nicolás Tolentino. While Duarte may not have been as ambitious or famous as Diego Durán, the honor of men like Durán may have inspired him to conceive of himself as more socially respectable.

Bishop Sánchez de Tagle suggested that perhaps alternating offices between Indians and mulattos would solve some confraternity problems. Duarte countered with the opinion that a financial solution would be more suitable, because the carelessness and poverty of the Indian brothers meant that they often did not pay their dues. Duarte recommended that the confraternity enforce the half-*real* membership dues more strictly and collect them regularly. He wanted to revoke the patents of confraternity brothers or sisters who did not pay their dues for three months. Duarte, with this suggestion, perhaps hoped to create a confraternity with more prosperous membership and more bureaucratic organization in order to keep the confraternity financially viable. The bishop decided that because the confraternity's finances were so precarious, he wanted it to submit financial statements for several years.[40] This case indicates that race still influenced choices Afromexicans made within confraternity life.

In other towns, the number of mulattos was larger than local Spanish populations, and conflicts about who should control the confraternities mulattos belonged to were not uncommon. In the hot lands of the colonial Diocese of Michoacán, located in the southwestern part of the modern state, people of African descent probably constituted the largest racial group by the late seventeenth century. Slaves and free mulattos had worked on sugar haciendas in this region of Michoacán since the 1550s. Sugar and cattle were the heart of the economy, and *encomenderos* [people with a royal grant to the labor of Indians] had gained control of the sugar economy in the second half of the sixteenth century. Their *trapiches* [sugar mills] began to dot the landscape of the towns of San Juan Peribán and Pinzándaro in the late sixteenth and early seventeenth centuries.[41] The indigenous population decreased dramatically after congregation, or forced resettlement into more geographically concentrated communities, in the late sixteenth century, and the Indians who remained were reduced to laboring in the sugar mills or working for cattle-growers.[42] The remaining indigenous population was not large enough to sustain the colonial enterprises, and plantation owners in San Juan Peribán and Pinzándaro quickly came to rely on imported slave labor from Africa. As the population of free mulattos grew, Spaniards struggled to control local confraternities, even though they continued to control the local economy.

There were only two lay religious organizations in San Juan Peribán in the seventeenth century, the Confraternity of the Holy Sacrament and an indigenous hospital. Afromexicans in this town did not have their own autonomous brotherhood. San Juan Peribán's confraternity seems to have been a Spanish organization, although the 1736 constitution did not mention racial limitations. Anyone who could make an initial donation of two pesos could join.[43] However, a 1672 case stated that this confraternity maintained a separate "*gremio* of mulatto and mestizo members."[44] These segregated members served frequently as deputies for the confraternity as a whole, although only Spaniards served as majordomos.

While this system worked for a time, it could not prevent an election dispute between the *casta* and Spanish members. The petitioners in the conflict argued that the candidate of the mestizos and mulattos had been elected instead of the candidate favored by the "leading Spanish gentlemen." The Spaniards chose a candidate they described as "an honorable Spanish person of substance, the owner of a sugar mill and plantation and devoted to the divine cult." In contrast, the candidate elected by mestizo and mulatto members should only be "considered" white, according to a witness. The reputation of this individual illustrates that public and private racial identities could come into conflict in the face of rules and traditions.[45] The Spanish members of the confraternity worked purposefully to maintain its identity as a Spanish confraternity, and they generally succeeded in doing so. The confraternity was described as Spanish in a 1776 list of confraternities in the Diocese of Michoacán.[46] All future documentation that mentioned Holy Sacrament mentioned only Spanish *hacendados* as majordomos; despite the fact that Spaniards were constituting a smaller and smaller percent of the population over the course of the eighteenth century, they continued to dominate in confraternity life.[47]

In contrast, Pinzándaro offers a rare example of a town dominated by mulattos. Located in a low-altitude hot region of western Michoacán, Pinzándaro produced sugar, cacao, and cattle. The decimation of the indigenous population had left the area almost deserted after the sixteenth century. Spaniards attempted to settle these hot lands at that point, but by the eighteenth century, their numbers were dwarfed by the growing populations of Africans and mulattos who were originally brought in as hacienda laborers and domestic servants.[48] In the early 1680s, an ecclesiastical visitor reported that Pinzándaro's population was made up of 59 Indians, 33 Spaniards, 210 mestizos, 2 blacks, 265 mulattos, and 1 *chino*: around half the population over the age of seven was labeled mulatto or black.[49] By 1743, no Indians at all survived in Pinzándaro and well over two-thirds of the population was called mulatto or mestizo.[50] Spanish church authorities considered Pinzándaro to be an ideally passive colonial settlement. Local Franciscans and various bishops of Michoacán, who invariably stopped in Pinzándaro on their tours through the region, worked to integrate the town into colonial religious practice.

In the late seventeenth and early eighteenth centuries, Pinzándaro's confraternities were open to members of all races. In records of his 1680 visit, Bishop Aguiar y Seixas mentioned only the black, mestizo, and mulatto Solitude confraternity. However, the town also had Holy Sacrament and Blessed Souls confraternities. The 1757 constitution of the confraternity of the Blessed Souls allowed male and female members "of whatever state and quality."[51] Although we do not know precise figures about the populations of these two towns, Pinzándaro was probably much smaller than Salvatierra; perhaps this is why its confraternities were less interested in racial divisions. The laborers in Pinzándaro seemed to view themselves, and be viewed by authorities, as mulattos. Unlike mulattos in Salvatierra and Valladolid, they did not seek to set themselves apart from other local residents by enforcing institutional divisions between mestizos and Indians.

But they did feel that they should have control over who held important offices in their confraternity. In a 1712 ecclesiastical court case, mulatto members of the Confraternity of the Solitude in Pinzándaro brought a case to the bishop disputing the election of a Spaniard as majordomo.[52] The mulatto majordomos strongly defended their position, opening their arguments with assertions that the confraternity was canonically approved and that "the said Confraternity of Our Lady of Solitude, is controlled by mulattos because they founded it and paid its expense with care and zeal, without the intervention of any Spaniard in its foundation, offices or burdens, as stated in the original election records."[53]

Witnesses who favored the Spanish majordomo in Pinzándaro sought to strengthen their argument by referring to patronage ties, just as Cristóbal Villamayor had done in late-seventeenth-century Parral. Pinzándaro's Spanish faction, which was supported by a *hacendado*, claimed that "as is publicly known and notorious in this entire jurisdiction . . . black slaves of the great hacienda" were the actual founders, not "free mulattos nor Spaniards." The Pinzándaro mulatto brothers took up their role in this paternalistic strategy and described themselves as "*pobres desamparados* [poor abandoned ones]." Although most of the testimony that slaves had founded Solitude came from dismissive Spaniards, one witness was an 80-year-old slave who had been born in 1632; he had lived through the entire era of this confraternity's existence and said that it had been founded on a hacienda, had been neglected, but then was reinstated by mulattos.[54]

This case provides insights into the financial arrangements and membership patterns of a rural confraternity. Unlike most urban non-Indian confraternities, Pinzándaro's Solitude earned its income from keeping livestock. After examining the original foundation documents, the court scribe stated that "after many free mulattos and slaves of several haciendas and areas (including some Spaniards) joined, the confraternity was in the hands of the mulattos that had joined and it lost its principal two or three times." The scribe observed that the mulattos involved in this case lacked the funds and financial stability to maintain a confraternity. (This association of race with economic weakness echoes testimonies from witnesses in the case of the dissenting brothers in Pátzcuaro's Saint Nicolás Tolentino confraternity several decades before.) In response, the mulatto brothers testified that they had had to sell some cattle to buy ornaments and clothes for the Virgin, which were justifiable expenses for a confraternity. They claimed that the sale of the cattle had nothing to do with "poverty or their color." Those who felt that mulattos should control the Solitude confraternity argued that the hacienda slaves were the ones who had wasted the funds of the confraternity; the free mulattos had actually brought the confraternity stability and, most important, orchestrated the bishop's approval of the confraternity (probably during the visit of Aguiar y Seixas in 1680.) The elderly slave stated that mulattos had been active in their collection of alms to finance the confraternity when it was located on the hacienda and was run by slaves. The ecclesiastical authorities who heard this case apparently accepted that Solitude was a mulatto institution, but further results of this case are not given in available documents.

The 1776 list of confraternities in the Diocese of Michoacán mentions only mulatto families for Pinzándaro, and the bishop's visit described these families as supportive to authorities in a local rebellion and "extremely affable and obedient."[55] An extensive case in the late eighteenth century over an inheritance involving the Confraternity of the Solitude reinforces the impression that mulattos were the leaders of the brotherhood. Questions of history and memory again emerged as the many witnesses (at least two-thirds of whom were mulatto) testified, some of whom claimed to be more than 100 years old.[56] Pinzándaro's long history of confraternal life, which was prominent in the memory of local residents in the late eighteenth century, helped these individuals acquire their reputation for peacefulness.

The increasingly visible presence of Afromexicans often led to fear or other negative reactions from other groups. Spaniards in the hot lowlands of Michoacán recognized that they were no longer the largest population group in some towns. Zitácuaro, which was located near Maravatío in the eastern part of the Diocese of Michoacán, was on the edge of the sugar-producing hot country. Like San Juan Peribán, Zitácuaro experienced friction because Spaniards felt threatened by an increasing population that was descended from hacienda slaves who had been brought into the region in the mid-1500s.[57] Disagreements escalated when Zitácuaro rose to prominence as the site of a miraculous image and shrine.

Spanish residents in Zitácuaro founded a Confraternity of the Immaculate Conception in 1651.[58] By the late seventeenth century, the confraternity enjoyed considerable wealth and owned cattle and slaves.[59] Throughout the seventeenth century, Spaniards officially controlled this confraternity. Their image of the Virgin and the precious glass box that contained it received special veneration.[60] Like San Juan Peribán, Zitácuaro did not seem to have an official Afromexican confraternity when Aguiar y Seixas visited in 1680. Both Spaniards and Indians had organizations of their own, but mulattos tried unsuccessfully to integrate themselves into the older Spanish Immaculate Conception Confraternity. By 1707, the Spanish brothers had begun to feel threatened by the presence of *castas* in their midst, whom they viewed as unsettled interlopers. They complained to the Bishop of Michoacán that "many mulattos, mestizos and others of vile or infamous quality [*infame calidad*] have been admitted" and were voting for their own candidates, disregarding the fact that Spaniards had founded and had traditionally had control of the brotherhood.[61] They pointed out that they had always shared the offices among themselves, "without intervention of any others who were not residents, nor any other kind of person of vile quality." The inclusion of the mulattos and mestizos caused the confraternity "great harm and damage" and the Spanish brothers were "disconsolate" because of the decrease in alms collected and the deterioration of the confraternity's property. They wanted the bishop to forbid non-Spanish members from taking out the precious image of the Virgin and carrying her box while they were collecting alms. The bishop agreed to these demands, ruling that "every year the rector, majordomo and other officials of the confraternity must be Spaniards and lifelong residents, not foreigners, nor *chinos*, mestizos, mulattos, or others of this quality." People of *infame calidad* could join the confraternity, but they could not vote. The bishop also ordered that all the confraternity's property be returned and that stricter care be taken in the use of and access to these valuables.[62] In Zitácuaro, despite the fact that *castas* were more numerous than Spaniards, they were prohibited from having access to the Virgin's statue, which was considered a truly valuable sacred object.

Salvatierra, Zitácuaro, Pinzándaro, Celaya, San Juan Peribán, and Valladolid varied in size and in type of local economy, yet the Afromexican population in each community experienced growth in the late seventeenth and eighteenth centuries. The changing demographics led to a need to change local confraternity structures. While race was often used as a weapon in the conflicts that emerged, other divisions along social and economic lines were equally salient in these disputes. Each community had property owners and workers, groups that were distinguished by both economic and racial differences. These racial divisions were not necessarily imposed by authorities; they seem to have been important to local confraternity members as well. In Salvatierra, the non-Spanish society divided within itself and did not unite against wealthier local Spaniards. Valladolid's mulattos disassociated themselves from local Indians. San Juan Peribán's Spaniards maintained control over their confraternity even as their numbers decreased. In Pinzándaro, the Spanish population decreased, but mulattos were ideal colonial subjects, according to the authorities. Confraternity disputes provide examples of the many possible permutations of racial divisions in New Spain.

Afromexican confraternities used a variety of methods to fund their confraternities and occasionally resorted to creative strategies to raise income to pay for important costs such as masses, fiestas on saints' days, and burial benefits for their members. In Parral, networks of local patronage helped the local *pardo* confraternity survive. Confraternities in larger towns, especially mining towns, made money through collecting alms. Some Afromexican confraternities imitated Indian confraternities and raised livestock. Hacienda confraternities depended upon *hacendados* to approve of, finance, and house their confraternities. If a hacienda did not have a confraternity, slaves could contribute to a nearby urban confraternity, as they did in the Orizaba region. These multifaceted approaches to financing confraternity life reflect the wide range of social and economic roles members played in New Spain and suggest how race may have played a role in evolving class distinctions.

While several historians have studied the ways in which confraternity investments such as loans, livestock, and rental properties financed these organizations, most have neglected the method most Afromexican confraternities used to raise funds: the collection of alms. The richest and most powerful confraternities in the viceregal capital resembled convents and monasteries in the volume of their financial dealings, which involved loans and properties worth thousands of pesos. They often took in thousands of pesos each year, many times the income of the poorer confraternities. By contrast, indigenous rural confraternities depended on livestock or agricultural produce for their income. These confraternities also owned land, and their income represented a village or community fund.[63]

The finances of confraternities led by individuals of African heritage in most cases resembled neither Indian rural confraternities nor elite urban Spanish institutions. Afromexican confraternities did not usually thrive in rural villages and were never tied directly to the community as a whole, other than in rare instances when the entire community was defined as black or mulatto, as was the case with Pinzándaro's Solitude confraternity. Even though confraternities such as Rosary in Valladolid sought to emulate wealthier Spanish brotherhoods, Afromexican confraternities did not resemble financially elite groups in larger towns and cities. Instead, Afromexican confraternities remained set apart from both groups by their reliance on income from alms and perhaps from a few properties that generated a small income. For example, Valladolid's Rosary brotherhood moved from being financially dependent on alms to a rent- and dues-based income. The typical urban confraternity, including those led by blacks and mulattos, subsidized its income with joining fees and membership dues. The cost of joining a confraternity of this kind ranged from four *reales* to two pesos. Most confraternities asked members to contribute a half-*real* every week, fortnight, or month.[64]

Confraternity constitutions occasionally specified different dues for members based on racial labels. Table 7.1 lists twenty-two confraternities with constitutions that designated distinct dues for Spanish, Indian, mulatto, black, and mestizo members. The dates of these constitutions and the confraternities' official foundings range from 1591 to the late eighteenth century. Seventeen out of the twenty-two confraternities with racially specific dues were founded in the second half of the seventeenth century, at the time when the concern over racial distinctions was at its peak, as was the number of new confraternities being founded. Most of these confraternities were located in the Diocese of Michoacán, although Taxco, Orizaba, and Maltrata also had confraternities with

Table 7.1. Seventeenth- and eighteenth-century confraternities in New Spain whose constitutions record membership dues by race

Confraternity	Founding date	Town and modern state	Spanish	Indian	Mulatto	Black	Mestizo
Most Holy Sacrament	1591	San Miguel, Guanajuato	3 pesos	2 pesos	2 pesos	2 pesos	unknown
Immaculate Conception	1641	San Francisco del Rincón, Guanajuato	2 pesos	1 peso	2 pesos	2 pesos	2 pesos
Saint Nicolás Tolentino	1644	Taxco, Guerrero	2 pesos	1 peso	2 pesos	2 pesos	2 pesos
Most Holy Sacrament	1648	San Juan Peribán, Michoacán	2 pesos	Free	2 pesos	2 pesos	unknown
Our Lady of Health	1656	Guaniqueo, Michoacán	3 pesos	12 reales	12 reales	12 reales	3 pesos
Our Lady of Remedies	1658	Tlalpuxagua, Michoacán	1 peso	4 reales	4 reales	4 reales	unknown
Holy Burial	1659	San Francisco del Rincón, Guanajuato	12 reales	1 peso	12 reales	12 reales	12 reales
Souls in Purgatory	1662	San Francisco del Rincón, Guanajuato	2 pesos	1 peso	2 pesos	2 pesos	2 pesos
Saint Joseph	1663	Nogales, Orizaba	2 reales	6 reales	3 reales	3 reales	unknown
Misericordia	1664	Irapuato, Guanajuato	1 peso	4 reales	1 peso	1 peso	unknown
Holy Sacrament	1664	San Francisco del Rincón, Guanajuato	1 peso	4 reales	4 reales	4 reales	4 reales
Our Lady of the Assumption	1667	Acultzingo, Veracruz	1 peso	4 reales	unknown	unknown	unknown
Holy Sacrament	1674	Maltrata, Veracruz	12 reales	1 peso	unknown	unknown	unknown
Our Lady of Guadalupe	1684	Pénjamo, Guanajuato	12 reales	6 reales	unknown	unknown	unknown
Jesus of Nazareth	1685	Tecpan, Michoacán	12 reales	1 peso	1 peso	1 peso	unknown
Jesus of Nazareth	1687	Cuitzeo, Michoacán	2 pesos	1 peso	12 reales	12 reales	12 reales
Jesus of Nazareth	1689	Nogales, Orizaba	2 pesos	5 reales	1 peso	1 peso	unknown
Souls in Purgatory	1694	San Juan Maravatío, Michoacán	12 reales	1 peso	12 reales	12 reales	12 reales
Souls in Purgatory	1720	Orizaba, Veracruz	1 peso	4 reales	1 peso	unknown	1 peso
Souls in Purgatory	1745	Zapotlán, Jalisco	2 pesos	1 peso	2 pesos	unknown	1 peso
Saint Joseph	1780	Real de Santiago Marfil, Guanajuato	5 reales	unknown	2 reales	unknown	2 reales
Souls in Purgatory	unknown	Apatzingán, Michoacán	2 pesos	1 peso	2 pesos	1 peso	2 pesos

Source: Casa de Morelos, Serie Constituciones, Caja 817, and Serie Cofradías, Cajas 818, 1250, 1256, 1264; Archivo Parroquial de Santa Prisca, Taxco, Libros de Cofradías; Archivo de la Parroquia de San Miguel, Orizaba, Libros de Cofradías; Archivo General de la Nacion.

dues that varied according to the race of its members. Any town with a growing mixed-race population and a clear distinction of wealth among races might have had confraternities that specified different dues according to race.

On the whole, the rules that specified dues based on race suggest that Indians were consistently the poorest members and that confraternities were open and embraced poorer members. The varying dues ranged from free entry for Indians who wanted to enter the Confraternity of the Holy Sacrament in San Juan Peribán to a fee of three pesos for Spaniards who wanted to enter the Confraternity of the Holy Sacrament in San Miguel el Grande.

Of the twenty-two constitutions that mention race-specific dues, nearly half neglected to mention differing dues for mestizo members. We do not know whether a mestizo member in these confraternities had to pay the same rate as a Spaniard or an Indian. However, the remaining twelve constitutions include eight that charged mestizos the same dues as Spanish members, supporting the thesis that mestizos were closest to Spaniards in economic status. Only four constitutions mentioned a lower rate for mestizos, and in three of these, mestizos paid what mulattos paid to enter the confraternity. Only in Zapotlán, which was located in a mining region in the Sierra de Michoacán, did mestizo brothers pay the same entry dues as Indians.

Almost every confraternity listed in table 7.1 specified dues for mulattos, but only sixteen mention entry fees for black members. The confraternity constitutions that did not address dues for blacks were all founded in the late seventeenth or eighteenth centuries. In most areas of New Spain, blacks represented a very small group in the population by the eighteenth century. Despite the fact that blacks were more likely to be slaves than mulattos were, only the Confraternity of the Souls in Purgatory in Apatzingan charged blacks less than they did mulattos. In this confraternity, blacks and Indians paid only one peso to join, while Spaniards and mulattos both paid two pesos.

Table 7.1 gives a sense of where different races fit in a hierarchy based on wealth and status in a given region. The different dues for different races institutionalize the social and economic roles in these towns to a degree by identifying the poorest and wealthiest local groups. Almost every confraternity that specified dues according to race was located in a town whose economy was based on mining or hacienda labor. Income in these regions was often characterized by a sharp divide between two groups: local residents who could earn money through either wage labor or ownership of mines or haciendas and slaves and others who had very little disposable income. Confraternities in San Miguel, Guaniqueo, Tlalpuxagua, Tecpan, and San Francisco del Rincón had the same entrance fees for Indians and mulattos and/or blacks and had higher fees for Spaniards. The practice of categorizing prospective members in this way may be an indication that most non-Spanish residents of these areas had low-paying jobs on haciendas and together formed the group that contained most of the poor in the town. Taxco, San Juan Peribán, Irapuato, and Orizaba charged Indians less than mestizos and mulattos and charged mulattos the same entry fees as Spaniards. This difference suggests that Indians were poorer and perhaps less integrated into urban life and wage labor in these towns and that mestizos and mulattos were better able to make a contribution approaching—if not equal to—that of a local Spaniard. The unique example is the Saint Joseph confraternity in Nogales, a sugar hacienda near Orizaba.[65] For some reason, Indians had to pay six reales to enter, while Spaniards only paid two reales. This role reversal seems so unlikely that perhaps it is a misprint and the Spaniards actually had to pay two pesos, the most expensive entry fee in this confraternity. The only other racial category their constitution used was for black and mulatto slaves, who each paid three reales. In Nogales, people with African racial labels were typically slaves, and perhaps they could not afford the same entrance fee as Indians. In contrast, the Confraternity of Jesus of Nazareth in the same town charged Spaniards two pesos, blacks and mulattos one peso, and Indians five reales to join, a more standard ranking of status from rich to poor. However this confraternity did not specifically mention that some members were slaves, so probably the constitution writers assumed that free Afromexican members made a better income than local Indians.

While these confraternities focused on racial divisions, confraternities in other regions united the poor of all races in efforts to provide charity to those who were even less fortunate than themselves. The Confraternity of the Solitude in Orizaba, several confraternities in Nogales near Orizaba, and the Confraternity of Saint Joseph in Cholula illustrate the ways in which confraternities that were founded and financed by enslaved populations managed to support themselves in the absence of access to generous urban donors or the small income from rent some Afromexican confraternities enjoyed.[66] In these areas, people of African descent did not earn the kind of income they did in mining or in more urban regions and did not have access to the social prestige—however limited—found in Valladolid. Confraternities near Orizaba and Cholula showed less concern with racial distinctions than confraternities in Michoacán and the Bajío region, perhaps in the interest of achieving their community and charitable goals. However, the economic distinctions in place in Orizaba were more rigid and overt and could not be negotiated through establishing rules or settling confraternity disputes in courts. In regions where slavery persisted, an increase in the Afromexican population did not lead to a similar increase in local power or change of position in the rigid racial hierarchy. Confraternities connected to haciendas had to maintain strong patronage ties to survive. Although the information about hacienda confraternities is fragmentary, it contributes to an overall picture of the diversity of confraternal practice.

The Confraternity of the Solitude, which was officially founded and led by mestizos and was based in the parish church of San Miguel in Orizaba, endured for nearly 200 years, from 1660 to the 1850s. The confraternity was led by mestizos, but it reached out to other social and racial groups in the region. In 1661, Indian members paid 6 *reales* and all other members paid one peso to join. In 1712, the brothers decided that they needed a stronger financial base and raised joining fees to one peso for Indians and twelve reales for all others. Through most of its history, this confraternity depended on membership dues and alms collection, although by the nineteenth century it had accumulated nine pieces of revenue-producing property.

From around 1706, Solitude accounts included a yearly donation from "black men and women and Indians of the Tuzpango sugar mill." Historian Patrick Carroll describes the Tuzpango hacienda, which had been a sugar plantation since 1560:

> In 1717 Tuzpango had 167 bondservants. The inventory listed them as carpenters, masons, potters, weavers, blacksmiths, refiners and field supervisors. . . . Some slaves on this plantation had positions of responsibility like master builder or master cauldron maker. . . . Spanish residents included an administrator, a surgeon, and a priest. Indian laborers from the neighboring village of Chiciguila did Tuzpango's most menial tasks such as clearing the land, planting, and cutting the cane. . . . Indians did not reside on the estate in large numbers.[67]

In the early eighteenth century, Tuzpango slaves, mainly men, were valued at above 30,000 pesos, but by mid-century, the number of slaves at the Tuzpango hacienda had fallen to 104 and their total monetary value had decreased 15,600 pesos. More slave women and children lived at the hacienda, and the decreasing number of new male slaves meant that the hacienda had begun to resemble a normal settlement, at least in the sex and age breakdown of its residents.[68]

Every year until around 1807, the servants and slaves of this sugar hacienda donated to the confraternity in Orizaba, the closest town. This amount peaked at 22 pesos, although some years the contribution was much smaller. At most, the hacienda workers provided about 10 percent of the confraternity's yearly income. Usually this donation arrived in a lump sum, but in some cases the accounts document donations from individual blacks and Indians.[69] Perhaps the slaves who donated held skilled positions such as carpenters, refiners, and supervisors on the hacienda that made it possible for them to contribute alms to a confraternity. Solitude records indicate that the confraternity paid for many burials of slaves and *morenos*.[70] Masters often freed slaves when they were sick or dying, and Tuzpango slaves may have depended on the Solitude confraternity for a proper burial. Those collaborative efforts indicate the ways in which urban mestizos and rural slaves and Indians forged a link in Orizaba that proved beneficial to all for decades.

The Confraternity of Saint Joseph in Cholula offers another example of both an unusual way of raising money to support a confraternity and a method for providing charitable services across racial and social divisions. Cholula, which is near Puebla, is known today for its pyramid and its pre-Hispanic market. In the seventeenth century, it was home to perhaps 1,000 people of African descent, and this number doubled in the eighteenth century. These people worked on fifty-eight haciendas and ranches in the jurisdiction.[71] An Inquisition document from 1650 mentions a local wool-weaving factory that hired people referred to as blacks and mulattos.[72] Fray Augustín de Vetancur, writing in 1697, listed Cholula's Spanish confraternities as "the most Holy True Cross, Souls in Purgatory, the Conception" and also mentioned Saint Joseph of the *morenos*.[73] The city's Indians controlled another thirteen confraternities.

Sergeant Juan Pinto, a free *pardo*, led the Saint Joseph confraternity in the 1720s and 1730s.[74] During the time Pinto was majordomo, the confraternity made a good income on what was called "the raffle prize [*premio de la rifa*]." For example, in one year the brothers took in 110 pesos and gave out thirteen. Except for the mention of the monetary prize, no other information exists regarding what this raffle meant or how it was organized. In the early 1730s, Saint Joseph made 500 pesos on its raffle each year. Deputies were elected specifically to administer the raffle. Saint Joseph used the income to provide entertainment in the form of lavish celebrations for several annual fiestas that included drums, clarinets, *chirimías* [a kind of clarinet], and fireworks. Fiesta decorations involved flowers, palm branches, and expensive gilded mirrors for Saint Joseph's altar. The confraternity also used its substantial income to pay for new ornaments—until an epidemic hit in 1736. That year, sixty members died, more than five times the normal mortality rate for this confraternity. Interestingly, although the confraternity was labeled *moreno* in 1697 and was led by a free *pardo*, almost all the funerals Saint Joseph paid for were for individuals described as Indians. This unusual financial arrangement characterized by money earned through a kind of gambling that was then spent on funerals for poorer community members and fiestas the entire town enjoyed illustrates a kind of communal charity not seen in the confraternities that were beset with racial conflicts and obsessed with the racial profile of their members and leaders.

Solitude in Orizaba and Saint Joseph in Cholula both had reputations as having leaders of a specific race, but the recipients of their charity often came from other groups, proving that people of indigenous and African descent could work together for positive goals in the colonial era. In Orizaba, urban mestizos helped pay for the burial of nearby slaves. In Cholula, *pardos*, including militia members, were able to help local Indians suffering from an epidemic. In these cases, charity was provided across racial barriers, even when the patrons were not wealthy Spaniards, but were instead *pardos* or mestizos.

However, as we saw in the cases of the Immaculate Conception in Parral and the Holy Sacrament in San Juan Peribán, most confraternities located on haciendas depended exclusively on the patronage of *hacendados* and faced a special set of challenges when they wanted to become independent. Master-slave ties were of course stronger in regions where slave-based economies remained in place into the eighteenth century. Both Parral and the sugar-growing areas of Michoacán depended on slave labor only for a short time, and they quickly developed a large supply of laborers who were free mulattos. In contrast, in well-established slave economies such as that surrounding Orizaba, Afromexican brothers remained dependent on and continued their paternalistic relationships with hacienda owners. This kind of relationship persisted into the eighteenth century at the sugar hacienda called, in various eras, the "ingenio de Orizaba, ingenio del Conde, Saint Juan Batista Nogales by 1743 and Nogales, villa."[75] Nogales is now a town on the outskirts of Orizaba; it was once the main settlement of the hacienda and was where its parish church dedicated to Saint Juan Bautista was located. It was founded by Viceroy Mendoza and later owned by the Count of the Valley of Orizaba as a royal gift to the family for service in the Americas and the Philippines and in the wars against the Chichimecas. The residents of Nogales probably lived in similar circumstances as those described for Tuzpango, which was also near Orizaba but had a more developed social and religious life. Nogales slaves experienced confraternal life on their hacienda and did not have to go to an urban area to look for involvement in confraternities; the slaves of Tuzpango depended on nearby Orizaba for access to confraternal life.

Saint Juan Bautista Nogales was a large hacienda, almost a small town: an inventory of the estate of the count of Orizaba described the hacienda as having "a veritable village in 1580, with the owner's house and the stone church, four big buildings for refining the sugar . . . little adobe houses for the Spaniards or black foreman, [and] cabins for other slaves and Indians." Hacienda property also included cane fields, woods, and areas for grazing cattle and sheep.[76]

Religious life offered options similar to those available to the faithful living in a small town. The parish church of San Juan Bautista had six confraternities, dedicated to the Souls in Purgatory, the Holy Sacrament, Jesus of Nazareth, Saint Joseph, Saint Anthony, and the Rosary.[77] Each of these had a racially distinct membership. Although many of the confraternity record books were lost in a 1716 fire that destroyed the church and may have been part of a rebellion, constitutions were re-copied and preserved.

Each of these confraternities drew its membership from different sectors of local hacienda society, a practice that reflects the distinct social and economic roles that grew from each individual's race. The most prestigious Afromexican confraternity may have been Blessed Souls in Purgatory, which was led in the 1700s by a free mulatto.[78] The surviving records of this confraternity mention the 1716 rebellion, calling it the work of "barbarians."[79] Throughout the eighteenth century, Blessed Souls was financed by its ownership of a herd of around 300 goats, along with small entrance fees. As was the case for all confraternities dedicated to the souls in purgatory, this confraternity dedicated itself to burials and prayers for the dead. Funerals were a major benefit of membership, and the confraternity provided wax, burial, mass, and a procession in which members carried their standard and other insignias. Blessed Souls lasted at least until the nineteenth century.

The confraternity of Jesus of Nazareth, which was established in 1689, was also founded with the patronage of the noble *hacendados* of Orizaba. The thirty-three original members included two members of the Vivero family, the lineage given the title of Counts of the Valley of Orizaba. However, most of the brothers were described as "free *pardos*, mestizos and Indians, and many other residents of this plantation."[80] While the counts served as deputies, the Indians also had a separate set of officials. The focus of this confraternity was a weekly procession and the fiesta of Corpus Christi.

The oldest confraternity on record for Nogales adhered closely to patterns of Afromexican confraternal practice seen in mining towns and other areas of New Spain with residents descended from African slaves. The Saint Joseph confraternity was founded in the 1650s by "male and female slaves of his lordship the count of the Valley of Orizaba."[81] The founders may have been Africans; several had surnames that referred to African regions such as Congo and Matamba. One founder was described as a creole named "Manuel Congo de Guzmán, sugar master." Saint Joseph seemed to be led by slaves until the post-independence era. As it did in seventeenth-century Afromexican confraternities in Valladolid, Zacatecas, and Veracruz, alms-collecting and female participation figured prominently in this confraternity's activities. Four sisters were chosen each year to care for the sick and to arrange candles and prepare members for their funeral. The confraternity imparted a sense of community with the ringing of the *ingenio* [sugar refinery] bell to summon those on the hacienda to attend the funerals of all members. Although the confraternity's constitution recognized the patronage of the count, the rules addressed this issue somewhat ambiguously. While Spaniards were allowed to join, they were not allowed to serve as officials. Constitutional provisions stated that deputies should be elected to represent Indians, black, and mulatto members, but "under no circumstances" could a Spaniard hold an office. The constitution also thanked the count for providing them with an image of Saint Joseph, but it ruled that alms had to be collected to add to the decoration of the image and its altar.[82] The confraternity's income came from a mix of urban and rural patterns; both alms and livestock provided money for Saint Joseph.

These diverse confraternities, each of which had different types of members, leaders, fund-raising techniques, and relationships with patrons illustrate that haciendas could support a fully developed, albeit restricted, confraternal life for their workers. *Hacendados* encouraged participation in this more stable confraternal life. These confraternities did not seem to undergo the same conflicts and problems of confraternities in other towns, where Afromexican confraternities sought autonomy and rejected patronage that reminded them of their previous slave status.

Confraternity constitutions and disputes demonstrate that the need to define racial distinctions was most intense from around 1650 to the early 1700s, at least in the Diocese of Michoacán. This period of conflict coincided with an increase in the Indian, mulatto, and mestizo populations and a decrease in the slave population. The racially articulated rules and discord described in this chapter suggest that racial divisions endured into the eighteenth century. This worked against the formation of an identity based on class. Differing perceptions of who could afford which entry fee for confraternity membership indicate the variety of ways in which race and class intersected. Afromexicans sometimes paid the same entry fees as Spaniards, but sometimes they paid a smaller fee that was similar or less than what Indians paid. However, charitable efforts in Orizaba and Cholula illustrate that *casta* confraternities could blur race barriers by offering patronage to less fortunate local residents. Not surprisingly, little-documented hacienda confraternities preserved colonial racial distinctions and patronage systems. Varying and subtle racial and social divisions could lead to expressions of superiority toward other groups, not only on the part of Spaniards but also in some cases on the part of mulattos toward Indians. Although some towns, such as Mexico City in 1692 and perhaps Valladolid in the late eighteenth century, had social and economic patterns that fostered some sense of plebeian unity that was expressed in political organizations and rebellions, this was not the case in many other smaller towns. The perpetuation of racial divisions evident in the rules of confraternities and conflicts that emerged in brotherhoods helped sustain the colonial system in the eighteenth century.

Conclusion

This project began with the question of whether or not Africans and their descendants acted as partners in the colonial enterprise or outsiders on the margins of colonial society. The question arose out of the presentation of slaves and freedmen in the historical literature as either "auxiliaries" to the conquest and domination of the indigenous people of Mexico or abusive vagabonds who harmed Indian communities for personal gain. Both of these interpretations create a dichotomy of either Spaniards or Africans versus Indians in New Spain's colonial society. Support for these views comes from several primary sources. Some Hispanicized Africans took part in sixteenth-century military expeditions. Afromexicans worked as overseers on some Spanish haciendas. Sixteenth-century viceroys reported that black, mulatto, and mestizo vagabonds abused Indian villagers. But how could enslaved people have functioned as weapons of domination when they sometimes did not speak Spanish, suffered from masters' abuse, and lacked access to justice and authority? And the existence of confraternities enmeshed in local religious and social structures disproves the idea that people of African descent were outsiders or criminals in New Spain.

Several scholars have already complicated the vision of Africans and their descendants as tools of Spanish domination. Cope's idea of a rise of plebeian consciousness and class divisions challenges the theory that conflicts in New Spanish society always revolved around race. However, Cope's approach does not take into account regional variation. While Cope's theory of the creation of a racially mixed plebeian class may hold true for seventeenth-century Mexico City and perhaps late-eighteenth-century Valladolid, it does not work for smaller towns in the Bajío region and the eastern sugar haciendas in the late seventeenth and early eighteenth centuries. Race continued to divide society as confraternities in these regions enforced racial exclusivity and local interpretations of racial divisions, although not always along lines of Spanish/mestizo/mulatto opposition to Indians. Even in Valladolid, eighteenth-century mulatto confraternity brothers disparaged Indian members while at the same time advocating the rights of plebeians.

Criminal and Inquisition records that involve cases of sorcery, blasphemy, and rebellion show that slaves and free people of color did not always submit to colonial rule or help carry out Spanish domination. While these sources reveal some details of the lives of *castas* who challenged colonial authority and show how Indians and *mulatos* shared a reputation for magic and illicit practices, they do not necessarily clarify the experience of the social conformists who constituted the overwhelming majority of Afromexican society. While misfits existed, Africans who survived their voyage and slavery produced descendants who, at least over several generations, generally conformed to Hispanic colonial rule and even hoped to achieve success within the system.

The idea that Afromexicans assimilated to Hispanic norms to different degrees depending on region and era helps clarify some of the contradictions inherent in the idea of an enslaved population that functioned as a tool of conquest. It is true that a "black Spaniard" who took part in the conquest did act as an auxiliary of the Spanish. But a *bozal* slave who had just arrived from Congo or Angola and did not speak Spanish, a *mulata* who was brought before the Inquisition for sorcery, or even a mulatto who was tried for being a vagabond was not an agent of conquest and Hispanic rule. Sooner or later, though, descendants of the black Spaniard, the African slave, the *mulata* sorceress, and the vagabond became a part of Spanish society, interacted with Indians and mestizos, were probably labeled *mulato*, and worked on or near a hacienda, in a city as a servant or craftsman, or in a mining region.

This study of regional differences and change over time adds complexity to our understanding of the roles Africans and their descendants played in New Spain's social and religious life. In the seventeenth century, distinctly Afromexican confraternity practices emerged that were characterized by female leadership, a stronger connection to African identities, distinctions between African and American birth, and manipulation of symbolic associations with slavery and humble status on the social hierarchy as a foundation for spiritual merit. Until the late seventeenth century, the constitutions and activities of Afromexican confraternities focused on community-building charity. But by the end of the seventeenth century, competitive social behavior had often replaced the earlier model. Examples from Valladolid and Parral illustrate the increasing prominence of Afromexicans who, over one or two generations, achieved a degree of status in Hispanic societies as free craftsmen.

In Mexico City, Parral, Veracruz, and the numerous towns described in chapter 7, several patterns emerged whereby free, urban workers who were generally called mulattos assimilated to Hispanic norms. Many of these individuals used Spanish institutions, especially the confraternity, to fit into and achieve prosperity in the Hispanic colonial world. Two individuals from two centuries,

Diego Durán and Juan Correa, illustrate two routes of Hispanicization and upward mobility.

Diego Durán represents the best example of the increasing success over several generations of a family with African origins. His paternal ancestors were probably slaves on sugar plantations outside the town of Pénjamo in the modern state of Guanajuato. Late in the 1600s, Diego's maternal great-grandparents moved to Valladolid. Not long after, the Duráns achieved success first as builders, then as master architects. Diego Durán and his family were unusually successful, but probably many men came from a similar mixed Indian and African rural heritage and sought out confraternities because they provided rare leadership opportunities for *castas*. In provincial towns such as Valladolid and Parral, *mulato* confraternities survived the eighteenth century and independence from Spain. In Valladolid, Durán was able to use his stature as a master architect and prominent confraternity leader to organize a plebeian political movement to support a government official.

In contrast, Mexico City, which had stronger ties to Spain and the wealth of the Spanish empire, provided an environment where wealthy Afromexicans could find success in the seventeenth century. These men were freed slaves or descendants of legitimate unions between Spaniards and women of color. Juan Correa, the son of a mulatto Spaniard and a black slave woman, achieved fame as a painter in the late seventeenth century, helped by connections through both parents to the ecclesiastical and civil bureaucracy of the capital. Juan Correa senior came from Cádiz, and his work as an Inquisition barber-surgeon shows his complete integration into Hispanic institutions. Mateo de Aguilar enjoyed similar prosperity as the son of a Spaniard and his black wife. However, this late-seventeenth-century success for mulattos in the capital did not mean lasting prominence as confraternity leaders. In contrast to the experience of Afromexicans in Valladolid and other provincial towns, successful mulattos in Mexico City, including confraternity leaders, perhaps more quickly joined Hispanic social circles or fell down the social ranks, to be absorbed in the plebeian masses Cope describes. Correa's descendants and other wealthy mulattos did not form a *pardo* elite in the eighteenth century: Correa's unusual talents brought him to the height of success for the colonial period; from there, his children and grandchildren could only move down in status unless they became nominally Spanish.

The lives of several other Afromexicans show the variety and complexity of the colonial experience for descendants of African slaves. Juan Bautista, who advocated a hospital for other mulattos in the late 1500s; Juan Roque, a successful property owner who sponsored a confraternity of African Zapes in early-seventeenth-century Mexico City; Sergeant Antonio Narváez, the persecuted mid-seventeenth-century leader of Parral's Afromexican confraternity; and Luis de la Serna, the slave and father of six who led a confraternity in Valladolid in the mid-1600s, each had different experiences of the colonial system. They may have rebelled in small personal ways or they may have supported the system. The only overarching theme that can be assigned to their lives is that they came into contact with a wide range of Spaniards, mestizos, and Indians and, regardless of racial labels, they all tried to help themselves, their families, and their friends survive and improve their situations.

Residents of every town and city from Parral to Veracruz incorporated Spanish institutions, including confraternities, into local public life. The degree of interest in confraternities in the eighteenth century varied across the regions and speaks to changes in religious practices of Spaniards in different towns and cities in New Spain. In some areas, such as Mexico City, the huge popularity of confraternities had declined by the eighteenth century among elite testators. Afromexican confraternities also faded away in the capital long before they disappeared in other towns. In Valladolid and Parral, *casta* confraternities began to resemble workingmen's organizations. Through the rejection of female-led, flagellant confraternities of the seventeenth century, Spanish trends influenced eighteenth-century Afromexicans, while at the same time Spaniards were discarding Spanish Baroque practices in favor of the French-influenced reforms noted in chapter 1.

This study of Afromexican confraternities brings up the difficult issue of colonial identity. Confraternities sometimes promoted ties to Africa early in the colonial period (before 1650), but they eventually fostered successful integration into colonial society. At first the primary activity of confraternities in the seventeenth century focused on meeting their enslaved members' desperate need for assistance in sickness and at death. Even more fundamentally, confraternities had two essential goals: bringing a diverse range of people into a Christian society and providing communal help for the souls of members. These goals were met by confraternities dedicated to the Holy Sacrament, which were open to all residents of any given town. The members and leaders of several confraternities in mining towns, such as Immaculate Conception in Parral and the Humility and Patience of Christ in San Luis Potosí, came from a wide variety of local workers, including Indians and mestizos. Although membership in a confraternity designated as Afromexican may have not been an individual's only source of personal or communal identity, race did influence an individual's experience in a confraternity. The term "mulatto," which suggests a Spanish-speaker of mixed descent, implies integration into colonial society. This label was much more commonly used by Spanish authorities in the eighteenth century than "black" or "*negro*." Confraternities did not maintain the label "black" or references to African cultures such as Zape into the eighteenth century.

In fact, confraternities led by Spaniards associated with regions in Spain and certain advocations of the Virgin were more concerned about holding on to a connection between the Old and New Worlds than Afromexican confraternities were. Afromexican confraternities also lacked ties to a specific locale, a characteristic of Indian rural confraternities. Thus, it could be argued that a confraternity referred to as *de los mulatos* more closely approximated an institution formed entirely out of a New World identity and the colonial experience, in contrast to Spanish confraternities that emphasized ties to Spain or Indian confraternities that may have helped maintain some pre-conquest associations. In the colonial period, New Spain was always divided by regions with different histories and patterns of economic development. Race and racial divisions in New Spain also varied by city, town, village, and region. No one town or individual can possibly express the variety of racial identities and hierarchies in formation in the colonial era.

Appendix

Afromexican confraternities founded in New Spain, 1586–1730s

Town	Church	Confraternity	Date Founded (if known)
Acambaro	Augustinian	Saint Nicolás Tolentino	by 1679
Acapulco	Parish Church	Saint Nicolás Tolentino	1691
Aguascalientes	Our Lady of Mercy(?)	Santa Efigenia	NA
Apa	Our Lady of Mount Carmel(?)	Our Lady of Mount Carmel	by 1683
Celaya	Hospital de San Juan de Dios	Our Lady of Tránsito	by 1679
Cerro San Pedro	Chapel of Saint Nicolás	Saint Nicolás Tolentino	1651
Chamacuaro	Augustinian	Saint Nicolás Tolentino	1667
Chilpancingo	Parish Church	Saint Nicolás Tolentino	by 1687
Mexico City	Santa Veracruz	Exaltation of the Holy True Cross and the Tears of Saint Peter	NA[1]
Mexico City	Hospital of the Marquis of the Valley	Our Lady of the Immaculate Conception	1600
Mexico City	Hospital de San Juan de Dios	Our Lady of the Sorrows	by 1706
Mexico City	Santa Catalina Martir	Precious Blood of Christ	1665
Mexico City	Mercedarian	Saint Joseph	by 1706
Mexico City	Augustinian	Saint Nicolás of Mount Calvary	by 1668
Mexico City	Mercedarian	Saint Efigenia	

continued

Town	Church	Confraternity	Date Founded (if known)
Mexico City	Dominican	Holy Christ of the Expiration	1602
Minas de San Pedro, Palmar de Vega	parish church	Saint Nicolás Tolentino	by 1679
Oaxaca	Hospital of Saint Damian/own church	Our Lady of the Snow	by 1660
Oaxaca	Carmen	Our Lady of Mount Carmel(?)	by 1671
Oaxaca	Blood of Christ	NA	NA
Ocotlan	parish church	Holy Burial	by 1709
Orizaba(?)	parish church	Our Lady of Solitude	1707
Patzcuaro	El Salvador	Most Holy Trinity	1642
Pinzándaro	Parish Church	Our Lady of Solitude	by 1680
Puebla de los Angeles	Jesuit college	Our Lady of the Annunciation	1663
Querétaro	Franciscan nuns	Our Lady of Tránsito	1686
Querétaro	Franciscan	Saint Benedict	by 1679
Salvatierra	Franciscan	Saint Nicolás Tolentino	1673
Salvatierra	Augustinian	Our Lady of Remedies	1643
Salvatierra	Parish Church	Saint Peter	1677
San Christobal, Chiapas	NA	Saint Nicolás Tolentino	NA
San Joseph Parral	Hospital de San Juan de Dios	Our Lady of the Immaculate Conception	1650s
San Juan Perivan	Parish Church	Holy Sacrament	1648
San Luis Potosí	Parish Church	Our Lady of Solitude	1606
San Luis Potosí	Parish Church	Humility and Patience of Christ	1657
San Miguel el Grande	parish church	Our Lady of Solitude	by 1668
San Miguel el Grande	Franciscan	Saint Benedict	1646
San Pedro Cholula	parish church	Saint Joseph	by 1720
Silao	Chapel of Saint Nicolás	Saint Nicolás Tolentino	NA
Sultepec	parish church	Our Lady of the Rosary	by 1685

Tampico	parish church	Saint Nicolás Tolentino	by 1683
Taxco	parish church	Saint Nicolás Tolentino	1644
Tejuipilco	parish church	Our Lady of Solitude	by 1685
Teloloapan	parish church	Saint Nicolás Tolentino	by 1685
Temescaltepec	parish church	Our Lady of Solitude	by 1685
Tepeaca	parish church	Virgin of the Charity	by 1643
Tlaxcala	Franciscan	Our Lady of the Rosary	1632
Toluca	Mercedarian	Our Lady of Mercy	by 1715
Toluca	Hospital de San Juan de Dios	Saint Efigenia	1698
Valladolid	Cathedral, Merced, Santa Veracruz	Incarnation of Our Lord and Saint Blaise	1610
Valladolid	Franciscan	Our Lady of the Rosary	1586
Valladolid	Augustinian	Saint Nicolás Tolentino	1635
Valle de Gasindo	Augustinian	Saint Nicolás Tolentino	by 1670
Varriquero	parish church	Our Lady of the Solitude	by 1705
Veracruz	Mercedarian	Our Lady of the Immaculate Conception and the Humility of Christ	1659
Veracruz	Franciscan	Saint Benedict and the Exaltation of the Cross	1636
Zacatecas	parish church	Our Lady of the Immaculate Conception	1661
Zacatecas	parish church	Saint John of the Penitence	1635
Zinagua	parish church	Saint John the Baptist	by 1730s

1. NA=Data not available

Source: Archivo General de la Nación; Casa de Morelos; Archivo Histórico del Arzobispado de México; Archivo de la Parroquia del Sagrario de Celaya; Archivo Histórico de la Provincia Franciscana de Michoacán; Archivo Histórico del Arquidiócesis de Oaxaca; Archivo Histórico del Arzobispado de San Luis Potosí; Archivo Histórico del Sagrario de San José de Toluca; Archivo Municipal del Hidalgo del Parral; Archivo Parroquial de San Pedro Cholula; Archivo Parroquial de Santa Prisca.

Notes

Introduction

1. Sandoval, *De instauranda aethiopum salute*, 107, 251. In the early 1600s, Sandoval founded the first Jesuit college in Cartagena to train missionaries to work with disembarking African slaves.

2. Ibid., 109, 196–97.

3. Cardozo, "The Lay Brotherhoods of Colonial Bahia," 12–30; Mulvey, "Slave Confraternities in Brazil"; Mulvey and Crouch, "Black Solidarity"; Russell-Wood, "Examination of Selected Statutes of Three African Brotherhoods"; Scarano, "Black Brotherhoods: Integration or Contradiction?"; Ribeiro, "Relations of the Negro with Christianity in Portuguese America"; Russell-Wood, "Black and Mulatto Brotherhoods in Colonial Brazil: A Study in Collective Behavior," 567–602. Howard's *Changing History* is another example of the importance of Afro-Latino organizations—in this case, political institutions.

4. For example, Muir, *Civic Ritual in Renaissance Venice*; Barnes, "De Poenitentibus Civitatis Massaliae"; Weissman, *Ritual Brotherhood*; Trexler, *Public Life in Renaissance Florence*; Banker, *Death in the Community*; Terpstra, *Lay Confraternities and Civic Religion in Renaissance Bologna*; Little, *Liberty, Charity, Fraternity*, 27, 57, 69, 80–81, 83; Flynn, *Sacred Charity*, 11–13.

5. I do not italicize the term "mestizo" because it is commonly used in English.

6. Lewis, *A Hall of Mirrors*.

7. Bennett, *Africans in Colonial Mexico*.

8. See von Mentz, *Pueblos de indios*; Valdez Aguilar, *Sinaloa: negritud y olvido*; Valdés, "Negros y mulatos en el noreste de México" and *Esclavos negros en Saltillo*; Soriano Hernández, "Aportes sobre el mestizaje de esclavos africanos en Chiapas colonial"; Redondo, *Negritud en Campeche*; Naveda Chávez-Hita, *Esclavos negros*; Herrera, *Presencia y esclavitud del negro en La Huasteca*; Gómez Danés, *Negros y mulatos en el Nuevo Reino de Leon, 1600–1795*; Gálvez Jiménez, *Celaya: Sus raíces africanas*; and Guevara Sanginés, *Guanajuato diverso*. See also Montiel, ed., *Encuentro nacional de afromexicanistas*. For a complete bibliography, see Vinson and Vaughn, *Afroméxico*.

9. Vinson, *Bearing Arms for His Majesty*.

10. Cope, *The Limits of Racial Domination*.

11. Vinson, *Bearing Arms for His Majesty*, 212–17, 226–28.

12. Ibid., 6.

13. Ibid., 4.

14. Vinson found that Afromexicans virtually monopolized these trades in some towns; Vinson, *Bearing Arms for His Majesty*, 114.

15. Menchaca, *Recovering History, Constructing Race*.

16. Vinson, *Bearing Arms for His Majesty*, 6.

17. Herman Bennett has argued more strongly for the existence of African communities

in New Spain in his Ph.D. dissertation, "Lovers, Family and Friends: The Formation of Afro-México, 1580–1810."

18. Lewis, *A Hall of Mirrors*, 33–34.

19. See the case of Mateo de Aguilar, a wealthy seventeenth-century testator in Mexico City, described in chapter 3.

20. Wilder, *In the Company of Black Men*, 77–78.

21. This social and cultural connection existed alongside other kinds of social ties that have been described in recent works dealing with people of African descent in Mexico. Herman Bennett argues that Africans and mulattos showed a sense of connection after being brought to New Spain by those they chose to marry and the witnesses they chose when they married. For other studies of race and class in New Spain, see Chance and Taylor, "Estate and Class in a Colonial City, Oaxaca in 1792"; Anderson, "Race and Social Stratification"; Jackson, "Race/Caste and the Creation of Meaning of Identity in Colonial Spanish America"; McCaa, "Calidad, Clase, and Marriage in Colonial Mexico"; Seed, "The Social Dimensions of Race"; and Chance, "The Ecology of Race and Class in Late Colonial Oaxaca."

22. Eire, *From Madrid to Purgatory*. Testaments show that Mexico City testators reached the peak of confraternal devotion by the mid-seventeenth century, a generation or two after their Spanish models. Brian Larkin's thesis on eighteenth-century wills charts the decline to its ultimate end in the nineteenth century. Larkin, "Baroque and Reformed Catholicism."

23. Lockhart, "Introduction," in *The Provinces of Early Mexico*, ed. Lockhart and Altman, 4–21.

24. Espejo-Ponce Hunt, "The Processes of Development of Yucatan, 1600–1700," 42–43.

Chapter 1. Blood Brothers: Afromexican Confraternities in the Seventeenth Century

1. "Religious Painting," in *Catholic Encyclopedia,* available online at www.newadvent.org, especially the section "The Baroque School."

2. Larkin, "Baroque and Reformed Catholicism," 37.

3. Moreno Navarro, *La antigua hermandad de los negros en Sevilla*, 50–52; and Sancho de Sopranis, *La cofradía de los morenos*. The confraternities in Triana and in Cádiz were dedicated to the Virgin of the Rosary.

4. Cortés López, *La esclavitud negra en la España peninsular del siglo XVI*, 20, 103.

5. Pike, *Aristocrats and Traders*, 1.

6. Ibid., 170, 172.

7. Cervantes, *Novelas ejemplares*, 40–41. Pike cites several other works of Cervantes that describe slaves in *Aristocrats and Traders*, 178–79.

8. Moreno Navarro, *La antigua hermandad de los negros en Sevilla*, 35.

9. Camacho Martinez, *La hermandad de los mulatos de Sevilla*, 60.

10. See chapter 3.

11. The source for all later accounts of the life of Aguiar y Seixas and his strange obses-

sions is his confessor, Joseph de Lezamis, who actually sought to portray the deceased archbishop in a saintly light in *Breve relacion*.

12. "Libro de la cofradía de Santa Efigenia, Toluca, 1698–1712," Archivo Histórico del Sagrario de San José de Toluca, caja 85, f. 5; "Libro de la cofradía de la preciosa sangre de Cristo, Apaseo, 1679–1772," Casa de Morelos (hereafter CM), caja 3, leg. 7, f. 4; "Constituciones de la cofradía del transito, Querétaro, 1686," Archivo General de la Nación (hereafter AGN), Bienes Nacionales, vol. 1028, exp. 6, f. 1; "Autos fechos sobre las constituciones de la cofradía de San Nicolas, Acapulco, 1691," AGN, Bienes Nacionales, vol. 1028, exp. 26, sf.

13. "Libro de la cofradía de San Nicolas Tolentino, Taxco, 1644–1699," Archivo Histórico de la Parroquia de Santa Prisca, caja 100, s.f.

14. "Libro de la Cofradía del santuario de la sta. Cruz del Calvario y Jesus Nazareno, Pátzcuaro, 1683–1721," CM, Cofradías, Asientos, caja 3, exp. 9.

15. Lezamis, *Breve relación*, chapter entitled "Humilidad y Pobreza" (no page numbers). However, this courtesy did not extend to women: he was eager to chastise a mestiza for not covering her head.

16. Lezamis, *Breve relación*, chapter entitled "De su castidad, mortificacion, y penetencia" (no page numbers).

17. "Libro de la cofradía de benditas animas, Itzapaluca," Archivo Histórico del Arzobispado de México (hereafter AHAM), caja 146CL, exp. 3.

18. The lack of interest Jesuits expressed in Afromexicans contrasts with their interest in Africans in Cartagena and Lima.

19. Butler, *Butler's Lives of the Saints*, I: 525–26.

20. Bowser, *The African Slave in Colonial Peru*, 179, 249.

21. See examples in "Libro de Bautismos de castas, Morelia, 1652–1670," LDS roll #644687. The feast day of Santa Efigenia is celebrated in Peru today; she is the patron of Afroperuvian dance.

22. See Grimes, *Symbol and Conquest*, 62–69.

23. Wilder, *In the Company of Black Men*, 122.

24. Butler, *Butler's Lives of the Saints* (1956), II: 30–31.

25. Fra-Molinero, *La imagen de los negros*, 77.

26. See "Libro de la cofradía de San Benito de Palermo, San Miguel del Grande, 1733–1793," Archivo Histórico de la Provincia Franciscana de Michoacán (hereafter AHPFM), frontispiece.

27. Fra-Molinero, *La imagen de los negros*, 77.

28. Ibid., 77, 90.

29. Ibid., 86, 99, 101.

30. Ibid., 92–3.

31. See numerous examples in "Visita de Aguiar y Seixas, 1679," CM, Visitas, caja 57, exp. 13.

32. "Confraternity of the Holy Rosary," in *Catholic Encyclopedia*, available online at www.newadvent.org.

33. García Ayluardo, "Confraternity, Cult and Crown," 132–39.

34. See Larkin, "Baroque and Reformed Catholicism," 34–55, for a detailed description of the senses and ritual in baroque New Spain.

35. Mitchell, *Passional Culture*, 73–74.

36. Trexler, *Public Life in Renaissance Florence*, 359–60.

37. Cohn, "The Black Death: End of a Paradigm," 705–6.

38. "Flagellants," in *Catholic Encyclopedia,* available online at www.newadvent.org.

39. Webster Verdi, *Art and Ritual in Golden Age Spain*, 25.

40. "Flagellants."

41. Henderson, *Piety and Charity in Late Medieval France*; Terpstra, *Lay Confraternities and Civic Religion in Renaissance Bologna*; Weissman, *Ritual Brotherhood.*

42. Weissman, *Ritual Brotherhood*, 27, 30, 53, 59, 88.

43. Ibid., 74–76, 123, 129, 151.

44. Henderson, *Piety and Charity in Late Medieval France*, 109–10.

45. Ibid., 152–54.

46. Webster Verdi, *Art and Ritual in Golden Age Spain*, 26–27.

47. Ibid., 27.

48. Flynn, *Sacred Charity*, 127–28.

49. Burkhart, *Holy Wednesday*, 43.

50. Flynn, *Sacred Charity*, 132–33.

51. Levine, *Vale of Tears*, 108.

52. Lopez Pulido, *The Sacred World of the Penitentes*, 22, 40.

53. Levine, *Vale of Tears*, 211–12.

54. Sepulveda, "La Cofradía de San Nicolás Tolentino," 8.

55. Ibid., 8–10.

56. I thank Bonnie Clark for this insight.

57. Larkin, "Baroque and Reformed Catholicism," 52.

58. Larkin's work cites several speeches of the Archbishops Nuñez and Lorenzano. Some of these sermons were made early in their tenure when their reforming tendencies were at their peak. Mexican practice may have appeared very foreign to them.

59. García Ayluardo, "Confraternity, Cult and Crown," 175–76.

60. Flynn, *Sacred Charity*, 141–45.

61. Burkhart, *Holy Wednesday*, 22, 29.

62. Flynn, *Sacred Charity*, 132.

63. Webster Verdi, *Art and Ritual in Golden Age Spain*, 15–16.

64. See many examples in "Visita de Francisco Rubio y Salinas, 1752–1753" and "Visita de Fray Joseph de Lanziego y Equilas, 1715," caja 20CL, both in AHAM.

65. "Libros de la cofradía de la Limpia Concepción y Santa Ana, Zacatecas, 1695–1858," Archivo de la Parroquia de Santo Domingo, Zacatecas, cajas 136 and 137. *Repartimientos de insignias* took place every year and were recorded regularly in these books.

66. "Libros de la cofradía de San Juan de la Penitencia, Zacatecas, 1651–1742," Archivo de la Parroquia de Santo Domingo, Zacatecas, caja 138, s.f.

67. Today "*cepo*" is translated as stocks, fetters, or shackles. However, the *Tesoro de la lengua castellano* written by Sebastián de Covarrubias Orozco and published in 1611 stresses the importance of the *cepo* as the small column of stone "where Our Redeemer was

bound to be beaten" (see edition edited by Felipe C. R. Maldoñado, 300–301). Covarrubias also mentions that *cepo* could mean stocks or fetters.

68. Appleton and Bridges, *Symbolism in Liturgical Art,* 29, 49, 55, 67, 93.

69. Ibid., 49.

70. "Libro de la cofradía de Nuestra Señora de la Candelaria, 1663–1679," LDS roll #708482, part 2, s.f.

71. "Libro de la cofradía del santo entierro, Taxco, 1602–1615," Archivo Histórico de la Parroquia de Santa Prisca, caja 100, book 2.

72. "Libro de la cofradía de San Juan de la Penitencia, Zacatecas, 1651–1742," Archivo Parroquial de Zacatecas, caja 138, Constitution.

73. Flynn, *Sacred Charity*, 128–30.

74. "Mandato del Obispo de Michoacán, San Luis Potosí, 1768," Archivo Histórico del Arzobispado de San Luis Potosí, caja 27, exp. 39, fs. 8–9.

75. "Petición de Pedro Joseph de Estrada y Bernadino Delgado, Zacatecas, 1753," Archivo del Estado de Zacatecas, Ayuntamiento, Cargos y Oficios, Gremios, s.f.

76. "Petición de la cofradía de la santisima Trinidad, Morelia, 1770," CM, caja 588, exp. 3. s.f.

77. "Petición de Josef Ventura Bertel, Veracruz, 1792," AGN, Reales Cedulas Originales, vol. 159, exp. 34, fs. 49–73.

78. Vinson, *Bearing Arms for His Majesty*, 206.

79. "Petición de Josef Ventura Bertel, Veracruz, 1792," AGN, Reales Cedulas Originales, vol. 159, exp. 34, fs. 49–73.

80. Fra-Molinero, *La imagen de los negros*, 97.

81. For Esperanza's story, see Bristol, "Negotiating Authority in New Spain," 137–49.

82. Ibid., 141.

83. "Constitución de la preciosa sangre de Cristo, Texcoco, 1713," AGN, Bienes Nacionales, vol. 444, exp. 4, f. 2.

84. "Constitución de la cofradía de nuestra señora de la soledad, Leon, 1584," CM, caja 589, leg. 4, s.f.; "Ordinario ecclesiastico contra Miguel de la Cruz, San Miguel el Grande, 1668," CM, caja 68, exp. 4, s.f.

85. "Oratorio de San Felipe Neri sobre imagen milagroso de ecce homo, San Miguel el Grande, 1733," CM, caja 581, leg. 4, s.f. refers to the date of founding and a long conflict over an image involving Soledad and the Oratorio of Saint Felipe Neri in the 1720s and 1730s.

86. See "Rosalino Antonio Zofallo mulato libre vecino de la villa de León sobre el derecho, León, 1790," CM, caja 595, leg. 136, fs. 1–5. See chapter 7 for further confraternal conflicts in this region.

87. "Memorial de todas las cofradías, Mexico City, 1706," AGN, Bienes Nacionales, vol. 1574, exp. 2, f. 15.

88. "Libro de la cofradía del Rosario, Orizaba, 1722," Archivo de la Parroquia de San Miguel, Orizaba, caja 119, exp. 2, s.f.

89. "Consitución de la cofradía de santissimo sacramento, Zapotlan, 1739," CM, caja 2, leg. 3, s.f.

90. "Constituciones de la cofradía del Rosario, Apantzingan, 1734," CM, caja 1256, exp. 13, s.f.

91. "Erección de la cofradía y esclavitud del santissimo sacramento, San Miguel Octopa, 1739," CM, caja 1256, exp. 21, s.f.

92. "Cartas de la esclavitud de la Virgen María, Puebla, 1669," Collección J. M. Lafragua, Benemérita Universidad Autónoma de Puebla, roll #4, leg. 163, s.f.

93. Alegre, *Historia de la Compañía de Jesus en Nueva España*, vol. II, 440–41.

94. "Libro de la Cofradía de Nuestra Señora del Carmen . . . Mexico City, 1610," Archivo Histórico de los Carmelitas Descalzos en México, Libros Imprentas Doctrinas 34, fs. 1–10.

95. Alegre, *Historia de la Compañía de Jesus en Nueva España*, vol. II, 440–41.

96. "Varios asuntos referentes al hospital de San Cosme y San Damiano, Oaxaca, 1660," Archivo Histórico de la Arquidiocesis de Oaxaca, caja 18, exp. 486, f. 2.

Chapter 2. Sisters: Women in Confraternities

1. "Proceso contra Magdalena Bolanos mulata libre acusada de pactar con el Diablo, Pinzándaro, 1778," CM, caja 834, exp. 21, f. 1–3. See chapter 7 for more information on the region of Pinzándaro.

2. Scholarship on nuns in Mexico goes back at least to early-twentieth-century analyses of Sor Juana Inéz de la Cruz. Other historians of Mexican women are Joséfina Muriel and Asunción Lavrin. Nuns have recently received more scholarly attention, especially surrounding the 300th anniversary of Sor Juana's death in 1995. Recent publications have emphasized writings produced by Hispanic nuns. See Arenal and Schlau, eds., *Untold Sisters*; Arenal and Schlau, eds., *Thin Lines, Bedeviled Words*; and Tudela, *Colonial Angels*.

3. See Lavrin, *Latin American Women: Historical Perspectives* and "Sexuality in Colonial Mexico: A Church Dilemma," in *Sexuality and Marriage in Colonial Latin America*, 3–22.

4. The connection between religious women and the public in colonial Peru is treated most compellingly in Burns, *Colonial Habits*.

5. An exception is the life of Rose of Lima. See Morgan, *Spanish American Saints*.

6. Cope, *The Limits of Racial Domination*, 36–37.

7. This change is explored more specifically for Valladolid in chapters 4 and 5.

8. López Muñoz, *Las cofradías de la parroquia de Santa María Magdalena de Granada*, 247.

9. Lockhart, *The Nahuas after the Conquest*, 218–29, especially 226–28, where Lockhart discusses seventeenth-century deputies in a cofradía in Tula. Indian women's leadership of confraternities continues to the present.

10. Wilder, *In the Company of Black Men*.

11. Carroll, *Blacks in Colonial Veracruz*, 22, 29.

12. Thornton, *A Kongolese Saint Anthony*.

13. Mulvey, "Slave Confraternities in Brazil," 46–47.

14. Landes, *The City of Women*.

15. Flynn, *Sacred Charity*, 135.

16. Terpstra, *Lay Confraternities and Civic Religion in Renaissance Bologna*, 130–32.

17. Dinan, "Overcoming Gender Limitations," 97–113.

18. See examples in "Libro de asientos de la cofradía Jesús Nazareno de las tres caidas, Orizaba, 1678–1715," caja 25 and "Libro de asientos de la cofradía de Benditas Animas, Orizaba," caja 115, both in Archivo de la Parroquia de San Miguel, Orizaba. Both show two-thirds female membership. The Confraternity of the Sweet Name of Jesus in Guanajuato had a mostly female membership (see "Libro de la cofradía de la dulce nombre de Jesús, 1730–1767," Guanajuato, CM, caja 1247). The Confraternity of the Cord of Saint Francis in Celaya had mostly female members (see "Libro de la cofradía de la cordon de San Francisco, Celaya, 1736," CM, caja 1247). Seventy-five percent of the members of the Confraternity of Our Lady of the Transformation in Zacatecas were female (see "Libro de asientos de cofrades de Nuestra Señora del Tránsito en el Convento de San Agustín, Zacatecas, 1721–1837," in Archivo de la Parroquia de Santo Domingo, Zacatecas, caja 146). The Confraternity of Saint Veracruz of Carpenters had mostly female members and was obviously not restricted to carpenters (see "Libro de Asientos de la cofradía de la Santa Veracruz de carpinteros, Zacatecas, 1673–1768," in Archivo de la Parroquia de Santo Domingo, Zacatecas, caja 152). Other confraternities for whom women constituted a large majority include the Confraternity of Our Lady of the Assumption in Acultzingo and the Confraternity of the Purification in Celaya (see "Libro de la Cofradía de Nuestra Señora de la Assumpción, Acultzingo, 1667–1776," LDS roll #725500 and "Informes sobre la cofradía de la Purificación, Celaya," CM, caja 833, leg. 5). Margaret Chowning also mentions several confraternities in Michoacán dominated by women in the late eighteenth century, including the Cofradía de la Merced in Valladolid (see "From Colonial Cofradías to Porfirian Pious Organizations").

19. Before 1550, the ecclesiastical hierarchy tried cloistering Nahua noblewomen in schools. This was abandoned until the moderately successful founding of the Convent of Corpus Christi for *indias cacicas* in 1724. See Lavrin, "Indian Brides of Christ: Creating New Spaces for Indigenous Women in New Spain," 225–61.

20. See also the "black nun" Esperanza, chapter 1.

21. "Profession of Gertrudis Joseph, Morelia, 1708," CM, Professiones.

22. "Solicita licencia para que seis indias o mulatas libres puedan servir en dicho convento, Mexico City, 1600," AGN, Bienes Nacionales, vol. 78, exp. 39, s.f.

23. "Un testador dispuso por clausula de su testamento que una mulata su esclava, Mexico City, 1640," AHN, vol. 725, Jacinto Curiel, #109, sf.

24. "Libros de la cofradía del Rosario, Mexico City, 1659–1761," AHAM, caja 146.

25. Further study of females as heads of households is necessary to clarify the social roles of *casta* women in general. See Arrom, *The Women of Mexico City*, 129–34.

26. Working-class Spaniards at this time also were not addressed as "Don" or "Doña." However, in Valladolid's notarial records, their surnames often connect them to well-known *casta* families, and I believe that many women property owners mentioned in these records were not Spanish.

27. See for example, "Venta de solar de Antonio Ramirez mulato libre a María de Pedraza, mulata libre soltera, Morelia, 1687," Archivo Histórico de Notarías, Morelia (hereafter AHNM), libro 39, f. 311; and "Venta de solar de Blasa Pérez mulata libre a doña Francisca de Figuerora, Morelia, 1708," AHNM, libro 55, f. 245, among many others.

28. See "Testament of María de Villegas, Morelia, 1760," AHNM, libro 121, f. 224;

"Testament of Durvina de Salceda, Morelia, 1711," AHNM, libro 58, f. 583; "Testament of Juana de Orozco y Conparan, Morelia, 1709," AHNM, libro 56, f. 208. Women in Valladolid continued to control property in the eighteenth century, even after they lost official control of confraternities. Perhaps they began to maintain covert economic control, similar to forms of subtle economic power Spanish women exercized through their large donations to all kinds of religious institutions.

29. "Venta de negra esclava Esperanza, Morelia, 1632," AHNM, libro 18, f. 198.

30. "Testament of Pascuala de Ochoa, Morelia, 1734," AHNM, libro 83, f. 29.

31. "Testament of Fracisco de Mondragón, Morelia, 1763," AHNM, libro 126, f. 275.

32. Behar's "Sexual Witchcraft, Colonialism, and Women's Powers" describes the perceptions of *morisca* or *mulata* women as sorceresses and makers of love potions.

33. San Luis Potosí, located 250 miles from Mexico City and 120 miles from Zacatecas and San Miguel Allende, was settled in the late sixteenth and early seventeenth centuries. In the colonial period, the journey from Mexico City to San Luis Potosí took two weeks. The population fluctuated due to ups and downs in the local mining industry. A 1680 visit by Bishop Aguiar y Seixas reported 2,812 *indios*, 1,472 *españoles*, 579 mestizos, 181 *negros*, 738 *mulatos*, and two *chinos*, for a total of 5,783 residents, *Visitas*, 1680, CM.

34. Palmer, *Slaves of the White God*, 76.

35. "Libro de la Cofradía de la Humildad y Paciencia de Cristo Nuestro Redentor, San Luis Potosí, 1657–1812," Archivo Histórico de la Parroquia del Sagrario, caja 146, sf.

36. "Constituciones de la cofradía de la coronación Veracruz, 1636," AGN, Ramo Clero Regular y Secular, vol. 16, exp. 6, fs. 475–85.

37. Ibid.

38. Ibid.

39. María Elena Díaz found that some seventeenth-century slaves in Cuba held the title of king throughout their lives, showing some recognition of "Old World rankings and status" and perhaps even "a small constituency among the local Diaspora of fellow enslaved Angolans willing to recognize [their] rank." See Díaz, *The Virgin, the King and the Royal Slaves of El Cobre*, 46–47.

40. Osowski, "Saints of the Republic."

41. "Libro de la cofradía de buen camino, Orizaba, 1722," Archivo de la Parroquia de San Miguel, Orizaba, caja 118, s.f. See chapter 7 for more information on Orizaba confraternities.

42. Another Confraternity of the Good Path existed in Veracruz, suggesting that the activities of the confraternity somehow helped people along the important road from Veracruz to the capital, as indicated by the name "Buen Camino [Good Path]." However, these activities were not specified. Advocations for confraternities often had more than spiritual implications. The muleteers of early-seventeenth-century Mexico City patronized a cofradía called Nuestra Señora de la Guía [Our Lady of the Guide]. See the books of José Rodríguez, notary #555, AN, for 1606 and 1607.

43. This is not the only case where this type of donation made an organization more mainstream. The same thing occurred when a black sister donated property to the Cofradía de Santa Ana in Zacatecas in the early eighteenth century and changed the cofradía from one designated as *de negros* to a Spanish brotherhood.

44. "Libro de Cofradía de la Escuela de Cristo del Santo Sepulcro, San Miguel Analco, 1792–1810," Archivo Parroquial de San Miguel Analco, Puebla.

45. This cofradía was dedicated to the worship of the rope belt of San Francisco. "Libro de la cofradía de nuestro Padre San Francisco fundada en la capilla de los naturales, 1670–1694," AHPFM, caja 10, s.f.

46. "Gertrudis Michaela Pícaro mayordoma, Maravatío, 1770," CM, caja 588, sf.

47. Gerhard, *A Guide to the Historical Geography of New Spain*, 172–74.

48. "Licenses, Morelia, 1730," CM, caja 1249, leg. 1, sf.

49. Cline, *Colonial Culhuacan*, 54.

50. "Libro de cofradía del Señor de Chavarrieta, Taxco, 1821," and "Libro de la hermandad de Nuestra Señora de Guadalupe, Taxco, 1735," both in Archivo Histórico de la Parroquia de Santa Prisca, Taxco, cajas 101 and 103, s.f.

51. "Constituciones de la cofradía de la coronación, Veracruz, 1636," AGN, Ramo Clero Regular y Secular, vol. 16, exp. 6, fs. 475–85.

52. "Libros de la cofradía de San Benito de Palermo, San Miguel el Grande, 1698–1793," AHPFM, cajas 16, 17, 18. San Miguel was located in the agriculturally prosperous Bajío region. In the colonial era, San Miguel was in the Diocese of Michoacán; now it is in the state of Guanajuato. In the 1500s, San Miguel was one of the most northern settlements in New Spain, an outpost against Chichimec resistance and eventually a stop on the way to mining towns farther north. Like other towns in the Bajío region, San Miguel had a large *casta* population that worked on the haciendas that surrounded the city.

53. "Libro de la cofradía de San Benito de Palermo, San Miguel el Grande, 1698–1793," AHPFM, caja 16.

54. See chapter 4 for the history of this cofradía and its decline in the eighteenth century.

55. "Documentos sobre la obra del retablo de la congregación de la esclavitud, Puebla, 1614–1789," Colección J. M. Lafragua, Benemérita Universidad Autónoma de Puebla, roll #6, leg. 155, sf.

56. Ibid., leg. 167.

57. "Libro de la Cofradía de la Humildad y Paciencia de Cristo Nuestro Redentor, San Luis Potosí, 1657–1812," Archivo de la Parroquia del Sagrario de Celaya, caja 146, s.f.

58. "Libro de la Cofradía de la Humildad y Paciencia de Cristo Nuestro Redentor, San Luis Potosí, 1657–1812," Archivo de la Parroquia del Sagrario de Celaya, caja 146, leg. 6, s.f.

59. Ibid.

60. "Cofradías y Archicofradías, San Luis Potosí, 1708," CM, caja 1255, leg. 3, sf.; "Cofradía de la Humildad, San Luis Potosí, 1828–1829," CM, caja 833, legs. 16 and 25.

61. "Libro de la Cofradía de la Humildad y Paciencia de Cristo Nuestro Redentor, San Luis Potosí, 1657–1812," Archivo Histórico de la Parroquia del Sagrario, caja 146, leg. 6, s.f.

62. "Dress was a visual measure of difference as it visually communicated self and social identities (religious, gendered, political, etc.) in contact and colonial period contacts. Yet not everyone agreed on 'proper' dress in such contexts; colonial officials regulated dress to distinguish colonized from colonizer, while colonial subjects . . . manipulated dress to blur

those divisions" (see Dipaolo Loren, "Social Skins: Orthodoxies and Practices of Dressing in the Early Colonial Lower Mississippi Valley," 172–89).

63. Thompson, ed., *Thomas Gage's Travels in the New World*, 68–69.

64. Konetzke, *Colección de documentos para la historia de la formación social de hispanoamérica*, 2:182–83.

65. Garner, "Zacatecas, 1750–1821," 69, 91.

66. "Libros de la Cofradía de San Juan de la Penitencia de mulatos, Zacatecas, 1651–1742," Archivo de la Parroquia de Santo Domingo, Zacatecas, caja 138, s.f.

67. Ibid.

68. Ibid.

69. "Libros de la Cofradía de Santa Ana de negros despues españoles, Zacatecas, 1695–1858," Archivo de la Parroquia de Santo Domingo, Zacatecas, cajas 136 and 137, s.f.

70. "Libro de la cofradía de San Nicolás Tolentino, Taxco, 1644–1699," Archivo Histórico de la Parroquia de Santa Prisca, caja 100, s.f.

71. Gerhard, *A Guide to the Historical Geography of New Spain*, 253–54. Gerhard reports that 100 Spanish *vecinos*, 900 Indian miners, and 700 negro slaves lived in and around Taxco in 1570, during the era of the area's peak years of silver production. The mines declined in production until 1748 and, like Parral, Taxco retained a large *casta* population through its lean years.

72. "Libro de la cofradía de San Nicolás Tolentino, Taxco, 1644–1699," Archivo Histórico de la Parroquia de Santa Prisca, caja 103, s.f.

73. Larkin, "Baroque and Reformed Catholicism," 168.

74. Ibid., 7–9.

75. Ibid., 161.

76. Ibid., 4–33.

77. See Note 18.

78. "Patentes de la Cofradía de San Nicolás Tolentino, Morelia, 1767–1798," CM, caja 1265, leg. 2, s.f.

79. Vinson, *Bearing Arms for His Majesty*, 80–81.

80. Two wills for Lorenzo Sendejas: Morelia, 1762, AHNM, libro 126, f. 179 and Morelia, 1791, AHNM, libro 189, f. 564.

81. "Petición para pedir limosnas, Morelia, 1663," CM, caja 7, leg. 5, sf.

82. Osowski, "Licensed Saints," 8–9.

83. See "Records of the Vela Perpetua, Morelia, 1800–1899," CM, cajas 818–36.

84. Chowning, "From Colonial Cofradías to Porfirian Pious Organizations."

Chapter 3. Africans in Mexico City: From Rebellion to Religious Conformity

1. Inez de la Cruz, *Obra selecta*, 234–41, 247–53.

2. Meléndez, "Sor Juana y los negros," in *Signos de Iberamérica*, 84–88.

3. See Fra-Molinero, *La imagen de los negros*, 19–53. Some dismiss the African pidgin used in Sor Juana's poems as condescension. It is perhaps more revealing to see how and where Africans surfaced in her work. Cope, *The Limits of Racial Domination*, 11.

4. Cruz, *Obras completas*, 241.

5. Harris, *Aztecs, Moors, and Christians*, 218–19. Sor Juana's characters are given names like "Flacico," a favorite name given to slave characters in Spanish literature. Fra-Molinero, *La imagen de los negros*, 13, 26.

6. Vinson, *Bearing Arms for His Majesty*, 50–51, tells the story of a very successful family of black militiamen.

7. See untitled document, Mexico City, 1635, Archivo General de Notarías, Mexico City (hereafter AN), Andres Moreno, notary #374, vol. 2480, f. 14 that shows documentation signed by a Japanese resident. "Testament of Juan de Prado, Mexico City, 1652," AN, Toribio Cobian, notary #110, vol. 726 bis., f. 22 mentions local Chinese and Japanese business associates.

8. Mondragón Barrios, *Esclavos africanos*, 49.

9. Cope, *The Limits of Racial Domination*, 10, 13.

10. Palmer, *Slaves of the White God*, 46.

11. On elite confraternities in New Spain, see Bazarte Martínez, *Las cofradías de españoles*; García Ayluardo, "Ceremonia y cofradía: La Ciudad de México durante el siglo XVIII"; García Ayluardo, "A World of Images: Cult, Ritual and Society in Colonial Mexico City," 77–93; Luque Alcaide, "Recursos de la cofradía de Aránzazu de México ante la corona"; Lavrin, "La congregación de San Pedro"; Lavrin, "Worlds in Contrast: Rural and Urban Confraternities in Mexico at the End of the Eighteenth Century."

12. Fra-Molinero, *La imagen de los negros*, 19–53.

13. Vinson, *Bearing Arms for His Majesty*, 67.

14. Mondragón Barrios, *Esclavos africanos*, 62–63.

15. For legal discrimination against Afromexicans, see Davidson, "Negro Slave Control and Resistance in Colonial Mexico," 235–53; Love, "Legal Restrictions on Afro-Indian Relations in Colonial Mexico"; and Dusenberry, "Discriminatory Aspects of Legislation in Colonial Mexico." For stereotypes of criminals, see Stern, "*Gente de Color Quebrado*."

16. Mondragón Barrios, *Esclavos africanos*, 52–55, 63.

17. Scholes and Adams, *Advertimientos generales que los virreyes dejaron a sus sucesores para el gobierno de Nueva España*, 100. I thank Professor Sarah Cline for this reference.

18. Torquemada, *Monarchia Indiana*, cited in Querol y Rosa, "Negros y mulatos," 124–25.

19. Naveda Chávez-Hita, *Esclavos negros*, 125–29.

20. Querol y Rosa, "Negros y mulatos," 127–53 details this rebellion.

21. "Cuaderno formado de las listas de las cofradías, Mexico City, 1788," AGN, Bienes Nacionales, vol. 1170, exp. 5, sf.

22. Querol y Rosa, "Negros y mulatos," 145. As did the Yoruban slaves in Bahia, these rebels protested in front of buildings representing authority. See Reis, *Slave Rebellion in Brazil*.

23. Querol y Rosa, "Negros y mulatos," 128–31.

24. "Que los negros y mulatos no tengan cofradías, Mexico City, 1612," AGN, Ramo Ordenanzas, vol. 1, exp. 164, f. 146.

25. "Para que durante la semana santa no salgan en esta ciudad de mexico las cofradías de sangre, ni se azote a nadie, Mexico City, 1612," AGN, Ramo Ordenanzas, vol. 1, exp. 173, f. 150.

26. Querol y Rosa, "Negros y mulatos," 131–34.

27. Ibid., 135–36.

28. It is interesting to note that Isidoro Moreno (who concurs with Fra-Molinero) argues that Spanish authorities did not fear Africans or the fact that they organized into confraternities in Seville. The presence of Indians and heavier dependence on African labor may have changed this perspective in New Spain. See Moreno Navarro, *La antigua hermandad de los negros en Sevilla*, 40–41.

29. Cope, *The Limits of Racial Domination*, 155–57.

30. Cope, *The Limits of Racial Domination*, 156, citing Taylor, *Drinking, Homicide and Rebellion*, 112.

31. Harris, *Aztecs, Moors, and Christians*, 232.

32. Thompson, ed., *Thomas Gage's Travels in the New World*, 69–70.

33. Querol y Rosa, "Negros y mulatos," 143–44.

34. Moreno Navarro, *La antigua hermandad de los negros en Sevilla*, 43.

35. Harris, *Aztecs, Moors, and Christians*, 128–29.

36. Beginning in the early seventeenth century, Afro-Brazilians also conducted a ceremony to elect a "king of the Congo" organized by the Rosary brotherhoods. Africans in Bahia and Recife appointed kings, queens, "governors of each tribal nation and a retinue of sub-delegates and military officers . . . [with] a certain traditional power and jurisdiction over the black population in the urban centers of Brazil. . . . The Kings of the Congo provided a system of indirect African government duplicating and preserving the traditional African customs which contributed to the integration and solidarity of the blacks of Recife. . . . In encouraging these practices the brotherhoods allowed for the emergence of a black elite who provided leadership." Mulvey, "Slave Confraternities in Brazil," 46–48. Portuguese authorities permitted these coronations until the 1700s, despite the crime and disorder that often ensued. A few seventeenth-century Afro-Cuban kings also functioned at least symbolically as elite local leaders.

37. Harris, *Aztecs, Moors, and Christians*, 153–54.

38. Sarinara, *Llanto del Occidente en el ocaso del mas claro sol de las Españas*, 108. Sarinara does not provide more details of the names of these confraternities, nor does he say how many there were.

39. "Memorial de todas las cofradías de españoles, mulatos e indios, Mexico City, 1706," AGN, Bienes Nacionales, vol. 574, exp. 2, sf.

40. Cope, *The Limits of Racial Domination*, 16, 20.

41. "Petición de vecinos mulatos, Mexico City, 1568," Archivo General de Indias, Special Sets, Microfilm Collection III, Bancroft Library, leg. 98.

42. Mondragón Barrios, *Esclavos africanos*, 57.

43. "Contra algunos mulatos que han formado cofradía y salido en posesion sin licencia, Mexico City, 1601," AGN, Bienes Nacionales, vol. 810, exp. 28, sf.

44. Testament of María de Saravia, Mexico City, 1682, AN, Andrés de Almoguera, notary #11, s.f.

45. García Ayluardo, "Confraternity, Cult," 217, 220.

46. "Testament of Juan Roque, Mexico City, 1634," AGN, Bienes Nacionales, vol. 1175, exp. 11, fs. 5–7.

47. Aguirre Beltrán, *Población negra*, 117. Today the descendants of the Zapes are called Kpwesi and live in Liberia.

48. Palmer, *Slaves of the White God*, 20–22.

49. Mondragón Barrios, *Esclavos africanos*, 32–39.

50. Fra-Molinero, *La imagen de los negros*, 26, 93.

51. "El mayordomo y los diputados morenos de la cofradía de nuestra señora, Mexico City, 1600," AGN, Bienes Nacionales, vol. 78, exp. 81, sf.

52. This entire section taken from the "Testament of Juan Roque, Mexico City, 1634," AGN, Bienes Nacionales, vol. 1175, exp. 11, fs. 5–7.

53. My argument that Afromexican identity formed through heritage and membership in confraternities contrasts with Herman Bennett's theories that Afromexican identity was strengthened through marriage until 1650. See Bennett, "Lovers, Family and Friends."

54. At this time the renters of the houses included a widow, a *mulata*, and five female slaves who were living alone.

55. "Constituciones y autos hechos por la jurisdicción, Mexico City, 1674," AGN, Hospital de Jesus, leg. 387, exp. 22, sf.

56. "Memoria de los altares y otras gracias concedidas, Mexico City, 1770," Biblioteca Nacional, Archivo Franciscano, caja 147, fs. 7–8; Vetancur, *Crónica de la provincia del Santo evangelio de México*, 36.

57. I thank Deb Cox and Sarah Cline for providing a photocopy of this patent.

58. "Testament of Juan Congo, Mexico City, September 6, 1651," AN, Toribio Cobian, #110, vol. 726 bis.

59. "Memoria de los altares y otras gracias concedidas, Mexico City, 1770," Biblioteca Nacional, Archivo Franciscano, caja 147, fs. 7–8.

60. "Cuaderno formado de las listas de las cofradías, Mexico City, 1788," AGN, Bienes Nacionales, vol. 1170, exp. 5, sf.

61. See chapter 1 for more details on this advocation.

62. "Cuaderno formado de las listas de las cofradías, Mexico City, 1788," AGN, Bienes Nacionales, vol. 1170, exp. 5, sf.

63. Ibid.

64. Pescador, *De bautizados a fieles difuntos*, 303, 309–10.

65. See Valdes, *Novena a la Preciosísima Sangre de Nuestro Señor Jesucristo*.

66. "Libro de recibos de la cofradía de la sangre, Mexico City, 1726–1727," AGN, Bienes Nacionales, vol. 190, exp. 6, sf.

67. "Antonio de Bruselas rector de la cofradía y hermandad de San Nicolás Tolentino se querella criminalmente, Mexico City, 1668," AGN, Matrimonios, vol. 9, exps. 11 and 12, fs. 303–8; "Autos hechos a pedimiento, Mexico City, 1672," AGN, Bienes Nacionales, vol. 79, exp. 1, sf.

68. "Constituciones de la nueva cofradía, Mexico City, 1713," AGN, Bienes Nacionales, vol. 444, exp. 3, sf.

69. Several historians of Hispanic religiosity have studied wills to gain insight into daily life and beliefs. In "Baroque and Reformed Catholicism," Brian Larkin analyzed 1,000 Mexico City wills, focusing on pious bequests. Larkin focused on large numbers of wills for the years 1696, 1737, 1779, and 1813.

This chapter depends more on the method Eire used to analyze 436 Madrid wills; he took samples from every decade from the 1520s to the 1590s. Eire, *From Madrid to Purgatory*, 57. I found Eire's method of analyzing wills from all decades of the seventeenth century most useful for several reasons. First, fewer wills are available for the seventeenth century compared to the eighteenth century. It would be impossible to find 250 wills for a single year or even a single decade before 1650. Second, Eire's comparison of samples by decades presents a greater opportunity to gauge change over time. Finally, choosing wills from certain years, especially periods of plague or other times when mortality was high, reveals the last wishes of people who did not live out their natural lifespan. Early deaths may have led to a pattern of bequests that was very different from the norm. People who lived during times less plagued by the threat of premature death may have joined confraternities later in life as they mentally and spiritually prepared themselves for death.

My sample analyzes 440 wills from the Notarial Archive in Mexico City; it includes approximately 40 wills for each decade from 1600 to 1700. From 1600 to the 1640s, only around 40 wills survive per decade, but after 1650, at least twice as many wills are recorded and preserved per decade. I chose to continue to record 40 wills for these later decades, selecting them randomly. Thus, the wills I analyzed are not comprehensive for the second half of the seventeenth century, but the sample includes nearly every available will from 1600 to 1650. Both Eire and Larkin provide statistics for confraternal devotion taken from their testament samples. My data combined with the information Eire and Larkin provided enabled me to compile a more complete 300-year history of how testators presented their confraternal and other pious affiliations at the hour of their death.

70. Larkin, "Baroque and Reformed Catholicism," 161.

71. "Testament of Doña Juana de la Mancha, Mexico City, 1672," Miguel de Ballestros, notary #62, vol. 464, f. 102.

72. See "Testament of Doncella Nicolasa de Guevara, Mexico City, July 28, 1656," AN, Nicolás de Arauz, notary #5, vol. 11; "Testament of Ana Jímenez, *soltera*, Mexico City, 1668," Juan de Cartagena Valdivia, notary #113, sf.

73. See Larkin, "Baroque and Reformed Catholicism," 89–98, and Eire, *From Madrid to Purgatory*, 127.

74. "Testament of Doña María de Castilla Altamirano, Mexico City, April 30, 1643," AN, Juan de Barrientos, notary #60.

75. Christian, *Local Religion in Sixteenth-Century Spain*, 188.

76. Ibid., 85, 96, 121, 194.

77. Ibid., 182.

78. "Testament of Marcos Pérez, Mexico City, 1645," AN, Francisco Flores, notary #228; "Testament of Dionisia de Pina, Mexico City, 1653," AN, Toribio Cobian, notary #110.

79. "Testament of Valentina de Morales, Mexico City, August 4, 1654," AN, Toribio Cobian, notary #110, vol. 727 bis.

80. "Testament of Agustín de Dueñas, Mexico City, 1692," AN, Bernave Sarmiento de Vera, notary #632, sf.

81. García Ayluardo, "Confraternity, Cult," 288.

82. This cofradía was described above as involved in some minor public conflicts. "Tes-

tament of José de Valle, Mexico City, 1693," AN, José Díaz de Rivera, notary #199, vol. 1315, fs. 6–7. I thank R. Douglas Cope for this reference.

83. "Testament of Juan Roque, Mexico City, 1634," AGN, Bienes Nacionales, vol. 1175, exp. 11, fs. 5–7.

84. For all documents connected to the life and social and family connections of Juan Correa, see Vargas Lugo and Curiel, eds., *Juan Correa*, vol. 2. Documents that relate to Juan Correa senior are on pages 31–42.

85. Ibid., 32.

86. Ibid., 47–48.

87. Ibid., 56.

88. Ibid., 45, 57, 64–65, 70.

89. Ruiz Gomar, "El gremio y la cofradía de pintores en la Nueva España," in Vargas Lugo, *Juan Correa*, 215.

90. Ibid., 43.

91. "Testament of Mateo de Aguilar, Mexico City, May 9, 1705," AN, José de Anaya y Bonillo, notary #13, vol. 64. I thank R. Douglas Cope for his generous assistance with this citation.

92. See "Will of Felipa Correa, Mexico City, 1701," AN, José Anaya y Bonillo, notary #13, vol. 60, fs. 311–13.

93. Vargas Lugo, *Juan Correa*, vol. 3, 117, 120, 124–24, 128–29, 132–33, 177.

94. Ibid., 124–35.

95. I have not included Mateo's *cofradía* in my list of Afromexican confraternities since it was only referred to in this will and was never given any other racial designation, at least in the documents I have found. The *cofradía* is listed in the 1706 catalogue of confraternities in the capital, but it is not described as racially distinct and is one of several confraternities that left little documentation. See "Memorial de todas las cofradías de españoles, mulatos e indios, Mexico City, 1706," AGN, Bienes Nacionales, vol. 1574, exp. 2, f. 5.

96. "Testament of Mateo de Aguilar, Mexico City, May 9, 1705."

97. Ibid. (A *vara* is equivalent to 83.598 centimeters or about 32.91 inches.)

98. "Testament of Petronila María, Mexico City, 1616," AN, Hernando de Arauz, notary #4, 1616; "Testament of José de Valle, Mexico City, 1693," AN, José Díaz de Rivera, notary #199, vol. 1315, fs. 6–7.

99. "Testament of Juan Congo, Mexico City, September 6, 1651," AN, Toribio Cobian, #110, vol. 726 bis. and José de Anaya y Bonilla, 1705, notary #13, vol. 64.

100. "Testament of Catalina de los Angeles, Mexico City, April 8, 1682," AN, Andrés de Almoguera, notary #11, vol. 29.

Chapter 4. Confraternities in Valladolid

1. The Confraternity of Saint Nicolás Tolentino is discussed in chapter 1.

2. "Testament of Pedro de Millan, Morelia, 1631," AHNM, libro 17, f. 88. Millan's will also gave 100 pesos to a *mulata* woman who was the daughter of a black woman, which suggests that she was his illegitimate daughter.

3. "Will of Gabriel López, Morelia, 1631," AHNM, libro 17, f. 110.

4. "Will of Alonso Núñez de Villavicencio, Morelia, 1632," AHNM, libro 18, f. 33.

5. "Will of Doña Geronima de Cisneros, Morelia, 1633," AHNM, libro 19, f. 133.

6. "Will of Enrique de Miranda, Morelia, 1634," AHNM, libro 17, f. 231.

7. "Testament of Juan Martínez, Morelia, 1634," AHNM, libro 20, sf.

8. "Testament of Pedro Martínez, Morelia, 1635," AHNM, libro 21, sf.

9. "Cuenta de recibo y gasto, Morelia, 1654," CM, caja 3, leg. 2, sf.

10. I thank Karen Melvin for information on the Mercedarian Order in Valladolid.

11. Christian, *Local Religion in Sixteenth-Century Spain*, 72, 131–32; Butler, *Butler's Lives of the Saints,* 1:239.

12. "Constituciones abrobadas para la cofradía, Morelia, 1726," CM, caja 1250, leg. 7, sf.

13. "Cuaderno de limosnas de la cofradía, Morelia, 1684," CM, caja 3, leg. 11, sf.

14. "Elecciones de la cofradía, Morelia, 1687–1691," CM, caja 5, leg. 5, sf.

15. "Luis de la Serna, mayordomo, pide licensia, Morelia, 1663," CM, caja 7, leg. 5, sf.

16. Their last request in the colonial period is in 1788. "Pide licensia para pedir, Morelia, 1788," CM, caja 1264, leg. 38, sf.

17. "Constituciones abrobadas para la cofradía, Morelia, 1726," CM, caja 1250, leg. 7, sf.

18. "Testament of Antonio Romero, Morelia, 1742," AHNM, libro 95, f. 322.

19. "Mayordomo y diputados de la cofradía Morelia, 1680," CM, caja 7, leg. 17, sf.

20. "Correspondencia de la cofradía, Morelia, 1739," CM, caja 581, leg. 8, sf.

21. "Cofradía de la Encarnación y San Blas, Morelia, 1749," CM, caja 582, leg. 3, sf.

22. The evidence for the *cofradía's* decline comes from "Joseph de Aguilar mayordomo y rector, Morelia, 1764," CM, caja 586, leg. 3, sf and caja 1267, leg. 24.

23. "Joseph de Aguilar mayordomo y rector, Morelia, 1764," CM, caja 586, leg. 3, sf.

24. See chapter 6 for examples of charges of unseemly behavior against an Afromexican confraternity.

25. "Patentes de la cofradía de la encarnación Morelia, 1822–1876," CM, caja 836, legs. 1 and 2; "Invitación a la función, Morelia, 1841," CM, caja 818, leg. 4, sf.

26. "Libro de Cofradía de Nuestra Señora de Rosario, Morelia, 1681," CM, caja 1, exp. 1.

27. Ibid.

28. Ibid.

29. "Libro de cuentas de la cofradía de Rosario de españoles, Morelia, 1677–1694," CM, caja 3, leg. 6, sf.

30. "Inventorio de Cofradías, Morelia, 1698–1710," CM, Diocesano Gobierno Religiosos Franciscanos, caja 86, sf.

31. Ibid.

32. "Libro de elecciones y constituciones, Morelia, 1733," CM, caja, 1246, leg. 9.

33. "Limosnas de la cofradía del Rosario, Morelia, 1664," CM, caja 3, leg. 3, sf.

34. "Blas Gomes, mayordomo de la cofradía, Morelia, 1667," CM, caja 7, leg. 7, sf.; and "Mateo Hernandez, mayordomo de la cofradía Morelia, 1664," CM, caja 7, leg. 19.

35. Italics added. "Cofradía de Rosario pide licensia, Morelia, 1679," CM, caja 7, leg. 27, sf. "Esta cofradía siempre se aman tenido y sustentado de limosnas q con licensias de los Señores obispos y illustrusimo cabildo se an pedido fuera desta jurisdicción para q en ella

y en esta ciudad no se recojen limosnas bastantes para el ornato y cera de la virgen santisima para sus missas para aniversarios que decimos para las almas de los pobres esclavos nuestros padres para socorro de enfermos que les asistimos y para cera en los entierros de pobres a que acudimos puntual y muy devotamente."

36. All seventeenth-century accounts for the mulatto Rosary are loose papers in CM, caja 3, leg. 3, sf. and caja 4, legs. 32, 33, and 48. Caja 4, legs. 43 and 44 and caja 5 have accounts for the Spanish Rosario that are more continuous and more substantial.

37. "Arrendamiento de ganado, Morelia, 1684," AHNM, libro 38, sf.

38. "Cuentas de la cofradía del Rosario, Morelia, 1732–1735," CM, caja 1252, legs. 16 and 17.

39. "Libro de elecciones y constituciones, Morelia, 1733," caja 1246, leg. 9, sf.

40. Ibid.

41. For the confraternity career of Diego Durán, see "Libro de elecciones y constituciones Morelia, 1733," caja 1246, leg. 9, sf. Another Sosa, Gregorio, was a smith that worked in Diego Durán's construction projects in the mid-eighteenth century; see Guzmán Pérez, "El Maestro Diego Durán," 60.

42. "Libro de Matrimonios, Morelia, 1759–1777," LDS roll #644854.

43. See the next chapter for more on Durán's life story.

44. "Diego Durán, mayordomo de la cofradía, Morelia, 1753," caja 582, leg. 2, sf.

45. "Aprobación de las cuentas, Morelia, 1775," CM, caja 1253, leg. 37, sf.

46. Margaret Chowning refers to members of this family in *Wealth and Power in Provincial Mexico*, 84, 85, 338.

47. "Mayordomo y diputados de la cofradía, Morelia, 1776," CM, caja 1267, leg. 16, sf.

48. "Cofradía del Rosario, Morelia, 1833 and 1837," caja 839, legs. 13 and 23.

49. "Mayordomos de la archicofradía, Morelia, 1846," CM, caja 690, leg. 43.

50. "Invitación de la función, Morelia," CM, caja 818, leg. 4, sf.; "Cuentas de la cofradía del Rosario, Morelia, 1829–1839," CM, caja 819, leg. 9, sf.

51. Election records for Rosario for the eighteenth century are in CM, caja 1255, leg. 5.

52. See Chowning, *Wealth and Power in Provincial Mexico*.

53. "Director de la cofradía del Rosario, Morelia, 1837," CM, caja 839, leg. 23, sf.

54. "Libro de elecciones de la cofradía de San Roque, Morelia, 1767–1847," CM, caja 1248, leg. 1, sf.

55. "Memorial de las cofradías, Morelia, 1833," CM, caja 689, leg. 30, sf.

56. Ibid.

Chapter 5. Moving toward Freedom in Valladolid

1. Ann Twinam, *Public Lives, Private Secrets* and "The Purchase of Whiteness—Some Revisionist Thoughts" (available online at http://sitemason.vanderbilt edu/files/k6EDBe/VACARGA%20twinamvacarga.pdf).

2. From a thorough investigation of census, baptism, and marriage records in colonial Oaxaca, John Chance concludes: "Paradoxically, the *sistema de castas* as a terminological system became more complex in the late eighteenth century, and the white elite were more preoccupied by it, at a time when race alone was no longer a reliable index to social rank. This does not mean that the stratification system was becoming more rigid, but only that

the elite was making a belated effort to maintain its position as a dominant white minority." Chance, *Race and Class in Colonial Oaxaca*, 176–77.

3. Cope, *The Limits of Racial Domination*, 123.

4. Cope, *The Limits of Racial Domination*, 106–24.

5. Super, "Miguel Hernández, Master of Mule Trains," 125–31.

6. See also Vinson, *Bearing Arms for His Majesty*, esp. chapter 4, which relates this discussion to militias in small and larger towns.

7. These impressions are taken from scanning the baptism records for Valladolid at the Latter Day Saints' Genealogical Library in Salt Lake City. Microfilm baptism books for seventeenth-century Valladolid are on rolls numbered 644686, 644688, 644850 and 644852. Because of the commonness of the name "de la Cruz" I have not attempted to look for confraternity members with this name in other kinds of records. See Cope, *The Limits of Racial Domination*, 62–63.

8. Cope, *The Limits of Racial Domination*, 58.

9. Palmer, *Slaves of the White God*, 46.

10. "Libro de bautismos, Morelia, 1549–1621," LDS roll #644686. The presence of fathers at Afromexican baptisms is summarized in Graph 5.3.

11. Ibid. Most of the children and many of the mothers are not given racial labels in these baptisms.

12. The term "*padres desconocidos* [unknown fathers]" is also widely used in the baptism records for mulattos born in Celaya from 1644 to 1700. See Gálvez Jiménez, *Celaya: Sus raíces africanas*, 66–67, 120.

13. See Lutz, *Santiago de Guatemala*, 83, 88–90, 92–94, for similar statistics in colonial Central America.

14. Chávez Carbajal, *Propietarios y esclavos negros en Michoacán*, 93–94.

15. Ibid., 98.

16. Proctor's "Slavery, Identity and Culture" supports these conclusions; see 2, 107–8.

17. Palmer, *Slaves of the White God*, 34.

18. Proctor, "Slavery, Identity and Culture," 31–32.

19. Ibid., 107–8.

20. "Libro de bautismos de castas, Morelia, 1652–1670," LDS roll #644687.

21. See Proctor's different analysis of low marriage rates among Afromexican women in "Slavery, Identity and Culture," 148–49.

22. "Libro de bautismos de castas, Morelia, 1709–1713," LDS roll #644689.

23. "Libro de bautismos de castas, Morelia, 1733–1737," LDS roll #644692. Because the number of yearly baptisms becomes so large at this time, my samples are more spread out in the eighteenth century.

24. Proctor, "Slavery, Identity and Culture," 31–32, 107–8.

25. Gerhard, *A Guide to the Historical Geography of New Spain*, 349.

26. "Libro de bautismos de castas, Morelia, 1758–1762," LDS roll #644701.

27. "Libro de bautismos de castas, Morelia, 1785–1789," LDS roll #644704.

28. Cope, *The Limits of Racial Domination*, 73.

29. For example, see the description below of the wives of Blas Gómez and Augustín de Arizaga.

30. Chávez Carbajal, *Propietarios y esclavos negros en Michoacán*, 124. "Libro de bautismos de castas, Morelia, 1636–1641," LDS roll #644686; "Libro de difuntos, Morelia, 1650–1670" LDS roll #644867.

31. All birth and death records for the family of Luis de la Serna come from "Libros de bautismos y difuntos, 1649–1708" LDS rolls #644688 and 644867.

32. "Elecciones de oficiales de la cofradía de la Encarnación, Morelia, 1664," CM, caja 6, Informes, leg. 5, sf.

33. All sacramental records for Joseph Gudino taken from "Libro de bautismos de castas, Morelia, 1652–1670," LDS roll #644687.

34. "Libro de matrimonias, Morelia, 1623–1642" LDS roll #644850.

35. "Juan de Barrio y su mujer, Morelia, 1662," AHNM, libro 31, f. 166.

36. "Carta de libertad, Morelia, 1662," AHNM, libro 32, f. 66.

37. "Libro de difuntos, Morelia, 1686," LDS roll #644867.

38. "Libro de matrimonios de castas, Morelia, 1662," LDS roll #644852.

39. "Libro de bautismos de castas, Morelia, 1650–1670," LDS roll #644687.

40. Ibid.

41. "Venta de negra esclava, Morelia, 1661," AHNM, libro 31, f. 165.

42. The names of the officials of the Rosary in the late 1660s gathered from Elecciones, CM, caja 3, exps. 4, 5, 14, and 15; caja 4, exps. 32, 33, 36, 41, and 48; caja 5, exps. 6 and 8.

43. See libros de bautismos, matrimonias, and difuntos, Morelia, LDS rolls #644852, 644867, 644687.

44. "Libro de bautismos de castas, Morelia, 1650–1670," LDS roll #644687.

45. "Libro de bautismos de castas, Morelia, 1653–1744," LDS roll #644852. A further connection between prominent families may be found in the marriage of a daughter of Blas Gómez to Antonio de Sosa in 1674, but if this is the same Blas, then the daughter Antonio married was from an earlier marriage, not his marriage to Isabel.

46. Díaz, *The Virgin, the King and the Royal Slaves of El Cobre*, 45.

47. Chávez Carbajal, *Propietarios y esclavos negros en Michoacán*, 99.

48. All baptism records for Antonio de Sosa taken from "Libro de bautismos de castas, Morelia, 1650–1670," LDS roll #644687.

49. "Libro de matrimonias, Morelia, 1679," LDS roll #644852.

50. See "Vende solar, mulato libre Miguel Tafolla, Morelia, 1766," AHNM, libro 131, f. 60.

51. "Libro de matrimonias, Morelia, 1653–1744," LDS roll #644852.

52. "Donación de casas Morelia, 1680," AHNM, libro 34, sf.

53. "Antonio Pardo, negro libre, compra solar, Morelia, 1704," AHNM, libro 51, f. 341 and "Libro de bautismos de castas, Morelia, 1652–1699," LDS roll #644689.

54. "Testament of Juana de Bustos, Morelia, 1663," AHNM, libro 32, sf.

55. "Testament of Francisco de Arrellano, Morelia, 1665," AHNM, libro 31, sf.

56. Chávez Carbajal, *Propietarios y esclavos negros en Michoacán*, 120.

57. "Testament of Francisca de Estrada, Morelia, 1699," AHNM, libro 45, f. 44.

58. "Testament of Phelipe de Bribescas, Morelia, 1703," AHNM, libro 50, f. 233.

59. "Testament of Juan de Villaseñor Cisneros, Morelia, 1705," AHNM, libro 52, f. 184.

60. "Venta de solar, Morelia, 1740," AHNM, libro 91, f. 275.

61. "Testament of Antonio Romero, Morelia, 1742," AHNM, libro 95, f. 322. Francisco Mondragón's will is in the same archive, libro 126, f. 275.

62. The notary Miguel de Mafra y Vargas made a special point of calling Durán *mulato* in the index of his 1760 book, although he used no label in the document itself. See "Deposito irregular, Morelia, 1760," AHNM, libro 121, f. 394. For the myth that Diego Durán worked in Taxco, see Toussaint, *Taxco*.

63. Guzmán Pérez, "El maestro Diego Durán," 21–91.

64. Tavera Alfaro, *Paseo por Morelia*, 125.

65. Guzmán Pérez, "El maestro Diego Durán," 31.

66. "Testament of Doña María Manuela Durán, Morelia, 1795," AHNM, libro 196, f. 140.

67. Guzmán Pérez, "El maestro Diego Durán," 29.

68. "Hermanos Nicolás Julian y Justo Pineda vende casa, Morelia, 1782," AHNM, libro 167, f. 633.

69. "Testament of Doña Margarita del Valle, Morelia, 1764," AHNM, libro 129, f. 157.

70. "Matrimonios de castas, Morelia, 1765," LDS roll #644854.

71. "Ordinarios sobre cuentas a pedimiento de los cofrades, Morelia, 1795," CM, caja 596, exp. 2.

72. Ibid. Durán did not get his dates right. He had led the confraternity from 1750. See chapter 4.

73. "Adiciones que los vocales de la cofradía del Rosario, Morelia, 1796," CM, caja 925, exp. 14.

74. "Testament of Doña María Manuela Durán, Morelia, 1795," AHNM, libro 196, f. 140. Durán's daughter was probably not Afromexican in appearance, and her unknown parentage freed her from probing suspicions.

75. "Libro de difuntos de castas, Morelia, 1711," LDS roll #644867.

76. "Thomas de la Huerta, maestro de arquitectura, Morelia, 1772," AHNM, libro 142, f. 140; and "Thomas Huerta, maestro alarife, Morelia, 1776," libro 151, f. 61.

77. "Luis Ruíz, maestro de sastre, Morelia, 1774," AHNM, libro 147, f. 174. Luis Ruíz was simply called "maestro" when he was elected as majordomo in 1776. See "Elecciones de la cofradía del Rosario, 1776," CM, Morelia, caja 1246, leg. 9.

78. Diego de Vargas, a deputy of the confraternity in 1711, is the first known master builder in this confraternity. "Diego de Vargas, maestro alarife, Morelia, 1745," AHNM, libro 100, f. 57. Also see Moisés Guzmán Pérez, "El maestro Diego Durán y la arquitectura colonial en Valladolid de Michoacán, siglo XVIII."

79. "Venta de sala y cuarto a Nicolás Pérez, maestro cantero, Morelia, 1764," AHNM, libro 129, f. 322.

80. Althouse, "The Power of Language," 88–92.

81. "Cofradías que se obligaran a pagar, Morelia, 1725," CM, caja 580, leg. 3, sf.

82. "Mayordomos de las cofradías, Morelia, 1781," CM, caja 1267, leg. 23.

83. "Mayordomos de las cofradías, Morelia, 1796," CM, caja 596, leg. 3.

84. "Joseph María Castro como mayordomo de la cofradía, Morelia, 1798," CM, caja 1268, leg. 5.

85. "En la ciudad de Valladolid, 15 de Septiembre, Morelia, 1766," AHNM, libro 132, f. 127.

Chapter 6. Patronage and the Pardo Confraternity in Parral

1. Parral's mine is called "la Negrita" or "la Prietita," both words for "little black one" or "little black girl."

2. The discovery of silver in Parral was delayed by Indian wars. West, *The Mining Community in New Spain*; Rocha Chávez, *Tres siglos de la historia*; Porras Muñoz, *El Nuevo Descubrimiento de San José del Parral*; and Villanueva Mayer, "The Black Slave in New Spain's Northern Frontier" are the most informative works on Parral's history. Villanueva Mayer's work is especially useful for bringing together many printed primary sources on the region. I thank Virginia Rocha Seáñz for her support and hospitality during my visit to Parral in 1998 and her father, Rubén Rocha Chávez, and grandfather, José Chávez, for cataloguing and maintaining Parral's municipal archives.

3. Although most of the Archivo Municipal del Hidalgo del Parral (hereafter AMHP) survives, few ecclesiastical records, such as confraternity record books, exist other than those cited here. The archive for the diocese, which is in Durango, does not have confraternity records for Parral.

4. Villanueva Mayer, "The Black Slave," 56–64.

5. Villanueva Mayer, "The Black Slave," 10, 13.

6. Municipal records begin in 1632; Villanueva Mayer, "The Black Slave," 15–16. All surviving Parral municipal records have been microfilmed. Although they are well indexed, numeric references to documents are erratic and follow no set style. If the number of the document is different from the year of the document, I cite the microfilm roll number here. I also cite the section of the roll and any other information available.

7. Gerhard, *The Northern Frontier of New Spain*, 171–72.

8. Villanueva Mayer, "The Black Slave," 39.

9. Parral baptism books have been photographed on microfilm and are catalogued and cited as LDS rolls 162529 to 162531. Parral baptisms, unlike those in Valladolid, were recorded in one book and are not divided by race. Because of gaps in the record and the smaller number of records, I decided to take long-term baptism samples for the seventeenth century. For the eighteenth century, because so many more baptisms were recorded, I took down five years of baptisms in intervals of two decades.

10. Althouse finds that in criminal records in Michoacán, the label mestizo was used less often than other labels and concludes that it would be the label that other *castas* would choose to assume (see "The Power of Language," 102).

11. "Testament of Antonio Juan Marquéz, Parral, July 20, 1641," AMHP, Protocolos, sf.

12. "Testament of Alonso de Castillo, Parral, 1642," AMHP, Protocolos, sf. This hospital is well documented in numerous bequests made in the early decades of Parral's existence. It is generally assumed that the Hospital de San Juan de Dios, which was founded with the help of the Immaculate Conception confraternity, was the first hospital in the region.

However, the Indian hospital had existed for at least forty years before the San Juanino hospital.

13. Cheryl English Martin describes the Immaculate Conception as "an opportunity [for confraternity members] to help one another, and provide a corporate identity and a place in the civic ritual of their community." The author contrasts eighteenth-century Chihuahua with Parral and feels that Parral's more gradual settlement and disorganized city government created space for the existence of the Immaculate Conception confraternity (*Governance and Society*, 186).

14. "Testament of Antonio Juan Márquez, Parral, July 20, 1641," AMHP, Protocolos, sf.

15. "Testament of Gusepe Gutierrez, Parral, 1651," AHMP, Causas Civiles, sf.

16. See "Testament of Francisco Frias, Parral, 1657," AHMP, exp. G12, sf.

17. The local story of this image says that an Indian discovered a large amount of silver after praying to the Virgin and donated it to fund construction of the building.

18. Arras Rodríguez, *Parral Colonial*, 231.

19. "Francisco Montaño de la Cueva, Parral, 1632," AMHP, Protocolos, sf.

20. AMHP, 1642, Civil, exp. G14, sf.

21. See Parral, 1637, AMHP, Civil, exp. G65, sf; Parral, 1638, AMHP, Civil, sf; Parral, 1647, AMHP, Administración, sf.

22. "Testament of Phelipe Montaño de la Cueva, Parral, 1676," AMHP, 1676C, Protocolos, sf. Phelipe's will says he was born in Extremadura. Francisco was also born in Spain, the son of another Knight of Santiago.

23. Villanueva Mayer, "The Black Slave," 61–62.

24. In "Crime and the Urban Poor: Mexico City in the Late Colonial Period" Michael Scardaville provides statistics to show that, at least for eighteenth-century Mexico City, Indians and *castas* were arrested less often than people who claimed European descent (see ix, 19–20).

25. "Contra Antonio de Narváez, Parral, 1660," AMHP, Civil, exp. G1, sf.

26. "Contra Juan de Dios, Parral, 1672," AMHP, 1672A, Criminal, exp. G33, sf.

27. "Contra Antonio de Narváez, Parral, 1677," AMHP, 1677C, Criminal, sf.

28. "Libro de Bautismos, Parral, 1634–1647," Book 1, LDS roll #162529.

29. Another Immaculate Conception deputy in the 1670s had the military title of captain. See "Declaration of Juan de Truxillo, Parral, Nov. 28, 1677," Archivo Parroquial de Hidalgo del Parral (hereafter APP), caja 4, leg. 2, sf.

30. "Contra Sargento Don Gonzalo de Carvajal por heridas, Parral, 1681," AMHP, 1681B, Criminal, sf.

31. "Poder que dan los diputados y mayordomos, Parral, June 4, 1685," AMHP, Protocolos, sf.

32. "Testament of María de la Rosa, Parral, 1692," AMHP, 1692A, Protocolos, sf.

33. "Testimony of Juan del Albirdes, Parral, Dec. 12, 1687," APP, caja 4, leg. 2, sf.

34. "Libro de bautismos, Parral, 1634–1647," Book 1, LDS roll #162529.

35. "Contra Diego Indio, Parral, 1651," AMHP, Criminal, sf. In the first decades of Parral's existence, the owners and servants of the Montaño de la Cueva hacienda were

involved in several violent crimes. See "Criminal por querella de Cristobal de Ximenes, Parral, 1637," AHMP, exp. B42, sf; "Robo contra Francisco Montaño de la Cueva, Parral, 1638," AMPH, Criminal, sf.

36. "María india criada, Parral, 1656," AMHP, Criminal, exp. 74, sf.

37. "Testimony of Don Cristóbal de Villamayor y Carvajal, Parral, Dec. 15, 1607," APP, caja 16B, leg. 1, sf.

38. "María india criada Parral, 1656," AMHP, Criminal, exp. 74, sf.

39. "Testament of Don Phelipe Montaño de la Cueva, Parral, 1676," AMHP, 1676C, Protocolos, sf.

40. See "Contra guardamina de Don Phelipe de la Cueva, Parral, 1661," AMHP, Criminal, sf, a case involving an assault on a slave.

41. Bula Apostolica cited in "Parral, Nov. 28, 1677," APP, caja 4, leg. 2, sf.

42. See "Heridas contra mulato esclavo, Parral, 1677," AMHP, Criminal, sf. Juan de Truxillo was a witness in another case involving an assault on a slave in the same year that Antonio de Narváez was implicated in theft, an incident described above.

43. All conflicts in the 1670s are in APP, caja 4, leg. 2, sf.

44. Urrecha is described as a Spanish resident in "Heridas contra Sargento Don Gonzalo de Carvajal, Parral, 1681," AMHP, exp. 26, sf. The 1681 criminal case indicates that Urrecha had connections to Don Gonzalo de Carvajal, Don Cristobal's brother. In that year, Urrecha and Carvajal had a dispute involving the rent of a mule. The dispute occurred after mass in "Sargento Mayor Don Gonzalo de Carvajal's chapel." While witnesses clearly saw the two fighting with swords, the blame for a wound Urrecha sustained shifted to "Antonio de Vargas, mulatto servant de Don Gonzalo." The authorities did not find Vargas until 1684.

45. See Rocha Chávez, *Tres siglos de la historia,* 89–99; and Muriel, *Hospitales de Nueva España*, vol. 2, 69–76. Several wills mention an Indian hospital, including "Testament of Ana Quijada, Parral, 1667"; "Testament of Baltasar de los Reyes, Parral, 1668"; Testament of Doña Antonio de Hermosillo, Parral, 1674"; all in AMHP, Protocolos.

46. Muriel, *Hospitales de Nueva España*, vol. 2, 69–71.

47. "Testament of Gonzalo de Carbajal, Parral, 1686," AMHP, 1686A, exp. G11, sf.

48. "Escritura otorgado de los Religiosos de San Juan de Dios Parral, 1684," AMHP, Protocolos, sf.

49. "Tomás de Ugarte, Vicario y Juez eclesiastico atento a lo pedido, Parral, Jan. 6, 1687," APP, caja 4, leg. 2, sf.

50. Ibid.

51. "Complaint of Don Cristóbal de Villamayor y Carvajal, Parral, Jan. 17, 1687," APP, caja 16B, leg. 1, sf.

52. "Auto que presenta el libro de la cofradía, Parral, Sept. 12, 1687," APP, caja 4, leg. 2, sf.

53. "Testimony of Juan de Albirdes, Parral, Dec. 12, 1687," APP, caja 4, leg. 2, sf.

54. "Testimony of Don Cristóbal de Villamayor y Carvajal, Parral, Dec. 15, 1687," APP, caja 16B, leg. 1, sf.

55. "Testimony of Juan de Albirdes, Parral, Dec. 20, 1687," APP, caja 4, leg. 2, sf.

56. "Testimony of Antonio de Urrecha, Parral, Jan. 9, 1688," APP, caja 4, leg. 2, sf.

57. "Testimony of Don Cristóbal de Villamayor y Carvajal, Parral, Jan. 28, 1688," APP, caja 4, leg. 2, sf.

58. Muriel, *Hospitales de Nueva España*, vol. 2, 76.

59. "Testament of Domingo de Renedo, mercader, Parral, 1686," AMHP, Protocolos, 1686A (a donation for construction); "Testament of Pedro de Rivera, Parral, 1687," AMHP, 1687B, Protocolos; Wills in AMHP, Protocolos for 1688B, "Testament of Sargento Mayor Juan Ignacio de la Vega, Parral, 1692," AMHP, 1692A, Protocolos; "Testament of Diego de Valdez, mercader, 1695, AMHP, 1688B, Protocolos; "Testament of Juana de Castilla, Parral, 1695," AMHP, 1688B, Protocolos; and Testament of a Capitan Lorenzo, Parral, 1696, AMHP, 1688B, Protocolos (donated 100 pesos, and requested burial in hospital).

60. Protocolos for the eighteenth century were usually done by a justice or another town leader who filled in the position of notary.

61. "Padrón, Parral, 1768," AMHP, sf.

62. "Padrón, Parral, 1788," AMHP, sf.

63. "Libro de bautismos, Parral, 1695–1716," LDS roll #162530.

64. "Libro de bautismos, Parral, 1746–1788," LDS roll #162531.

65. Robinson, "Population Patterns in a Northern Mexican Mining Region," 92.

66. McCaa, "Calidad, Clase, and Marriage in Colonial Mexico," 477–501.

67. Robinson, "Population Patterns in a Northern Mexican Mining Region," 83–95.

68. Ibid., 87.

69. "Padrón, Parral, 1788," AMHP, 1785A, exp. G2, sf.

70. Robinson, "Population Patterns in a Northern Mexican Mining Region," 87.

71. Ibid., 89–90.

72. "Testimony of Joseph de Carvajal, Parral, Feb. 18, 1718," APP, caja 4, labeled as roll #10, 2:2.37, sf.

73. "Testament of Ana Díaz Félix, Parral, 1712, AHMP, Protocolos (left four candelabras to the hospital); "Testament of Juan de Rivera, Parral, 1717," AHMP, 1718B, exp. 20; "Testament of Josepha Muñoz Parral, 1721," AMHP, 1721B, Protocolos (asked to be buried in the hospital).

74. "Permission from Don Pedro Tapia, bishop elect, Durango, April 14, 1714," in AHMP, 1718B, Protocolos, sf.

75. "Sobre templo de San Juan de Dios, Parral, 1723," AHMP, 1723D, leg. 145F, sf.

76. This is the first time the term *pardos* was used to describe members of the Immaculate Conception confraternity.

77. "Sobre toros, comedias y fiestas, Parral, 1724," AHMP, 1724A, Administración, exp. 107, sf.

78. Harris, *Aztecs, Moors, and Christians*, 23–25, 220.

79. All documentation for Immaculate Conception's activities from 1746 to the end of the eighteenth century comes from AMHP, 1746–1795, Administración, exp. GL.

80. "Petition of Francisco Pacheco, Parral, 1788," AMHP, 1746, Administración, exp. GL, sf.

81. Ibid.

82. Pacheco testified that "Pope Pius V in his bull beginning De salute gregsi dominic, paragraph five, clearly declares that bullfights are falsely considered to honor and glorify the saints"; ibid.

83. Ibid.

84. "Lista de soldados, Parral, 1779," AHMP, 1779A, Administración, exp. 101, sf.

85. "Petition of José Muñoz and Leandro Mosqueda, Parral, 1788," AMHP, 1746, Administración, exp. GL.

86. Robinson, "Population Patterns," 85, 89.

Chapter 7. Conflict and Accommodation in Confraternities

1. "Autos fechos sobre las constituciones, Acapulco, 1691," AGN, Bienes Nacionales, vol. 1028, exp. 26, sf. Italics added.

2. "Listas de cofradías, 1706," AGN, Cofradías, vol. 6, fs. 278–79.

3. García Ayluardo, "Confraternity, Cult," 42. Flynn describes early examples of these contradictory outcomes in the case of medieval Zamora, a city used as a base for colonization efforts during the Reconquista. Flynn argues that "it was the fate of [Zamora's] people to try to incorporate diverse elements into society, and it was primarily through the religious confraternities that they succeeded. Confraternal programs dissolved regional differences enough to create a common cultural outlook among inhabitants by the later Middle Ages." Flynn, *Sacred Charity*, 14–15. Confraternities stand as an example of how the Spanish used the model and culture of the Reconquista as a foundation for their actions in the New World. Confraternities brought outsiders and newcomers into society, just as confraternities on the frontiers of the Reconquista had done. Flynn found that confraternities in medieval Zamora divided people by geographic location within a town, by place of origin, and by profession. Confraternities in New Spain also functioned as places for immigrants to gather and share experiences.

4. Lockhart and Altman, eds., *Provinces of Early Mexico*, "Introduction," 25.

5. Chance, *Race and Class in Colonial Oaxaca*, 103.

6. Vinson, *Bearing Arms for His Majesty*, 2–5.

7. Chance, "The Ecology of Race and Class in Late Colonial Oaxaca," 93–115.

8. Garcia Ayluardo, "Confraternity, Cult and Crown," 222. Afro-Brazilian confraternities rotated offices between people born in Angola and Brazil (see Mulvey, "Slave Confraternities in Brazil," 61).

9. "Documentos sobre la obra del retablo de la congregación de la esclavitud, Puebla, 1614–1789," Colleción J. M. Lafragua, Benemérita Universidad Autónoma de Puebla Roll 6, leg. 155, sf. See also Alegre, *Historia de la Compania de Jesus*, 440–41.

10. "Cofradía de San Nicolás Zinándaro, Morelia, 1780," CM, caja 593, leg. 112, sf.

11. "Constitución de la Cofradía de Benditas Almas, Cuzamala, 1686," CM, caja 6, sf.

12. "Constitución de la Cofradía de la Coronación y San Benito, Veracruz, 1636," AGN, Clero Regular y Secular, vol. 16, exp. 6, fs. 475–85.

13. "Constitución de la cofradía de la concepción y la humildad y paciencia de Cristo, Veracruz, 1792," AGN, Reales Cedulas Originales, vol. 159, exp. 34, fs. 49–73. Sincere thanks to Ben Vinson for his help in tracking down this citation.

14. Vinson, *Bearing Arms for His Majesty*, 29.

15. See chapter 2.

16. Constitution in "Libro de la cofradía de San Benito, San Miguel el Grande, 1646," AHPFM, caja 17, sf.

17. "Constitución de la cofradía de los remedios, Santiago Tlalpuxagua, 1658," CM, caja 6, exp. 11, sf.

18. This may have even been a standard rule, because the exact same wording is used in the 1658 constitution for the Hermandad de la Misericordia founded in Irapuato. A similar desire for Indian leadership is in the constitution of the cofradía de la Candelaria founded in 1685 in Tuxpan and in the 1687 founding of the Confraternity of Jesus of Nazareth in Cuitzeo. All of these founding documents are in CM, caja 6.

19. "Constitución de la cofradía de benditas animas de purgatorio, San Francisco Xiquilipa, 1693," CM, caja 6, exp. 44, sf.

20. "Libro de la cofradía de la preciosa sangre de Cristo, Apaseo, 1679," CM, caja 3, exp. 7, sf. Celaya also had an Afromexican confraternity in the local Hospital de San Juan de Dios (see appendix 1) and a substantial black population in the early seventeenth century. After 1644, people of African descent who were born in Celaya were invariably given the label *mulato* at baptism. See Gálvez Jiménez, *Celaya: Sus raíces africanas*, 53, 60–61.

21. "Constitución de la cofradía de benditas almas, Tuxantla, 1691," CM, caja 6, exp. 42, sf.

22. "Fundación de la cofradía de señor sacramentado, Celaya, 1794," CM, caja 1258, leg. 53, sf.

23. Gerhard, *A Guide to the Historical Geography of New Spain*, 66.

24. Colin Palmer uses the statements of viceregal authorities as evidence of the use of this stereotype (see *Slaves of the White God*, 64, 132). Cope denounces the myth of the threatening *casta* in *The Limits of Racial Domination*, 4–7, 15–21. See also "Petición de los mulatos y morenos vecinos Pátzcuaro, 1642," CM, caja 7, exp. 1, sf.

25. Gerhard, *A Guide to the Historical Geography of New Spain*, 66.

26. "Sumarios de bienes de cofradías, Morelia, 1836," CM, caja 834, leg. 36. Salvatierra also had a *vela perpetua* in the nineteenth century (see CM, caja 817, leg. 9).

27. "Petición de Magdalena de la Cruz Villalobos, natural y vecino desta ciudad, Salvatierra, 1657," CM, caja 86, leg. 11, sf. This petition cites the case of a widow of a free black; she complained about the large donation he had made to the cofradía de Tránsito, which was founded for the poor in the Hospital de San Juan de Dios.

28. "Fundación de la cofradía de la humilidad y paciencia de Cristo, Salvatierra, 1663," CM, caja 6, leg. 17, sf.

29. "Pedro Ruano, en nombre de los mulatos y mestizos, Salvatierra, 1677," CM, caja 6, leg. 22, sf.

30. "Fundación de la cofradía de los remedios, Salvatierra, 1643," CM, caja 2, leg. 6, sf.

31. "Testimonio de Ambrosio Vásquez, Salvatierra, 1671," CM, caja 86, leg. 13, sf.

32. This case also provides rare insights into how clerics were involved in confraternity affairs.

33. All of Ambrosio's supporters were mature men of thirty-eight to fifty years old. Older men were commonly among those called upon to testify in cases that involved Af-

romexican confraternities, one of the many indications that these organizations created and preserved respect and social status.

34. "Testimonio de Juan Rodríguez, majordomo, Salvatierra, 1673," CM, caja 5, leg. 2, sf.

35. "Visita del Obispo, Michoacán, 1702," CM, caja 490, exp. 1.

36. "Fundación de San Nicolás, Morelia, 1657," CM, caja 6, leg. 15; and "Mayordomos de las cofradías, Morelia, 1796," CM, caja 596, leg. 3. The earlier date was mentioned in the context of a conflict over who should have seniority in processions.

37. CM, Gobierno, Religiosos, Agustinos, leg. 11. I thank Karen Melvin for this citation.

38. "Testimonio de Mathias Nicolás Duarte, Morelia, 1766," CM, caja 586, leg. 4, sf.

39. Ibid. Italics added.

40. "Presentación de Mathias Nicolás Duarte, Morelia, 1769," CM, caja 588, leg. 2, sf.

41. López Lara, *El Obispado de Michoacán*, 190; and Althouse, "The Power of Language," 32.

42. Gerhard, *A Guide to the Historical Geography of New Spain*, 387–88.

43. "Constitución de la cofradía del Santissimo Sacramento, San Juan Peribán, 1736," CM, caja 1250, leg. 5, sf.

44. "Petición de la cofradía del Santissimo Sacramento, Morelia, 1672," CM, caja 68, leg. 49, sf.

45. See Ann Twinam, *Public Lives, Private Secrets*.

46. Bechtloff, *Las Cofradías de Michoacán*, 339–40.

47. "Petición del mayordomo de la cofradía del Santissimo Sacramento, San Juan Peribán, 1735," CM, caja 581, leg. 5, sf.

48. Gerhard, *A Guide to the Historical Geography of New Spain*, 251.

49. Carillo Cazeres, *Partidos y padrones del obispado de Michoacán*, 19.

50. Gerhard, *A Guide to the Historical Geography of New Spain*, 251.

51. "Fundación de la cofradía de Benditas Animas, Pinzándaro, 1757," CM, caja 1257, leg. 30, sf.

52. "Testimonio sobre las elecciones, Pinzándaro, 1712," CM, caja 1267, leg. 1.

53. Ibid.

54. Ibid.

55. Bechtloff, *Las Cofradías de Michoacán*, 268–69.

56. "Proceso contensio sobre la cofradía de la Soledad, Pinzándaro, 1772," CM, caja 590, leg. 1.

57. See Chevalier, *Land and Society*, 77–81.

58. "Fundación de la cofradía de Nuestra Señora de la Limpia Concepción, Zitácuaro, 1651," AHPFM, caja 3, exp. 1.

59. "Censo de la cofradía de la santissima virgen milagrosa, Zitácuaro, 1681," CM, caja 5, leg. 14, sf.

60. "Libros de gastos de la cofradía de la virgen, Zitácuaro, 1651–1666," AHPFM, caja 3, exp. 2 and 3.

61. "Testimonio de un pedimiento presentados por los cofrades españoles, Zitácuaro, 1707," AHPFM, caja 3, exp. 5.

62. All citations from AHPFM, exps. cited above. The case over who owned the image and had access to it continued many years, but this dispute involves the Spanish brothers and the Franciscans of Zitácuaro who argue a prior claim over the image.

63. Rugeley, *Of Wonders and Wise Men*, 144–45; Taylor, *Magistrates of the Sacred*, 301–23; Lockhart, *The Nahuas after the Conquest*.

64. Larkin, "Baroque and Reformed Catholicism," 162. This contrasts greatly with the confraternity of priests in Mexico City, which allowed laypeople to join for 500 pesos.

65. The record books of confraternities in Nogales are microfilmed on LDS rolls #726443 and 726444.

66. "Libros de la Cofradía de la Soledad, 1707–1851," Archivo Parroquial de San Miguel, Orizaba, Veracruz, cajas 121 and 122.

67. Carroll, *Blacks in Colonial Veracruz*, 72.

68. Ibid., 73–77.

69. "Libros de la Cofradía de la Soledad, 1707–1851," Archivo Parroquial de San Miguel, Orizaba, Veracruz, cajas 121 and 122.

70. Ibid.

71. Gerhard, *A Guide to the Historical Geography of New Spain*, 114–15.

72. Inquisición, AGN vol. 435, exp. 154, fojas 287–90. This case prosecuted an *obraje* owner for forcing the blacks to work on holidays.

73. Vetancur, *Crónica de la provincia del Santo Evangelio de Mexico*, 56.

74. "Libro de la cofradía de San Joseph, Cholula, 1732–1752," Archivo Parroquial de San Pedro Cholula, book 617. In 1746, this confraternity's inventory included ten old books of confraternity records. Although these were not available for researchers to use, they indicate that the confraternity had a very long history before the eighteenth century.

75. Gerhard, *A Guide to the Historical Geography of New Spain*, 206–7.

76. Chevalier, *Land and Society*, 82, 289.

77. See LDS rolls #726443 and 726444.

78. "Libro de la cofradía de benditas animas, Nogales, 1722–1738," LDS roll #726443.

79. Rebellions were common in this region in the eighteenth century. See Patrick Carroll, "Mandinga, 1735–1827," 488–505.

80. Copy of 1689 constitution in "Libro de la cofradía de Jesús Nazareño, Nogales, 1723–1761," LDS roll #726443.

81. Copy of 1663 constitution in "Libro de la cofradía de San Joseph, Nogales, 1736–1770," LDS roll #726443.

82. Ibid.

Bibliography

Archives and Private Collections

Archivo de Ayuntamiento de Morelia.
Archivo de la Parroquia del Sagrario de Celaya.
Archivo de la Parroquia de San Miguel, Orizaba.
Archivo de la Parroquia de Santo Domingo, Zacatecas.
Archivo del Estado de Zacatecas.
Archivo General de la Nación, Mexico City (AGN).
Archivo General de Notarías, Mexico City (AN).
Archivo Histórico de la Ciudad de Veracruz.
Archivo Histórico de la Provincia Franciscana de Michoacán (AHPFM).
Archivo Histórico del Arquidiocesis de Oaxaca.
Archivo Histórico del Arzobispado de México (AHAM).
Archivo Histórico del Arzobispado de Michoacán, Casa de Morelos, Morelia (CM).
Archivo Histórico del Arzobispado de San Luis Potosí.
Archivo Histórico del Estado de Querétaro.
Archivo Histórico del Estado de San Luis Potosí.
Archivo Histórico de los Carmelitas Descalzos en México.
Archivo Histórico del Sagrario de San José de Toluca.
Archivo Histórico de Notarías, Morelia (AHNM).
Archivo Municipal del Hidalgo del Parral (AMHP).
Archivo Municipal de Puebla.
Archivo Parroquial de Cerro San Pedro.
Archivo Parroquial de Hidalgo del Parral (APP).
Archivo Parroquial del Sagrario, San Luis Potosí.
Archivo Parroquial de San Angel Analco, Puebla.
Archivo Parroquial de San Pedro Cholula.
Archivo Parroquial de San Sebastián, San Luis Potosí.
Archivo Histórico de la Parroquia de Santa Prisca, Taxco.
Archivo Parroquia de Santa Veracruz, México D.F.
Bancroft Library, University of California, Berkeley.
Biblioteca Nacional, Mexico City.
Church of Jesus Christ, Latter Day Saints Genealogical Library, Salt Lake City, Utah, and Oakland, California.
Colección J. M. Lafragua, Benemérita Universidad Autónoma de Puebla.
Fondo Luis Guzman Castaneda, Oaxaca.

Nettie Lee Benson Latin American Collection, University of Texas, Austin.

Dissertations

Althouse, A. P. "The Power of Language: Socioethnic Labeling, Social Relations, and Identity in the Patzcuaro Region, 1680–1740." Ph.D. diss., Stanford University, 1997.

Barnes, Andrew. "De Poenitentibus Civitatis Massaliae. The Counter Reformation, Religious Change, and the Confraternities of Penitents of Marseille, 1499–1792." Ph.D. diss., Princeton University, 1983.

Belanger, Brian Conal. "Secularization and the Laity in Colonial Mexico: Querétaro, 1598–1821." Ph.D. diss., Tulane University, 1990.

Bennett, Herman L. "Lovers, Family, and Friends: The Formation of Afro-Mexico, 1580–1810." Ph.D. diss., Duke University, 1993.

Black, Charlene. "Saints and Social Welfare in Golden Age Spain: The Imagery of the Cult of Saint Joseph." Ph.D. diss., University of Michigan, 1995.

Brady, Robert LeDon. "The Emergence of a Negro Class in Mexico, 1524–1640." Ph.D. diss., University of Iowa, 1965.

Bristol, Joan. "Negotiating Authority in New Spain: Blacks, Mulattos, and Religious Practice in the Seventeenth Century." Ph.D. diss., University of Pennsylvania, 2001.

Brockington Gutierrez, Lolita. "The Haciendas Marquesanas in Tehuantepec: African, Indian and European Labor and Race Relations." Ph.D. diss., University of North Carolina at Chapel Hill, 1982.

Brooks, Francis. "Parish and Cofradía in Eighteenth-Century Mexico." Ph.D. diss., Princeton University, 1976.

Christenson, Allen J. "Scaling the Mountain of the Ancients: The Altarpiece of Santiago Atitlan, Guatemala." Ph.D. diss., University of Texas, Austin, 1998.

Dieterich, David Henry. "Brotherhood and Community on the Eve of the Reformation: Confraternities and Parish Life in Liege, 1450–1540." Ph.D. diss., University of Michigan, 1982.

Gallagher, Ann Miriam. "The Family Background of the Nuns of Two 'Monasterios' in Colonial Mexico: Santa Clara, Querétaro and Corpus Christi, Mexico City (1724–1822)." Ph.D. diss., Catholic University of America, 1972.

Garcia Ayluardo, Clara. "Confraternity, Cult and Crown in Colonial Mexico City, 1700–1810." Ph.D. diss, University of Cambridge, 1989.

Garner, Richard. "Zacatecas: 1750–1821: The Study of a Late Colonial Mexican City." Ph.D. diss., University of Michigan, 1970.

Horowitz, Elliott S. "Jewish Confraternities in Seventeenth-Century Verona: A Study in the Social History of Piety." Ph.D. diss., Yale University, 1982.

Larkin, Brian Richard. "Baroque and Reformed Catholicism: Religious and Cultural Change in Eighteenth-Century Mexico." Ph.D. diss., University of Texas, Austin, 1999.

Melvin, Karen. "Urban Religions: Mendicant Orders in New Spain's Cities, 1570–1800." Ph.D. Diss, University of California, Berkeley, 2005.

Osowski, Edward W. "Saints of the Republic: Nahua Religious Obligations in Central Mexico, 1692–1810." Ph.D. diss., Pennsylvania State University, 2002.

Proctor, Frank T. "Slavery, Identity and Culture: An Afro-Mexican Counterpoint, 1640–1763." Ph.D. diss., Emory University, 2003.

Scardaville, Michael C. "Crime and the Urban Poor: Mexico City in the Late Colonial Period." Ph.D. diss., University of Florida, 1977.

Sella, Barbara Anna. "Piety and Poor Relief: Confraternities in Medieval Cremona, c. 1334–1499." Ph.D. diss., University of Toronto, 1996.

Serna Herrera, Juan Manuel de la. "From Slaves to Citizens: Blacks and Mulattoes in Querétaro at the End of the Eighteenth Century." Ph.D. diss., Tulane University, 1999.

Super, John Clay. "Querétaro: Society and Economy in Early Provincial Mexico, 1590–1630." Ph.D. diss., University of California, Los Angeles, 1973.

Valdes, Denis Nodin. "The Decline of the *Sociedad de Castas* in Mexico City." Ph.D. diss., University of Michigan, 1978.

Villanueva Mayer, Vincent. "The Black Slave in New Spain's Northern Frontier: San Joseph del Parral, 1632–1676." Ph.D. diss., University of Utah, 1975

Vinson, Ben. "Bearing Arms for His Majesty: The Free-Colored Militia in Colonial Mexico." Ph.D. diss., Columbia University, 1998.

Printed Sources

Aguilar Criado, Encarnación. *Las hermandades de Castilleja de la Cuesta: Un estudio de antropología cultural.* Sevilla, Spain: Servicio de Publicaciones del Ayuntamiento de Sevilla, 1983.

Aguirre Beltrán, Gonzalo. *Cuijla: Esbozo etnográfico de un pueblo negro.* Mexico City: Secretaria de Educación Publica, Cultura: Fondo de Cultura Económica, 1958.

———. *El negro esclavo en Nueva España.* Mexico City: Fondo de Cultura Económica, 1994.

———. Población negra de México, 1519–1810. Mexico City: Ediciones Fuente cultural, 1946.

Alberro, Solange. *Inquisición y sociedad 1571–1700.* Mexico City: Fondo de Cultural Económica, 1988.

———. "Negros y mulatos en los documentos inquisitoriales: Rechazo y integración." In *El trabajo y los trabajadores en la historia de México*, edited by Elsa Frost and Josefina Zoraida Vásquez, 132–61. Mexico City: Colegio de México, 1979.

Alegre, Francisco Javier. *Historia de la Compañía de Jesus en Nueva España.* 3 vols. Mexico City: J. M. Lara, 1841.

Alvarez Rey, Leandro, ed. *Las Cofradías de Sevilla en el siglo XX.* Seville, Spain: Secretariado de Publicaciones de la Universidad de Sevilla, 1992.

Anderson, Rodney. "Race and Social Stratification: A Comparison of Working-Class Spaniards, Indians, and *Castas* in Guadalajara, Mexico, in 1821." *Hispanic American Historical Review* 68, no. 2 (May 1988): 211–43.

Angulo Iñiguez, Diego, Enrique Marco Dorta, and Mario José Buschiazzo. *Historia del Arte hispanoamericano*. 3 vols. Barcelona, Spain: Salvat, 1950.

Appleton, LeRoy H., and Stephen Bridges. *Symbolism in Liturgical Art*. New York: Scribner, 1959.

Arenal, Electa, and Stacey Schlau, eds. *Thin Lines, Bedeviled Words: Monastic and Inquisitional Texts by Colonial Mexican Women*. Madrid: Editorial Castalia, 1992.

———. *Untold Sisters: Hispanic Nuns in Their Own Works*. Translated by Amanda Powell. Albuquerque: University of New Mexico Press, 1989.

Arras Rodríguez, Hector. *Parral Colonial*. Chihuahua, Mexico: Talleres Graficos del Gobierno del Estado, 1990.

Arrom, Silvia Marina. *The Women of Mexico City, 1790–1857*. Stanford, Calif.: Stanford University Press, 1985.

Avila Chong, Luz O. "Manifestaciones religioso-populares de las fiestas patronales del Santo Cristo de Esquípulas de Antón." *Revista Lotería* 375 (January–February 1990): 85–94.

Bainbridge, Virginia R. *Gilds in the Medieval Countryside: Social and Religious Change in Cambridgeshire, c. 1350–1558*. Woodbridge, UK: Boydell Press, 1996.

Bakewell, P. J. *Silver Mining and Society in Colonial Mexico: Zacatecas, 1546–1700*. Cambridge: Cambridge University Press, 1971.

Banker, James R. *Death in the Community: Memorialization and Confraternities in an Italian Commune in the Late Middle Ages*. Athens: University of Georgia Press, 1988.

Barkin, Florence. "Black Slave Trade in the Seventeenth-Century Real of San Joseph de Parral." Occasional Paper. Tempe, Ariz.: Center for Latin American Studies, 1977.

Barr, Cyrilla. *The Monophonic Lauda and the Lay Religious Confraternities of Tuscany and Umbria in the Late Middle Ages*. Kalamazoo: Medieval Institute Publications, Western Michigan University, 1988.

Bauer, A. J., ed. *La Iglesia en la economía de América Latina, siglos XVI al XIX*. Mexico City: Instituto Nacional de Antropología e Historia, 1986.

Bazarte Martínez, Alicia. *Las cofradías de españoles en la ciudad de México (1526–1860)*. Mexico City: Universidad Autónoma Metropolitana, 1989.

Bechtloff, Dagmar. "La formación de una sociedad intercultural: Las cofradías en el Michoacán colonial." *Historia Mexicana* 43:2 (October–December 1993): 251–63.

———. *Las cofradías de Michoacán durante la epoca de la colonia: La religion y su relación politica y económica en una sociedad intercultural*. Translated by Joaquín Francisco Zaballa Omana. Zinacantepec, Mexico: El Colegio de Michoacán, 1996.

Beezley, William H., Cheryl English Martin, and William E. French, eds. *Rituals of*

Rule, Rituals of Resistance: Public Celebrations and Popular Culture in Mexico. Wilmington, Del.: Scholarly Resources, 1994.

Behar, Ruth. "Sexual Witchcraft, Colonialism, and Women's Powers." In *Sexuality and Marriage in Colonial Latin America,* edited by Asunción Lavrin. Lincoln: University of Nebraska Press, 1989.

Belanger, Brian C. "Between the Cloister and the World: The Franciscan Third Order of Colonial Querétaro." *Americas* 49, no. 2 (October 1992): 157–77.

Belena, Eusebio Bentura, ed. *Recopilación sumaria de todos los autos acordadas de la real audiencia.* Mexico City: Zúñiga y Ontiveros, 1787.

Benitez Bolorinos, Manuel. *Las cofradías medievales en el Reino de Valencia, 1329–1458.* Alicante, Spain: Universidad de Alicante, Secretariado de Publicaciones, 1998.

Bennett, Herman L. "A Research Note: Race, Slavery, and the Ambiguity of Corporate Consciousness." *Colonial Latin American Historical Review* 3, no. 2 (Spring 1994): 207–13.

———. *Africans in Colonial Mexico: Absolutism, Christianity, and Afro-Creole Consciousness, 1570–1640.* Bloomington: Indiana University Press, 2003.

Black, Christopher. *Italian Confraternities in the Sixteenth Century.* Cambridge: Cambridge University Press, 1989.

Blázquez Domínguez, Carmen, Carlos Contreras Cruz, and Sonia Pérez Toledo, eds. *Población y estructura urbana en México, siglos XVIII y XIX.* Xalapa, Mexico: Universidad Veracruzana, 1996.

Boschi, Caio Cesar. *Os leigos e o poder: Irmandades leigas e politica colonizadora em Minas Gerais.* Sáo Paulo, Brazil: Editora Atica, 1986.

Bossy, John. *Christianity in the West, 1400–1700.* Oxford: Oxford University Press, 1985.

Bowser, Frederick. *The African Slave in Colonial Peru, 1524–1650.* Stanford, Calif.: Stanford University Press, 1974.

Boyer, Richard. "Cast [*sic*] and Identity in Colonial Mexico. A Proposal and an Example." Occasional Paper. Storrs, Conn.: Center for Latin American & Caribbean Studies, University of Connecticut; Providence, R.I.: Center for Latin American Studies, Brown University; Amherst, Mass.: Latin American Studies Program, University of Massachusetts, 1997.

Brading, D. A. *Church and State in Bourbon Mexico: The Diocese of Michoacán, 1749–1810.* Cambridge: Cambridge University Press, 1994.

———. *Miners and Merchants in Bourbon Mexico.* Cambridge: Cambridge University Press, 1971.

Briceño Perozo, Mario. "En el bicentenario de la insurrección de los negros, zambos y mulatos de la serranía de Coro: El código negro." *Boletín de la Academia Nacional de la Historia* 78, no. 310 (April–June 1995): 23–33.

Brown, Patricia Fortini. "Honor and Necessity: The Dynamics of Patronage in the Confraternities of Renaissance Venice." *Studi Veneziani* XIV. Pisa, Italy: Giardini Editori, 1987.

Burkhart, Louise. *Holy Wednesday: A Nahua Drama from Early Colonial Mexico*. Philadelphia: University of Pennsylvania Press, 1996.

Burns, Kathryn. *Colonial Habits: Convents and the Spiritual Economy of Cuzco, Peru*. Durham, N.C.: Duke University Press, 1999.

Butler, Alban. *Butler's Lives of the Saints*. London: Burns and Oates, 1956.

Cáceres Gómez, Rina. "La Puebla de los pardos en el siglo XVII." *Revista de Historia* 34 (July–December 1996): 83–113.

Cahill, David P. "Popular Religion and Appropriation: The Example of Corpus Christi in Eighteenth-Century Cuzco." *Latin American Research Review* 31, no. 2 (1996): 67–110.

Calvo, Thomas. *Poder, religión y sociedad en la Guadalajara del siglo XVII*. Guadalajara, Mexico: Universidad de Guadalajara, 1992.

———, ed. *Historia y población en México (siglos XVI–XIX)*. Mexico City: Colegio de México, 1994.

Camacho Martínez, Ignacio. *La hermandad de los mulatos de Sevilla: Antecedentes históricos de la Hermandad del Calvario*. Seville, Spain: Area del Cultura del Ayuntamiento de Sevilla, 1998.

Cardenas, Alejandra. *Hechiceria, saber y transgresion: Afromestizas ante la inquisicion (Acapulco: 1621–1622)*. Chilpancingo, Mexico: Imprenta Candy, 1997.

Cardozo, Manoel S. "The Lay Brotherhoods of Colonial Bahia." *Catholic Historical Review* (April 1947–January 1948): 12–30.

Carillo Cazeres, Alberto. *Michoacán en el otoño del siglo XVII*. Zamora, Mexico: Colegio de Michoacán, 1993.

———. *Partidos y padrones del obispado de Michoacán, 1680–1685*. Morelia, Mexico: Gobierno del Estado de Michoacán, 1996.

Carrero Rodríguez, Juan. *Diccionario cofrade: Más de 2.000 palabras y expresiones de la Semana Santa de Sevilla*. Sevilla, Spain: Hermandad y Cofradía de Nazarenos de Nuestro Padre Jesús de las Penas y María Santísima de los Dolores, 1980.

Carroll, Patrick James. *Blacks in Colonial Veracruz: Race, Ethnicity, and Regional Development*. Austin: University of Texas Press, 1991.

———. "Los mexicanos negros, el mestizaje y los fundamentos olvidados de la 'raza cósmica': una perspectiva regional." *Historia Mexicana* 44, no. 3 (January–March 1995): 403–38.

———. "Mandinga: The Evolution of a Mexican Runaway Slave Community, 1735–1827." *Comparative Studies in Society and History* 19, no. 4 (1977): 488–505.

Carvalho, José Geraldo Vidigal de. "A igreja e a escravidão: As irmandades de Nossa Senhora do Rosário dos Preitos." *Revista do Instituto Histórico e Geográfico Brasileiro* 361 (October–December 1988): 490–509.

Castañon Gonzalez, Guadalupe. "La integración y asimilación de los africanos a la Nueva España a partir de la historiografia sobre la esclavitud." In *Segundo Congreso*

Nacional de la Asociación Latinamericana de Estudios Afroasiáticos. Mexico City: Colegio de México, 1985.

Cavero Dominguez, Gregoria. *Las cofradías en Astorga durante la edad media*. Leon, Mexico: Universidad de Leon, 1992.

Cervantes Saavedra, Miguel de. *Novelas ejemplares*. Madrid, Spain: Castalia, 1982.

César Dachary, Alfredo, and Stella M. Arnaiz Burne. "La frontera caribe de México en el XIX: Una historia olvidada." *Siglo XIX: Cuadernos* 3, no. 7 (October 1993): 33–62.

Chance, John. "The Ecology of Race and Class in Late Colonial Oaxaca." In *Studies in Spanish American Population History*, edited by David J. Robinson, 93–117. Boulder, Colo.: Westview Press, 1981.

———. *Race and Class in Colonial Oaxaca*. Stanford, Calif.: Stanford University Press, 1978.

Chance, John, and William B. Taylor. "Cofradías and Cargos: An Historical Perspective on the Mesoamerican Civil-Religious Hierarchy." *American Ethnologist* 12, no. 1 (1985): 1–26.

———. "Estate and Class in a Colonial City: Oaxaca in 1792." *Comparative Studies in Society and History* 19, no. 4 (1977): 454–87.

Charney, Jean Paul. "A Sense of Belonging: Colonial Indian Cofradías and Ethnicity in the Valley of Lima, Peru." *The Americas* 54, no. 3 (January 1998): 379–407.

Chávez Carbajal, María Guadalupe. *Propietarios y esclavos negros en Michoacán (1600–1650)*. Morelia, Mexico: Universidad Michoacana, 1994.

Chevalier, François. *Land and Society in Colonial México: The Great Hacienda*. Berkeley: University of California Press, 1963.

Chowning, Margaret. "From Colonial Cofradías to Porfirian Pious Organizations: A View from the Provinces." Paper presented at the Latin American Studies Association Conference, Cambridge, Mass., 2001.

———. *Wealth and Power in Provincial Mexico: Michoacán from the Late Colony to the Revolution*. Stanford, Calif.: Stanford University Press, 1999.

Christian, William. *Local Religion in Sixteenth-Century Spain*. Princeton, N.J.: Princeton University Press, 1981.

Cline, S. L. *Colonial Culhuacan, 1580–1600*. Albuquerque: University of New Mexico Press, 1986.

Cohn, Samuel K. "The Black Death: End of a Paradigm." *American Historical Review* 107, no. 3 (June 2002): 703–38.

Cooper, Donald B. "A Selective List of the Colonial Manuscripts (1564–1800) in the Archives of the Department of Health and Welfare, Mexico City." *Hispanic American Historical Review*, XLII, no. 3 (August 1962): 385–414.

Cope, R. Douglas. *The Limits of Racial Domination: Plebian Society in Colonial Mexico City, 1660–1720*. Madison: University of Wisconsin Press, 1994.

Cortés Alonso, Vicenta. "La imagen del otro: Indios, blancos y negros en el México del siglo XVI." *Revista de Indias* 51, no. 192 (May–August 1991): 259–92.

Cortés Jacome, María Elena. "Tendencia de la vida familiar del grupo mulato novohispano, siglo XVIII." In *Segundo Congreso Nacional de la Asociación Latinamericana de Estudios Afroasiáticos*, edited by Guillermo Quartucci Núñez, 217–48. Mexico City: Colegio de México, 1985.

Cortés López, José Luis. *La esclavitud negra en la España peninsular del siglo XVI*. Salamanca, Spain: Universidad de Salamanca, 1989.

Cottler, Susan M. *Preliminary Survey of the Mexican Collection*. Salt Lake City: University of Utah, 1978.

Covarrubias Orozco, Sebastián. *Tesoro de la lengua castellano*. Edited by Felipe C. R. Maldoñado. Madrid, Spain: Editorial Castalia, 1994.

Crouch, David J. F. *Piety, Fraternity, and Power: Religious Gilds in Late Medieval Yorkshire, 1389–1547*. Woodbridge, UK: York Medieval Press, 2000.

Davidson, David. "Negro Slave Control and Resistance in Colonial México, 1519–1650." *Hispanic American Historical Review* 46, no. 3 (August 1966): 235–53.

Díaz, María Elena. *The Virgin, the King and the Royal Slaves of El Cobre: Negotiating Freedom in Colonial Cuba, 1670–1780*. Stanford, Calif.: Stanford University Press, 2000.

Dinan, Susan. "Overcoming Gender Limitations: The Daughters of Charity in Early Modern Catholicism." In *Early Modern Catholicism: Essays in Honor of John W. O'Malley, S.J.*, edited by Kathleen M. Comerford and Hilmar M. Pabel, 114–30. Toronto: University of Toronto Press, 2001.

Dipaolo Loren, Diana. "Social Skins: Orthodoxies and Practices of Dressing in the Early Colonial Lower Mississippi Valley." *Journal of Social Archeology* 1, no. 2 (2001): 172–89.

Donnelly, John Patrick, and Michael W. Maher. *Confraternities and Catholic Reform in Italy, France and Spain*. Kirksville, Mo.: Thomas Jefferson University Press, 1999.

Dusenberry, William H. "Discriminatory Aspects of Legislation in Colonial Mexico." *Journal of Negro History* 33, no. 3 (1948): 284–302.

Eire, Carlos M. N. *From Madrid to Purgatory: The Art and Craft of Dying in Sixteenth-Century Spain*. Cambridge: Cambridge University Press, 1995.

Engerman, Stanley L., and Eugene Genovese, eds. *Race and Slavery in the Western Hemisphere*. Princeton: Princeton University Press, 1975.

English Martin, Cheryl. *Governance and Society in Colonial Mexico: Chihuahua in the Eighteenth Century*. Stanford, Calif.: Stanford University Press, 1996.

———. *Rural Society in Colonial Morelos*. Albuquerque: University of New Mexico Press, 1985.

Espejo-Ponce Hunt, Marta. "The Processes of Development of Yucatán, 1600–1700." In *Provinces of Early Mexico: Variants of Spanish American Regional Evolution*, edited by James Lockhart and Ida Altman. Los Angeles: University of California Press, 1976.

Fanti, Mario. *Confraternite e citta a Bologna nel Medioevo e nell'eta moderna*. Roma, Italy: Herder, 2001.

Farriss, Nancy. *Maya Society under Colonial Rule: The Collective Enterprise of Survival*. Princeton: Princeton University Press, 1984.

Fernández Repetto, Francisco, and Genny Negroe Sierra. *Una población perdida en la memoria: Los negros de Yucatan. Raíces y expression de su identidad*. Mérida, Mexico: Universidad Autónoma de Yucatán, 1995.

Flynn, Maureen. *Sacred Charity: Confraternities and Social Welfare in Spain, 1400–1700*. Ithaca: Cornell University Press, 1989.

Foster, George. "Cofradía and Compadrazgo in Spain and South America." *Southwestern Journal of Anthropology* 9, no. 1 (Spring 1953): 1–28.

Fra-Molinero, Baltasar. *La imagen de los negros en el teatro del siglo de oro*. Mexico City: Siglo XXI, 1995.

Galpern, A. N. *The Religions of the People in Sixteenth-Century Champagne*. Cambridge, Mass.: Harvard University Press, 1976.

Gálvez Jiménez, Mónica Leticia. *Celaya: Sus raíces africanas*. Guanajuato, Mexico: La Rana, 1995.

Gante, Risela de, Guadalupe Olivera, and Mariano Torres. *Inventario del archivo parroquial de San Pedro Cholula*. Puebla, Mexico: Universidad Autónoma de Puebla, 1984.

García Ayluardo, Clara. "Ceremonia y cofradía: La Ciudad de México durante el siglo XVIII." In *Identidad y prácticas de los grupos de poder en México, siglos XVII–XIX: Seminario de formación de grupos y clases sociales*, edited by Rosa María Meyer Cosio. Mexico City: Instituto Nacional de Antropología e Historia, 1999.

———. "A World of Images: Cult, Ritual and Society in Colonial Mexico City." In *Rituals of Rule, Rituals of Resistance: Public Celebrations and Popular Culture in Mexico*, edited by William H. Beezley, Cheryl English Martin, and William E. French, 77–93. Wilmington: Scholarly Resources, 1994.

Garibay Alvarez, Jorge. *Archivo parroquial del Sagrario, Leon, Guanajuato*. México City: Archivo General de la Nación, 1981.

Garrido, Isauro Manuel. *La ciudad de Toluca*. Toluca, Mexico: Biblioteca Enciclopedia del Estado de México, 1975.

Gerhard, Peter. *A Guide to the Historical Geography of New Spain*. Rev. ed. Norman: University of Oklahoma Press, 1993.

———. *The Northern Frontier of New Spain*. Norman: University of Oklahoma Press, 1982.

———. *The Southeast Frontier of New Spain*. Rev. ed. Norman: University of Oklahoma Press, 1993.

Gibson, Charles. *The Aztecs under Spanish Rule: A History of the Indians of the Valley of Mexico*. Stanford: Stanford University Press, 1964.

Gil Albarracín, Antonio. *Cofradías y hermandades en la Almería moderna: Historia y documentos*. Almería-Barcelona, Spain: Griselda Bonet Girabet, 1997.

Gómez Danés, Pedro. *Negros y mulatos en el Nuevo Reino de León, 1600–1795*. Monterrey, Mexico: Gobierno de Nuevo León, Archivo General del Estado, 1996.

González Franco, Glorinela, María del Carmen Olvera, and Ana Eugenia Reyes y Cabañas. *Artistas y artesanos a través de fuentes documentales*. Vol. 1. Mexico City: Instituto Nacional de Antropología e Historia, 1994.

González Méndez, Vicente. *Los Reyes, Tingüindín, Tancitaro, Tocumbo y Peribán*. Morelia, Mexico: Gobierno del Estado de Michoacán, 1980.

González Ponce, Enrique. *Catálogo del ramo de cofradías y archicofradías*. Mexico City: Departamento de Publicaciones del Archivo de la Nación, 1977.

González Sánchez, Isabel. *El obispado de Michoacán en 1765*. Morelia, Mexico: Comité Editorial del Gobierno de Michoacán, 1985.

González y González, Luis. *La vuelta a Michoacán en 500 libros*. Zamora, Mexico: Colegio de Michoacán, 1994.

Greenleaf, Richard E. "The Inquisition Brotherhood: Cofradía de San Pedro Mártir of Colonial Mexico." *The Americas* 40, no. 2 (October 1983): 171–208.

Grimes, Ronald. *Symbol and Conquest: Public Ritual and Drama in Santa Fe, New Mexico*. Ithaca, N.Y.: Cornell University Press, 1976.

Guevara Sangínes, María. *Guanajuato diverso: sabores y sinsabores de su ser mestizo (siglos XVI a XVI)*. Guanajuato, Mexico: La Rana, 2001.

Guzmán Pérez, Moisés. "El maestro Diego Durán y la arquitectura colonial en Valladolid de Michoacán, siglo XVIII." In *Arquitectura, comercia, ilustración y poder en Valladolid de Michoacán*, edited by Moisés Guzmán Pérez, 21–91 . Mexico City: Instituto Nacional de Antropología e Historia.

Harris, Marvin. *Patterns of Race in the Americas*. New York: Walker, 1964.

Harris, Max. *Aztecs, Moors, and Christians: Festivals of Reconquest in Mexico and Spain*. Austin: University of Texas Press, 2000.

Henderson, John. *Piety and Charity in Late Medieval Florence*. Oxford: Clarendon Press, 1994.

Herrera, María Luisa. *Presencia y esclavitud del negro en La Huasteca*. Mexico City: Editorial Porrua, 1989.

Howard, Philip A. *Changing History: Afro-Cuban Cabildos and Societies of Color in the Nineteenth Century*. Baton Rouge: Louisiana State University, 1998.

Huerta, María Teresa. "Estructuras de clases y de trabajo." In *Balance y perspectivas de la historiografía social en México*, edited by María Teresa Huerta, 124–48. Mexico City: Instituto Nacional de Antropología e Historia, 1980.

Humboldt, Alexander von. *Political Essay on the Kingdom of New Spain*. Translated by John Black. Norman: University of Oklahoma Press, 1972.

Hunefeldt, Christine. *Paying the Price of Freedom: Family and Labor among Lima's Slaves, 1800–1854*. Berkeley: University of California Press, 1994.

Illades, Carlos. *Hacia la república del trabajo: La organización artesanal en la ciudad de México, 1853–1876*. Mexico City: Colegio de México, 1987.

Inez de la Cruz, Sor Juana. *Obra selecta*. Edited by Luis Sáinz de Medrano. Barcelona, Spain: Planeta, 1987.

Israel, J. I. *Race, Class and Politics in Colonial Mexico*. London: Oxford University Press, 1975.

Jackson, Robert Howard. "Race/Caste and the Creation and Meaning of Identity in Colonial Spanish America." *Revista de Indias* 55, no. 203 (January–April 1995): 149–73.

Jiménez Gómez, Juan Ricardo. *Catálogo de expedientes de la Alcaldia Mayor Querétaro, Siglo XVI*. Mexico City: Archivo General de la Nación, 2000.

Jiménez Guerrero, José, ed. *Cofradías, historia, sociedad: Estudios sobre la Semana Santa Malaguena*. Malaga, Spain: Editorial Sarria, 1997.

Junquera, Carlos. "Pervivencia de las religiones africanas en Perú." *Ibero-Amerikanisches Archiv* 2, no. 10 (1984): 175–88.

Klein, Herbert S. *African Slavery in Latin America and the Caribbean*. Oxford: Oxford University Press, 1986.

Konetzke, Richard. *Colección de documentos para la historia de la formación social de hispanoamérica*. 3 vols. Madrid, Spain: Consejo Superior de Investigaciones Científicas, 1962.

Konrad, Herman. *A Jesuit Hacienda in Colonial Mexico: Santa Lucía, 1576–1767*. Stanford, Calif.: Stanford University Press, 1980.

Lacombe, Lourenço Luís. "Ordens religiosas, irmandades e confrarias." *Revista do Instituto Histórico e Geográfico Brasileiro* 288 (July–September 1970): 69–80.

Landes, Ruth. *The City of Women*. New York: Macmillan, 1947.

Lara Tenorio, Blanca. *La esclavitud en Puebla y Tepeaca (1545–1630)*. Mexico City: INAH, Centro Regional de Puebla-Tlaxcala, 1976.

Laurans, Guy. *L'humilité et la gloire: Contribution à l'étude sociologique des Confréries de Pénitents en Bas-Languedoc*. Nîmes, France: Lacour, 1999.

Lavrin, Asunción. "Indian Brides of Christ: Creating New Spaces for Indigenous Women in New Spain." *Mexican Studies/Estudios mexicanos* 15, no. 2 (Summer 1999): 225–60.

———. "La congregación de San Pedro—Una cofradía urbana del México colonial, 1604–1730." *Historia Mexicana* 16, no. 14 (1980): 562–99.

———. "Worlds in Contrast: Rural and Urban Confraternities in Mexico at the End of the Eighteenth Century." In *The Church and Society in Latin America*, edited by Jeffrey A. Cole, 99–124. New Orleans, La.: Center for Latin American Studies, Tulane University, 1984.

———, ed. *Latin American Women: Historical Perspectives*. Westport, Conn.: Greenwood Press, 1978.

———. *Sexuality and Marriage in Colonial Latin America.* Lincoln: University of Nebraska Press, 1989.

Levine, Robert M. *Vale of Tears: Revisiting the Canudos Massacre in Northeastern Brazil, 1893–1897.* Berkeley: University of California Press, 1992.

Lewis, Laura. *A Hall of Mirrors: Power, Witchcraft, and Caste in Colonial Mexico.* Durham, N.C.: Duke University Press, 2003.

Lezamis, Joseph de. *Breve relación de la vida y muerte del illmo. y rmo. Señor Doctor D. Francisco de Aguiar y Seijas.* Mexico City: Doña María de Benavides, 1699.

Linage Conde, Antonio. *Las cofradías de Sepúlveda.* Segovia, Spain: Caja de Ahorros y Monte de Piedad de Segovia, 1986.

Little, Lester K. *Liberty, Charity, Fraternity: Lay Religious Confraternities at Bergamo in the Age of the Commune.* Northampton, Mass.: Smith College, 1988.

Lockhart, James. *The Nahuas after the Conquest: A Social and Cultural History of the Indians of Central Mexico, Sixteenth through Eighteenth Centuries.* Stanford, Calif.: Stanford University Press, 1992.

Lockhart, James, and Ida Altman, eds. *Provinces of Early Mexico: Variants of Spanish American Regional Evolution.* Los Angeles: University of California Press, 1976.

López Cano, Pilar Martínez, Gisela von Wobeser, and Guillermo Muñoz, eds. *Cofradías, capellanias y obras pias en la America colonial.* Mexico City: Universidad Nacional Autónoma de México, 1998.

López González, Pedro, ed. *Las cofradías en Nayarit: Capt. Juan López Portillo y Rojas, pionero del desarrollo socioeconomico de Tepic en el siglo XVII.* Tepic, Nayarit, Mexico: n.p., 1980.

López Gutierrez, Antonio J. *Los archivos de las hermandades religiosas: Manual de organización de fondos.* Seville, Spain: G.E.A., 1993.

López Lara, Ramón. *El Obispado de Michoacán en el siglo XVII: Informe inédito de beneficios, pueblos y lenguas.* Morelia, México: Fimax, 1973.

López Muñoz, Miguel Luis. *Las cofradías de la parroquia de Santa María Magdalena de Granada en los siglos XVII y XVIII.* Granada, Spain: Universidad de Granada, 1992.

López Pulido, Alberto. *The Sacred World of the Penitentes.* Washington, D.C.: Smithsonian Institution Press, 2000.

Love, Edgar. "Legal Restrictions on Afro-Indian Relations in Colonial Mexico." *Journal of Negro History* 55, no. 2 (April 1970): 131–39.

Lundius, Jan. "Rural Cofradías: A Comparative Study of Syncretism, Fertility Beliefs, and Communal Worship among Peasants in the Dominican Republic and the Mayan Regions." *Ibero Americana* (Sweden), 23, no. 1–2 (1993): 39–88.

Luque Alcaide, Elisa. "Recursos de la cofradía de Aránzazu de México ante la corona, 1729–1763." *Revista de Indias* 56, no. 206 (January–April 1996): 205–18.

Lutz, Christopher H. *Santiago de Guatemala, 1541 to 1773: City, Caste and the Colonial Experience.* Norman: University of Oklahoma Press, 1994.

MacLeod, Murdo J. "Papel social y económico de las cofradías indígenas de la colonia en Chiapas." *Mesoamérica* 4, no. 5 (June 1983): 64–86.

Martz, Linda. *Poverty and Welfare in Hapsburg Spain: The Example of Toledo*. Cambridge: Cambridge University Press, 1983.

Masferrer Kan, Elio R. "Criterios de organización andina, Recuay siglo XVII." *Bulletin de l'Institut français d'études andines* 13, nos. 1–2 (1984): 47–61.

Mayer, Vincent. "The Black on New Spain's Northern Frontier: San José de Parral 1631 to 1643." Occasional Paper. Durango, Colo.: Center of Southwest Studies, 1974.

McCaa, Robert. "Calidad, Clase, and Marriage in Colonial Mexico: The Case of Parral, 1788–1790." *Hispanic American Historical Review* 64 (August 1984): 477–502.

McCaa, Robert, Stuart B. Schwartz, and Arturo Grubessich. "Race and Class in Colonial Latin America: A Critique." *Comparative Studies in Society and History* 21, no. 3 (1979): 421–33.

Megged, Amos. *Exporting the Catholic Reformation: Local Religion in Early-Colonial Mexico*. Leiden, Netherlands: Brill, 1996.

———. "Poverty and Welfare in Mesoamerica during the Sixteenth and Seventeenth Centuries: European Archetypes and Colonial Translations." *Colonial Latin American Historical Review* 6, no. 1 (Winter 1997): 1–29.

Meléndez, Concha, ed. *Signos de Iberoamérica*. San Juan de Puerto Rico: Editorial Cordillera, 1970.

Mellafe, Rolando. *Negro Slavery in Latin America*. Translated by J.W.S. Judge. Berkeley: University of California Press, 1975.

Menchaca, Martha. *Recovering History, Constructing Race: The Indian, Black and White Roots of Mexican Americans*. Austin: University of Texas Press, 2001.

Mentz, Brígida von. *Pueblos de indios, mulatos y mestizos, 1770–1870*. Mexico City: CIESAS, 1988.

Meyers, Albert, and Diane Elizabeth Hopkins, eds. *Manipulating the Saints*. Hamburg, Germany: Wayasbah, 1988.

Meyers, Albert, and Olinda Celestino. *Las cofradías en el Perú: Región central*. Frankfurt, Germany: Verlag Vervuert, 1981.

Mintz, Sidney, and Richard Price. *An Anthropological Approach to the Afro-American Past: A Caribbean Perspective*. Philadelphia: Institute for the Study of Human Issues, 1976.

Mitchell, Timothy. *Passional Culture: Emotion, Religion and Society in Southern Spain*. Philadelphia: University of Pennsylvania Press, 1990.

Mondragón Barrios, Lourdes. *Esclavos africanos en la Ciudad de México: El servicio doméstico durante el siglo XVI*. Mexico City: Conaculta, 1999.

Montiel, Luz, ed. *III Encuentro nacional de afromexicanistas*. Colima, Mexico: Gobierno del Estado, 1993.

———. *VI Encuentro nacional de afromexicanistas*. Colima, Mexico: Gobierno del Estado, 2001.

———. *Presencia africana en México*. Mexico City: Consejo Nacional para la Cultura y los Artes, 1994.

Montoya, Salvador. "Milicias negras y mulatas en el reino de Guatemala, siglo XVIII." *Caravelle* 49 (1987): 93–104.

Moreno Navarro, Isidoro. *Cofradías y hermandades andaluzas: Estructura, simbolismo e identidad*. Seville, Spain: Editoriales Andaluzas Unidas, 1985.

———. *La antigua hermandad de los negros en Sevilla: Ethnicidad, poder y sociedad*. Seville, Spain: Universidad de Sevilla, 1997.

Morgan, Ronald Jay. *Spanish American Saints and the Rhetoric of Identity, 1600–1810*. Tucson: University of Arizona Press, 2002.

Morin, Claude. *Michoacán en la Nueva España de siglo XVII: Crecimiento y desigualidad en una economía colonial*. Mexico City: Fondo de Cultura Económica, 1979.

Mörner, Magnus. *Race and Class in Latin America*. New York: Columbia University Press, 1970.

———. *Race Mixture in the History of Latin America*. Boston: Little, Brown, 1967.

Muir, Edward. *Civic Ritual in Renaissance Venice*. Princeton, N.J.: Princeton University Press, 1981.

Mulvey, Patricia. "Slave Confraternities in Brazil: Their Role in Colonial Society." *The Americas* 39, no. 1 (July 1982): 39–68.

Mulvey, Patricia, and Barry Crouch. "Black Solidarity: A Comparative Perspective on Slave Sodalities in Latin America." In *Manipulating the Saints*, edited by Albert Meyers and Diane Elizabeth Hopkins, 51–65. Hamburg, Germany: Wayasbah, 1988.

Muriel, Josefina. *Hospitales de Nueva España*. 2 vols. Mexico City: Instituto de Historia, 1960.

Naveda Chávez-Hita, Andrea. *Esclavos negros en las haciendas azucareras de Córdoba, Veracruz, 1690–1830*. Xalapa, Mexico: Universidad Veracruzana, Centro de Investigaciones Históricas, 1987.

Nettel Ross, M. *Colonización y poblamiento del Obispado de Michoacán, período colonial*. Morelia, Mexico: Gobierno del Estado, Instituto Michoacano de Cultura, 1995.

Ngou-Mve, Nicólas. *El Africa bantu en la colonización de México (1595–1640)*. Madrid, Spain: Consejo Superior de Investigaciones Científicas, 1994.

Osowski, Edward. "Licensed Saints." Unpublished paper given at Latin American Studies Association Conference, Dallas, April 2003.

Ouweneel, Arj, and Simon Miller, eds. *The Indian Community of Colonial Mexico: Fifteen Essays on Land Tenure, Corporate Organizations, Ideology and Village Politics*. Amsterdam, Netherlands: CEDLA, 1990.

Palmer, Colin. *Slaves of the White God*. Cambridge, Mass.: Harvard University Press, 1976.

Paniagua Pérez, Jesús. "Cofradías limeñas: San Eloy y La Misericordia, 1597–1733." *Anuario de Estudios Americanos* 52, no. 1 (1995): 13–35.

Peña, Gabriela Alejandra. *La evangelización de indios, negros y gente de castas en Córdoba del Tucumán durante la dominación española, 1573–1810*. Córdoba, Argentina: Facultad de Filosofía y Humanidades, Universidad Católica de Córdoba, 1997.

Pérez Castro, Ana Bella, and Lorenzo Ochoa Salas. "Mestizaje cultural en la sierra alta de Hidalgo, México." *Cuadernos Americanos* 35, n.s. (September–October 1992): 84–98.

Pescador C., Juan Javier. *De bautizados a fieles difuntos: Familia y mentalidades en una parroquia urbana, Santa Catarina de México, 1568–1820*. Mexico City: Colegio de México, 1992.

———. "Devoción y crisis demográfica: La Cofradía de San Ygnacio de Loyola, 1761–1821." *Historia Mexicana* 29, no. 3 (1990): 767–802.

———. "La nupcialidad urbana preindustrial y los límites del mestizaje: Características y evolución de los patrones de nupcialidad en la ciudad de México, 1700–1850." *Estudios Demográficos y Urbanos* 7, no. 1 (January–April 1992): 137–68.

Pescatello, Ann, ed. *The African in Latin America*. Washington, D.C.: University Press of America, 1975.

Pérez-Rocha, Emma, and Gabriel Moedano Navarro. *Aportaciones a la investigación de archivos del México colonial y a la bibliohemerografía afromexicanista*. Mexico City: Instituto Nacional de Antropología e Historia, 1992.

Pérez Toledo, Sonia. *Los hijos del trabajo: Los artesanos de México, 1780–1853*. Mexico City: Colegio de México, 1996.

Pike, Ruth. *Aristocrats and Traders: Sevillian Society in the Sixteenth Century*. Ithaca, N.Y.: Cornell University Press, 1972.

Porras Muñoz, Guillermo. *El nuevo descubrimiento de San José del Parral*. Mexico City: Universidad Nacional Autónoma de México, 1988.

Powers, Karen Vieira. "The Battle for Bodies and Souls in the Colonial North Andes: Intraecclesiastical Struggles and the Politics of Migration." *Hispanic American Historical Review* 75, no. 1 (February 1995): 31–56.

Price, Richard, ed. *Maroon Societies: Rebel Slave Communities in the Americas*. Baltimore, Md.: Johns Hopkins University Press, 1979.

Querol y Rosa, Luis. "Negros y mulatos de Nueva España: Historia de su alzamiento en México en 1612." *Anales de la Universidad de Valencia* 12, no. 90 (1931–1932): 121–62.

Rabell Romero, Cecilia Andrea. "Matrimonio y raza en una parroquia rural: San Luis de la Paz, Guanajuato, 1715–1810." *Historia Mexicana* 42, no. 1 (July–September 1992): 3–44.

Ramos-Baquero, Angeles. "Ordenanzas, cofradía y gremio de plateros en Panama durante el periodo colonial." *Revista Cultural Loteria* 413 (July 1997): 25–48.

Redondo, Brígido. *Negritud en Campeche*. Campeche, Mexico: Ediciones de la LIV Legislatura, 1994.

Reis, João José. *Slave Rebellion in Brazil: The Muslim Uprising of 1835 in Bahia.* Translated by Arthur Brakel. Baltimore, Md.: Johns Hopkins University Press, 1993.

Ribeiro, René. "Relations of the Negro with Christianity in Portuguese America." *The Americas* 14, no. 4 (1958): 454–84.

Robinson, D. J. "Population Patterns in a Northern Mexican Mining Region: Parral in the Late Eighteenth Century." In *Historical Geography of Latin America: Papers in Honor of Robert C. West*, edited by William V. Davidson. Baton Rouge, La.: School of Geoscience, 1980.

———. *Research Inventory of the Mexican Collection of Colonial Parish Registers.* Salt Lake City: University of Utah Press, 1980.

Rocha Chávez, Ruben. *Perfil de una singular ciudad.* Parral, Mexico: Imprenta Parral, 1993.

———. *Tres siglos de la historia: Biografia de una ciudad.* Ciudad Juarez, Mexico: Lux, 1989.

Rocha, Leopoldo da. *As confrarias de Goa, seculos XVI–XX: Conspecto histórico-juridico.* Lisbon, Portugal: Centro de Estudos Históricos Ultramarinos, 1973.

Rodríguez, Manuel Alfredo. "Los pardos libres en la colonia y la independencia." *Boletín de la Academia Nacional de la Historia* 75, no. 299 (July–September 1992): 33–62.

Rodríguez Mateos, Joaquín. "Las cofradías de Peru en la modernidad y el espiritu de la contrarreforma." *Anuario de Estudios Americanos* 52, no. 2 (1995): 15–29.

Romero Samper, Milagrosa. *Las cofradías en el reformismo de Carlos III.* Madrid, Spain: Fragua, 1991.

Rosal, Miguel Angel. "Negros y pardos en Buenos Aires, 1811–1860." *Anuario de Estudios Americanos* 51, no. 1 (1994): 165–84.

Rout, Leslie B. *The African Experience in Spanish America.* Cambridge: Cambridge University Press, 1976.

Rubin, Vera, and Arthur Tuden, eds. *Comparative Perspectives on Slavery in New World Plantation Societies.* New York: New York Academy of Sciences, 1977.

Rugeley, Terry. *Of Wonders and Wise Men: Religion and Popular Cultures in Southeast Mexico, 1800–1876.* Austin: University of Texas Press, 2001.

Russell-Wood, A.J.R. "Black and Mulatto Brotherhoods in Colonial Brazil: A Study in Collective Behavior." *Hispanic American Historical Review* 54, no. 4 (November 1974): 567–602.

———. "Prestige, Power, and Piety in Colonial Brazil: The Third Orders of Salvador." *Hispanic American Historical Review* 69, no. 1 (February 1989): 61–89.

Sabourín Fornaris, Jesús. "Blancos, negros y mulatos en 'El siglo de las luces.'" *Revista de la Biblioteca Nacional José Martí* 24, nos. 1–2 (January–August 1982): 211–34.

Sacerdote anónimo. *Novena a la preciosisima sangre de Christo, en que se consagran las potencias y sentidos a la misma Sangre de Christo.* Mexico City: Jauregui, 1786.

Salvucci, Richard. *Textiles and Capitalism in Mexico: An Economic History of the Obrajes, 1539–1840.* Princeton: Princeton University Press, 1987.

Sánchez Herrero, José, ed. *Las cofradías de Sevilla: Historia, antropología, arte*. Seville, Spain: Servicio de Publicaciones de la Universidad de Sevilla, 1985.

Sancho de Sopranis, Hipólito. *La cofradía de los morenos de Cádiz*. Tangier, Morocco: Instituto General Franco para la Investigación Hispano-Arabe, 1940.

Sandoval, Alonso de. *De instauranda aethiopum salute*. Edited by Angel Valtierra. Bogotá: Biblioteca de la Presidencia de Colombia, 1956.

Sarinara, Isidro. *Llanto del Occidente en el ocaso del mas claro sol de las Españas*. Mexico City: Viuda de Bernando Calderon, 1666.

Scarano, Julita. "Black Brotherhoods: Integration or Contradiction?" *Luso-Brazilian Review* 16, no. 1 (Summer 1979): 1–17.

Scholes, France V., and Eleanor B. Adams. *Advertimientos generales que los virreyes dejaron a sus sucesores para el gobierno de Nueva España, 1590–1604*. Mexico City: Porrúa, 1956.

Schroeder, Susan. "Nahuas and the Bona Mors at the Colegio de San Gregorio." Paper presented at the 17th International Congress of the History of Religions, Chicago, Illinois, 1995.

Schwaller, John Frederick. "Constitution of the Cofradía of Tula, Hidalgo, 1570." *Estudios de Cultura Náhuatl* 19 (1989): 217–44.

Seed, Patricia. "The Social Dimensions of Race: Mexico City, 1752." *Hispanic American Historical Review* 62, no. 4 (1982): 569–606.

Sepulveda, María Teresa. "La Cofradía de San Nicolás Tolentino." *Anales de INAH* 54 (1976): 5–22.

Smith, E. Valerie. "The Sisterhood of Nossa Senhora da Boa Morte and the Brotherhood of Nossa Senhora do Rosario: African-Brazilian Cultural Adaptations to Antebellum Restrictions." *Afro-Hispanic Review* 11, nos. 1–3 (1992): 58–69.

Sobrino, Tomas. *Documentación medieval del cabildo de San Benito de Avila*. Avila, Spain: Institución "Gran Duque de Alba" de la Excma, 1991.

Somohano Martínez, Lourdes. *Sistemas de aprendizaje gremial en obrajes y talleres artesanales en Querétaro (1780–1815)*. Querétaro, Mexico: Gobierno del Estado, 2001.

Soriano Hernández, Silvia. "Aportes sobre el mestizaje de esclavos africanos en Chiapas colonial." *Cuadernos Americanos* 43, Nueva época (January–February 1994): 80–93.

Sotomayor, María Lucía. "Organización socio-política de las cofradías." *Revista Colombia Antropología* 29 (1992): 155–89.

Stern, Peter. "*Gente de color quebrado*: Africans and Afromestizos in Colonial Mexico." *Colonial Latin American Historical Review* 3, no. 2 (Spring 1994): 185–205.

Stiles, Neville, and Agustín Estrada Monroy. "Ordenanzas de la Cofradía de San José de Guatemala, 1632." *Estudios de Cultura Náhuatl* 21 (1991): 339–54.

Super, John C. *La vida en Querétaro durante la colonia, 1531–1810*. Mexico City: Fondo de Cultura Económica, 1983.

———. "Miguel Hernández, Master of Mule Trains." In *Colonial Spanish America: A Documentary History*, edited by William B. Taylor and Kenneth Mills, 125–31. Wilmington, Del.: Scholarly Resources, 1998.

Tavera Alfaro, Xavier. *Paseo por Morelia: Guía histórica y artística de los edificios monumentos de la antigua Valladolid.* Morelia, Mexico: Morevallado, 1967.

Taylor, William B. *Drinking, Homicide and Rebellion in Colonial Mexican Villages.* Stanford, Calif.: Stanford University Press, 1979.

———. "The Foundation of Nuestra Señora de Guadalupe de los Morenos de Amapa." *The Americas* 26 (1979): 439–46.

———. *Magistrates of the Sacred: Priests and Parishioners in Eighteenth-Century Mexico.* Stanford, Calif.: Stanford University Press, 1996.

Terpstra, Nicholas. *Lay Confraternities and Civic Religion in Renaissance Bologna.* Cambridge: Cambridge University Press, 1995.

———. *The Politics of Ritual Kinship: Confraternities and Social Order in Early Modern Italy.* Cambridge: Cambridge University Press, 2000.

Thompson, Eric, ed. *Thomas Gage's Travels in the New World.* Norman: University of Oklahoma Press, 1985.

Thornton, John K. *A Kongolese Saint Anthony: Doña Beatriz Kimpa Vita and the Antonian Movement, 1684–1706.* Cambridge: Cambridge University Press, 1998.

———. "On the Trail of Voodoo: African Christianity in Africa and the Americas." *The Americas* 44, no. 3 (1988): 261–78.

Toussaint, Manuel. *Taxco. Su historia y sus monumentos.* Mexico City: Secretaria de la Hacienda, 1931.

Trexler, Richard C. *Public Life in Renaissance Florence.* New York: Academic Press, 1980.

Tudela, Vera Sampson. *Colonial Angels: Narratives of Gender and Spirituality in Mexico: 1580–1750.* Austin: University of Texas Press, 2000.

Twinam, Ann. *Public Lives, Private Secrets: Gender, Honor, Sexuality, and Illegitimacy in Colonial Spanish America.* Stanford, Calif.: Stanford University Press, 1999.

———. "Purchase of Whiteness—Some Revisionist Thoughts." Working paper originally presented at Virginia-Carolinas-Georgia Colonialists Group (VACARGA), Vanderbilt Univerisity, Nashville, Tenn., April 2–3, 2004. http://sitemason.vanderbilt.edu/files/k6EDBe/VACARGA%20twinamvacarga.pdf.

Uchmany, Eva Alexandra. "El mestizaje en el siglo XVI novohispano." *Historia Mexicana* 37, no. 1 (July–September 1987): 29–48.

Valdés, Carlos Manuel. *Esclavos negros en Saltillo, siglos XVII a XIX.* Saltillo, Mexico : Ayuntamiento de Saltillo, 1989.

———. "Negros y mulatos en el noreste de México." *Review of Latin American Studies* 4, no. 2 (1991): 252–63.

Valdés, José Francisco. *Novena a la Preciosisima Sangre de Nuestro Señor Jesucristo.* Mexico City: Felipe de Zúñiga y Ontiveros, 1787 and 1796.

Valdez Aguilar, Rafael. *Sinaloa: Negritud y olvido.* Culiacán, Mexico: El Diario de Sinaloa, 1993.

Valdiosera Berman, Ramón. "Cruz, iglesia y muerte." *Artes de México* 21, no. 184 (n.d.): 71–72.

Vargas, Raul. *Catálogo del archivo de la parroquia de Santiago Apostol de Silao, Guanajuato*. Mexico City: Archivo General de la Nación, 1983.

Vargas Lugo de Bosch, Elisa, and Gustavo Curiel, eds. *Juan Correa: Su vida y su obra.* Mexico City: Universidad Nacional Autónoma de Mexico, 1990.

Varon, Rafael. "Cofradías de indios y poder local en el Perú colonial: Huaraz, siglo XVII." *Allpanchis*. 17, no. 20 (1982): 127–46.

Vega, Enrique Esquivel. *Peribán y su antigua jurisdicción: Los Reyes Tingüindin, Charapán, San Francisco de Peribán, Metamorfosis de un Pueblo*. Guadalajara, Mexico: Valenzuela, 1985.

Vetancur, Agustín de. *Crónica de la provincia del Santo Evangelio de México*. Mexico City: Porrúa, 1971.

Victoria Moreno, Dionisio. *El convento de la Purísima Concepción de los Carmelitos Descalzos en Toluca*. Toluca, Mexico: Biblioteca Enciclopédica del Estado de México, 1979.

Villaseñor y Sánchez, Joseph Antonio de. *Teatro americano: Descripción general de los reynos y provincias de la Nueva España y sus jurisdiciones*. Mexico City: Editorial Trillas, 1992.

Vinson, Ben, III. *Bearing Arms for His Majesty: The Free-Colored Militia in Colonial Mexico*. Stanford, Calif.: Stanford University Press, 2001.

———. "Free Colored Voices: Issues of Representation and Racial Identity in the Colonial Mexican Militia." *Journal of Negro History* 80, no. 4 (1994): 170–82.

Vinson, Ben, III, and Bobby Vaughn. *Afroméxico: El pulso de la población negra en México: Una historia recordada, olvidada y vuelta a recordar*. Translated by Clara García Ayluardo. Mexico City: Fondo de Cultura Económica, 2004.

von Germeten, Nicole. "Death in Black and White: Testaments and Confraternal Devotion in Seventeenth-century Mexico City." *Colonial Latin America Historical Review* 12, no. 3 (Summer 2003): 275–301.

Wade, Peter. *Blackness and Race Mixture: The Dynamics of Racial Identity in Colombia.* Baltimore, Md.: Johns Hopkins University Press, 1993.

———. *Race and Ethnicity in Latin America*. London: Pluto Press, 1997.

Webster Verdi, Susan. *Art and Ritual in Golden Age Spain*. Princeton, N.J.: Princeton University Press, 1995.

———. "Art, Ritual, and Confraternities in Sixteenth-Century New Spain: Penitential Imagery at the Monastery of San Miguel, Huejotzingo." *Anales del Instituto de Investigaciones Estéticas* 19, no. 70 (Spring 1997): 5–43.

Weissman, Ronald F. E. *Ritual Brotherhood in Renaissance Florence*. New York: Academic Press, 1982.

West, Robert. *The Mining Community in New Spain: The Parral Mining District.* Berkeley: University of California Press, 1949.

———. *Sonora: Its Geographical Personality.* Austin: University of Texas Press, 1993.

Wilder, Craig Steven. *In the Company of Black Men: The African Influence on African American Culture in New York City.* New York: New York University Press, 2001.

Winfield Capitaine, Fernando. "La cofradía de Cristo Negro de Otatitlán en el siglo XVIII." *La Palabra y el Hombre* 89 (January–March 1994): 43–54.

———, ed. *Esclavos en el Archivo Notarial de Xalapa, Veracruz, 1700–1800.* Xalapa, Mexico: Universidad Veracruzana, 1984.

Wright, Winthrop R. *Café con Leche: Race, Class and National Image in Venezuela.* Austin: University of Texas Press, 1990.

Zafra Oropeza, Aurea. *Las cofradías de Cocula.* Guadalajara, Mexico: Ayuntamiento Constitucional de Guadalajara: Editorial Agata, 1996.

Zahino Peñafort, Luisa, ed. *El Cardenal Lorenzano y el IV concilio provincial mexicano.* Mexico City: Porrúa, 1999.

Zamora, Araceli, Asunción Ruiz, Ramon Torres, and Miguel Ferro Herrera. *Catálogo de Libros Notariales, 1587–1938.* Querétaro, Mexico: Archivo Histórico del Estado de Querétaro, 1996.

Index

Nicole von Germeten is a professor of history at Oregon State University.

Laborers in the Vineyard of the Lord: The Beginnings of the AME Church in Florida, 1865–1895, by Larry Eugene Rivers and Canter Brown Jr. (2001)

Between Cross and Crescent: Christian and Muslim Perspectives on Malcolm and Martin, by Lewis V. Baldwin and Amiri YaSin Al-Hadid (2002)

The Quest for the Cuban Christ: A Historical Search, by Miguel De La Torre (2002)

For a Great and Grand Purpose: The Beginnings of the AMEZ Church in Florida, 1864–1905, by Canter Brown Jr. and Larry Eugene Rivers (2004; first paperback edition, 2025)

Afro-Cuban Religiosity, Revolution, and National Identity, by Christine Ayorinde (2004)

From Garvey to Marley: Rastafari Theology, by Noel Leo Erskine (2005)

Hell Without Fires: Slavery, Christianity, and the Antebellum Spiritual Narrative, by Yolanda Pierce (2005; first paperback edition, 2021)

Where Men are Wives and Mothers Rule: Santería Ritual Practices and Their Gender Implications, by Mary Ann Clark (2005)

Around the Family Altar: Domesticity in the African Methodist Episcopal Church, 1865–1900, by Julius H. Bailey (2005)

Black Blood Brothers: Confraternities and Social Mobility for Afro-Mexicans, by Nicole von Germeten (2006; first paperback edition, 2026)

African American Atheists and Political Liberation: A Study of the Sociocultural Dynamics of Faith, by Michael Lackey (2007)

The African American Religious Experience in America, by Anthony B. Pinn (paperback edition, 2008)

The Ethiopian Prophecy in Black American Letters, by Roy Kay (2011)

Saved and Sanctified: The Rise of a Storefront Church in Great Migration Philadelphia, by Deidre Helen Crumbley (2012; first paperback edition, 2013)

www.ingramcontent.com/pod-product-compliance
Lightning Source LLC
LaVergne TN
LVHW100911220826
846271LV00024B/124
9780813081793